Antitrust Economics

Antitrust Economics:
Mergers, Contracting, and Strategic Behavior

Oliver Williamson

Basil Blackwell

Copyright © Oliver Williamson, 1987

First published in this form 1987

Basil Blackwell Ltd
108 Cowley Road, Oxford, OX4 1JF, UK

Basil Blackwell Inc.
432 Park Avenue South, Suite 1503
New York, NY 10016, USA

British Library Cataloguing in Publication Data

Williamson, Oliver E.
  Essays in antitrust economics.
  1. Antitrust law——United States
  I. Title
  347.303'72   KF1649
  ISBN 0-631-15363-2

Library of Congress Cataloging-in-Publication Data

Williamson, Oliver E.
  Essays in antitrust economics.

  Includes index.
  1. Industrial organization (Economic theory)
  2. Antitrust law—Economic aspects. I. Title.
  HD2326.W49 1987   338.8   87-5153
  ISBN 0-631-15363-2

Typeset in 10 on 11 pt Times
by Photo·graphics, Honiton, Devon
Printed in Great Britain by TJ Press Ltd, Padstow

Contents

Preface

The past twenty-five years have witnessed a dramatic increase of interest in, and economic talent applied to, the study of industrial organization – of which antitrust economics is a part. Grim assessments of the state of industrial organization were nonetheless expressed as recently as fifteen years ago. Thus Victor Fuchs, in his foreword to the National Bureau of Economics Research volume on *Policy Issues and Research Opportunities in Industrial Organization*, opened with the query 'Whither industrial organization?', to which he responded that 'all is not well with this once flourishing field' (1972, p. xv). Today's answer is that industrial organization is alive and well and is the queen of applied microeconomics.

Much has happened in the intervening years. Indications that industrial organization was undergoing major change had already appeared by 1972. The market power era of the 1960s was actively being contested by those who offered efficiency analysis as an alternative to the reigning monopoly predisposition.

This preoccupation with market power and the associated low regard for efficiency were byproducts of the prevailing practice of describing business firms – large and small, ancient and modern – as production functions. Deeper inquiry into the purposes served by hierarchical forms of organization of firms was thus thought to be unneeded and unhelpful. The ruling tradition within both theoretical, and applied microeconomics was that the firm was a 'black box'.

Although Ronald Coase had vigorously contested that view, his opinion was widely ignored. Dissent was nevertheless building. Thus Vernon Smith declared in 1974 that the older style microtheory had come to an impasse and would be supplanted (or at least supplemented) by a new microtheory that 'will, and should, deal with the economic foundations of organization and institution, and this will require us to have an economics of information and a more sophisticated treatment of the technology of transacting' (1974, p. 321).

Such developments were already in progress. Some of these entailed new forms of efficiency reasoning, whereupon efficiency arguments were brought to bear on a wider range of issues than had been previously examined in these terms. Earlier excesses of entry barrier reasoning were also being challenged. But that entry barrier analysis had been overdone did not mean that there was nothing there. Delimiting these issues required, however, that a more meticulous economics of 'strategic behavior' be invented. This too was beginning to take shape.

The decades of the 1970s and 1980s have witnessed broader applications of partial equilibrium welfare economics, the progressive development of the economics of information, related developments in transaction cost economics, and a burgeoning literature dealing with strategic behavior. Industrial organization has attracted many of the best doctoral candidates during this interval and has become the envy of applied microtheory.

It has been my good fortune to have been associated with such an energetic field. The essays in this book speak to some of the developments in industrial organization that I have worked on, with special emphasis on those that have application to antitrust.

The essays are organized in four parts. The first four essays deal with mergers. The importance of economies of production and transaction costs are featured in all four of these essays. The central issues are these: How should economies be assessed? What forms do they take? What is the relevance of internal organization to both of the foregoing? And what are the antitrust enforcement ramifications?

The second set of essays deals with the technology of transacting. Any issue that can be posed directly or indirectly as a contracting problem is usefully addressed in transaction cost economizing terms. A surprisingly large number of problems of interest to antritrust economics fall within the purview.

Issues of strategic behavior are dealt with in the third set of essays. Both uses and abuses of strategic reasoning are illustrated.

The last set of essays offer commentary on the enforcement changes that have evolved over the past quarter of a century. Although I support most of the changes that have occurred, I am nevertheless concerned that antitrust shows signs of overshooting. Hard-headed antitrust enforcement is the object. The public interest is poorly served by 'balancing' the excesses of monopoly reasoning of an earlier era with excesses of competitive reasoning today.

Oliver E. Williamson
Yale University

Part I
Mergers

The first essay in this section uses the apparatus of partial equilibrium welfare economics to assess a merger that simultaneously affords prospective economies and increases, at least temporarily, market power. This essay had its origins in a memorandum that I drafted in 1967 for the head of the Antitrust Division of the US Department of Justice (at a time when I was serving as his Special Economic Assistant). Contrary to the prevailing view that small market power effects would invariably swamp economies, the 'naive model' demonstrated the opposite. Although there was considerable initial (and even continuing) resistance to the view that merger enforcement should be revised so as to make sympathetic provision for economies, this position has progressively taken hold.

The second essay deals with a subject to which I have had frequent occasion to return: vertical integration. My interest in this issue also owes its origins to the year that I spent with the Antitrust Division. Vertical mergers and, even more, vertical market restrictions were at that time regarded with deep suspicion by antitrust. So as to better sort things out, I offered a seminar on vertical relationships the following year when I returned to the University of Pennsylvania. Although the students and I who worked our way through the literature were not persuaded by much of what we found, fashioning a coherent alternative was not obvious either.

I had occasion to return to these issues two years later when I taught a more general course dealing with the economics of organization. The students and I in this second course spent a considerable amount of time on the market failure literature. What were the sources of market failure and what were the ramifications for economic organization?

Although Coase and Arrow had insisted that transaction costs were germane and even central to these queries, operationalizing transaction costs had been notoriously difficult. The second essay employs a comparative contracting approach to vertical integration in which differential transaction costs are featured. Investment attributes – with special emphasis on the condition of 'asset specificity' – play a key role in the comparative contracting argument.

The third essay was written for the National Bureau of Economics Colloquium to which I made reference in the preface. It argues that the comparative contracting approach should be brought to bear more generally. Not only is vertical integration better understood in these terms, but the often deprecated conglomerate form of organization and certain dominant firm outcomes are usefully examined in a contracting framework. In each instance, the view of the firm as a production function needed to make way for the modern corporation as a governance structure.

The last essay focuses on vertical merger guidelines. Changes in antitrust enforcement between 1968, when the initial merger guidelines were issued, and 1982, when the merger guidelines were first revised, are examined. The observed changes in the guidelines not only reflect greater respect for efficiency, but they specifically reflect the influence of transaction cost reasoning.

1

Economies as an Antitrust Defense: The Welfare Trade-Offs

Suppose that a merger (or other combination) is proposed that yields economies but at the same time increases market power. Can the courts and antitrust agencies safely rely, in these circumstances, on a literal reading of the law which prohibits mergers 'where in any line of commerce or any section of the country, the effect of such acquisition may be substantially to lessen competition, or to tend to create a monopoly,'[1] or does this run the risk of serious economic loss? In the usual merger where both effects are insubstantial this problem is absent.[2] But in the occasional

Reprinted with the author's amendments from *American Economic Review*, LVIII (March 1968), pp. 18–36, by kind permission of the American Economic Association.

[1] Public Law 899, Sec. 7, 38 Stat. 731, as amended; 15 USC 18.

[2] Donald Dewey has observed in this connection that most mergers 'have virtually nothing to do with either the creation of market power or the realization of scale economies' (Dewey, 1961, p. 257). Jesse Markham agrees that since 1930 monopolization has not been a principal merger objective, but finds that 'some mergers have undoubtedly come about as adjustments to major innovations ...: the first great wave of mergers followed a period of rapid railroad building, and the wave of the 1920s came with the rise of the motor car and motor truck transportation and a new advertising medium, the home radio' (Markham, 1955, pp. 181–2). It might be useful briefly to summarize some of the ways in which efficiencies might result from combination. These would include miscalculation, shifts in demand, technological developments, displacement of ineffective managements, and mixtures thereof.

As an example of miscalculation consider two firms that have entered a market at an efficient plant scale but have incorrectly estimated the volume necessary to support an efficient distribution system. Combination here could lead to efficiencies but might also have some market power effects (reducing competition between the two but possibly enhancing their competitive position with respect to their rivals). A significant, persistent decline in demand might produce a condition of excess capacity in which combination would permit economies but would also have market power consequences. As discussed in section III, an increase in demand might induce a change from job shop to assembly line type operations with vertical integration consequences. Technological developments may similarly provide opportunities for a significant reorganization of resources into more efficient configurations – the electronic digital computer being a recent example. Finally, merger may be the most expeditious way of displacing an inefficient by a more efficient management – but the benefits here may only be of a short-run variety. A manifestly inefficient management would, hopefully, be displaced by other means if, by reason of the market power consequences of a combination, the merger route were closed. (cont'd overleaf)

case where efficiency and market power consequences exist, can economies be dismissed on the grounds that market power effects invariably dominate? If they cannot, then a rational treatment of the merger question requires that an effort be made to establish the allocative implications of the scale economy and market power effects associated with the merger.

The initial indication of the Supreme Court's view on this question came on the occasion of the first merger case to come before it under the 1950 amendment to section 7 of the Clayton Act. In a unanimous opinion, the Court took the position in *Brown Shoe* that not only were efficiencies no defense, but a showing that a merger resulted in efficiencies could be used affirmatively in attacking the merger since small rivals could be disadvantaged thereby (*Brown Shoe* v. *United States*, 1962, p. 374). Opportunities to reconsider this position have presented themselves since, *Proctor & Gamble* being the most recent.

Justice Douglas, in delivering the opinion of the Court, observed that Procter & Gamble 'would be able to use its volume discounts to advantage in advertising Clorox,' and went on to state that 'economies cannot be used as a defense to illegality. Congress was aware that some mergers which lessen competition may also result in economies but it struck the balance in favor of protecting competition' (*Federal Trade Commission* v. *Procter & Gamble Co.*, 1967, pp. 1230–1). Although in reference to congressional intent may relieve the Court of the responsibility for making trade-off valuations, this does not fully dispose of the issue. What trade-off calculus did Congress employ that produced this result?

In a concurring opinion to the Clorox decision, Justice Harlan provides the first hint that efficiencies may deserve greater standing. At least with respect to conglomerate or product-extension mergers 'where the case against the merger rests on the probability [as contrasted, apparently, with a certainty] of increased market power, the merging companies may attempt to prove that there are countervailing economies reasonably probable which should be weighed against the adverse effects' (*Federal Trade Commission* v. *Procter & Gamble Co.*, 1967, pp. 1240–1). But inasmuch as the economies in Clorox were in his opinion merely pecuniary rather than real, which distinction is of course appropriate, he concluded that Procter's efficiency defense was defective (p. 1243).

Even if Justice Harlan's position were the prevailing one, it is clear that economies would be an acceptable antitrust defense for only a restricted set of structural conditions. Since the relevant economic theory, although widely available, has never been developed explicitly on this issue, such a result is not unexpected. Indeed, lacking a basis for evaluating net effects, for the Court to hold that the anticompetitive consequences

---

A merger can, of course, produce diseconomies as well. What I have previously characterized as the 'control loss' phenomenon appears to be an increasing function of firm size (Williamson, 1967, pp. 11–31). See also parts H and I, section II below.

of a merger outweigh any immediate efficiency advantages is only to be expected. An institution acting as a caretaker for the enterprise system does not easily exchange what it regards as long-term competitive consequences for short-term efficiency gains.

The merits of the Supreme Court's position on mergers are at the heart of the recent Bork and Bowman v. Blake and Jones debate (Blake and Jones, 1965a, pp. 377–400; Blake and Jones, 1965b, pp. 422–66; Bork and Bowman, 1965, pp. 363–76; Bork, 1965, pp. 401–16). Although this dialogue deals directly with the critical issues, its failure to produce a consensus is at least partly due to the fact that essential aspects of the relevant economic model were not supplied. Lacking a trade-off relation, Bork is forced to assert that 'Economic analysis does away with the need to measure efficiencies directly. It is enough to know in what sorts of transactions efficiencies are likely to be present and in what sorts anticompetitive effects are likely to be present. The law can then develop objective criteria, such as market shares, to divide transactions [into those predominantly one type or other]' (Bork, 1965, p. 411). But this obviously leaves the mixed cases, which are the hard ones, unresolved. Blake and Jones, by contrast, conclude that 'claims of economic efficiency will not justify a course of conduct conferring excessive market power. The objective of maintaining a system of self-policing markets requires that all such claims be rejected' (Blake and Jones, 1965, p. 427). But what are the standards for 'excessive' market power and 'self-policing' markets? And are these really absolute or do they reflect an implicit trade-off calculation? And if it is the latter, should we (if we can) make this trade-off explicit?

Indeed, there is no way in which the trade-off issue can be avoided. To disallow trade-offs altogether merely reflects a particularly severe *a priori* judgment as to net benefits. Moreover, it is doubtful that a goal hierarchy scheme of the sort proposed by Carl Kaysen and Donald Turner has acceptable properties. As they formulate the problem, higher level goals strictly dominate lower level goals, so that only when the latter are available without sacrifice in the former is lower level goal pursuit allowed (Kaysen and Turner, 1959, pp. 44–5). Inasmuch as they rank efficiency and progressiveness above reductions in market power, an absolute defense would appear to obtain when, for any structural condition present or prospective, it could be shown either that economies have not yet been exhausted or that discreteness conditions (indivisibilities) would not efficiently permit a separation (Kaysen and Turner, 1959, pp. 44–6, 58, 78). But this may be to construe their intentions too narrowly; for it is with antitrust actions that result in substantial efficiency losses (Kaysen and Turner, 1959, pp. 44, 133) and involve too great a sacrifice in performance (Kaysen and Turner, 1959, p. 58) that they are especially concerned. Although these distinctions are important, they are not ones for which goal hierarchy analysis is well suited to deal. Trade-off analysis, by contrast, is designed to cope with precisely these types of issues.

The relevant partial equilibrium model with which to characterize the trade-offs between efficiency and price effects together with a representative set of indifference relations are developed in section I of this chapter. A variety of essential qualifications to this naive model are then presented in section II. Extensions of the argument, which is developed initially in horizontal merger terms, to deal with questions of dissolution as well as vertical and conglomerate mergers, are given in section III. The conclusions follow in section IV.

I.   The Naive Trade-off Model

The effects on resource allocation of a merger that yields economies but extends market power can be investigated in a partial equilibrium context with the help of figure 1.1. The horizontal line labeled AC_1 represents the level of average costs of the two (or more) firms before combination,

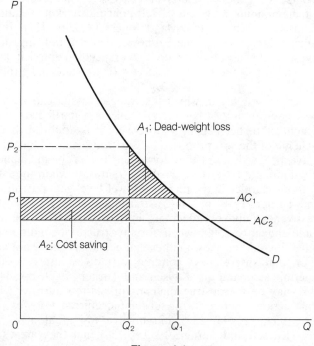

Figure 1.1

while AC_2 shows the level of average costs after the merger. The price before the merger is given by P_1 and is equal to k (AC_1) where k is an index of pre-merger market power and is greater than or equal to unity. The price after the merger is given by P_2 and is assumed to exceed P_1 (if it were less than P_1 the economic effects of the merger would be strictly positive).[3] Assume for our purposes here that pre-merger market power is negligible $(k = 1)$.

The net welfare effects of the merger are given (approximately) by the two shaded areas in the figure. The area designated A_1 is the familiar dead-weight loss that would result if price were increased from P_1 to P_2, assuming that costs remain constant. But since average costs are actually reduced by the merger, the area designated A_2, which represents cost savings, must also be taken into account. The net allocative effect is given by the difference, $A_2 - A_1$, of these two areas.[4]

The area A_2 is given by $(AC_2 - AC_1)Q_2$, or $[\Delta(AC)]Q_2$, while A_1 is given approximately by $\frac{1}{2}(P_2 - P_1)(Q_1 - Q_2)$, or $\frac{1}{2}(\Delta P)(\Delta Q)$. The net economic effect will be positive if the following inequality holds:

$$[\Delta(AC)]Q_2 - 1/2(\Delta P)(\Delta Q) > 0. \tag{1.1}$$

Dividing through by P_1Q_1, substituting for $\Delta Q/Q_1$ the expression $\eta(\Delta P/P_1)$, where η is the elasticity of demand, and recognizing that $P_1 = AC_1$, we obtain

$$\frac{\Delta(AC)}{AC} - \frac{1}{2}\eta\frac{Q_1}{Q_2}\left(\frac{\Delta P}{P_1}\right)^2 > 0. \tag{1.2}$$

If this inequality holds, the net allocative effect of the merger is positive. If the difference is equal to zero the merger is neutral. If the inequality is reversed the merger is negative.

In words, the inequality shown in equation (1.2) says that if the decimal fraction reduction in average costs exceeds the square of the decimal fraction increase in price premultiplied by one-half times the elasticity of demand times the ratio of the initial to final outputs, the allocative effect

---

[3] This is a simple but basic point. It reveals that market power is only a necessary and not a sufficient condition for undesirable price effects to exist. It would be wholly irrational to regard an increase in the price to average cost ratio $(P_2/AC_2 > P_1/AC_1)$ as grounds for opposing a merger if, at the same time, the post-merger price were less than the pre-merger level $(P_2 < P_1)$ and the qualifications discussed in section II are insubstantial.

[4] My use of dead-weight loss is somewhat restrictive. Inefficiency is also a dead-weight loss. For convenience of exposition, however, I refer to the Marshallian triangle as the dead-weight loss and compare this to the cost-saving (efficiency) aspects of a merger. Estimating the value of consumers' surplus by the Marshallian triangle follows the common (and broadly defensible) practice of suppressing the income effects associated with a price change. The net social benefit associated with a particular cost–price configuration is defined as total revenue plus consumers' surplus less social cost, where social and private costs are assumed to be identical (externalities and producers' surplus are both assumed to be zero).

of the merger (judged in naive terms) is positive. The cost reductions necessary to offset price increases for various values of the elasticity of demand are shown in table 1.1.

Table 1.1 Percentage cost reductions [($\Delta(AC)/AC$) × 100] sufficient to offset percentage price increases ($\Delta P/P$ × 100) for selected values of η

η ($\Delta P/P$) × 100	2	1	1/2
5	0.26	0.12	0.06
10	1.05	0.50	0.24
20	4.40	2.00	0.95
30	10.35	4.50	2.10

For example, if price were to increase by 20 per cent, then running across the row [($\Delta P/P$) × 100] = 20 we observe that if η is 2 a cost reduction of 5 per cent will be sufficient to offset the price increase, while if η is 1 only a 2 per cent cost decrease is needed to neutralize the price effect, and if η is $\frac{1}{2}$, a cost reduction of 1 per cent is sufficient. More generally it is evident that a relatively modest cost reduction is usually sufficient to offset relatively large price increases even if the elasticity of demand is as high as 2, which is probably a reasonable upper bound. Indeed, if a reduction in average costs on the order of 5 to 10 per cent is available through merger, the merger must give rise to price increases in excess of 20 per cent if $\eta \cong 2$, and in excess of 40 per cent if $\eta \cong \frac{1}{2}$, for the net allocative effects to be negative. Moreover, it should be noted, if the merger reduces average costs by x per cent and the post-merger price increases by y per cent, the post-merger price to average cost differential slightly exceeds $x + y$ per cent. Thus, expressing price with respect to the post-merger level of average costs yields an even greater differential than is reflected by the relations stated above. The naive model thus supports the following proposition: a merger which yields nontrivial real economies must produce substantial market power and result in relatively large price increases for the net allocative effects to be negative.

II. Qualifications

Our partial equilibrium analysis suffers from a defect common to all partial equilibrium constructions. By isolating one sector from the rest of the economy it fails to examine interactions between sectors. Certain economic effects may therefore go undetected, and occasionaly behavior which appears to yield net economic benefits in a partial equilibrium analysis will result in net losses when investigated in a general equilibrium context. Such a condition has been shown to exist in an economy in which monopoly exists in many sectors. Thus, whereas partial equilibrium analysis indicates that an increase in the monopoly price in any one sector invariably yields a loss, viewed more generally such an isolated price increase may actually lead to a desirable reallocation of resources.[5] Conceivably, therefore, a merger that has monopoly power and cost-saving consequences could yield benefits in *both* respects[6] – although it is probably rare that operational content can be supplied to this qualification. But were there no other considerations, such bias as our partial equilibrium construction produces would be to under-estimate the net economic gains of combination.

This does not, however, exhaust the range of qualifications. Among the other factors that can or should be taken into account are pre-existing market power, inference and enforcement expense, timing incipiency, weighting, income distribution, extra-economic political objectives, techno-logical progress, and the effects of monopoly power on managerial discretion.

A. PRE-EXISTING MARKET POWER

We continue to employ the conventional partial equilibrium welfare function; to wit, welfare is expressed as $W = (TR + S) - (TC - R)$, where, under appropriate restrictions, the terms in the first set of parentheses reflect social benefits (total revenue plus consumers' surplus) and those in the second reflect social costs (total pecuniary costs less intramarginal rents). Assuming that R is negligible, this can be restated as $W = (TR - TC) + S$, or inasmuch as $TR - TC$ profits, as $W = \pi + S$, where π denotes profits. Any change in welfare is then given by

$$\Delta W = (\pi_2 - \pi_1) + (S_2 - S_1).$$

Let k be the pre-existing market power parameter, where $k = P_1/AC_1$. It can be shown that ΔW can be expressed as

$$\Delta(AC)Q_2 - [\tfrac{1}{2}\Delta P + (k - 1)AC_1]\Delta Q. \tag{1.3}$$

The parallel test expression to equation (1.2) is whether

---

[5] This is the familiar 'second-best' argument. For a discussion of second-best qualifications in treating the monopoly problem, and references to this literature, see Ferguson (1964, pp. 16–17, 49–51).

[6] This is more likely if (a) the factor markets of the industry in question are competitive, (b) the firms involved in the merger produce strictly for final demand, and (c) significant relations with sectors in which distortions exist are mainly ones of substitutabiity rather than complementarity.

$$\frac{\Delta(AC)}{AC_1} - \left[\frac{1}{2}k\left(\frac{\Delta P}{P_1}\right) + (k-1)\right] \eta \frac{\Delta P}{P_1} \cdot \frac{Q_1}{Q_2} \qquad (1.4)$$

is greater or less than zero.

The question now to be addressed is what values of k might reasonably obtain? Consider in this connection Joe Bain's treatment of entry barriers in the 'very high', 'substantial', and 'moderate or low categories (1956, p. 170):

It is hazardous to assign any absolute values to the entry barriers corresponding to these three rankings, but the very roughest guess would be as follows: (1) that in the 'very high' category, established firms might be able to elevate price 10 per cent or more above *minimal* costs while forestalling entry; (2) that with 'substantial' barriers, the corresponding percentage might range a bit above or below 7 per cent; (3) that in the 'moderate to low' category the same percentage will probably not exceed 4, and will range down to around 1 per cent. (Emphasis added)

This suggests that k may ordinarily be expected to fall in the range 1.00 to 1.10. Table 1.2 shows the percentgae cost reductions sufficient to offset various percentage price increases for selected demand elasticities (assumed to be constant in the relevant range) and values k of 1.05 and 1.10.

Table 1.2 Percentage cost reductions $[(\Delta AC/AC_1) \times 100]$ sufficient to offset percentage price increases $[(\Delta P/P_1) \times 100]$ for selected values of η and $k = 1.05$ and 1.10

	$\eta = 2$		$\eta = 1$		$\eta = \frac{1}{2}$	
$\Delta P/P_1 \times$	$k =$	$k =$	$k =$	$k =$	$k =$	$k =$
100	1.05	1.10	1.05	1.10	1.05	1.10
5	0.78	1.31	0.38	0.64	0.19	0.31
10	2.15	3.26	1.03	1.55	0.50	0.76
20	6.82	9.23	3.10	4.20	1.48	2.00
30	14.28	18.27	6.21	7.95	2.90	3.57

As is evident from an inspection of tables 1.1 and 1.2, the cost savings required to offset price increases are significantly greater if pre-merger market power prevails. The enforcement agencies are thus well advised to give special scrutiny to the monopolistic subset. Still, the existence of pre-merger market power is not enough, by itself, to upset the basic conclusions of the naive model.

B. INFERENCE AND ENFORCEMENT EXPENSE

The relevant effects are those which take the form of real rather than pecuniary economies. Also, since evaluating a claim that economies exist will itself absorb real resources, it seems reasonable to impose a requirement that the net gain exceed some threshold value before such a defense will even be entertained. This, in conjunction with qualifications C through E below, would appear to meet Donald Turner's point that if economies are to be invoked as a defense 'the law might well require clear and convincing evidence that the particular merger would produce substantial economies that could not be achieved in other ways' (Turner, 1965, p. 1328). As the tools for assessing economies are progressively refined (and the incentive to make such improvements is obvious once an efficiency defense – even in principle – is granted), this threshold level should be reduced accordingly. Still, protection for the legal process may be essential.

A four-stage program to implement an economies defense is proposed. At a minimum, the antitrust agencies and the courts should explicitly recognize the merits of an economies defense in principle, even though they may disallow it as a practical defense. This would at least forestall perverse treatment of economies before the law. The effects of even such a modest change might well be considerable. As Kaysen has pointed out, 'policy change comes about, in large part, by the way in which the enforcing agencies select cases and frame issues for courts and commissions to decide' (Kaysen, 1968, p. 85).

Second, although an economies defense would be disallowed, it could be introduced for 'explanatory completeness.[7] This would hopefully encourage companies to reveal the efficiency consequences of mergers more completely, so that the importance of allowing an economies defense could be better assessed. The legal process would be protected, and an idea of the magnitude of the implicit trade-offs might begin to emerge.

A more ambitious undertaking, but one which would still provide substantial protection to the legal process, would be to allow an economies defense for certain types of mergers. Justice Harlan has suggested that an economies defense should be available for conglomerate or product-extension mergers (*Federal Trade Commission* v. *Procter & Gamble Co.*, 1967, pp. 1240–1). As experience is accumulated, this might be eventually extended to include other types of mergers. With respect to vertical and horizontal mergers, for example, *Merger Guidelines* could be rewritten to acknowledge a band of uncertainty within which an economies defense would be available: above a specified set of market share values, a merger

---

[7] As Bork points out, the courts have, occasionally, permitted this (1966, p. 390, n. 40).

would be disallowed; below a second set of values, a merger would be permitted; within the range between, an economies defense, subject to an appropriate set of threshold stipulations, would be entertained. Proceeding in a gradualist way of this sort would appear to conform to the objective proposed by Bok (1960, pp. 348–9):

While the basic values and objectives of Section 7 should presumably remain unchanged by court or agency, the methods and standards used to achieve these ends must evolve to keep pace with developments in our knowledge concerning the nature and effects of mergers. . . . The issue . . . is fundamentally one of timing; the question is whether *at present* we stand to gain from rules which seek to capture the subtler images of reality evoked by the complexities of economic theory.

Finally, an economies defense (appropriately qualified) might be admitted quite generally. Even, however, if this last stage is never reached, the process is worth setting in motion. Stage one involves merely an immediate expression of positive regard for economies by the antitrust agencies and the courts – a step which is unambiguously desirable. There are clear benefits and no evident costs.

C. TIMING

Significant economies will ordinarily be realized eventually through internal expansion if not by merger. Growth of demand can facilitate this internal adjustment process; the necessity for part of the industry to be displaced in order that efficient size be achieved is relieved in a growing market. Thus, although a merger may have net positive effects immediately (cost savings exceed the dead-weight loss), when allowance is made for the possibility of internal expansion these effects can become negative eventually (the cost savings persist, but these could be realized anyway, and the dead-weight loss could be avoided by prohibiting the merger).

Designating the dead-weight loss effects of the merger by $L(t)$ and the cost savings by $S(t)$, the argument would be that the value of $S(t)$ falls while $L(t)$ persists over time. Thus, taking the discounted value of net benefits (V) we have

$$V = \int_0^T [S(t) - L(t)]\, e^{-rt}\, dt \qquad (1.5)$$

and if initially $S(t)/L(t) > 1$, but eventually $S(t)/L(t) < 1$, this can easily become negative.

For purposes of illustration, let P_3 be the price that would obtain if the economies were realized, with a delay, by internal expansion, and define

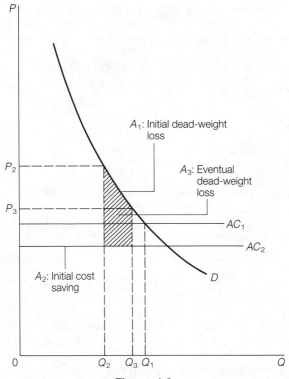

Figure 1.2

an attenuation coefficient a by the ratio $a = (P_2 - P_3)/(P_2 - AC_2)$. P_2 and AC_2 are specified; the value that a takes on thus depends on the post-expansion price P_3. If $P_3 = AC_2$, in which case $a = 1$, internal expansion results in the full attenuation of the market power effects that a merger, if permitted, would produce; no attenuation exists if $a = 0$ (since here $P_3 = P_2$); partial attenuation occurs if a falls in the interval $0 < a < 1$.

For each value that P_3 (and hence a) takes on, the question becomes: How soon must the internal expansion occur for the merger to have net negative allocative consequences? The relevant benefit and loss regions to be examined are those shown in figure 1.2.

Again let S be the initial cost savings of the merger (the rectangle designated as A_2) and L be the initial dead-weight loss (the triangle designated as A_1). When the internal expansion is completed and the price P_3 obtains, the dead-weight loss of the merger becomes the shaded region A_3. Let T' be the switch-over point such that, on allocative grounds,

Table 1.3 Switch-over values (T') for selected values of $\bar{S}/\bar{L}$ and of the attenuation coefficient (a)

a \ $\bar{S}/\bar{L}$	1.5	2	3	6
0.0	0.0	0.0	0.0	0.0
0.3	7.2	4.7	3.0	1.5
0.7	11.1	7.1	4.6	2.7
1.0	12.0	7.9	5.1	3.0

one is indifferent between going the internal expansion route or permitting the merger, and let the discount rate be 10 per cent. Substituting the values $\bar{S}$, $\bar{L}$, and A_3 into equation (1.5), the critical values of T' are those for which the discounted value of the net benefits of the merger are equal to zero. To wit:

$$V(T') = \int_0^{T'} (\bar{S} - \bar{L})\, e^{-rt} dt - \int_{T'}^{\infty} A_3 e^{-rt}\, dt = 0. \qquad (1.6)$$

Solution values of T' in this expression, for selected values of $\bar{S}/\bar{L}$ and a, require that the magnitude of the initial price increase and the elasticity of demand be specified. Assume for this purpose that demand has unit elasticity in the relevant range and that the merger gives rise to a 10 per cent rise increase, which is probably a rough upper bound. The switch-over (indifference) values that obtain for selected values of $\bar{S}/\bar{L}$ and a under these assumptions are shown in table 1.3.

The lower the value of T', the more quickly must economies be realized by internal expansion for a merger to have net negative allocative consequences. As would be expected, early internal expansion becomes more essential as the ratio of initial cost savings to the initial dead-weight loss ($\bar{S}/\bar{L}$) increases and as the attenuation coefficient (a) decreases. Roughly, the values of T' that appear on and to the right of the main diagonal are sufficiently small that one should have reasonable confidence that potential economies will be realized in the next few years for a merger to be disallowed on account of timing considerations alone.[8]

---

[8] Note that the solution values of T' depend on the choice of $\Delta P/P_1$, r, and η – increasing as either $\Delta P/P_1$ and η increase, decreasing as r increases. My guess is that the selected values of r and η are probably close, but that the choice of $\Delta P/P_1$ tends toward an upper bound. Hence, 'typical' values of T' will be lower than those shown.

D. INCIPIENCY

It is likewise vital to consider not merely the market power effects of any single merger taken in isolation, but whether the merger is representative of a trend. If a series of such mergers can reasonably be expected, the judgment of whether to permit any given combination should properly be cast in an industry context – in which case the anticipated economy and market power effects throughout the industry should be examined. Since, if economies are available by combining one pair of firms they will often be available more generally, this may frequently be an important consideration. The notion of incipiency thus has special relevance in administering the law on mergers where economies are claimed.

This proposition might usefully be contrasted with that of Bork and Bowman (1965, p. 594):

The difficulty with stopping a trend toward a more concentrated condition at a very early stage is that the existence of the trend is prima facie evidence that greater concentration is socially desirable. The trend indicates that there are emerging efficiencies or economies of scale – whether due to engineering and production developments or to new control and management techniques – which make larger size more efficient. This increased efficiency is valuable to the society at large, for it means that fewer of our available resources are being used to accomplish the same amount of production and distribution. By striking at such trends in their very earliest stages the concept of incipiency prevents the realization of those very efficiencies that competition is supposed to encourage.

Their evaluation of the social desirability of a trend suggests a certain insensitivity to the relevant scale economy–market power trade-off considerations, and they appear to read the significance of a trend somewhat too loosely; it may also indicate an emerging awareness that market power advantages might be realized through a series of combinations.[9] Moreover, whereas they seem to suggest that to disallow a merger is to prevent the realization of scale economies altogether, ordinarily it is not a question of whether economies will be realized but when and with what market power effects. Thus, while Bork and Bowman may be correct in charging that scale economy justifications have not been given sufficient weight in the recent enforcement of the merger law, they are also guilty of a certain heavy-handedness in their own treatment of the incipiency question.

---

[9] This is George Stigler's point in his treatment of 'Monopoly and Oligopoly by Merger' (1958). Bork concedes this possibility in his response to Blake and Jones (1965, p. 412); but his principal emphasis, which is probably correct, is that a trend signals emerging economies.

E. WEIGHTING

The economies that a merger produces are usually limited strictly to the combining firms. But the market power effects of a merger may sometimes result in a price increase across a wider class of firms. Where this occurs, a weighting factor should be introduced into expression (1.2) to reflect this condition. The criterion becomes

$$\left(\frac{Q_2}{Q_T}\right)\frac{\Delta(AC)}{AC} - \frac{1}{2}\eta\frac{Q_1}{Q_2}\left(\frac{\Delta P}{P_1}\right)^2 > 0 \tag{1.2'}$$

where Q_2 is the output of the merging firms and Q_T is the total quantity of industry sales for which the price increase becomes effective.

F. INCOME DISTRIBUTION

An additional qualification to our analysis involves income distribution effects. The rectangle in figure 1.1 bounded by P_2 and P_1 at the top and bottom respectively and O and Q_2 on the sides represents a loss of consumers' surplus (gain in monopoly profits) that the merger produces. On the resource allocation criteria for judging welfare effects advanced above, the distribution of these profits becomes a matter of indifference. For specific welfare valuations, however, we might not always wish to regard consumer and producer interests symmetrically – although since, arguably, antitrust is an activity better suited to promote allocative efficiency than income distribution objectives (the latter falling more clearly within the province of taxation, expenditure, and transfer payment activities), such income distribution adjustments might routinely be suppressed. If they are not, the trade-off between efficiency gains and distributive losses needs explicitly to be expressed. Thus, while economies would remain a defense, any undesirable income distribution effects associated with market power would be counted against the merger rather than enter neutrally as the naive model implies.

Inasmuch as the income redistribution which occurs is usually large relative to the size of the dead-weight loss, attaching even a slight weight to income distribution effects can sometimes influence the overall valuation significantly. Thus, expressing the dead-weight loss ($L = \frac{1}{2}(\Delta P)(\Delta Q)$) as a ratio of the income distribution effect ($I = (\Delta P)Q$), and substituting into this ratio the expression for the elasticity of demand (η), the fraction $L/I = \frac{1}{2}(\Delta P/P)\,\eta$ obtains. It is therefore obvious that, except where the elasticity of demand is 'high', the dead-weight loss as a fraction of the income distribution effect is relatively small – certainly less than unity. Hence, if as is probably common, the income redistribution which results when market power is increased is regarded unfavorably, an appropriate weighting of this factor will, at least occasionally, upset a net valuation which on resource allocation grounds is positive.

Note in this connection that the transfer involved could be regarded unfavorably not merely because it redistributes income in an undesirable way (increases the degree of inequality in the size distribution of income), but also because it produces social discontent. This latter has serious efficiency implications that the above analysis does not take explicitly into account. This same point also appears to have gone unnoticed in the entire Bork and Bowman v. Blake and Jones exchange (Blake and Jones, 1965a, pp. 377–400; Blake and Jones, 1965b, pp. 422–66; Bork and Bowman, 1965, pp. 363–76; Bork, 1965, pp. 401–16). Distinguishing social from private costs in this respect may, however, be the most fundamental reason for treating claims of private efficiency gains skeptically.

G. POLITICAL CONSIDERATIONS

Combinations which involve firms that are already very large in absolute terms might be resisted on grounds that these raise extra-economic problems of political significance. There is not, however, any obvious way in which to integrate these into the analysis. Rather, although the political implications of control over wealth are a matter for serious concern, these are separable from the economic problems posed by control over markets; a different calculus is required to deal with each. The necessary political judgment, ideally, is one for Congress to make. Possibly, as Carl Kaysen has suggested, this would take the form of a prohibition against expansion by merger of the largest 50 or 100 corporations (1965, p. 37).

The issue here reaches beyond the social discontent matter raised above. Thus, whereas social discontent can be reduced, in principle at least, to efficiency-equivalent (net value product) terms, the political implications of the control over wealth involve a judgment of how the quality of life in a democracy is affected by size disparities. The latter is less easily (or even appropriately) expressed in efficiency terms. The issue is nevertheless important, and failure to deal with it may be unresponsive to the position taken by Blake and Jones. Inasmuch as several of the counterexamples that they pose in their critique of Bork and Bowman appear deliberately to have been selected from the giant firm universe (Blake and Jones, 1965, pp. 425–7), possibly it is mergers within this subset that concern them most. Should economies be allowed as a defense, therefore, the rule proposed by Kaysen would limit such a defense in a way which would presumably relieve this aspect of their concern.

H. TECHNOLOGICAL PROGRESS; AND

I. MANAGERIAL DISCRETION

The highly conjectural nature of qualifications H and I makes it unclear at this time what weight ought to be assigned to them. It is at least arguable that the prevailing uncertainties are too great to give any effect to these two factors at this time. They are, nevertheless, potentially of such significance that to dismiss them may run the risk of serious error. In consideration of this potential importance, additional research which would permit us better to evaluate their actual significance would seem warranted. The manner in which each would influence the estimate of net effects is sketched out below.

Consider technological progress first. Such increases in market power that result in predictable effects on technological progress should, if they can easily, be taken into account. The present evidence, while hardly abundant, suggests that, as a general rule, the research and development expenditures of the four largest firms in an industry are neither as large proportionately nor as productive as those of their immediately smaller rivals.[10] But this fails to answer the question of what market structures most enhance progressiveness. The evidence on this latter is somewhat mixed.[11] It seems unlikely, however, that subsequent investigation will upset the basic proposition that progressiveness is promoted by at least some elements of competition at virtually every stage of an industry's development – if for no other reason than that competition tends to assure

[10] With respect to size, Mansfield found that the ratio of innovations to firm size reached a maximum at about the sixth largest firm for the petroleum and coal industries, and at a much lower rank for steel (1963, p. 566). Elsewhere Mansfield reports that the largest firms in petroleum, drugs, and glass spent somewhat less on R&D, relative to sales, than did somewhat smaller firms; in chemicals they spent somewhat more; in steel they spent less, but the difference was not statistically significant (1964, p. 334). Scherer concludes from his study of patent behavior in a group of 448 firms selected from the Fortune list of the largest 500 industrial corporations in 1955 that 'the evidence does support the hypothesis that corporate bigness is especially favorable to high inventive output' (1965, p. 1114). Turning to productivity, Mansfield concludes that 'in most industries, the productivity of an R&D program of given scale seems to be lower in the largest firms than in somewhat smaller firms' (1963, p. 338). Comanor found that diseconomies of scale in the pharmaceutical industry were encountered at even moderate firm sizes (1965, p. 190). For a recent review of this literature, see Johnson (1966, pp. 169–71).
[11] Hamburg (1966, chapter 4) and Horowitz (1962, pp. 330–1) report a positive correlation between R&D expenditures and industrial concentration. Scherer finds a much weaker but slightly positive association (1965, pp. 1119–21). Kendrick concludes from an examination of Terleckyj's data that there is no significant correlation between productivity changes and industrial concentration (1961, p. 179). Stigler found in an earlier study 'hints that industries with lower concentration had higher rates of technological progress' (1956, p. 278), while I, using Mansfield's data, found a negative correlation between the proportion of innovations introduced by the four largest firms and industrial concentration (Williamson, 1965).

that variety in research approaches will be employed. Local or regional monopolies may provide partial exceptions (since here the requisite variety will be available nationally, although the rate at which innovations are implemented may nevertheless lag if competitive pressures are lacking), but monopoly, or near-monopoly, would not seem to be the perfect instrument for technical progress in industries for which the relevant market is national.

Lacking additional evidence, it would not seem injudicious to assume that mergers between relatively small-sized firms rarely have negative (and may frequently have positive) effects on progressiveness, whatever the condition of concentration. This judgment probably holds for most mergers involving lower–middle sized firms as well. Thus it is mainly in the relatively large firms, particularly those in moderately to highly concentrated national markets (which, of course, are also ones where market power effects may be important), that the effects of a merger on technological progress deserve special attention.

Whether the effects be positive or negative, the necessary extension to the model is identical. Assume therefore that a merger is proposed involving a large firm in a concentrated industry, and that while it yields economies it also predictably decreases the rate of progressiveness. Holding constant for the moment the effects on price, how large a change in the rate of technical progress would be required to offset the available economy of scale advantage? To obtain a crude estimate of this, let θ be the ratio of the immediate post-merger to pre-merger average costs (so that $1 - \theta$ is the immediate decimal fraction reduction in average costs), g_1 be the rate of productivity increase in the absence of the merger, and g_2 the rate if the merger is approved (where $g_1 \geqslant g_2$), $Q(t)$ be the output in period t, and let r be the social discount rate. Then the merger will have neutral effects if the discounted value of costs under each condition is the same. This requires that the equality given below should hold:[12]

$$\int_0^\infty [(AC)Q(t)e^{-g_1 t}]e^{-rt}dt = \int_0^\infty [\theta(AC)Q(t)e^{-g_2 t}]e^{-rt}dt. \quad (1.7)$$

Assuming that output increases exponentially at the rate δ, athe critical value of g_2 is given by

$$g_2 = \theta g_1 - (1 - \theta)(r - \delta). \quad (1.8)$$

If, for example, the values of θ, g_1 and $r - \delta$ were 0.90, 0.03, and 0.07

---

[12] The argument assumes that only the yield and not the expenditures on R&D are affected by the combination. Although any expenditure difference could go either way, one would expect in general that the higher rate of progress would be associated with a higher expenditure stream, in which case the indicated allocative advantage associated with the more progressive structure would be correspondingly reduced.

respectively, the critical value of g_2 would be 0.02. Were g_2 to fall below this value, an indicated economy of 10 per cent would not be sufficient to offset the cumulative productivity loss associated with the merger, to say nothing of the market power effects that the merger produces. If indeed the selected values of g_1 and $r - \delta$ are at all representative, a predictable decrease in the rate of productivity advance by one-third or more would thus be sufficient to disallow a merger for which an efficiency advantage as large as 10 per cent could be expected.[13]

Consider now the managerial discretion argument. Here the direction of the effect is not so much a matter for dispute as is its quantitative significance. The argument is that market power provides a firm with the opportunity to pursue a variety of other-than-profit objectives. Although this is an 'old' argument, its persistence at least suggests the possibility that it may not be without merit.[14] Whether qualitatively there is anything to it turns essentially on the behavioral proposition that where competition in the product market presents no significant threat to survival, the resources of the firm are absorbed in part as corporate consumption activities by those members of the firm who are knowledgeable of discretionary opportunities, powerfully situated, and disposed to be assertive (Williamson, 1964; 1967). Its quantitative significance rests on a judgment over whether the conspicuous evidence is sufficiently strong.[15]

If indeed a predictable relaxation in the least-cost posture of a firm which has acquired market power through merger can be made, the estimated cost savings that appear in equation (1.5) should be adjusted accordingly. Economies which are available in theory but, by reason of market power, are not sustainable are inadmissible.

III. Extensions

Although the foregoing analysis has been concerned exclusively with horizontal mergers, the argument applies generally to problems in which

[13] If the beneficial economies of scale are available only to the combining firms, while the negative progressiveness effects are felt throughout the industry, the above results underestimate the extent of economies necessary to produce indifference.

[14] As Arthur Hadley observed in 1897, 'The tendency of monopoly to retard the introduction of industrial improvement is . . . a more serious thing than its tendency to allow unfair rates. This aspect of the matter has hardly received proper attention. We have been so accustomed to think of competition as a regulator of prices that we have lost sight of its equally important function as a stimulus to efficiency. Wherever competition is absent, there is a disposition to rst content with old methods, not to say slack ones. In spite of notable exceptions this is clearly the rule' (1897, p. 383).

[15] This presently is the weakest part of the argument. For a recent survey of the data, see Leibenstein (1966, pp. 392–415).

market power–efficiency trade-offs exist. Dissolution, vertical mergers, and conglomerate mergers can all be treated within this general framework.

A. DISSOLUTION

The argument here is perfectly straightforward. It is simply not sufficient in a monopolization case for which dissolution is the indicated relief that (a) a persistent monopoly condition ($P_1 > AC_1$) exist, and (b) a reduction in price following dissolution ($P_2 < P_1$) be expected. It is necessary in addition that the gains realized by the price reduction be sufficient to offset any losses in economies that result. The relevant test is that shown in equation (1.3) – modified, as may be necessary, by the qualifications discussed in section II above.

B. VERTICAL MERGERS

It is important to note in dealing with vertical mergers that the conventional analysis of vertical integration, which takes a historical definition of an industry as given, often leads to incorrect results. The logical boundaries of a firm are not necessarily those which have been inherited but rather are defined by the condition that the firm be unable to arrange a transaction internally more cheaply than the market.[16] This is not something which is given once-for-all but depends both on technology and the extent of the market. Thus what may be regarded as 'vertical integration' under a historical definition of an industry might, in many instances, more accurately be characterized as a reorganization into a more efficient configuration. For example, as technology evolves processes that are more fully automated or as demand for a commodity increases sufficiently to warrant continuous processing techniques, combinatorial economies may result by serially linking activities within a single firm that had previously been done in separate specialty firms.[17] A transformation of this sort accomplished in part through vertical mergers is probably common in the production of commodities which shift from sequential job shop to continuous assembly line type operations.

[16] As Ronald Coase has pointed out, 'a firm will tend to expand until the costs of organizing an extra transaction within the firm become equal to the costs of carrying out the same transaction by means of an exchange on the open market or the costs of organizing in another firm' (1952, p. 341).

[17] Stigler argues that increasing the extent of the market will often lead to disintegration of manufacturing processes since now the market will be sufficient to support a specialized firm (1951, pp. 188–90). Although this may often occur, there is also the countervailing tendency to maintain or extend integration where coordination among the parts in the face of market uncertainties is critical – as it often is where assembly line operations are employed. See Coase (1952, p. 337).

That vertical integration can produce real economies is a result of the fact that the market does not perform its exchanges costlessly. Going to the market involves search costs, contracting costs, misinformation costs, delay costs, transfer costs, interface costs, and so on,[18] and these must be balanced against the costs of organizing a transaction internally. Where the former exceed the latter, 'vertical integration' is indicated. But of course this is vertical integration in only an apparent sense: in fact it represents a rationalization of the firm into an optimum economic unit.

The historical organization of an industry can ordinarily be presumed to reflect adequately basic efficiencies where significant market or technological developments have been lacking. And even where such recent changes have occurred, an efficiency defense is not automatic. Furthermore, if an efficiency defense can be supplied, any market power consequences that a vertical merger produces need also to be considered.[19] Again the basic trade-off calculation is that given by equation (1.3) – modified as necessary by the qualifications discussed in section II.

C. CONGLOMERATE MERGERS

The principal ways in which conglomerate mergers can produce efficiencies have been given previously by M. A. Adelman (1961, pp. 241–2) and Turner (1965, pp. 1323–39, 1358–61). The ways in which conglomerate mergers may produce market power are also discussed by Turner.[20] All that remains, essentially, is to deal with the trade-off question. Again the rules for estimating net benefits are substantially those given above.

IV. Conclusions

Most mergers produce neither significant price nor efficiency consequences, and where this is true the analysis of this chapter has limited relevance. Where both occur, however, and if without merger the transition to an efficient industrial configuration is apt to be both painful and delayed, an efficiency defense deserves consideration. This does not of course mean that the mere existence of economies is sufficient to justify

---

[18] Coase discusses some of these (1952, pp. 336–7). (For an early example in which the costs of going to the market were examined in a common law proceeding, see *Hadley* v. *Baxendale*.) In addition, if suppliers possess market power, going to the market may involve pecuniary expenses that could be avoided by integrating backward into supply activities.

[19] Stigler identifies barriers to entry that take the form of increased capital and/or knowledge requirements as potential anticompetitive consequences of a vertical merger (1951, p. 191).

[20] For a more recent treatment of the economies and market power effects of conglomerate organization, see Williamson (1970).

a merger. But since a relatively large percentage increase in price is usually required to offset the benefits that result from a 5 to 10 per cent reduction in average costs, the existence of economies of this magnitude is sufficiently important to give the antitrust authorities pause before disallowing such a merger.

There are, however, as indicated in section II, a variety of qualifications that may upset this general conclusion in any particular case. The argument, thus, is not dispositive; a crude feel for the quantitative significance of the relevant factors is all that can be claimed.[21]

---

[21] Moreover, the argument does not pretend to be exhaustive. Product variety considerations, for example, have been suppressed: any predictable change in product variety attributable to the merger should appropriately be reflected in the welfare valuation. Inasmuch, however, as product variety changes could go either way (an increase or decrease in product variety is possible), since neither is apt to be evident *ex ante*, and as such effects as do obtain are likely to be small, it seems reasonable to proceed, for the present at least, as though product variety will remain unchanged. This is the usual, if implicit, assumption in most welfare loss valuations. For a recent contribution to the product differentiation literature that might, were the matter to be regarded as operationally significant, eventually be brought to bear on these issues, see Wright (1969).

2

The Vertical Integration of Production: Market Failure Considerations

The study of vertical integration has presented difficulties at both theoretical and policy level of analysis. That vertical integration has never enjoyed a secure place in value theory is attributable to the fact that, under conventional assumptions, it is an anomaly: if the costs of operating competitive markets are zero, 'as is usually assumed in our theoretical analysis' (Arrow, 1969, p. 48), why integrate?

Policy interest in vertical integration has been concerned mainly with the possibility that integration can be used strategically to achieve anticompetitive effects. In the absence of a more substantial theoretical foundation, vertical integration, as a public policy matter, is typically regarded as having dubious if not outright antisocial properties. Technological interdependencies or, possibly, observational economies, constitute the principal exceptions.

The technological interdependency argument is both the most familiar and the most straightforward: successive processes which, naturally, follow immediately in time and place dictate certain efficient manufacturing configurations; these, in turn, are believed to have common ownership implications. Such technical complementarity is probably more important in flow process operations (chemicals, metals, etc.) than in separable component manufacture. The standard example is the integration of iron and steel making, where thermal economies are said to be available through integration. It is commonly held that where 'integration does not have this physical or technical aspect – as it does not, for example, in integrating the production of assorted components with the assembly of

Research on this chapter has been supported by a grant from the Brookings Institution. It is part of the larger study referred to in footnote 1. Helpful comments from Noel Edelson, Stefano Fenoaltea, Julius Margolis, and Almarin Phillips are gratefully acknowledged.

Previously published in *American Economic Review*, LXI (May 1971), pp. 112–3, by kind permission of the author and of the American Economic Association.

those components – the case for cost savings from integration is generally much less clear' (Bain, 1968, p. 381).

There is, nevertheless, a distinct unease over the argument. This is attributable, probably, to a suspicion that the firm is more than a simple efficiency instrument, in the usual scale economies and least-cost factor proportions senses of the term, but also possesses coordinating potential that sometimes transcends that of the market. It is the burden of the present argument that this suspicion is warranted. In more numerous respects than are commonly appreciated, the substitution of internal organization for market exchange is attractive less on account of technological economies associated with production but because of what may be referred to broadly as 'transactional failures' in the operation of markets for intermediate goods. This substitution of internal organization for market exchange will be referred to as 'internalization'.

The two principal prior contributions on which the argument relies are Coase's seminal discussion on 'The Nature of the Firm' (1937) and Arrow's more recent review of market versus nonmarket allocation (1969). As will be evident, I agree with Malmgren (1961) that the analysis of transaction costs is uninteresting under fully stationary conditions and that only when the need to make unprogrammed adaptations is introduced does the market versus internal organization issue become engaging.

But while Malmgren finds that the advantage of the firm inheres in its capacity to control information and achieve plan consistency among interdependent activities, which may be regarded as an information processing advantage, I mainly emphasize the differential incentive and control properties of firms in relation to markets. This is not to suggest that information processing considerations are unimportant, but rather that these incompletely characterize the distinctive properties of firms that favor internal organization as a market substitute.

I. Internal Organization: Affirmative Aspects

A complete treatment of vertical integration requires that the limits as well as the powers of internal organization be assessed. As the frictions associated with administrative coordination become progressively more severe, recourse to market exchange becomes more attractive, *ceteris paribus*. It is beyond the scope of this chapter, however, to examine the organizational failure aspect of the vertical integration question.[1] Rather it is simply assserted that, mainly on account of bounded rationality and greater confidence in the objectivity of market exchange in comparison

[1] I discuss the organizational failure dimension of this issue in Markets and Hierarchies (1975). Policy implications of the argument are also examined there.

with bureaucratic processes, market intermediation is generally to be preferred over internal supply in circumstances in which markets may be said to 'work well'.[2]

The properties of the firm that commend internal organization as a market substitute would appear to fall into three categories: incentives, controls, and what may be referred to broadly as 'inherent structural advantages'. In an incentive sense, internal organization attenuates the aggressive advocacy that epitomizes arm's length bargaining. Interests, if not perfectly harmonized, are at least free of representations of a narrowly opportunistic sort; in any viable group, of which the firm is one, the range of admissible intraorganizational behavior is bounded by considerations of alienation. In circumstances, therefore, where protracted bargaining between independent parties to a transaction can reasonably be anticipated, internalization becomes attractive.[3]

Perhaps the most distinctive advantage of the firm, however, is the wider variety and greater sensitivity of control instruments that are available for enforcing intrafirm in comparison with interfirm activities (Williamson, 1970). Not only does the firm have the constitutional authority and low-cost access to the requisite data which permit it to perform more precise own-performance evaluations (of both a contemporaneous and *ex post* variety) than can a buyer, but its reward and penalty instruments (which include selective use of employment, promotion, remuneration, and internal resource allocation processes) are more refined.

Especially relevant in this connection is that, when conflicts develop, the firm possesses a comparatively efficient conflict resolution machinery. To illustrate, fiat is frequently a more efficient way to settle minor conflicts (say differences of interpretation) than is haggling or litigation. *Inter*organizational conflict can be settled by fiat only rarely, if at all. For one thing, it would require the parties to agree on an impartial arbitrator, which agreement itself may be costly to secure. It would also require that rules of evidence and procedure be established. If, moreover, the occasions for such interorganizational settlements were to be common, the form of organization converges in effect to vertical integration, with the arbiter

[2] An intermediate market will be said to work well if, both presently and prospectively, prices are nonmonopolistic and reflect an acceptable risk premium, and if market exchange experiences low transaction costs and permits the realization of essential economies. To the extent that the stipulated conditions do not hold, internal supply becomes relatively more attractive, *ceteris paribus*.

[3] Common ownership by itself, of course, does not guarantee goal consistency. A holding company form of organization in which purchaser and supplier are independent divisions, each maximizing individual profits, is no solution. Moreover, merely to stipulate joint profit maximization is not by itself apt to be sufficient. The goal needs to be operationalized, which involves both rule-making (with respect, for example, to transfer pricing) and the design of efficacious internal incentives. For a discussion, see Williamson (1970).

becoming a manager in fact if not in name. By contrast, *intra*organizational settlements by fiat are common (Whinston, 1964, pp. 410–14).

The firm may also resort to internalization on account of economies of information exchange. Some of these may be due to structural differences between firms and markets. Others, however, reduce ultimately to incentive and control differences between internal and market organization. It is widely accepted, for example, that communication with respect to complex matters is facilitated by a common training and experience and if a compact code has developed in the process. Repeated interpersonal interactions may permit even further economies of communication; subtle nuances may come through in familiar circumstances which is an unfamiliar relationship could be achieved only with great effort. Still, the drawing of an organizational boundary need not, by itself, prevent intensely familiar relations from developing between organizations. Put differently, but for the goal and control differences described above, the informational advantages of internal over market organization are not, in this respect, apparent. Claims of informational economies thus should distinguish between economies that are attributable to information flows *per se* (structure) and those which obtain on account of differential veracity effects (see part D, section II).

II.   Market Failure Considerations

What are referred to here as market failures are failures only in the limited sense that they involve transaction costs that can be attenuated by substituting internal organization for market exchange. The argument proceeds in five stages. The first three are concerned with characterizing a successively more complex bargaining environment in which small numbers relations obtain. The last two deal with the special structural advantages which, either naturally, or because of prevailing institutional rules, the firm enjoys in relation to the market.

A. STATIC MARKETS

Consider an industry that produces a multicomponent product, assume that some of these components are specialized (industry specific), and assume further that among these there are components for which the economies of scale in production are large in relation to the market. The market, then, will support only a few efficient-sized producers for certain components.

A monopolistic excess of price over cost under market procurement is commonly anticipated in these circumstances – although, as Demsetz (1968) has noted, this need not obtain if there are large numbers of suppliers willing and able to bid at the initial contract award stage. Assume, however, that large numbers bidding is not feasible. The postulated conditions then afford an 'apparent' incentive for assemblers to integrate backward or suppliers to integrate forward. Two different cases can be distinguished: bilateral monopoly (oligopoly) and competitive assembly with monopolistic supply. The former is considered here; the latter is treated in part C.

Bilateral monopoly requires that both price and quantity be negotiated. Both parties stand to benefit, naturally, by operating on rather than off the contract curve – which here corresponds to the joint profit-maximizing quantity (Fellner, 1947). But this merely establishes the amount to be exchanged. The terms at which this quantity will be traded still need to be determined. Any price consistent with nonnegative profits to both parties is feasible. Bargaining can be expected to ensue. Haggling will presumably continue until the marginal private net benefits are perceived by one of the parties to be zero. Although this haggling is jointly (and socially) unproductive, it constitutes a source of private pecuniary gain. Being, nevertheless, a joint profit drain, an incentive to avoid these costs, if somehow this could be arranged, is set up.

One possible adaptation is to internalize the transaction through vertical integration; but a once-for-all contract might also be negotiated. In a perfectly static environment (one that is free of disturbances of all kinds), these may be regarded with indifference: the former involves settlement on component supply price while merger requires agreement on asset valuation. Bargaining skills will presumably be equally important in each instance (indeed, a component price can be interpreted in asset valuation terms and conversely). Thus, although vertical integration may occur under these conditions, there is nothing in the nature of the problem that requires such an outcome.

A similar argument in these circumstances also applies to adaptation against externalities: joint profit considerations dictate that the affected parties reach an accommodation, but integration holds no advantage over once-for-all contracts in a perfectly static environment.

Transforming the relationship from one of bilateral monopoly to one of bilateral oligopoly broadens the range of bargaining alternatives, but the case for negotiating a merger agreement in relation to a once-for-all contract is not differentially affected on this account. The static characterization of the problem, apparently, will have to be relaxed if a different result is to be reached.

B. CONTRACTUAL INCOMPLETENESS

Let the above conditions be enriched to include the stipulation that the product in question is technically complex and that periodic redesign and/

or volume changes are made in response to changing environmental conditions. Also relax the assumption that large numbers bidding at the initial contract award stage is infeasible. Three alternative supply arrangements can be considered: a once-for-all contract, a series of short-term contracts, and vertical integration.

The dilemma posed by once-for-all contracts is this: lest independent parties interpret contractual ambiguities to their own advantage, which differences can be resolved only by haggling or, ultimately, litigation, contingent supply relations ought exhaustively to be stipulated. But exhaustive stipulation, assuming that it is feasible, is itself costly. Thus although, if production functions were known, appropriate responses to final demand or factor price changes might be deduced, the very costliness of specifying the functions and securing agreement discourages the effort. The problem is made even more severe where a changing technology poses product redesign issues. Here it is doubtful that, despite great effort and expense, contractual efforts reasonably to comprehend the range of possible outcomes will be successful. An adaptive, sequential decision process is thus indicated. If, however, contractual revisions or amendments are regarded as an occasion to bargain opportunistically, which predictably they will be, the purchaser will defer and accumulate adaptations, if by packaging them in complex combinations their true value can better be disguised; some adaptations may be foregone altogether. The optimal sequential decision-making process can in these respects be distorted.

Short-term contracts, which would facilitate adaptive, sequential decision making, might therefore be preferred. These pose problems, however, if either (a) efficient supply requires investment in special-purpose, long-life equipment, or (b) the winner of the original contract acquires a cost advantage, say by reason of 'first mover' advantgaes (such as unique location or learning, including the acquisition of undisclosed or proprietary technical and managerial procedures and task-specific labor skills).

The problem with condition (a) is that optimal investment considerations favor the award of a long-term contract so as to permit the supplier confidently to amortize his investment. But, as indicated, long-term contracts pose adaptive, sequential decision-making problems. Thus optimal investment and optimal sequential adaptation processes are in conflict in this instance.

It might be argued that condition (b) poses no problems since initial bidders will fully reflect in their original bids all relevant factors. Thus, although anticipated downstream cost advantages (where downstream is used both here and subsequently in the sense of time rather than place) will give rise to small numbers competition for downstream supply, competition at the initial award stage is sufficient to assure that only competitive returns will be realized over the entire supply interval. One might expect, therefore, that the low bidder would come in at a price below cost in the first period, set price at the level of alternative supply price in later periods, and earn normal returns over-all. Appropriate changes can be introduced easily at the recontracting interval.

A number of potential problems are posed, however. For one thing, unless the total supply requirements are stipulated, 'buying in' strategies are risky. Also, and related, the alternative supply price is not independent of the terms that the buyer may subsequently offer to rivals. Moreover, alternative supply price is merely an upper bound; an aggressive buyer may attempt to obtain a price at the level of current costs on each round. Haggling could be expected to ensue. Short-term contracts thus experience what may be serious limitations in circumstances where nontrivial first-mover advantages obtain.

In consideration, therefore, of the problems that both long- and short-term contracts are subject to, vertical integration may well be indicated. The conflict between efficient investment and efficient sequential decision making is thereby avoided. Sequential adaptations become an occasion for cooperative adjustment rather than opportunistic bargaining; risks may be attenuated; differences between successive stages can be resolved more easily by the internal control machinery.

It is relevant to note that the technological interdependency condition involving flow process economies between otherwise separable stages of production is really a special case of the contractual incompleteness argument. The contractual dilemma is this: on the one hand, it may be prohibitively costly, if not infeasible, to specify contractually the full range of contingencies and stipulate appropriate responses between stages. On the other hand, if the contract is seriously incomplete in these respects but, once the original negotiations are settled, the contracting parties are locked into a bilateral exchange, the divergent interests between the parties will predictably lead to individually opportunistic behavior and joint losses. The advantages of integration thus are not that technological (flow process) economies are unavailable to nonintegrated firms, but that integration harmonizes interests (or reconciles differences, often by fiat) and permits an efficient (adaptive, sequential) decision process to be utilized. More generally, arguments favorable to integration that turn on 'supply reliability' considerations commonly reduce to the contractual incompleteness issue.[4]

---

[4] It is sometimes suggested that breach of contract risk affords an additional reason for integration: the small supplier of a critical component whose assets are insufficient to cover a total damage claim leaves the purchaser vulnerable. But this is an argument against small suppliers, not contracting quite generally; the large, diversified supplier might well have superior risk pooling capability to that of the integrated firm. The risks of contractual incompleteness, however, remain and may discourage purchasing from large, diversified organizations. For a discussion of 'ideal' contracts in this connection, see Arrow (1965, pp. 52–3).

C. STRATEGIC MISREPRESENTATION RISK

Contractual incompleteness problems develop where there is *ex ante* but not necessarily *ex post* uncertainty. Strategic misrepresentation risks are serious where there is uncertainty in both respects. Not only is the future uncertain but it may not be possible, except at great cost, for an outside agency to establish accurately what has transpired after the fact. The advantages of internalization reside in the facts that the firm's *ex post* access to the relevant data is superior, it attenuates the incentives to exploit uncertainty opportunistically, and the control machinery that the firm is able to activate is more selective.

Affirmative Occasions for Integration

Three affirmative occasions to integrate on account of strategic misrepresentation risk and two potentially anticompetitive consequences of integration can be identified.

1 *Moral hazard.* The problem here arises because of the conjoining of inharmonious incentives with uncertainty – or, as Arrow puts it (1969, p. 55), it is due to the 'confounding of risks and decisions.' To illustrate, consider the problem of contracting for an item the final cost and/or performance of which is subject to uncertainty. One possibility is for the supplier to bear the uncertainty. But, he will undertake a fixed price contract to deliver a specified result, the costs of which are highly uncertain, only after attaching a risk premium to the price. Assume that the buyer regards this premium as excessive and is prepared on this account to bear the risk himself. The risk can easily be shifted by offering a cost-plus contract. But this impairs the incentives of the supplier to achieve least-cost performance; the supplier may reallocate his assets in such a way as to favor other work to the disadvantage of the cost-plus contract.

Thus, although, if commitments were self-enforcing, it might often be institutionally most efficient to divide the functions of risk bearing and contract execution (that is, cost-plus contracts would have ideal properties), specialization is discouraged by interest disparities. At a minimum, the buyer may insist on monitoring the supplier's work. In contrast therefore to a fixed-price contract, where it is sufficient to evaluate end-product performance, cost-plus contracts, because they expose the buyer to risks of inefficient (high cost) contract execution, require that *both* inputs and outputs be evaluated.

Internalization does not eliminate the need for input evaluation. Rather, the advantage of internalization, for input monitoring purposes, resides in the differential ease with which controls are exercised. An external agency, by design, lacks recourse to the internal control machinery:

proposed remedies require the consent of the contractor and then are highly circumscribed; unrestricted access by the buyer to the contractor's internal control machinery (including selective use of employment, promotion, remuneration, and internal resource allocation processes) is apt to be denied. In consideration of the costs and limitations of input monitoring by outsiders, the buyer may choose instead to bear the risk and perform the work himself. The buyer thus internalizes, through backward vertical integration, a transaction which, but for uncertainty, would move through the market. A cost-type contract for internal procurement is arranged.

2 *Externalities/imputation*. The externality issue can be examined in two parts. First, has a secure, unambiguous, and 'appropriate' assignment of property rights been made? Second, are the accounting costs of imputing costs and benefits substantial? If answers to these questions are affirmative and negative respectively, appropriability problems will not become an occasion for vertical integration. Where these conditions are not satisfied, however, integration may be indicated.

The assignment aspect of this matter is considered in part E below. Here it is assumed that an efficacious assignment of property rights has been made and that only the expense of imputing costs and benefits is at issue. But indeed this is apt often to be the more serious problem. High imputation expenses which discourage accurate metering introduce ambiguity into transactions. Did party A affect party B and if so in what degree? In the absence of objective, low-cost standards, opposed interests can be expected to evaluate these effects differently. Internalization, which permits protracted (and costly) disputes over these issues to be avoided, may on this account be indicated.

3 *Variable proportions distortions*. Consider the case where the assembly stage will support large numbers; fewness appears only in component supply. Whether monopolistic supply prices provide an occasion for vertical integration in these circumstances depends both on production technology and policing expense. Variable proportions at the assembly stage afford opportunities for nonintegrated assemblers to adapt against monopolistically priced components by substituting competitively priced factors (McKenzie, 1951). Although conceivably the monopolistic component supplier could stipulate, as a condition of sale, that fixed proportions in assembly should prevail, the effectiveness of such stipulations is to be questioned – since, ordinarily, the implied enforcement costs will be great. Where substitution occurs, inefficient factor proportions, with consequent welfare losses, will rseult. The private (and social) incentives to integrate so as to reduce total costs by restoring efficient factor combinations are evident.

Anticompetitive Consequences

Anticompetitive effects of two types are commonly attributed to integration: price discrimination and barriers to entry (Stigler, 1968, p. 303).

1 *Price discrimination*. The problem here is first to discover differential demand elasticities, and secondly to arrange for sale in such a way as to preclude reselling. Users with highly elastic demands which purchase the item at a low price must not be able to service inelastic demand customers by acting as middle-man; all sales must be final. Although vertical integration may facilitate the discovery of differential elasticities, it is mainly with respect to the non resale condition that it is regarded as especially efficacious.

Integration, nevertheless, is a relatively extreme response. Moreover, price discrimination is clearly practised in some commodities without recourse to vertical integration (witness electricity and telephone service). What are the distinguishing factors? Legality considerations aside, presumably it is the cost of enforcing (policing) terms of the contract that are at issue. Some commodities apparently have self-enforcing properties – which may obtain on account of high storage and repacking costs or because reselling cannot be arranged inconspicuously. The absence of self-enforcing (policing) properties is what makes vertical integration attractive as a means of accomplishing discrimination.

2 *Entry barrier effects*. That the vertical integration of production might be used effectively to bar entry is widely disputed. Bork (1969, p. 148) argues that 'In general, if greater than competitive profits are to be made in an industry, entry should occur whether the entrant has to come in at both levels at once or not. I know of no theory of imperfections in the capital market which would lead suppliers of capital to avoid areas of higher return to seek areas of lower return.' But the issue is not one of profit avoidance but rather involves cost incidence. If borrowers are confronted by increasingly adverse rates as they increase their finance requirements, which Hirshleifer suggests is a distinct possibility (1970, pp. 200–1), cost may not be independent of vertical structure.

Assuming that vertical integration has the effect of increasing capital requirements, the critical issues are to what extent and for what reasons the supply curve of finance behaves in the way postulated. The following conjecture is offered as a partial explanation: unable to monitor the performance of large, complex organizations in any but the crudest way or to effect management displacement easily except on evidence of seriously discreditable error, investors demand larger returns as finance requirements become progressively greater, *ceteris paribus*. Thus the costs of policing against the contingency that managers will operate a rival enterprise opportunistically are, on this argument, at least partly responsible for the reputed behavior of the supply curve of capital. In consideration of this state of affairs, established firms may use vertical integration strategically to increase finance requirements and thereby to discourage entry if potential entrants feel compelled, as a condition of successful entry, to adopt the prevailing structure – as they may if the industry is highly concentrated.

D. INFORMATION PROCESSING EFFECTS

As indicated in section I, one of the advantages of the firm is that it realizes economies of information exchange. These may manifest themselves as information impactedness, observational economies, or what Malmgren (1961) refers to as the 'convergence of expectations'.

Information Impactedness

Richardson illustrates the problems of information impactedness by reference to an entrepreneur who was willing to offer long-term contracts (at normal rates of return, presumably) but which contracts others were unprepared to accept because they were not convinced that he had 'the ability, as well as the will, to fulfill them. He may have information sufficient to convince himself that this is the case, but others may not' (Richardson, 1960, p. 83). He goes on to observe that the perceived risks of the two parties may be such as to make it difficult to negotiate a contract that offers commensurate returns to each; objective risks are augmented by contractual risks in these circumstances. Integration undertaken for this reason is akin to self-insurance by individuals who know themselves to be good risks but are priced out of the insurance market because of their inabiilty, at low cost, to 'reveal' this condition to insurers.

Observational Economies

As Radner indicates, 'the acquisition of information often involves a "set-up cost", i.e., the resources needed to obtain the information may be independent of the scale of the productin process in which the information is used' (Radner, 1970, p. 457). Although Radner apparently had horizontal firm size implications in mind, the argument also has relevance for vertical integration. If a single set of observations can be made that is of relevance to a related series of production stages, vertical integration may be efficient.

Still, the question might be raised, why common ownership? Why not an independent observational agency that sells information to all comers? Or, if the needed information is highly specialized, why not a joint venture? Alternatively, what inhibits efficient information exchange between successive stages of production according to contract? In relation, certainly, to the range of intermediate options potentially available, common ownership appears to be an extreme response. What are the factors which favor this outcome?

One of the problems with contracts is that of specifying terms. But even if terms could be reached, there is still a problem of policing the agreement. To illustrate, suppose that the common information collection responsibilities are assigned by contract to one of the parties. The purchasing party then runs a veracity risk: information may be filtered and possibly distorted to the advantage of the firm that has assumed the information collection responsibility. If checks are costly and proof of contractual violation difficult, contractual sharing arrangements manifestly experience short-run limitations. If, in addition, small numbers prevail so that options are restricted, contractual sharing is subject to long-run risks as well. On this argument, observational economies are mainly to be attributed to strategic misrepresentation risks rather than to indivisibilities.

Convergence of Expectations

The issue to which the convergence of expectations argument is addressed is that, if there is a high degree of interdependence among successive stages of production and if occasions for adaptation are unpredictable yet common, coordinated responses may be difficult to secure if the separate stages are operated independently. March and Simon (1958, p. 159) characterize the problem in the following terms:

> Interdependence by itself does not cause difficulty if the pattern of interdependence is stable and fixed. For, in this case, each subprogram can be designed to take account of all the subprograms with which it interacts. Difficulties arise only if program execution rests on contingencies that cannot be predicted perfectly in advance. In this case, coordinating activity is required to secure agreement about the estimates that will be used as the basis for action, or to provide information to each subprogram unit about the activities of the others.

This reduces, in some respects, to a contractual incompleteness argument. Were it feasible exhaustively to stipulate the appropriate conditional responses, coordination could proceed by contract. This is ambitious, however; in the face of a highly variable and uncertain environment, the attempt to program responses is apt to be inefficient. To the extent that an unprogrammed (adaptive, sequential) decision process is employed instead, and in consideration of the severe incentive and control limitations that long-term contracts experience in these circumstances (see part B above), vertical integration may be indicated.

But what of the possibility of short-term contracts? It is here that the convergence of expectations argument is of special importance. Thus assume that short-term contracts are not defective on account either of investment disincentives or first-mover advantages. It is Malmgren's (1961) contention that such contracts may nevertheless be vitiated by the absence of structural constraints. The costs of negotiations and the time required to bring the system into adjustment by exclusive reliance on market (price) signals are apt to be great in relation to that which would obtain if successive states were integrated and administrative processes employed as well or instead.

E. INSTITUTIONAL ADAPTATIONS

Institutional adaptations of two types are distinguished: simple economic and extra-economic.

Simple Economic

As has been noted by others, vertical integration may be a device by which sales taxes on intermediate products are avoided, or a means by which to circumvent quota schemes and price controls (Coase, 1937, pp. 338–9; Stigler, 1968, pp. 136–7). But vertical integration may also be undertaken because of the defective specification of property rights.

Although the appropriate assignment of property rights is a complex question, it reduces (equity considerations aside) to a simple criterion: What assignment yields maximum total product (Coase, 1960, p. 34)? This depends jointly on imputation and negotiation expenses and on the incentives of the compensated party. So as to focus on the negotiation expense aspect, assume that imputation expenses are negligible and set the incentive question aside for the moment.[5] An 'appropriate' assignment of property rights will here be defined as one which automatically yields compensation in the amount of the external benefit or cost involved, while an 'inappropriate' assignment is one that requires bargaining to bring the parties into adjustment. Thus if A and B are two parties and A's activity imposes costs on B, the appropriate assignment of property

[5] As Coase has emphasized (1960, pp. 32–3, 41), compensation can impair the incentives of the compensated party that experiences an external cost to take appropriate protective measures. Parties that are assured of compensation will be content to conduct business as usual. Such a practice easily contributes to greater social cost than would obtain were compensation denied. A sensitivity to what, in a broad sense, might be regarded as contributory negligence is thus required if the system is to be brought fully into adjustment. Clairvoyance with respect to contributory negligence would of course permit the courts to supply those who experience the external cost with requisite incentives to adapt appropriately. Since, however, such clairvoyance (or even unbiasedness) cannot routinely be presumed, internalizing the transaction through vertical integration may be indicated for this reason as well. (Interestingly, a symmetrical problem is not faced where the externality is a benefit. Stipulating that compensation shall be paid induces Meade's (1952) orchard grower not merely to extend his production appropriately, but also to shift from apples to peaches if this is socially advantageous.)

rights is to require A to compensate B. If instead property rights were defined such that A is not required to compensate B, and assuming that the externality holds at the margin, efficient adaptation would occur only if B were to bribe A to bring his activity into adjustment – which entails bargaining. Only if the costs of such bargaining are neglected can the alternative specifications of property rights be said to be equivalent. For similar reasons, if A's activity generates benefits for B, the appropriate specification of property rights will be to require B fully to compensate A. Harmonizing the otherwise divergent interests of the two parties by internalizing the transaction through vertical merger promises to overcome the haggling costs which result when property rights are left either undefined or inappropriately specified.

Other

Risk aversion refers to the degree of concavity in the utility valuation of pecuniary outcomes. Decision makers who are risk averse will be concerned not merely with the expected value, but also with the dispersion in outcomes associated with alternative proposals: the greater the dispersion, the lower the utility valuation. *Ceteris paribus*, decision makers who are the less risk averse will presumably assume the risk-bearing function. Even, however, if attitudes toward risk were identical – in the sense that every individual (for any given set of initial endowments) would evaluate a proposal similarly – differing initial asset positions among the members of a population could warrant a specialization of the risk-bearing function, with possible firm and market structure effects (Knight, 1965).

Arrow calls intention to norms of social behavior, including ethical and moral codes. He observes in this connection that 'It is useful for individuals to have some trust in each other's word. In the absence of trust, it would become very costly to arrange for alternative sanctions and guarantees, and many opportunities for mutually beneficial cooperation would have to be foregone' (1969, p. 62). One would expect, accordingly, that vertical integration would be more complete in a low-trust than a high-trust culture, *ceteris paribus*.

III.   Conclusions

That product markets have remarkable coordinating properties is, among economists at least, a secure proposition. That product markets are subject to failure in various respects and that internal organization may be substituted against the market in these circumstances is, if somewhat less familiar, scarcely novel. A systematic treatment of market failure as it bears on vertical integration, however, has not emerged.

Partly this is attributable to inattention to internal organization: the remarkable properties of firms that distinguish internal from market coordination have been neglected. But the fragmented nature of the market failure literature as it bears on vertical integration has also contributed to this condition; the extensive variety of circumstances in which internalization is attractive tends not to be fully appreciated.

The present effort attempts both to address the internal organization issue and to organize the market failure literature as it relates to vertical integration in a systematic way. The argument, however, by no means exhausts the issues that vertical integration rises. For one thing, the discussion of market failures may be incomplete in certain respects. For another, a parallel treatment of the sources and consequences of the failures of internal organization as they relate to vertical integration is needed. Third, the argument applies strictly to the vertical integration of production; although much of it may have equal relevance to backward vertical integration into raw materials and forward integration into distribution, it may have to be delimited in significant respects. Fourth, game-theoretic considerations, which may permit the indicated indeterminacy of small numbers bargaining situations to be bounded, have been neglected. Finally, nothing in the present analysis establishes that observed degrees of vertical integration are not, from a social welfare standpoint, excessive. It should nevertheless be apparent that a broader *a priori* case for the vertical integration of production exists than is commonly acknowledged.

3

Antitrust Enforcement and the Modern Corporation

My discussion of policy issues and research opportunities in industrial organization is principally concerned with issues where the analyses of firm and market structures overlap, with special attention to matters that fall within the ambit of antitrust enforcement. I take the position that a re-examination of the implicit assumptions of conventional firm and market models is needed if antitrust analysts are accurately to assess the properties of the modern corporation and the markets within which it operates. I suggest, in this connection, that an 'institutional failures' orientation – to include an assessment of the failures of internal organization (administrative processes) as well as failures of product and capital markets – can usefully be adopted by students of antitrust economics.

Among the matters that come under review is the influence of product market failures (of both conventional and unconventional sorts) on the dominant firm condition and on vertical integration. Failures in the capital market as these relate to conglomerate organization are also examined. But no discussion of firm and market structures is complete without calling attention to the limits of internal organization. Markets, after all, do not fail absolutely, but only in relation to some nonmarket alternative (Arrow, 1969, p. 48). Focusing, as I attempt to, on the transactional relations that occur within and between firms and markets makes especially evident that internal organization and market processes can, for many purposes, usefully be regarded as substitutes.

The differences between this and the usual industrial organization approach warrant explication. It is not, I think, a caricature to say that the internal organization of the firm, including the allocation of functions between firms and markets, is of concern to traditonal analysis mainly as

Research on this chapter has been supported by a grant from The Brookings Institution. It is part of a larger study also supported by Brookings. The opinions expressed are my own.

Previously published in *Policy Issues and Essays on Research Opportunities in Industrial Organization*, ed. Victor R. Fuchs. (National Bureau of Economic Research, New York, 1972, pp. 16–33).

this can be said to influence 'market power' and 'offensive business conduct'. By contrast, I treat the question of organizational design as intrinsically interesting and inseparably associated with efficiency considerations. Firms become devices for alleviating market frictions (failures) by internalizing activities that might otherwise be performed by the market. The limitations of firms for these purposes, while real, are a function of organization form. The study of organizational innovations, consequently, is a matter of special interest. Altogether, the approach that I am advocating is one of 'transactional analysis of a comparative–institutional sort.' While there is no essential conflict between this and 'market power analysis' of the usual variety (indeed they ought to be regarded as complements), the research programs suggested by each are quite different.

I conclude that an incomplete treatment of the dominant firm problem in economics has led to an incorrect characterization of the monopoly problem by the law, and that antitrust has been undiscriminating in its treatment of both vertical and conglomerate structures. In more numerous respects than are generally recognized, vertical integration and conglomerate organization permit transactional failures (in the product and capital markets, respectively) to be attenuated.

I. Dominant Firm Industries

A. ISSUES

Antitrust is on its most familiar ground when dealing with conventional monopoly problems that take the form of horizontal market power. The underlying economic theory here is thought to be relatively well developed and its applications obvious. Still, neither the courts nor the enforcement agencies have been prepared seriously to challenge pre-existing market power that takes the form of a dominant firm.

As the law is currently interpreted, dominance does not constitute a Section 2 monopoly violation if the structure in question is attributable to 'a superior product, business acumen, or historic accident.'[1] Although, in practice, the courts may never explicitly entertain defenses to dominance along any of these lines, merely to offer them in principle has enforcement significance: the enforcement agencies are precluded from using any of these hypothetical defenses as an affirmative reason for bringing a case. That, in these circumstances, dominant firm complaints rely mainly on alleged conduct offenses is only to be expected. This often reduces them, however, to contrived cases, and legitimate issues are suppressed.

---

[1] *United States* v. *Grinnell Corp.*, 384 US 563, 571 (1966).

B. EVALUATION

Dominant firm industries will be defined, provisionally, to be industries for which the output of the dominant firm has persistently exceeded 60 per cent of the industry total. The dominant firms in such industries will ordinarily enjoy supernormal rates of return – at least potentially if not actually.[2] Two issues are especially relevant in assessing the dominant firm condition: How did dominance develop? What remedies, if any, ought to be invoked?

The usual assumption, implicit if not explicit, in most treatments of the dominant firm issue is that 'competition works' – at least in the limited sense that extant and potential rivals can be relied upon to perform self-policing functions by responding appropriately to opportunities for private gain. But for circumstances in which economies of scale are large in relation to the market, patent protection exists, or illegal practices are employed, persistent dominance with monopoly returns is not to be expected. Still, reference by the Court to business acumen and historic accident defenses reveals a chink in the workability argument that just possibly warrants closer attention. Ought differential expertise and chance event effects to be regarded as manifestations of market failure, and what are the policy implications?

It is proposed here that differential expertise in amounts sufficient to support dominance be regarded as a failure in the market for managerial talent. This can take either of two forms. First, the requisite talents may simply be scarce. Thus although it is usually assumed that the supply of managerial talent is quite adequate (Kaysen and Turner, 1959, pp. 9, 117), at least occasionally this may not be true. Marschak, in a related context, puts the issue as follows; 'There exist almost unique, irreplaceable research workers, teachers, administrators; just as there exist unique choice locations for plants and harbors. The problem of unique or imperfectly standardized goods ... has been neglected by the textbooks' (1968, p. 14). The possibility that the dominant firm has gained ascendancy because of the inimitable quality of its management at least warrants consideration.

This is not, however, the only possibility. The dominant firm may have displayed no special management expertise but existing and potential rivals, on which the responsibiity for self-policing functions devolves, may have been uncommonly inept. Persistent ineptitude of this sort is an indication that the self-policing functions of rivalry have lapsed. Such discreditable performance on the part of principal rivals during critical

---

[2] Sometimes these firms may be run slack, in which case reported profit will not disclose the full supernormal profit potential.

formative stages of an industry's development will be referred to as default failure.

Whether, however, a default failure outcome is more than a hypothetical possibility – to be conceded in principle but not observed in practice – is perhaps to be doubted. Relevant in this connection is the experience of the diesel locomotive industry, where an argument not only can be, but has been, advanced that the dominance by General Motors in diesel locomotive manufacture is to be explained by default failure among the steam locomotive firms.[3] Although this record needs to be more thoroughly developed and documented, I find the evidence more than suggestive that General Motors' dominance of this industry was the result of ineptitude on the part of the steam locomotive manufacturers and imperceptiveness among potential rivals.

Consider now the historic accident defense. Dominance that results from an unusual run of luck will be referred to as chance event failure. The dominant firm and its rivals may be performing in a fully creditable (yet unexceptional) manner, but the dominant firm is thrust ahead by an unusual sequence of fortuituous events.

The extensive literature on stochastic determinants of firm size is relevant in this connection. The usual and simplest assumption here is that all firms in an industry prospectively have access to identical mean growth rates, with actual rates being assigned at random from a common probability distribution. In the absence of serial correlation, a firm that experiences high growth in one period may easily 'draw' a low growth rate in the next; no special advantage need obtain. Occasionally, however, a firm may enjoy an unusual run of luck; a series of super-normal rates are strung together. Where this happens, the lucky firm can be thrust into a position of dominance. Moreover, the dominance outcome, once realized, may not easily be undone by continued application of the same stochastic mechanism: 'Once the most fortunate firms climb well ahead of the pack, it is difficult for laggards to rally and rectify the imbalance, for by definition, each firm – large and small – has an equal chance of growing by an equal percentage amount' (Scherer, 1970, p. 127). If indeed the variance in growth rates declines as an industry matures and technical progress slackens, the prospect that a dominant firm outcome once established will subsequently be upset (in any short period of time) by chance market processes is correspondingly impaired.

As a policy matter, it would seem appropriate to regard both default and chance event failures that result in dominance as indications that the

---

[3] See the testimony, including exhibits, of C. R. Osborne in *A Study of the Antitrust Laws*. Hearings before the Senate Subcommittee on Antitrust and Monopoly of the Committee on the Judiciary, 84th Cong., 1st Sess., Part 8, 9 December 1955, Washington, DC, 1956, pp. 3948–97.

self-policing properties of the market, in these respects, have broken down. Intervention by the Government on grounds of 'residual responsibility' to restore a more competitive outcome is arguably appropriate. New bases upon which to rest a Section 2 violation that do not rely exclusively or primarily on conduct offenses would in this way become available to the enforcement agencies. Moreover, structural relief, where either default or chance event failures are established (and countervailing considerations do not obtain), is presumably warranted. Altogether, more assertive antitrust enforcement toward the dominant firm industries would emerge.

It might be noted that Turner (1969) has recently reached a similar policy conclusion concerning dominant firm industries – albeit on somewhat different grounds. Turner appeals to 'reasonableness' considerations in suggesting that, but for scale economy or unexpired patent defenses, 'it is appropriate to put a time limit on continuing monopoly power that rests in part on earlier success, regardless of how the early success was achieved' (p. 1219). The advantage of the present argument is that implementing such a proposal is more attractive where significant default or chance event failures can be shown to have occurred.

The position of Posner (1969, pp. 1596–8) on persistent monopoly can also be assessed in the light of the above argument. Posner objects to Section 2 dissolution proceedings as a means for dealing with persistent dominance on the grounds that monopoly positions not supported by scale economies, predatory behavior, superior skill, or foregone monopoly gains will *usually* be eliminated by market processes. One can agree, especially if the time horizon stipulated is sufficiently long. If, however, a dominant firm position, once secured, may be undone by unassisted market processes only with difficulty, a policy of waiting for self-correcting measures to be effective in a market where the dominance outcome has resulted from chance event or default failures is, perhaps, excessively passive. Unusual measures may be indicated when the unusual event obtains.[4]

---

[4] Posner argues elsewhere that inasmuch as 'a recent study (Brozen, 1970) found that a high level of concentration in an industry tends to dissipate by natural forces within an average period of 10 years ... [and since] the average length of a divestiture proceeding in a monopolization case involving a major regional or national market is 8 years, ... it seems unlikely that administrative methods of deconcentration will work significantly more rapidly than the market' (1970, p. 417, n. 50). The argument has merit but relies heavily on average market tendencies which, in the particular cases of very high concentration that we are concerned with here, may be unwarranted. It also takes prevailing judicial practices as given, despite reform proposals concerning this matter [see, for example, the Neale Task Force Report, 1969).

C. RESEARCH OPPORTUNITIES

However one comes out on the policy ramifications of the argument, it is a matter of scientific interest that a series of *focused* industry studies of the dominant firm industries be conducted. Can default or chance event failures reasonably be established, or is the dominant firm outcome invariably to be attributed to scale economies, unexpired original patents, or illegal conduct? The matter can be approached directly, by examining both the properties of the decisions taken by the dominant firm's principal rivals (default failure) and the stochastic experience of the industry (chance events),[5] and indirectly, by assessing the conventional scale economy, patent, and conduct conditions. But for nontrivial scale economy, patent, or conduct effects, or unless management superiority claims can be supported, default or chance event failures are presumably to be inferred. Claims of management superiority are difficult to evaluate in any simple way, but the study of organizational innovations, with special attention to changes in organization form, may sometimes permit indirect inferences to be made. (See in this connection Chandler, 1966 and Williamson, 1970.)

None of this requires that the relief question be reached. If, however, as a policy matter, the question of dissolution is seriously to be considered, it is further necessary to examine both the human and physical assets in the dominant firm. Should a study reveal that the requisite managerial and technical capabilities are impacted, in the sense that these cannot easily be assembled by unassisted market processes, any dissolution effort ought presumably to attempt to transfer human as well as physical capital in amounts sufficient to assure viability.

II. Vertical Integration[6]

A. ISSUES

The study of vertical integration has presented difficulties at both theoretical and policy levels of analysis. Vertical integration has never enjoyed a secure place in value theory because under conventional assumptions it is an anomaly: If the costs of operating competitive markets are zero, 'as is usually assumed in our theoretical analysis' (Arrow, 1969, p. 48), why integrate?

Policy interest in vertical integration has been concerned mainly with the possibility that integration can be used strategically to achieve

---

[5] Examination of unanticipated technical and market developments as well as product life cycle effects are relevant to an assessment of chance event failures.

[6] The argument in this section relies extensively on chapter 2, this volume.

anticompetitive effects. In the absence of a more substantial theoretical foundation, vertical integration, as a public policy matter, is typically regarded as having dubious if not outright antisocial properties. Technological interdependencies (as in flow process operations) or, possibly, observational economies, constitute the principal exceptions.

There is, nevertheless, as distinct unease over the argument. This is attributable, probably, to a suspicion that the firm is more than a simple efficiency instrument, in the usual scale economies and efficient factor proportions senses of the term, but also possesses coordinating potential that sometimes transcends that of the market. It is the burden of the present argument that this suspicion is warranted.

B. EVALUATION

That product markets have remarkable coordinating properties is, among economists at least, a secure proposition. That product markets are subject to failure in various respects and that internal organization may be substituted against the market in these circumstances is, if somewhat less familiar, scarcely novel. A systematic treatment of market failure as it bears on vertical integration, however, has not emerged.

Partly this is attributable to inattention to internal organization: the remarkable properties of firms that distinguish internal from market coordination have been englected. But the fragmented nature of the market failure literature as it bears on vertical integration has also contributed to this condition; the extensive variety of circumstances in which 'internalization' (the substitution of internal organization for the market) is attractive tends not to be fully appreciated.

The properties of the firm that commend internal organization as a market substitute would appear to fall into three categories: incentives, controls, and what may be referred to broadly as 'inherent structural advantages'. In an incentive sense, internal organization attenuates the aggressive advocacy that epitomizes arm's length bargaining. Interests, if not perfectly harmonized, are at least free of representations of a narrowly opportunistic sort; in any viable group, of which the firm is one, the range of admissible intraorganizational behavior is bounded by considerations of ostracism. In circumstances, therefore, where protracted bargaining between independent parties to a transaction can otherwise be anticipated, internalization becomes attractive.

Perhaps the most distinctive advantage of the firm, however, is the wider variety and greater sensitivity of control instruments that are available for enforcing intrafirm in comparison with interfirm activities. Not only is the firm able to perform more precise own-performance evaluations (both contemporaneous and *ex post*) than can a buyer, but its reward and penalty instruments (which include selective use of employment, promotion, remuneration, and internal resource allocation processes) are more refined. Moreover, when conflicts develop, the firm possesses a comparatively efficient conflict resolution machinery.

To illustrate, fiat is frequently a more efficient way to settle minor conflicts (say, differences of interpretation) than is haggling or litigation. *Inter*organizational conflict can be settled by fiat only rarely, if at all. For one thing, the parties would have to agree on an impartial arbitrator, an agreement which itself might be costly to secure. Also rules of evidence and procedure would have to be established. If, moreover, the occasion for such interorganizational settlements were to be common, the form of organization converges in effect to vertical integration, with the arbiter becoming a manager in fact if not in name. By contrast, *intra*organizational settlements by fiat are common (Whinston, 1964, pp. 410–14).

The firm may also resort to internalization on account of defects in the prevailing institutional arrangements. The dysfunctional consequences of faulty property rights specifications, for example, may be overcome by common ownership. Also the firm may offer a more efficient communication network.

The firm, however, also experiences genuine limitations in relation to the market. Mainly on account of bounded rationality and greater confidence in the objectivity of market exchange in comparison with bureaucratic processes, market mediation is generally to be preferred over internal supply in circumstances in which markets may be said to 'work well'. Therefore the question is, when may markets be expected to display defects? Which brings us to the matter of market failure.

This aspect of the argument has been developed at some length elsewhere.[7] It reduces to the following series of propositions: the substitution of internal organization for product market exchange becomes relatively more attractive (a) as contractual incompleteness risks become great, (b) as the risks of strategic misrepresentation in interfirm transactions increase, and (c) where market exchange suffers from what may be referred to as 'intrinsic inefficiency,' especially as this bears on the convergence of expectations. Small numbers of traders, product complexity, and technical and market uncertainties exacerbate these conditions and thereby encourage the internalization of transactions.

Typically, the conclusion of the conventional analysis of vertical integration – which focuses principally on market power considerations – is that, but for flow process operations where materials handling economies are said to be available, the sources of cost saving from integration are 'unclear'. Transactional analysis, by contrast, reveals that vertical integration may permit the realization of transactional economies over a much wider class of activities. The critical point, as a policy matter, is

---

[7] The interested reader is referred to chapter 2.

that in consideration of the variety of circumstances in which product market failures can occur and the potentially attractive properties that internal organization possesses as a market substitute, the *a priori* case for vertical integration is much more extensive than is commonly realized. If, therefore, contrary to the usual assumptions, vertical integration between successive stages of production often permits real cost savings, its economic consequences in this respect cannot be regarded with indifference. Vertical merger guidelines,[8] which make no apparent allowance for these effects but focus exclusively on the potential anticompetitive consequences of vertical integration, may, accordingly, warrant reconsideration.

C. RESEARCH OPPORTUNITIES

The argument above, assuming that it is correct, by no means exhausts the issues that vertical integration raises. For one thing, a parallel treatment of the sources and consequences of the failures of internal organization as they relate to vertical integration is needed.[9] In addition, the above argument requires qualification in that it applies strictly to the vertical integration of production. Although much of it may have equal relevance to backward integration into raw materials and forward integration into distribution, I conjecture that the affirmative case for vertical integration may often be less compelling where control over raw materials or distributional channels is involved and that the anticompetitive potential of vertical integration into either of these stages is especially great. A more discriminating approach toward vertical mergers – depending not merely on market shares but also on the stage of economic activity affected and the absolute size of the organization – could easily emerge.

Also relevant to an understanding of vertical integration is the study of intermediate forms of market organization that fall between full integration and arm's length bargaining. Such an investigation may be especially

---

[8] See the *Merger Guidelines of the Department of Justice, 1968*; see also Stigler (1968, pp. 302–4).

[9] Of special interest in this connection is the matter of foreclosure. It is often said that vertical integration poses an antitrust problem because nonintegrated firms are foreclosed from securing business that would otherwise be open to competition. Unfavorable market power and unfair competition effects are said to obtain. The economic rationale for these claims has frequently been unclear, however; other students of vertical integration have expressed doubts that foreclosure has any unfavorable economic effects whatsoever. I submit that distinguishing between economic and bureaucratic rationality may help to clarify the issues. Behavior that appears to lack merit, and consequently is dismissed when regarded in economic terms, may not be so bizarre when evaluated as a bureaucratic phenomenon. This distinction between economic and bureaucratic rationality may also be useful in examining other business conduct practices. It is elementary that, where opportunity sets are large, bureaucratic preferences may govern.

productive in revealing the limits of the firm as an integrating device. The franchise system is of special interest, both in organizational and antitrust terms. What are the incentive and other properties that make it an attractive form of organization? In what types of circumstances does this occur? What contractual limitations (customer, product, territorial, etc.) facilitate efficient exchange and might reasonably be allowed, and when do such limitations have anticompetitive effects? Distinguishing pecuniary price from 'full price' (in the sense of Becker, 1965, may be essential for assessing the monopolistic consequences of such restrictions.

The argument could also be brought to bear on historic trends toward vertical integration (including disintegration) in individual industries. Are these developments mainly to be explained by reference to technical scale economies and diseconomies (cf. Stigler, 1951, or by the interfirm versus intrafirm *transactional approach* proposed here (and originally advocated by Coase, 1937)? Have recent developments in the study of transactional costs and market failures, together with an emerging appreciation of the properties of firms that commend internal organization as a product market substitute, now made it possible to apply transactional analysis to explain historic trends in vertical integration and related firm and market structures effectively? Put differently, is transactional analysis a research strategy whose time has come?

III. Conglomerate Organization

A. ISSUES

Industrial organization specialists have been actively concerned with the conglomerate phenomenon at least since Edwards's 1955 treatment of the subject. As Edwards saw it, conglomerate bigness gave rise to monopoly power in subtle but significant ways. Stocking, however, in commenting on the various and diffuse effects described by Edwards, found that most of the alleged anticompetitive consequences could be traced to original monopoly power of a conventional sort. He conceded, nevertheless, that the conglomerate corporation posed significant institutional issues for which conventional theory was inadequate (Stocking, 1955, pp. 358–9).

The dialogue has continued, most recently being a subject for high-level regulatory review in connection with the Merger Guidelines of the Department of Justice, two Presidential Task Force reports dealing with current antitrust problems, and a Federal Trade Commission Staff Report. The emphasis throughout, both in the earlier literature as well as the more recent policy treatments of the issue, has been on the alleged anticompetitive consequences of the conglomerate form of organization.

Such a narrow focus is perhaps appropriate if, as an efficiency matter, the distribution of functions between firms and markets can be regarded with indifference; the principal issues then can be reduced to an application of basic (or extended) monopoly theory to the particular circumstances at hand. If, however, internalization often has significant effects on efficiency, such an approach is arguably too narrow.[10]

B. EVALUATION

Whereas vertical integration involves the substitution of administrative for market processes in response to product market failures, the conglomerate can be regarded mainly as a substitution of internal for market organization in response to failures in the capital market.[11] The capital market has two general functions to perform: funds metering and the supply of incentives, of both reward and penalty types. The extent to which the capital market is engaged in funds metering, however, is severely limited by prevailing retained earnings practices. Baumol concludes from his study of this function that 'the stock market is only infrequently given the opportunity to discipline directly the vast majority of the nation's leading corporations' (Baumol, 1965, p. 76).[12] An examination of the incentive properties of the capital market also reveals defects. The external relation that the capital market bears to the firm places it at a serious information disadvantage and thus, because of high imputation costs, limits the efficacy of selective reward procedures. This external relation also prevents the capital market from intervening selectively to correct local conditions. Management displacement, which is an extreme corrective response, incurs significant original and secondary costs.

The conglomerate internalizes both incentive and metering functions. As an internal control mechanism with constitutional authority, expertise, and low-cost access to the requisite data, it is able both to employ

[10] I have argued elsewhere that organizational innovation, of which the conglomerate is a recent manifestation, often has had (and can be expected to have) remarkable efficiency consequences (Williamson, 1970). The argument, as it applies to the transformation of the enterprise from a unitary to a multidivisional form at least, is supported by the application of *a priori* theory to the problems of managing complex, hierarchical, human organizations; by Alfred Chandler, Jr.'s, historical survey of early twentieth-century corporate developments (Chandler, 1966); by natural selection considerations; and by a casual review of the conspicuous evidence.

[11] The extent to which this substitution can be expected to be efficacious depends on the internal structure of the firm and the control apparatus employed. The argument here is restricted to divisionalized conglomerate organizations in which strategic decision-making functions (including resource allocation) are assigned to a strong general office and in which a sensitive internal control apparatus has been assembled. For an elaboration, see Williamson (1970).

[12] Also relevant in this connection is the Baumol et al. (1970) article concerning marginal rates of return to alternative sources of funds. The finding that very low rates of return are associated with internal sources of capital reinforces the argument in the text that the funds-metering function of the capital market is incompletely realized.

additional reward and penalty instruments and to exercise these in selective and preventative ways that are unavailable to an external control agent. As a funds-metering instrument, the conglomerate (ideally) assigns cash flows on the basis of prospective yields instead of allowing them to be retained by the sectors from which they originate. In both these respects, therefore, the conglomerate (potentially at least)[13] can be regarded as a miniature capital market. In the absence, therefore, of countervailing considerations not already reflected in current merger policy toward conglomerates, and assuming that the enforcement of the merger statutes with regard to horizontal and vertical combinations is to remain severe, a more sympathetic attitude toward conglomerate organization would seem to be warranted. Not only are the immediate efficiency gains in funds metering and the supplying of incentives to be valued, but an active market for corporate control (Manne, 1965) is also promoted.

Recent policy proposals concerning conglomerates,[14] however, appear to give no weight to these factors. Based on alleged reciprocity and cross-subsidization dangers together with expressed concern over potential competition effects, enforcement criteria have been tentatively advanced which, if implemented, would relieve several hundred large firms from the forces of competition in the capital market, forces which probably ought to be supported rather than suppressed. Protective efforts by the enforcement agencies to defeat takeover efforts where members of the 'business establishment' are the target firms are similarly suspect.[15] Exclusive antitrust concern with competition in the product market (narrowly regarded), to the neglect of competition in the capital market, can result in a perversion of the enforcement process. If, as I have argued elsewhere (1970, pp. 145–50), conglomerate mergers pose genuine public policy issues (in both economic and sociopolitical respects) mainly in a systems sense involving acquisitions by already giant-sized firms, the indicated delimitation of conglomerate merger enforcement is to direct it explicitly toward the giant-sized subset.

Of course not all firms in the giant-sized subset would be affected either by a dominant firm program of the sort suggested in section I or by a tougher policy toward mergers involving giant-sized enterprise. Unless other economic grounds are advanced, therefore, or unless antitrust were to expand its scope to include noneconomic considerations, many giant-sized enterprises would elude the antitrust enforcement net. For those who take the position that antitrust should not be converted into an instrument for reconstituting firm size for sociopolitical reasons, such an escape is altogether appropriate. However one comes out on this matter,

[13] See the qualifications in Williamson (1970, chapter 10).
[14] Especially the Neale Task Force Report (1969) and the FTC Staff Study (1969).
[15] For an illustration, see Williamson (1970, pp. 100–2, 171).

it is relevant to observe that antitrust is not the only policy instrument that can be brought to bear. The voluntary divestiture programs that some large corporations have recently been observed to engage in are of special interest in this regard.[16]

Some, perhaps many, of these voluntary divestitures have been undertaken in response to pressing cash needs in the face of high interest rates. Others, however, may well have been undertaken out of recognition that large size and proliferating variety eventually result in diseconomies. The parent organization is induced on this account voluntarily to split off some of its operating divisions – either as independent economic entities, as spinoffs (in which some financial interest is retained), or for acquisition by others. This process of 'mitosis' represents a variety of organizational self-renewal that warrants a sympathetic public policy response. Not only does it promise operating efficiencies, and on this account alone is to be valued, but it also serves to relieve legitimate sociopolitical concerns over wealth concentration tendencies in the largest corporations.

C. RESEARCH OPPORTUNITIES

As a research matter, an effort to categorize conglomerate merger activity according to motive and effect is needed. The discussion above emphasizes economic efficiency dimensions of the conglomerate, but it is clearly a more complex phenomenon than that. Many of these issues relate more to tax and securities regulations than to industrial organization per se and might therefore better be pursued by other specialists. A full treatment of the conglomerate phenomenon nevertheless requires that these other factors be assessed.

Of greater interest to industrial organization specialists is the influence of internal structure on performance. Studies of the effects of industry structure on performance are part of the core commitment of industrial organization; cross-sectional studies relating industry structure to performance are common. It is proposed here, however, that the internal structure of the firm (organization form) be introduced as an explanatory variable and that the conglomerate be regarded less as a distinctive organization form itself than as a diversified manifestation of either the multidivisional or free-form structure (Williamson, 1970, pp. 142–3, 162).

Although the analysis of organization form itself is at a very primitive stage of development (and, consequently, only the crudest variety of classification scheme exists),[17] it would be interesting to examine the

---

[16] See *Forbes*, 15 May 1970, pp. 214–20; also *Business Week*, 15 August 1970, pp. 86–7.

[17] The following structural distinctions would seem appropriate from the outset: unitary form, multidivision form, free form, and 'other.' For a discussion, see Williamson (1970). The need to create additional categories may be evident as the study of internal structure proceeds.

influence of internal structure on performance in the following respects: comparative growth and profit rates among rival firms; marginal rates of return to alternative sources of funds; evidence relating to slack (internal efficiency), perhaps especially in relation to business conditions; evidence relating to internal operating practices, such as cross-subsidization; evidence bearing on 'offensive' marketing practices, such as reciprocity.[18] It is probably essential, for the purposes of such studies, to make allowance for firm size effects.

Of related interest is the historical evolution of the multidivision form. Chandler (1966) traces much of this in descriptive terms, but a more formal assessment of this organizational innovation, including its diffusion, would seem to be indicated. Which firms with what characteristics have been first to employ multidivisionalization in their respective industries, and what factors explain the degree of rapidity with which imitation by rivals has occurred?

An effort to discover the quantitative significance of organizational innovation as it affects aggregate growth rates would be ambitious but not necessarily intractable. What fraction of the residual term in conventional growth models can reasonably be imputed to organizational developments?

Also of interest in this regard is the link between technical and organizational innovation. In what respects have developments of the organizational innovation type altered the locus of technical innovative activity and with what performance consequences? To what extent and in what circumstances does technical innovation take an interorganizational rather than intraorganizational route? Is interfirm exchange – in which different firms with distinctive attributes participate in the invention, development, and final supply stages – really viable? What factors impair its effective operation, and what are the policy implications?[19]

The purpose, locus, frequency, and magnitude of voluntary divestiture efforts need more thoroughly to be documented. Also, consideration ought to be given to means by which to supply incentives that make voluntary divestiture more attractive; this may indeed be the most promising approach to the bigness per se issue. At a minimum, existing tax disincentives to voluntary divestiture ought to be reviewed. Freeing the market for corporate control ought also to be considered as a means by which to encourage very large firms to trim their operations when excessive size and variety are reached; anxious to forestall takeover,

---

[18] Again, the distinction between economic and bureaucratic rationality referred to in footnote 9 may be useful. There are bureaucratic reasons to expect performance in these respects to vary systematically with organization form, while the conventional theory of the form is mainly silent on these matters.

[19] For an elaboration of the issues discussed in this paragraph, see Turner and Williamson. Also see Nelson, Peck, and Kalachek (1967).

otherwise passive firms may be induced voluntarily to exercise restraint. The limits of competition in the capital market in this respect, however, need more fully to be assessed.

The multinational corporation might also be examined in an institutional failures context. To what extent is it a response to alleged imperfections in the capital market? What organizational structures have evolved to support this form of operation, and what limitations (organizational failures) does it experience? What present and potential antitrust problems are posed, and is a corresponding multinational extension of the antitrust enforcement machinery indicated? Even if many of the projections of 'world dominance' by multinational corporations are regarded as unrealistic – in that they reflect insufficient appreciation of the limits of internal organization – serious public policy issues may, in individual instances at least, nevertheless be posed.

IV. Conclusions

It is argued that the study of firm and market structures, and the application of antitrust policy thereto, can benefit from a more systematic examination of the sources and consequences of market failure and by a more thorough assessment of the powers and limits of internal organization. More specifically, product market failure analysis ought to admit to the possibility of default and chance event failures – especially with reference to dominant firm industries. Similarly, the 'transactional' limitations that interfirm exchange is subject to, warrant explication as these bear on vertical integration. The substitution of internal organization against failures in the capital market, especially as this relates to an assessment of conglomerate organization, likewise deserves attention. The influence of organization form on enterprise performance, and of organizational innovation in general, also merit study. Of particular public policy interest is the possibility of inducing or otherwise supporting voluntary divestiture by giant-sized enterprises.

A survey of the literature on the modern corporation reveals that industrial organization specialists have mainly been bystanders. Partly this is to be explained by the prevailing opinion that the industry, not the firm, is the relevant unit of analysis. But however correct this may be for some purposes, it is less obviously true in others. If one of the most remarkable attributes of American capitalism is its adaptive capacity to invent efficient and viable organization forms in response to changing technological, market, and organizational conditions, to characterize the system in conventional industry terms, to the neglect of internal organization, easily misses much of what accounts for its most significant accomplishments.

4

Vertical Merger Guidelines: Interpreting the 1982 Reforms

Fourteen years separate the original Justice Department Merger Guidelines of 30 May 1968, the last day of Donald Turner's term as head of the Antitrust Division, and the Merger Guidelines of 14 June 1982, which were issued in the second year of William Baxter's tenure. Because merger policy plays an essential role in antitrust enforcement, the promulgation of new Merger Guidelines provides an important means of assessing changes in that area. Inasmuch as a decade appears to be a useful interval for evaluating antitrust developments,[1] a comparison of the recent with the earlier Guidelines should help to disclose what kinds of progress in antitrust enforcement (if any) have occurred within the interval.

In addition, an examination of the recent Guidelines may help to evaluate the proposition that ideas drive outcomes in antitrust law.[2] Economic scholarship has considerably reshaped the economic rationale

Reprinted with permission from California Law Review, 71 (March 1983). Copyright © 1983 by California Law Review, Inc.

[1] For an argument that a decade is a useful interval in which to measure changes in antitrust law, see chapter 13.

[2] O. E. Williamson, 'On the political economy of antitrust: Grounds for cautious optimism', in *The Political Economy of Antitrust*, ed. R. Tollison (1980), p. 77. This viewpoint is disputed by G. J. Stigler, 'The economists and the problem of monopoly', *Am. Econ. A. Proc.*, (May 1982), pp. 1,7 ('Economists have their glories, but I do not believe that the body of American antitrust law is one of them').

for vertical integration during the past decade.[3] A comparative examination of the 1968 and 1982 vertical Merger Guidelines should therefore be instructive in determining whether antitrust enforcement policy follows antitrust scholarship.

I. The 1982 Vertical Merger Guidelines

A. MAIN PROVISIONS

The 1982 Guidelines distinguish between two broad classes of mergers, horizontal and nonhorizontal. The latter category includes both conglomerate and vertical mergers. This is a change from the classification in the 1968 Guidelines, which distinguished horizontal, conglomerate, and vertical mergers.

The main antitrust problem posed by conglomerate and vertical mergers is that they may reduce actual or perceived potential competition. The Justice Department evidently believes that potential competition problems are insubstantial unless the Herfindahl–Hirschman index (HHI) in the acquired firm's market exceeds 1800[4] and the market share of the acquired firm exceeds 5 per cent.[5] The threshold for challenging conglomerate and vertical mergers is thus set at these levels.

The Department, in my judgment, would have been better advised to maintain the conventional three-way classification of mergers – horizontal, vertical, and conglomerate – rather than dividing mergers only into horizontal and nonhorizontal types. To be sure, conglomerate and vertical mergers are troublesome in antitrust respects mainly in the degree to

---

[3] The main developments and contributions have been summarized as follows: 'The most popular [argument for vertical integration] has been that if economies of scope between successive stages due to technological or organizational interrelationships are strong enough, these activities should be provided under joint ownership (e.g., Chandler (1966)). Other arguments for Vertical Integration have been the avoidance of factor distortions in monopolized markets (e.g., Vernon and Graham (1971), Warren-Boulton (1974), Schmalensee (1973)); uncertainty in the supply of the upstream good with the consequent need for information by downstream firms (Arrow (1975)); and the transfer of risks from one sector of the economy to another (Crouhy (1976), Carlton (1979)). Furthermore it has been pointed out that transaction costs might create important incentives for vertical integration (e.g., Coase (1937), Williamson (1971, 1975)).'
P. Kleindorfer and G. Knieps, 'Vertical integration and transaction-specific sunk costs', *European Economic Review*, 19 (1982), p. 71.
My emphasis here is mainly with the transaction cost ramifications of this literature. For specific references to the relevant literature in this area, see footnotes 33–4, *infra*.

[4] An HHI of 1800 corresponds roughly to a four-firm concentration ratio of 70%. US Dept. of Justice, Merger Guidelines, III(A), 47 Fed. Reg. 28,493, 28,497 (1982), reprinted in *California Law Review*, 71(1983) pp. 649, 655–7 (hereinafter cited without cross-reference as Guidelines).

[5] Ibid., IV(A), 47 Fed. Reg. at 28,499–500, *California Law Review*, 71 (1983), pp. 660–2.

which they pose potential competition problems.[6] But this is little more than incidental. Much more important to an understanding of the antitrust concerns posed by these mergers are the *sources* of the competition difficulties they can create. Conglomerate and vertical mergers differ substantially in this respect – as the Guidelines effectively, if obscurely, concede. Thus, the operational content of the nonhorizontal Merger Guidelines exists less in the common threshold levels than it does in the subsequent two-part breakdown of nonhorizontal mergers, which distinguishes between 'elimination of specific potential entrants' and 'competitive problems from vertical mergers.'[7]

Entry Barriers

Vertical integration of a firm can create entry barriers by making it more difficult for nonintegrated rival firms[8] that are otherwise qualified to compete to remain effective competitors. These entry barriers include greater difficulty of contracting, adverse effects of scale economies, and increased cost of capital.

The ease with which a rival firm at one stage of an industry (stage I) can contract for its requirements[9] in another stage (stage II) depends upon whether nonintegrated capacity at stage II is large (or can easily be increased). If ample nonintegrated stage II capacity is not in place and will not appear without special effort, the stage I rival firm must contemplate simultaneous entry at both stages. The acquisition by merger of previously nonintegrated stage II capacity can thus force an otherwise qualified stage II rival to choose between integrated entry and no entry at all. Whether integrated entry is significantly deterred will then depend upon cost of capital and scale economies.

To its credit, the Justice Department observes that the need for additional capital, by itself, does not constitute a barrier to entry into the primary market (here, stage I), as long as the necessary funds are available at a cost commensurate with the level of risk in the secondary market.[10] But the Department correctly recognizes that integreated entry that includes an unfamiliar stage is apt to carry a risk premium. This is because

[6] Vertical mergers can also pose problems if they increase the price in the downstream market, although this is not a likely outcome. Moreover, conglomerate organization may facilitate reciprocal buying – though again, this is a slender reed upon which to rest a case against conglomerates.

[7] Guidelines, IV(A), (B), 47 Fed. Reg. at 28,499, 28,500, *California Law Review*, 71 (1983), pp. 660, 662.

[8] Throughout this chapter, the term 'rival' will refer to either an actual or potential rival.

[9] Such contracting might be backward into earlier stages of production, laterally into other components required at a given stage, or forward into fabrication and distribution of the product.

[10] Guidelines, IV(B)(1)(b)(i), 47 Fed. Reg. at 28.501, *California Law Review*. 71 (1983), p. 663.

lenders may 'doubt that would-be entrants to the primary market have the necessary skills and knowledge to succeed in the secondary market and, therefore, in the primary market.'[11] The Guidelines note that this problem is exacerbated when a high percentage of the capital assets in the secondary market are long-lived and specialized to that market, and are therefore difficult to recover in the event of failure.

The Department also acknowledges that scale economies could create an entry barrier if a firm is forced to enter at two stages simultaneously because another firm has vertically integrated into the secondary market. It posits a situation in which the capacities of minimum-efficient-scale plants in the primary and secondary markets differ significantly. For example, if the capacity of a minimum-efficient-scale plant in the secondary market were greater than the needs of such a plant in the primary market, entrants would have to choose between inefficient operation at the secondary level and a larger scale than necessary at the primary level. The secondary level inefficiency would result because the firm would be either operating an efficient plant at an inefficient output, or producing an efficient level of output from an inefficiently small plant. If the firm chose instead to be efficient at the secondary level, it would oversupply its primary level needs. Either effect, the Department concludes, could cause a significant increase in the entering firm's operating costs.[12]

To this, however, the Department adds in a footnote that 'this problem would not exist if a significant outside market exists at the secondary level. In that case, entrants could enter with the appropriately scaled plants at both levels, and sell or buy in the market as necessary.'[13]

Collusion

Vertical integration is most likely to facilitate collusion in conjunction with forward integration into retail distribution. Thus, the Department's concern is that collusion in the upstream market is most likely to result because of the integrated firm's ability to monitor price.[14] This is troublesome if vertical integration into retail distribution is extensive and the upstream market is concentrated – where 1800 HHI is the level above which concentration is believed to pose a collusion concern.[15]

[11] Ibid.

[12] IV(B)(1)(b)(ii), 47 Fed. Reg. at 28,501, *California Law Review*, 71 (1983), p. 663.

[13] Ibid., n. 47, 47 Fed. Reg. at 28,501 n. 47, *California Law Review*, 71 (1983), p. 663, n. 47.

[14] Ibid., IV(B)(2)(a), 47 Fed. Reg. at 28,501, *California Law Review*, 71 (1983), p. 664.

[15] The recent Guidelines should, but do not, elaborate on why collusion becomes a serious concern at an HHI of 1800.

Rate Regulation

Acquisition of a supplier by a regulated utility might permit the utility to evade rate regulation, because '[a]fter the merger, the utility would be selling to itself and might be able arbitrarily to inflate the prices of internal transactions.'[16] These practices should be difficult for regulators to monitor. Thus, although the Department is sensitive to 'genuine economies of integration,' it will 'consider challenging mergers that create substantial opportunities for such abuses.'[17]

B. COMPARISON AND INTERPRETATION

In the 1968 vertical Merger Guidelines, the Justice Department indicated that it would examine the market shares of both upstream (supplying) and downstream (purchasing) firms. The Department stated that it would ordinarily challenge mergers between a supplying firm that accounted for at least 10 per cent of sales in its market and one or more purchasing firms totalling at least 6 per cent of purchases in the market.[18]

The 1982 vertical Merger Guidelines make no such upstream–downstream distinction. Instead, they focus entirely on the *acquired* firm's market. Vertical acquisitions are subject to challenge only in a concentrated market, that is, where the HHI in the acquired firm's market exceeds 1800. Where this occurs, the acquisition of a 5 per cent firm may be challenged.

The presumption that a vertical merger poses antitrust problems only if the acquired firm is operating in a concentrated market constitutes a substantial shift in vertical merger policy. It is grounded on the proposition that in markets where concentration is low or moderate, nonintegrated rivals will be able easily to contract for their requirements and hence will not be disadvantaged. The vertical Merger Guidelines are thus in accord with recent economic scholarship on contracting and strategic behavior that indicates that efforts by established firms to discipline actual competition and discourage potential competition are troublesome only in highly concentrated industries where entry is difficult.[19]

More generally, the recent Guidelines place emphasis on the ease of contracting, which is to say that transaction cost considerations are

---

[16] Guidelines, IV(B)(3), 47 Fed. Reg. at 28,501, *California Law Review*, 71 (1983), pp. 664–5.

[17] Ibid., 47 Fed. Reg. at 28,502, *California Law Review*, 71 (1983), p. 665.

[18] US Dept of Justice, Merger Guidelines – 1968, para. 12 (30 May 1968), reprinted in *Trade Reg. Rep.* (CCH) 2 paragraph 4510, p. 6886 (1982).

[19] Joskow and Klevorick (1979, pp. 213, 245–9); Ordover and Willig (1981, p. 301); chapters 6 and 9. Although this literature is mainly concerned with predatory pricing, the same reasoning applies to strategic behavior generally.

implicitly assigned a key role.[20] This is especially evident in the discussion of the cost of capital analyzed above.[21]

Rather than incurring these cost-of-capital penalties, firms that have demonstrated qualifications only at stage I may attempt to satisfy their stage II requirements by contract. The question then becomes whether the stage II product will be made available on competitive terms. The structure of the industry plainly has a bearing on this. If economies of scale are large in relation to the size of the nonintegrated fringe and if integrated firms are few and supply principally or exclusively their own needs, the would-be stage I entrant can anticipate difficulties in securing his second-stage requirements on parity terms.

The recent Guidelines also make the sophisticated point that investments in the secondary market are risky in the degree to which 'capital assets in the secondary market are long-lived and specialized to the market.'[22] This point is also in accord with recent developments in transaction cost economics in which asset specificity plays a key role. The issues here are developed somewhat more fully below.

II. Antecedents

The 1982 Merger Guidelines differ significantly from the 1968 Guidelines' counterpart. If, as I argued at the outset, antitrust enforcement follows antitrust scholarship, a change in the economic interpretation of vertical integration should have occurred during this interval. It will therefore be useful to compare the pre-1968 and post-1970 interpretations of vertical integration in the industrial organization literature.

---

[20] See Guidelines, IV(B)(1)(b), 47 Fed. Reg. at 28,500–01, *California Law Review*, 71 (1983), pp. 662–3. See text accompanying footnotes 32–46, *infra*.

[21] Lenders may raise capital costs for potential entrants if they 'doubt' that such entrants are fully qualified because prior competence has been demonstrated at only one of the stages. This may occur even though a potential entrant may be objectively qualified to enter at two stages of an industry because of the competence of its employees and management. The problem here is that it can prohibitively costly for qualified entrants who lack a track record at the secondary stage to show their qualifications.

Such an objectively qualified firm would still be financed on low-risk terms in a world of complete information. In the real world, however, the potential two-stage entrant would face high costs for acquiring knowledge of the technology and the operating skills associated with secondary stage activity. Were the relevant information easily accessible (from blueprints, manuals, and the like), and were it easily digested rather than embedded in the experienced work force (in which workers are costly to move in team configurations), the potential entrant would not be at a disadvantage to existing two-stage rivals in the secondary market.

[22] Guidelines, IV(B)(1)(b)(i), 47 Fed. Reg. at 28,501, *California Law Review*, 71(1983), p. 663.

A. PRE-1968 VIEWS ON VERTICAL INTEGRATION

The period 1950 to 1970 has been described by Coase as the applied price theory era in industrial organization.[23] The leading texts[24] were preoccupied with 'the study of pricing and output policies of firms, especially in oligopolistic situations (often called a study of market structure).'[25] The firm, for these purposes, was essentially viewed as a production function.

Such a technological approach conceded merit to vertical integration where successive stages were joined by a 'physical or technical aspect.'[26] The integration of stages where such a technological linkage was missing, by contrast, was considered to create antitrust problems. Where technological cost savings were not apparent, anticompetitive purpose was arguably the driving force. It was easy, therefore, to conclude that public policy concern was warranted whenever vertical integration involved an 'appreciable degree of market control at even one stage of the production process.'[27] Specifically, Stigler stated that when a firm has at least 20 per cent of an industry's output, its acquisition of more than 5 per cent of the output capacity of firms from which it buys or to which it sells can be presumed to violate antitrust laws.[28]

The 1968 vertical Merger Guidelines, which set the limits at 10 per cent and 6 per cent, are plainly in this spirit. They were either informed by and reflected this line of scholarship, or the correspondence between the two is a remarkable coincidence.

B. POST-1970 DEVELOPMENTS

Although the technological orientation toward vertical integration predominated among industrial organization specialists, there were dissenters who viewed vertical integration in transaction cost terms. Coase first promulgated such a view in 1937.[29] In principle, according to Coase, any

---

[23] Coase, (1972).

[24] Bain (1968); Stigler (1968).

[25] Coase, *supra* footnote 23, p. 62.

[26] Bain explicitly made this technological argument. Bain, *supra* footnote 24, p. 381. Stigler advanced a life cycle view of vertical integration, but the contractual benefits of unified ownership over market exchange are nowhere developed in transaction cost terms. The main argument instead turns upon technological economies of scale, and attention then focuses upon the use of integration to evade sales taxes and defeat quota schemes and other methods of nonprice rationing. Stigler, (1951).

[27] Stigler, 'Mergers and preventive antitrust policy', *University of Pennsylvania Law Review*, 104 (1955), pp. 176, 183.

[28] Ibid., p. 183.

[29] J. G. Coase, 'The nature of the firm', *Economica* 4, (1937), p. 386, reprinted in *Readings in Price Theory*, eds G. Stigler and K. Boulding (1952), p. 331.

transaction can be accomplished through either market or internal procurement. Whether a firm should produce for its own needs or purchase turns largely upon the transaction costs associated with each alternative. Specifically, Coase stated that transactions for which the administrative costs of internal organization were less than the costs of mediating an exchange by contract would be removed from markets and organized internally. Otherwise, market mediation would be observed.

This nontechnological approach to vertical integration remained outside the mainstream of operational microeconomics for two reasons.[30] First, most economists were still unpersuaded of the merits of transaction cost economics. Second, those who recognized merit in Coase's formulation could only acknowledge post hoc that transactions were consistent with the formulation. They were unable to use it to predict which transactions would be organized internally and which would be subject to market mediation.[31]

During the past decade, however, transaction cost economics has gained widespread use, and is now an effective means of predicting how transactions will be structured. The next section will describe transaction cost economics and its methods for analyzing problems of industrial organization. It will then explain the transaction cost ramifications for vertical integration, and will finally assess the correspondence between these developments and the recent vertical Merger Guidelines.

Operationalizing Transaction Cost Economics

1 *Premises of transaction cost economics.* Transaction cost economics is a comparative institutional assessment of alternative means of contracting. Coase believed that a deeper understanding of industrial organization would result from concentrating on what activities firms undertake, and from discovering the characteristics of the grouping of activities within firms. He also thought that because market arrangements are the alternative to intrafirm organization, it would be beneficial to study contractual arrangements between firms, such as long-term contracts, leasing, and licensing arrangements of various kinds.[32]

The basic transaction cost mechanics for assessing a firm's decisions of whether to produce or purchase its requirements were first set out in 1971.[33] They have been refined and elaborated since.[34]

Transaction cost economics rests on three propositions. First, the study

[30] Coase lamented some 35 years after its publication that his original article was 'much cited and little used.' Coase, *supra* footnote 23, p. 63.
[31] Alchian and Demsetz (1972, p. 783).
[32] Coase, *supra* footnote 23, p. 73.
[33] See chapter 2.
[34] Williamson, (1975); Klein, Crawford and Alchian (1978, p. 297); *Journal of Economic Behavior and Organization*, 3 (1980), p. 233.

of economic organization requires that social scientists come to terms with what might be called 'human nature as we know it.'[35] Second, transactions need to be 'dimensionalized,' that is, the relevant dimensions with respect to which transactions differ must be identified, and their bearing on transaction costs must be determined. Third, carefully matching governance structures (generally, firms and markets) with the attributes of transactions can result in transaction cost economies.

The rudimentary behavioral assumptions for describing human nature owe their origins to organization theory (Herbert Simon) and to political science (Niccolo Machiavelli). Although Simon acknowledges that human agents are 'intendedly rational,' which is the prevailing assumption throughout economics, he also insists that human competence is limited. Where human cognitive limitations are severe in relation to the complexity of the problems being faced, a condition of 'bounded rationality' occurs.[36] Machiavelli describes a phenomenon that might be called 'opportunism' when he advises his prince that 'a prudent ruler ought not to keep faith when by so doing it would be against his interest, and when the reasons which made him bind himself no longer exist.'[37]

Bounded rationality and opportunism place great strain on the convenient fiction of comprehensive market contracting. Nonmarket forms of governance – nonstandard forms of contracting, specialized mediation (such as arbitration), and complex hierarchical structures (administrative organization) – arise in response to these limitations.

2 *Determining governance structures.* Neoclassical analysis fails to consider either bounded rationality or opportunism.[38] In contrast, transaction cost economics makes explicit provision for both. Accordingly, whereas neoclassical analysis generally takes the organization of economic activity as given, thus ignoring the comparative institutional assessment of alternative modes of contracting, transaction cost economics expressly focuses upon assigning governance structures to transactions which will economize on transaction costs.

Comparative institutional analysis not only requires that transactions be dimensionalized, but that *ex ante* and *ex post* supply conditions be distinguished. Conventional microtheory focuses strictly on the former. Market contracting is said to be efficacious if large numbers of qualified suppliers tender bids at the outset. Transaction cost economics, by contrast, examines both *ex ante* and *ex post* supply conditions. If production

---

[35] Knight (1965, p. 270).
[36] Simon (1957).
[37] N. Machiavelli, *The Prince* (1952), New York, New American Library, p. 92.
[38] See Diamond, 'Comments', *Frontiers of Quantitative Economics*, 1 (1971), p. 29 [response to K.J. Arrow, 'Political and economic evaluation of social effects and externalities', *Frontiers of Quantitative Economics*, 1, (1971), p. 3].

of the item necessitates significant investments in transaction-specific assets,[39] as contractual asymmetry develops between the initial winning bidder and all other bidders. The contractual relationship between buyer and seller is then transformed into a relationship of bilateral exchange during contract execution and at each time of renewal. Bilateral transactions are predictably beset with problems related to opportunism during contract execution, such as performing only to the letter of the contract or agreeing to efficient adaptations only upon renegotiation of terms. Internal organization (unified governance) often supplants autonomous contracting (market governance) for this reason.

Moreover, the influence of asset specificity on economic organization is not uniform. Different types of asset specificity have different ramifications for governance. Four types of asset specificity include:[40]

(a) *Site specificity*. When successive stages are located in close proximity to one another, common ownership generally results. This occurs because of an asset immobility condition, that is, the set-up or relocation costs of a station are great. Thus, once the assets are placed, their owners are operating in a bilateral exchange relation for the useful life of the assets.

(b) *Physical asset specificity*. If the assets are mobile and their specificity is attributable to their physical features (e.g., specialized dies), market procurement may still be feasible if the buyer owns the assets and solicits production bids. Lock-in problems are avoided because if contractual difficulties develop between buyer and seller, the buyer can reclaim the dies and reopen the bidding.

(c) *Human asset specificity*. Conditions that give rise to this type of asset specificity, such as learning-by-doing or problems of moving human assets in team configurations, favor common ownership. Integrated ownership coupled with a long-term employment relationship, rather than autonomous outside contracting, will generally govern such transactions.

(d) *Dedicated assets*. Investment in dedicated assets involves expanding an existing plant on behalf of a particular buyer. Buyers are understandably reluctant to make earmarked investments in the physical plant of their suppliers, and unified ownership is thus rare. The trading hazards to which suppliers are exposed are often mitigated by expanding the

---

[39] Transaction-specific assets are durable investments that are specialized to the contracting parties. Their value in best alternative uses (or by alternative users) is much lower than in their intended use. General purpose assets, by contrast, are diverted to alternative uses or users at little sacrifice of value.

[40] See O. E. Williamson, 'Vertical integration – and related variations on a transaction cost economics theme' (1982) (Unpublished manuscript) (University of Pennsylvania Center for the Study of Organizational Innovation Discussion Paper No. 129).

contractual relation to effect 'equilibration.' Nonstandard contracting, such as reciprocity or barter, sometimes appears for this reason.

Technology thus has a bearing on transaction cost reasoning, but only to the extent that it contributes to an asset specificity condition. Contracts that are supported by asset-specific investments are ones in which the parties have an interest in maintaining the continuity of the exchange, lest the productive value of these assets be sacrificed by premature contract termination. Vertical integration plainly helps preserve the continuity of a complex contracting relationship, and is best understood as a response to these underlying continuity needs. It is thus wrong to conclude that vertical integration presents antitrust problems unless attended by the 'physical or technical aspects' to which earlier scholarship referred.[41] Such technological aspects are neither necessary nor sufficient for vertical integration to yield valued transaction cost economies.

Public Policy

A transaction cost approach shows that vertical integration can yield cost savings over a wider range of circumstances than the earlier technological/ market-power approach indicated. Thus, a more permissive view of vertical integration is warranted in light of recent transaction cost scholarship. The 10 per cent and 6 per cent limits of the 1968 Guidelines find no support at all when the issues are framed in transaction cost terms.

Vigilance with respect to possible anticompetitive effects of vertical integration nevertheless remains important. But these effects also have transaction cost origins. If the leading firms in a highly concentrated stage I were to integrate into an otherwise competitive stage II activity, the nonintegrated sector of the market may be so reduced that only a few firms of efficient size can service the stage II market. Then, entry would be deterred by the potential entrant's having to engage in small-numbers bargaining with those few nonintegrated stage II firms. Furthermore, the alternative of integrated entry will be unattractive because prospective stage I entrants that lack experience in stage II activity would incur high capital and start-up costs were they to enter both stages themselves. But if stages I and II were of low or moderate concentration, a firm entering either stage can expect to strike competitive bargains with either integrated or nonintegrated firms in the other stage, because no single integrated firm can enjoy a strategic advantage in such transactions, and because it is difficult for the integrated firms to collude. Thus, anticompetitive effects are likely to exist in highly concentrated industries; but because vertical

[41] See *supra* text accompanying footnotes 26–8.

integration in low or moderately concentrated industries is likely to promote efficiency, it will rarely pose an antitrust issue.[42]

The 1982 Guidelines

The 1982 vertical Merger Guidelines correspond in three significant respects to the developments in transaction cost economics discussed above. First, the Guidelines express concern over the competitive consequences of a vertical merger only if the acquired firm is operating in an industry in which the HHI exceeds 1800. The presumption is that nonintegrated stage I firms can satisfy their stage II requirements by negotiating competitive terms with stage II firms where the HHI is below 1800. The Guidelines thus focus exclusively on the monopolistic subset, which is congruent with transaction cost reasoning. Second, the anticompetitive concerns in the Guidelines regarding costs of capital, (contrived) scale diseconomies, and the use of vertical integration to evade rate

---

[42] The full argument can be found in Williamson, *supra* footnote 34, pp. 115–16:
'Except for the rather special case where a regulated firm has integrated backward into equipment supply, which needs to be assessed in the context of the regulatory milieu, vertical integration poses antitrust issues of two kinds: price may be adversely affected and the condition entry may be impaired. It needs, however, to be appreciated that adverse effects of neither kind will obtain unless a nontrivial degree of monopoly exists. Accordingly, the enforcement of antitrust with respect to vertical integration ought to be restricted to the monopolistic subset. Elsewhere, the maintained hypothesis ought to be that vertical integration has been undertaken for the purpose of economizing on transaciton costs ...

Entry impediments of two types can arise where the leading firms in stage I integrate (backward or forward) into what could otherwise be a competitively organized stage II activity. For one thing, the residual (nonintegrated) sector of the market may be so reduced that only a few firms of efficient size can service the stage II market. Firms that would otherwise be prepared to enter stage I may be discouraged from coming in by the prospect of having to engage in small-numbers bargaining, with all the hazards that entails, with these few nonintegrated stage II firms. Additionally, if prospective stage I entrants lack experience in stage II related activity, and thus would incur high capital costs were they to enter both stages themselves, integrated entry may be rendered unattractive. The integration of stages I and II by leading firms is then anticompetitive, in entry aspects at least, if severing the vertical connection would permit a competitive (large-numbers) stage II activity to develop without loss of scale economies.

Vertical integration in industries with low to moderate degrees of concentration does not, however, pose these same problems. Here a firm entering into either stage can expect to strike competitive bargains with firms in the other stage whether they are integrated or nonintegrated. The reasons are that no single integrated firm enjoys a strategic advantage with respect to such transactions and that collusion by the collection of integrated firms (in supply or demand respects) is difficult to effectuate. Vertical integration rarely poses an antitrust issue, therefore, except as the industry in question is highly concentrated or, in less concentrated industries, collective refusals to deal are observed. But for such circumstances, vertical integration is apt to be of the efficiency promoting kind.'

regulation are all consonant with transaction cost reasoning.[43] Finally, the Guidelines make express reference to the importance of asset specificity, although the analysis is less fully developed than it might be.

Despite this striking correspondence, the Guidelines are not fully consonant with transaction cost reasoning. The transaction cost rationale for challenging a 5 per cent acquisition whenever the HHI exceeds 1800 is not self-evident. Furthermore, the Guidelines make no provision for an economies defense, even where asset specificity is demonstrably great. It is true that there are hazards in allowing an economies defense, especially if economic evidence must be presented in court.[44] These hazards can be mitigated, however, if the Justice Department declines to bring cases where economies are clearly driving organizational outcomes.[45]

III. Conclusion

The 1968 vertical Merger Guidelines reflected the then-prevailing technological orientation toward vertical integration. Because the requisite 'physical or technical aspects' were commonly missing and transaction cost economies were disregarded, severe limits on vertical mergers were thought to be in the public interest. The acquisition of a 6 per cent downstream firm by a 10 per cent upstream firm was thus presumptively unlawful.

In the 1970s, the technological orientation toward vertical integration gave way to the comparative institutional assessment of contracting inherent in transaction cost economics. This approach focused on the purposes vertical integration can serve. Vertical integration realizes transaction cost economies where the parties are, in effect, reduced to bilateral trading because of an asset specificity condition. The transaction cost approach also identifies anticompetitive abuses of vertical integration. Such abuses can arise because of strategic pre-emption (fringe markets are reduced, resulting in rivals being forced to sell or secure supplies on bilateral terms), and because implicit contracts to collude are easier to enforce if rivals are identically integrated. Backward vertical integration may also be suspect in regulated industries if regulators are unable to

---

[43] The concern is that the regulator will be unable to evaluate the reasonableness of the costs incurred and prices charged by an integrated supplier because the relevant information is costly to obtain and difficult to evaluate. Such concerns would vanish were regulators comprehensively knowledgeable (not subject to bounded rationality) or if regulated firms would disclose all relevant information candidly (not subject to opportunism).

[44] Some of these are discussed in O. E. Williamson, 'Economies as an antitrust defense revisited', *University of Pennsylvania Law Review*, 125 (1977), pp. 699, 701–3.

[45] General Motors' acquisition of Fisher Body after a contracting relationship experienced strain is described by Klein, Crawford, & Alchian, *supra* footnote 34, pp. 308–10.

evaluate underlying cost conditions except at great expense.

That the 1982 vertical Merger Guidelines are much more permissive than the 1968 vertical Merger Guidelines arguably reflects an appreciation for a wider set of efficiency benefits than had previously been recognized. The recent Guidelines are also much more precise in identifying the problems that vertical mergers in dominant firm or highly concentrated industries can present. I doubt that the recent Guidelines would read as they do had there not been a shift from market power to efficiency analysis in the intervening years. Accordingly, although I do not want to make too much of 'one observation,' the evidence is consistent with the hypothesis that ideas drive outcomes in antitrust law.[46]

---

[46] For related arguments and evidence, see *supra* footnotes 1, 2. See also Bork (1978); Liebeler (1978, p. 1231); Muris (1980, p. 381); Posner (1979, p. 925); A. Fisher and R. Lande, 'Efficiency considerations in merger enforcement.' (Unpublished manuscript, forthcoming in *California Law Review* 71 (1983), pp. 1580–1696.)

Part II

Contracting

My sense that transaction cost economics speaks to many of the critical issues in antitrust is further developed in comparative contracting terms in the first essay that appears in this section. Of special importance is the use of a contracting approach to examine oligopoly. I was early persuaded that vertical integration was usefully thought of as an internal contracting alternative to intermediate product market exchange. That conglomerate firms (with the appropriate internal structure) could be thought of as miniature internal capital markets was a natural next step. But oligopoly seemed to be resistant to transaction cost reasoning.

Upon reformulating the oligopoly problem in contracting terms, however, I discovered that the critical factors that determined whether a coalition would succeed well or poorly could be discerned. This formulation had the further advantage that dominant firms could be distinguished from oligopolies in terms of their governance/contracting efficacy.

The second essay explicates a transaction cost rationale for vertical market restrictions – tie-ins, block booking, reciprocity, franchises, etc. – and further identifies the circumstances where such restrictions are problematic. I use the *Schwinn* case to illustrate both sides of the issue. Interestingly, the *Schwinn* case was the first antitrust case that I was asked to work on when I joined the Antitrust Division in September 1966. Although I advised against the line of argument taken in the Government's brief, the advice came too late and/or was unpersuasive. Happily, however, the *Schwinn* opinion was reversed ten years later by *GTE–Sylvania*.

The last essay in this section examines alternative monopoly and efficiency approaches to the study of contract, with special emphasis on transaction cost economics. A simple contracting schema is devised whereby the critical elements of contract – technology, price, and governance – are interactively displayed. What I refer to as the study of 'contracting in its entirety' is also discussed. Finally, I introduce, but scarcely develop, what is one of the deep, unsettled puzzles of contract: the problem of contrived contractual inconsistency. More work on this issue is sorely needed.

5

The Economics of Antitrust: Transaction Cost Considerations

Economic analysis is commonly, though somewhat arbitrarily, divided into macroeconomic and microeconomic categories. The former is concerned with highly aggregative economic issues – such as national income, employment, and inflation – while the latter deals with the behavior of individual consumers, firms, and markets. To the extent that economics is thought to have a bearing on antitrust analysis and policy, the firm and market models of received microtheory are thought, by economists and lawyers alike, to supply the relevant foundations.[1]

Although I am in general agreement with this position. I contend that received microtheory sometimes needs to be augmented by introducing transaction cost considerations. Failure or refusal to make allowance for transaction costs, in circumstances where these are arguably nonnegligible, can lead to error. Not only is an understanding of the issues impaired, but incorrect policy prescriptions will sometimes result.

Copyright © reserved by the author. Research on this chapter has been supported by a grant from the National Science Foundation. Parts of the chapter are based on a lecture given at the University of California at Los Angeles on 10 January 1974 in conjunction with the *Major Issue Lecture Series* program 'Large Scale Enterprise in a Changing Society'. Previously published in *University of Pennsylvania Law Review* 122 (1974), pp. 1439–96. ©1974 by the University of Pennsylvania.
[1] To be sure, these models are sometimes tailored before applying them to particular antitrust problems. Examples of the application of received microtheory to antitrust issues are E. Singer, *Antitrust Economics* (1968), Englewood Cliffs: Prentice Hall. W. Baxter, Legal restrictions on exploitation of the patent monopoly: An economic analysis, *Law Journal*, 76 p. 267. See also chapter 8.

One of the attractive attributes of the transaction cost approach[2] is that it reduces, essentially, to a study of contracting – which means that the contracting expertise of lawyers developed in other contexts can be drawn upon. Issues such as the following are addressed: When will a related set of transactions be completed most efficaciously by negotiating contracts between firms (across a market), and when will merger or integration (internal organization) be preferred? In what respects, if any, do pre-existing firm and market structures impede or facilitate the ability of new firms to negotiate the necessary market contracts for labor, capital, materials, and intermediate products to effectuate successful entry? While these types of issues can be addressed in an unconvoluted way using the transaction cost apparatus, the models of received microtheory, in which transaction costs are suppressed, are often ill-suited and sometimes misleading.

I begin with a brief review of received microtheory before setting out the elements of the transaction cost approach. The examination of vertical integration, oligopoly, and conglomerate organization from the transactional point of view suggests antitrust policies somewhat different from those advanced by scholars employing the conventional microtheory approach. Although not exhausting the applications of the transaction cost approach to the study of antitrust issues,[3] the chapter will hopefully give the reader a sense of the relevance of this approach to the antitrust area.

I. The Basic Approaches

It is widely thought that 'the economic background required for understanding antitrust issues seldom requires detailed mastery of economic refinements'[4] – meaning, presumably, that the standard economic models of firms and markets found in intermediate microtheory textbooks will

---

[2] More generally, the issues posed involve an assessment of markets and hierarchies. For a discussion of these issues, see O. E. Williamson, 'Markets and hierarchies: Some elementary considerations', *American Economic Review*, 63, May 1973, p. 316; O. E. Williamson, 'Markets and Hierarchies: Analysis and Antitrust Implications' (August 1973) (Unpublished paper held by author). This approach is similar to that advocated by J. Commons, *Institutional Economics* (1934), who took the position that the transaction constituted the ultimate unit of investigation. Commons, however, had to fashion many of his transactional concepts himself, while I am able to draw, 40 years later, on much more extensive literatures in both economics and organization theory. This is a considerable advantage.

[3] For example, the marketing practices of Arnold, Schwinn & Co., to which the Antitrust Division objected, can usefully be examined in transaction cost terms. See *United States* v. *Arnold, Schwinn & Co.*, 388 US 365 (1967).

[4] P. Areeda, *Antitrust Analysis*, 4 (1967).

normally be sufficient for antitrust purposes. I doubt that this is the case. Conventional analysis sometimes needs to be augmented and at other times supplanted by express consideration of transactional problems.

A. RECEIVED MICROTHEORY[5]

Demand curves (average revenue curves), average cost curves, and the marginal curves of revenue and cost drawn to each of these constitute the basic modeling apparatus for most antitrust treatments of firms and markets. Implicit in this model are efficiency assumptions of two kinds. First, it is assumed that the firm realizes the maximum output of product from each feasible combination of factor inputs (mainly labor and capital). That is, it operates on its production function. Failure to operate on the production function would imply wasteful use of inputs; this is assumed away. Second, given the prices of productive factors, it is assumed that the firm chooses the least-cost combination of factors for each possible level of output. The total cost curve, from which average and marginal. cost curves are derived, is constructed in this way.

In circumstances where economies of scale are large in relation to the size of the market, a condition of natural monopoly (or perhaps oligopoly) may be said to exist. The monopolist or the oligopolists who supply goods and services in such a market will be sufficiently large that small percentage changes in their output will perceptibly affect the market price. Price is thus subject to strategic determination. However, in circumstances where economies of scale are exhausted at firm sizes that are small in relation to the market, each firm will regard price as given[6] and a condition of competitive market supply, in which price will be equal to marginal cost, will obtain.

Intermediate types of markets, such as duopoly or oligopoly, are modeled by making appropriate assumptions about the nature of the technology and the interfirm relations which develop.[7] Depending on the underlying technology and the behavioral assumptions that are employed,

---

[5] In setting out what I think to be the main distinctions between the conventional and transactional approaches, I concede at the outset that my discussion of received microtheory is highly simplified. It is the theory of the firm that appears in the conventional intermediate price theory textbook. Inasmuch as I often find such a tactic to be a source of considerable irritation when reviewing the work of others who study the behavior of the modern corporation, I resort to it with some reluctance. My defense is that the simplified presentation is an economical way to expose the issues.

[6] This assumes that the firms in question behave in an independent (noncollusive) manner.

[7] Among the leading types of models for these purposes are Cournot models and their variants, and entry barrier models, which make allowance for potential competition. For an elegant review and extension of Cournot models, see L. Telser, *Competition, Collusion, and Game Theory (1972)*. A classic example of entry barrier models is Modigliani (1958), p. 215.

the prices and outputs that will be associated with alternative market structures can be succinctly derived. The social welfare implications of each, moreover, can be established by characterizing the benefits and costs resulting from the structure in question in appropriate social welfare terms.[8] The types of trade-offs that antitrust must contend with in circumstances where monopoly power and production economies both obtain can then be displayed in a relatively straightforward manner.[9]

Implicit throughout most analyses of this kind is that the nature of the firm – with respect, for example, to what it will make and what it will buy – is simply taken as given. Matters of internal organization (hierarchical structure, internal control processes) are likewise ignored. The firm is thereby reduced to little more than a production function to which a profit maximization objective has been assigned. That many interesting problems of firms and markets are suppressed or neglected as a result should come, perhaps, as no surprise.

B. THE TRANSACTION COST APPROACH[10]

The transactional approach may be stated compactly as follows: (a) markets and firms are alternative instruments for completing a related set of transactions; (b) whether a set of transactions ought to be executed between firms (across markets) or within a firm depends on the relative efficiency of each mode; (c) the costs of writing and executing complex contracts across a market vary with the characteristics of the human decision makers who are involved with the transaction on the one hand, and the objective properties of the market on the other; (d) although the human and transactional factors which impede exchanges between firms (across a market) manifest themselves somewhat differently within the firm, the same set of factors applies to both. A symmetrical analysis of trading, therefore, requires that the transactional limits of internal organization as well as the transactional sources of market failure be acknowledged. Moreover, just as market structure matters in assessing the efficacy of trades in the marketplace, so internal structure matters in assessing internal organization.

The transaction cost approach is interdisciplinary, drawing extensively on contributions from both economics and organization theory. The market failure,[11] contingent claims contracting,[12] and recent organizational

[8] For a discussion of partial equilibrium welfare economics, see A. Harberger, 'Three basic postulates for applied welfare economics: An interpretive essay', *Journal of Economic Literature*, 9 (1971), p. 785.

[9] See chapter 1.

[10] The discussion in this section draws on chapter 2 and Williamson, *supra*, footnote 23.

[11] See e.g., Arrow (1969).

[12] See e.g., J. Meade, *The Controlled Economy* (1971), London: Allen & Unwin, pp. 147–88.

design[13] literatures supply the requisite economic background. The administrative man[14] and strategic behavior[15] literatures are the main contributions from organization theory.

With this basis the transaction cost approach attempts to identify a set of market or transactional factors which together with a related set of human factors explain the circumstances under which complex contracts involving contingent claims will be costly to write, execute, and enforce. Faced with such difficulties, and considering the risks that simple, and therefore incomplete, contingent claims contracts pose,[16] the firm may decide to bypass the market and resort to hierarchical modes of organization. Transactions that might otherwise be handled in the market would then be performed internally and governed by administrative processes.

Uncertainty and small numbers exchange relations, in which one party's choice of trading partners is restricted, are the transactional factors to which market failure is ascribed. Unless joined by a related set of human factors, however, such transactional conditions need not impede market exchange. The pairing of uncertainty with bounded rationality and the joining of small numbers with what I will refer to as opportunism are especially important.

Consider first the pairing of bounded rationality with uncertainty. The principle of bounded rationality has been defined by Herbert Simon as follows: '*The capacity of the human mind for formulating and solving complex problems is very small compared with the size of the problems whose solution is required for objectively rational behavior in the real world. ...*'[17] It refers both to neurophysiological limits on the capacity to receive, store, retrieve, and process information without error[18] and to

---

[13] See e.g., Hurwicz (1972), p. 297.

[14] See, e.g., Simon (1957). For a discussion of the limits of internal organization, see O. E. Williamson, 'Limits of internal organization, with special reference to the vertical integration of production', in *Industrial Management: East and West* (1973), p. 199.

[15] See e.g., E. Goffman, *Strategic Interaction* (1969). Philadelpia: University of Pennsylvania Press.

[16] This is merely a necessary but not sufficient condition for internal organization to supplant the market. Internal organization also experiences distortion. Shifting a transaction from the market to a firm requires that a net efficiency gain be shown.

[17] Simon (1957), p. 198 (emphasis in original).

[18] The implications for contractual purposes of joining bounded rationality with uncertainty are suggested by the following description of the decision process: 'For even moderately complex problems ... the entire decision tree cannot be generated. There are several reasons why this is so: one is the size of the tree. The number of alternative paths in complex decision problems is very large.... A second reason is that in most decision situations, unlike chess, neither the alternative paths nor a rule for generating them is available.... A third reason is the problem of estimating consequences.... For many problems, consequences of alternatives are difficult, if not impossible, to estimate. The comprehensive decision model is not feasible for most interesting decision problems.'
J. Feldman and H. Kanter, 'Organizational decision-making', (cont'd overleaf)

definitional limits inherent in language. If these limits make it very costly or impossible to identify future contingencies and to specify, *ex ante*, appropriate adaptations thereto, long-term contracts may be supplanted by internal organization. Recourse to the internal organization of transactions permits adaptations to uncertainty to be accomplished by administrative processes as each problem arises. Thus, rather than attempt to anticipate all possible contingencies from the outset, the future is permitted to unfold. Internal organization in this way economizes on the bounded rationality attributes of decision makers in circumstances where prices are not 'sufficient statistics'[19] and uncertainty is substantial.

Rather, however, than resort to internal organization when long-term contingent claims contracts are thought to be defective (too costly or perhaps infeasible), why not employ short-term contracts instead? Appropriate adaptations to changing market circumstances can then be introduced at the contract renewal interval, thereby avoiding the prohibitive costs of *ex ante* specification. The pairing of opportunism with small numbers exchange relations, however, creates other obstacles to market transactions.

Developing this set of issues is somewhat involved and the interested reader is referred to discussions elsewhere of the types of contracting problems that give rise to vertical integration.[20] Suffice it to observe here that (a) opportunism refers to a lack of candor or honesty in transactions,

---

in *Handbook of Organizations* ed. J. March (1965), Chicago: Rand McNally & Co., p. 615. The infeasibility, or prohibitive cost, of describing the comprehensive decision tree and making *ex ante* optimal choices at every node means that collusive agreements must, except in implausibly simple circumstances, be highly incomplete documents.

A specific illustration of bounded rationality in the large corporation is afforded by the statement of R. H. Davies, President of Electric Autolite Company at the time of the Ford-Autolite merger. He testified on deposition as follows: 'Electric Autolite was "concerned" because, when Champion Spark Plug Company "went public" in 1958, "the figures that came out were very large – showing very large profits" and "when Ford saw those figures and saw how much profit there was in it" Electric Autolite "felt" that "the very essence of that much profit going to a supplier would be enough to make Ford think in terms of integration."'

Trial Memorandum for Defendant Ford Motor Co. pp. 14–15, *United States* v. *Ford Motor Co*. 286 F. Supp. 407, 435 (E.D. Mich. 1968) (violation of Clayton Act found), 315 F. Supp. 372 (E.D. Mich. 1970) (divestiture ordered), aff'd 405 US 562 (1972). The example is interesting because it suggests that as large and successful a firm as the Ford Motor Company, with its staff of engineers, cost accountants, and financial analysts, failed to discern the underlying profitability of spark plug manufacture until Champion went public (Champion was the first spark plug firm to go public). In a world of unbounded rationality, such disclosure would be unnecessary to stimulate Ford's interest.

[19] In circumstances, however, where prices are sufficient statistics, see T. Koopmans, *Three Essays on the State of Economics*, New York: McGraw-Hill (1957), pp. 41–54, reliance on the price system serves to economize on bounded rationality. See F. Hayek, 'The use of knowledge in society', *American Economic Review*, 35 (1945), p. 519.

[20] Williamson, *supra*, footnote 10.

to include self-interest seeking with guile; (b) opportunistic inclinations pose little risk to trading partners as long as competitive (large numbers) exchange relations obtain; (c) many transactions which at the outset involve a large number of qualified bidders are transformed in the process of contract execution – often because of economies of scale and accrued cost-advantages attributable to successful bidders learning more about the job as they perform their work (learning by doing) – so that a small numbers supply condition effectively obtains at the contract renewal interval; and (d) short-term contracting is costly and risky when opportunism and small numbers relations are joined. The argument will be developed further in other sections of this chapter.

In consideration of the problems that both long- and short-term contracts are subject to – by reason of bounded rationality and uncertainty in the first instance and the pairing of opportunism with small numbers relations in the second–internal organization may be used instead. With internal organization, issues are handled as they arise rather than in an exhaustive contingent planning fashion from the outset.[21] The resulting adaptive, sequential decision-making process is the internal organizational counterpart of short-term contracting and serves to economize on bounded rationality. That opportunism does not pose the same difficulties for such internal, sequential supply relations that it does when negotiations take place across a market is because (a) internal divisions do not have pre-emptive claims on profit streams, but act under common ownership and supervision to more nearly maximize joint profits instead, and (b) the internal incentive and control machinery is much more extensive and refined than that which obtains in market exchanges.[22] The firm is thereby better able to take the long view for investment purposes (and hence is more prepared to put specialized plant and equipment in place) while simultaneously adjusting to changing market circumstances in an adaptive, sequential manner.

Having said this, I hasten to add that if internal organization serves frequently to attenuate bounded rationality and opportunism problems, it does not eliminate either condition. Of special relevance in this connection are two propositions: (a) the limitations of internal organization

[21] This is oversimple. Internal organization also provides for contingencies by developing what are referred to as 'performance programs,' which are sometimes quite elaborate. Such programs are more easily adapted to unforeseen contingencies than are interfirm contracts, for the reasons given in the text. For a discussion of performance programs, see J. March and H. Simon, *Organizations* (1958), New York: John Wiley.

[22] Williamson (1970), pp. 120–35. Internal organization affords two further benefits: it helps to overcome conditions where one party holds information not available to the other without some expense (information impactedness), because internal audits are more powerful than external, and is sometimes able to reduce uncertainty by promoting convergent expectations. Both of these are important but less basic to the present argument than the effects of internal organization on bounded rationality and opportunism.

in both bounded rationality and opportunistic respects vary directly with firm size, organization form held constant,[23] but (b) organization form – that is, the way in which activities in the firm are hierarchically structured – matters.[24] The import of this latter proposition is developed in the discussion of conglomerates in section IV.

Moreover the choice between firm and market ought not to be regarded as fixed. Both firms and markets change over time in ways which may render an initial assignment of transactions to firm or market inappropriate. The degree of uncertainty associated with the transactions in question may diminish; market growth may support large numbers of suppliers in competition with one another, and information disparities between the parties often shrink. Also, changes in technology may occur, altering the degree to which bounded rationality limits apply. Thus, the efficacy of completing transactions by hierarchies or markets should be reassessed periodically.

C. AN EXAMPLE: PRICE DISCRIMINATION

The differences between received microtheory and the transaction cost approach can be illustrated by examining the familiar problem of price discrimination. As will be evident, the transaction cost approach does not abandon but rather augments the received microtheory model.

Assume for this illustration that the market in question is one in which economies of scale are large in relation to the size of the market, in which case the average cost curve falls over a considerable output range. Assume, in particular, that demand and cost conditions are as shown in figure 5.1. The unregulated monopolist who both maximizes profits and sells his output at a single, uniform price to all customers will restrict output below the social optimum[25] (shown by Q^* in figure 5.1)[26] at which marginal cost equals price. Instead, the monopolist will produce only to the point (Q_m) at which marginal cost equals marginal revenue so that an excess of price over marginal cost obtains.

It is sometimes argued, however, that price discrimination will correct the allocative efficiency distortion in a monopoly situation. The monopolist who can segregate his market in such a way that each customer is made to pay his full valuation (given by the demand curve) for each unit of output has the incentive to add successive units of output until the price paid for the last item sold just equals the marginal cost. The fully

---

[23] See Williamson, *supra*, footnote 14.

[24] See Chandler (1962); Williamson, *supra* footnote 22.

[25] So-called 'second best' issues are assumed away here and throughout the article.

[26] So that a break-even problem will not be posed if output is set at Q^*, I assume that scale economies are exhausted before this output is reached.

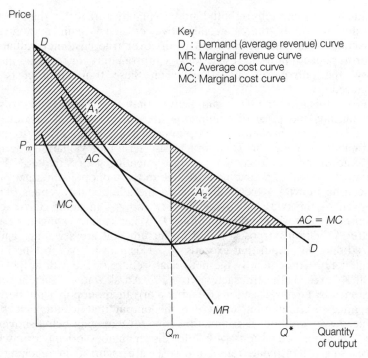

Figure 5.1

discriminating monopolist will thus be led to expand output from the
restricted position of a nondiscriminating monopolist (Q_m) to the social
optimum point (Q^*). Although income distribution will be affected in the
process (in possibly objectionable ways), the output distortion is removed
and an allocative efficiency gain is realized.[27]

Evaluating this allocative efficiency claim gives us our first opportunity
to contrast the conventional analysis of received microtheory with a
transactions cost approach. Implicit in the above conventional microtheory
argument is an assumption that the costs of both discovering true customer
valuations for the product and of enforcing restrictions against resale (so
that there can be no arbitrage) are negligible and can be disregarded.
Such costs vanish, however, only if either (a) customers will honestly self-
reveal preferences and self-enforce nonresale promises (no opportunism)
or (b) the seller is omniscient (a strong variety of unbounded rationality).

---

[27] If the output of the industry in question is used as an intermediate rather than strictly
as a final product, factor distortions at other stages of production may be induced. See
McKenzie (1951), p. 785. For simplicity, let these be assumed away.

Inasmuch as assumptions of both kinds are plainly unrealistic, the question naturally arises: Is there an allocative efficiency gain if nontrivial transaction costs must be incurred to discover true customer valuations and/or to police nonresale restrictions? Unfortunately for received microtheory, the outcome is uncertain when these transaction costs are introduced.

To see this, assume (for simplicity), that the transaction costs of accomplishing full price discrimination are independent of the level of output: the costs are either zero, in which event no effort to price discriminate is made, or T, in which case customer valuations become fully known and enforcement against cheating is complete.[28] Price discrimination will of course be attractive to the monopolist if a net profit gain can be shown – which will obtain if the additional revenues (which are given by the two shaded regions, A_1 and A_2, in figure 5.1) exceed the costs of achieving discrimination, T. What is interesting for social welfare evaluation purposes is that an incremental gross welfare gain is realized only on output that exceeds Q_m. This gain is given by the lower triangle (A_2). Consequently the net social welfare effects will be positive only if A_2 exceeds the transaction costs, T. An allocative efficiency loss, occasioned by high transaction costs, but a private monopoly gain, derived from price discrimination applied to the output that would have been produced even without discrimination (this revenue gain being shown by A_1), is therefore consistent with fully discriminatory pricing in circumstances where nontrivial transaction costs are incurred in reaching the discriminatory result. More precisely, if T is less than A_1 plus A_2 but more than A_2 alone, the monopolist will be prepared to incur the customer information and policing costs necessary to achieve the discriminatory outcome, because *his* profits will be augmented ($A_1 + A_2 > T$), but these same expenditures will give rise to a net *social* welfare loss ($A_2 < T$).[29]

In circumstances where T is zero or negligible, of course, this contradiction does not arise. But the results of received microtheory rest crucially on such an assumption. If, arguably, the assumption is not

---

[28] Generalizing the analysis by expressing the transaction costs of discerning true customer valuations and policing resale restrictions as a continuous function of output is relatively easy but yields little that the simplified assumptions do not. (One difference to be noted is that the price discriminating output will be less than the social optimum, Q^*.) The analysis can likewise be generalized to make the degree of precision of price discrimination a decision variable.

[29] The discussion in the text assumes, implicitly, that the uniform pricing monopolist can price at P_m without inducing entry. If, however, the entry forestalling price ($\bar{P}$) is less than P_m, the initial position to be evaluated is a larger output and lower price than that discussed above. For fixed T, the welfare gains of price discrimination are further reduced. (In all likelihood an entry threat will attenuate the private gains as well.)

satisfied, transaction costs need expressly to be taken into account before a welfare assessment is ventured.

II. Vertical Integration

The discussion of market exchange versus internal organization in the preceding section suggests that internal organization has attractive properties in circumstances where long-term contracts are not feasible, because contractual contingencies overwhelm the limited planning capacities of parties subject to bounded rationality, and where short-term contracts pose hazards, because of the conjunction of opportunism with a small numbers exchange condition. Prospective interfirm contracting difficulties are thus responsible for the decision to integrate. The details of such a transactional approach to vertical integration have been worked out elsewhere.[30]

It should be appreciated, however, that this has not been the prevailing rationale for vertical integration among economists. More often the argument runs in terms of technological considerations. Two such arguments are examined below and are rejected in favor of the transactional approach. The possibility that vertical integration might inhibit potential entry is then explored and the incentive to integrate as a means by which to circumvent government controls (taxes, quotas) is briefly trated. I conclude this section with a statement of the antitrust enforcement implications of the argument.

A. A LIFE CYCLE ANALYSIS

George Stigler deduces, from his explication of Adam Smith's theorem, that the division of labor is limited by the extent of the market, that vertical integration is related to an industry's life cycle: vertical integration will be extensive in firms in young industries: disintegration will be observed as an industry grows; and reintegration will occur as an industry passes into decline.[31] These life cycle effects are illustrated by reference to a multiprocess product in which each procss involves a separable technology and hence its own distinct cost function.[32] Some of the processes display falling cost curves, others curves that rise continuously, and still others U-shaped cost curves.

[30] Williamson, *supra* footnote 10.
[31] G. J. Stigler, 'The division of labor is limited by the extent of the market', *Journal of Political Economy*, 59 (1951), p. 185.
[32] Stigler employs the separability assumption for convenience; relaxing it complicates but does not alter the general argument.

Stigler then asks, why does the firm not exploit the decreasing cost activities by expanding them to become a monopoly? He answers by observing that, at the outset, the decreasing cost functions may be 'too small to support a specialized firm or firms.'[33] But, unless the argument is meant to be restricted to global or local monopolies, for which there is no indication, resort to a specialized firm does not exhaust the possibilities. Assuming that there are at least several firms in the business, why does one of them not exploit the available economies, to the mutual benefit of all the parties, by producing the entire requirement for the group? The reasons, I submit, turn on transaction costs inherent in interfirm rivalry.

If, for example, the exchange of specialized information between the parties is involved (Stigler specifically refers to 'market information' as one of the decreasing cost possibilities) strategic misrepresentation issues are posed. The risk here is that the specialist firm will disclose information to its rivals in an incomplete and distorted manner. Because the party buying the information can establish its accuracy only at great cost, possibly by collecting the original data themselves, the exchange fails to go through. If, however, rivals were not given to opportunism, the risk of strategic distortion would vanish and the technologically efficient specialization of information could proceed.

The exchange of physical components that experience decreasing costs is likewise discouraged where both long-term and short-term contracts incur prospective transactional difficulties. Long-term contracts are principally impeded by bounded rationality considerations: the extent to which uncertain future events can be expressly taken into account – in the sense that the cost of appropriate adaptations can be estimated and contractually specified – is simply limited. Since, given opportunism, incomplete long-term contracts predictably pose interest conflicts between the parties, other arrangements are apt to be sought.

Spot market (short-term) contracting is an obvious alternative. Such contracts, however, are hazardous if there are only a small number of suppliers, which (by assumption) holds true for the circumstances described by Stigler. The buyer then incurs the risk that the purchased product of service will, at some later time, be supplied under monopolistic terms. Industry growth, moreover, need not eliminate the tension of small numbers bargaining if the item in question is one for which learning by doing is important and if the market for human capital is imperfect.[34] Delaying own-production until own-requirements are sufficient to exhaust scale economies would, considering the learning costs of undertaking own

---

[33] Stigler, *supra* footnote 31, p. 188.
[34] For a discussion of learning by doing, see P. Doeringer and M. Piore, *Internal Labor Markets and Manpower Analysis* (1971) Boston: D. C. Heath.

production at this later time, incur substantial transition costs. It may, under these conditions, be more attractive from the outset for each firm to produce its own requirements – or, alternatively, for the affected firms to merge.[35] Absent present or prospective transaction costs of the sorts described, however, specialization by one of the firms (monopoly supply), to the mutual benefit of all, would presumably occur. Put differently, technology is no bar to contracting; it is transactional considerations that are decisive.

Aspects of the above argument can be illustrated with the help of figure 5.2. The average costs of supplying the item in question by a specialized outside supplier at time 1 are shown by the curve AC_1^s. Firms that are already in the industry can supply the same item at the average costs shown by AC_1^x. The curve AC_1^s is everywhere above the curve AC_1^x because

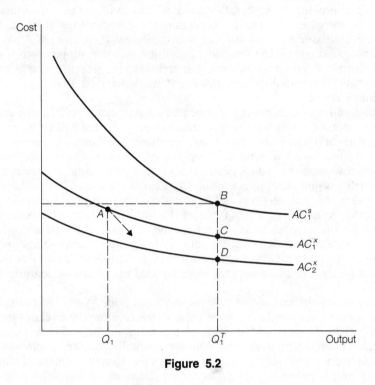

Figure 5.2

---

[35] Mergers would permit the firms involved to realize economies of scale with respect to the decreasing cost activity in question. Such mergers might also, however, result in market power. That such mergers are attractive in a private benefit sense is clear, but social net benefits need not obtain. See Williamson, *supra* footnote 9.

firms already in the industry avoid the setup costs which a specialized outside supplier would incur. Each of the firms in the industry generates requirements for the item at time 1 of Q_1^i. The total industry requirement at time 1 is Q_1^T.

The implicit comparison that Stigler makes in his explanation for vertical integration is point A versus point B. Thus although having a specialized supplier service the whole industry (produce Q_1^T would permit economies of scale to be more fully exploited, the declining cost advantage is more than offset by the setup costs. Therefore, the average costs of the specialized supplier (at B) exceed the average costs that each individual firm would incur by supplying its own requirements (at A). My argument, however, is that point A should also be compared with point C – where point C shows the average costs of supplying the requirements for the entire industry by one of the firms that is *already in* the industry. Such a firm does not incur those setup costs which disadvantage the outside specialist supplier. Given the decreasing cost technology that Stigler assumes, the average costs at C are necessarily less than those at A. Why then not have one of the firms already in the industry supply both itself and all others? The impediments, I submit, are the hazards of interfirm contracting (of both long-term and spot market types) that have been described above.

The comparison, moreover, can be extended to include a consideration of the curve AC_2^x, which represents the average costs that will be incurred by a firm at time 2 that has been supplying continuously during the interval from time 1 to time 2. The curve AC_2^x is everywhere lower than AC_1^x by reason of advantages gained from learning by doing. To the extent that such learning advantages are not or cannot be shared with others,[36] they will accrue only to firms that have undertaken own-production during the period in question. Thus if one of the firms in the industry becomes the monopoly supplier to all others at time 1, and if at time 2 the other firms become dissatisfied with the monopoly supplier's terms, the buying firms cannot undertake to supply their own requirements at a later date on cost parity terms because they have not had the benefit of learning by doing.

Note finally the arrow that points away from point A toward point D. If the industry is expected to grow (plainly the case for the circumstances described by Stigler) and if each of the firms in the industry can be expected to grow with it, then each firm, if it supplies its own requirements (Q_1^i) at time 1 and incurs average costs of A, can, by reason of both growth and learning by doing, anticipate declining own-supply, costs –

---

[36] Again, this is because the market for human capital is imperfect. Firm X cannot simply hire firm Y's experienced employees away without incurring very considerable transfer costs. The learning by doing knowledge is thus impacted in firm Y.

perhaps to the extent that each substantially exhausts the economies of scale that are available. Since supplying its own requirements avoids the transactional hazards of procuring its supply from a market with only a few trading partners, vertical integration of the items with a decreasing cost technology is all the more to be expected.

B. TECHNOLOGICAL INTERDEPENDENCY

Of the various rationales for vertical integration that have been advanced, the technological interdependency argument is both the most familiar and straightforward: successive processes which naturally follow immediately in time and place dictate certain efficient manufacturing configurations; these, in turn, are held to have common ownership implications. Such technical complementarity is probably more important in flow process operations, such as chemicals and metals, than in separable component manufacture. The standard example is the integration of the making of iron and steel, where thermal economies are said to be available through integration. It is commonly held that where 'integration does not have this physical or technical aspect – as it does not, for example, in integrating the production of assorted components with the assembly of those components – the case for cost savings from integration is generally much less clear.'[37]

I submit, however, that such technological interdependency is neither essential for cost savings to be realized by integration nor typical of most integrated activities. Consider Adam Smith's pin-making example.[38] Pin manufacture involved a series of technologically distinct operations such as wire straightening, cutting, pointing, and grinding. In principle, each of these activities could be performed by an independent specialist and work passed from station to station by contract. The introduction of buffer inventories at each station, moreover, would decrease the coordination requirements and thereby reduce contractual complexity. Each worker could then proceed at his own pace, subject only to the condition that he maintain his buffer inventory at some minimum level. A series of independent entrepreneurs rather than a group of employees, each subject to an authority relation, would thus perform the tasks in question.

Transaction costs militate against such an organization of tasks, however. For one thing, it may be possible to economize on buffer inventories by having the entire group act as a unit, under common direction, with respect to such matters as work breaks and variable rates of production. Although rules could be worked out in advance and make explicit in the contract, or the authority to make such decisions could be rotated among

---

[37] J. Bain, *Industrial Organization* (1968), New York: John Wiley, p. 381.
[38] A. Smith, *The Wealth of Nations* ed. Cannan (1937), London: Methuen, pp. 4–5.

the members of the group, coordination might usefully be assigned to a 'boss,' who oversees the entire operation and can more easily judge the fatigue and related work attitudes in the group.

The more pressing reasons for replacing autonomous contracting by an employment relation, however, turn on adaptability considerations. Suppose one of the individuals becomes ill (real or feigned) or becomes injured. Who nominates and chooses a replacement, or otherwise arranges to pick up the slack, and how is compensation determined? Reaching agreement on such matters is apt to be relatively costly compared to having a boss reassign the work among the members of the group or make other ad hoc arrangements on the group's behalf. Similarly, what is to be done if an individual declines to deliver the requisite quantity or quality to the next station? How are penalties determined? Litigation is apt to be costly and time consuming, and to what avail if the individual lacks the requisite assets to compensate for the losses attributable to his deviant behavior? Again, remedies and adaptations under an employment relation, where an individual has much weaker property claims to a work station, are likely to be quicker and less costly to effectuate.

The problem, more generally, is that autonomous contracting in small numbers circumstances is fraught with difficulties if unforeseen events requiring adaptation frequently appear, especially if the parties are given to opportunism. Rather than endure the costs that can be expected to arise when a series of bilateral contracts are negotiated among a group of individuals each of whom enjoys, in the short run at least, a monopoly position, a firm will integrate such related activities instead. Central ownership of the work stations and an employment relation between the workers and entrepreneur will facilitate adaptation.[39]

C. THE CONDITION OF ENTRY

Stigler observes that 'it is possible that vertical integration increases the difficulty of entry by new firms, by increasing the capital and knowledge necessary to conduct several types of operation rather than depend on rivals for supplies or markets.'[40] Others, however, take exception to this argument. Robert Bork, for example, contends that 'In general, if greater than competitive profits are to be made in an industry, entry should occur whether the entrant has to come in at both levels or not. I know of no theory of imperfections in the capital market which would lead suppliers of capital to avoid areas of higher return to seek areas of lower return.'[41]

---

[39] The specialization of risk bearing and strategic decision making may also favor common ownership and the replacement of autonomous contracting by an employment relation.

[40] Stigler, *supra* footnote 31, p. 191.

[41] Bork (1969), pp. 139, 148.

Similarly, Ward Bowman observes that 'difficulties of access to the capital market that enable X to offer a one dollar inducement (it has a bankroll) and prevent its rivals from responding (they have no bankroll and, though the offering of the inducement is a responsible business tactic, for some reason cannot borrow the money) ... [have] yet to be demonstrated.'[42] As I hope to make apparent, these and related arguments of the received microtheory variety go through only if transaction cost considerations are suppressed. The pairing of bounded rationality with uncertainty and the joining of opportunism with a condition of 'information impactedness' (where one party to a transaction has access to information that the other party can obtain only at some expense, if at all) are the neglected factors.[43]

The phenomenon to be explained is not merely an increase of the financial requirements, as Stigler indicates, but an adverse alteration of the terms under which capital becomes available. Borrowing by the firm to finance additional plant and equipment is, of course, unlike borrowing by the consumer to purchase a house. The firm borrows funds in anticipation of realizing a prospective stream of earnings. These prospective earnings, as well as the resale value of the assets in question, are used to support the loan in question. The homeowner, by contrast, is not ordinarily able to augment his earnings by purchasing a house. Thus, whereas the householder who successively increases the size of his mortgage eventually incurs adverse capital costs, because the risks of default are greater, the firm need not likewise be impeded. Why then, if at all, does vertical integration by established firms disadvantage prospective entrants on account of capital market 'defects'?

An assessment of the issues will be facilitated by setting out the specific alternatives. Suppose that two distinct stages of production can be identified in the industry in question (designated I and II respectively). Assume further that stage I in the industry is essentially monopolized while stage II may or may not be integrated. The question now is whether a potential entrant who has developed a technologically satisfactory stage I substitute and has an established reputation in activity related to stage I will be unaffected by the integrated condition of stage II. Consider, in particular, the following contrasting conditions: (a) the monopolistic stage I producer is not integrated, in which case the prospective new entrant can come into stage I only and sell his product to stage II producers (suitably expanded, if that is necessary or absorption of the additional stage I production), and (b) the monopolistic stage I producer is integrated

[42] W. Bowman, *Patent and Antitrust Law: A Legal and Economic Appraisal* (1973), Chicago: University of Chicago Press, p. 59. The discussion in this section follows Williamson, Book Review, *Yale Law Journal*, 83 (1974), p. 647.

[43] Examples of information impactedness are given in this section and the sections that follow. For a specific illustration, see especially the text on implementation under uncertainty in section III subsection *infra*.

into stage II so that either (i) the new entrant himself must come in at both stages or (ii) independent new entrants appear simultaneously at both stages. If Bork and Bowman are correct, the cost of capital ought to be independent of these conditions.

To contend that the terms of finance are the same under condition b(i) as they are under condition a implies that the capital market has equal confidence in the new entrant's qualifications to perform stage II activities as it does in firms that are already experienced in the business. Except in circumstances where experienced firms are plainly inept, this is tantamount to saying that experience counts for nought. This, however, is implausible for transactions that involve large, discrete investments rather than small but recurring commitments of funds. Thus, although a series of small, recurring transactions can be monitored reasonably effectively on the basis of *ex post* experience, this is much less easy for transactions of the large, discrete variety – which are the kind under consideration here. Reputation, which is to say prior experience, is of special importance in establishing the terms of finance for transactions that involve alrge, discrete commitments of funds.

The significance that lenders and investors attach to reputation can be traced in part to the incompleteness of information regarding the qualifications of applicants for financing. Faced with incomplete information, suppliers of capital are vulnerable to opportunist representations. Unable to distinguish between those unknown candidates who have the capacity and the will to execute the project successfully from opportunists who assert that they are similarly qualified, when objectively (omnisciently) they are not, the terms of finance are adjusted adversely against the entire group. Furthermore, and of special relevance to the issue at hand, if lenders are not omniscient then, as between two candidates for financing, both of whom would be judged by an omniscient assessor to have identical capacities and wills to execute the project, but only one of whom has a favorable and widely known performance record, the unknown candidate will find that he is disadvantaged.[44]

Moreover, where both candidates are equally suspect, but one has access to internal sources of financing while the other does not, the candidate requiring outside financing may be unable to proceed. In this connection, timing can be of critical significance. If one firm moves to

[44] As H. B. Malmgren has noted, in a related context, 'Some firms will see opportunities, but be unable to communicate their own information and expectations favorably to bankers, and thus be unable to acquire finance, or need to pay a higher charge for the capital borrowed. Bankers and investors of funds in turn will be attracted to those firms which have shown in the past an ability to perceive and exploit effectively new opportunities, as against new firms which can only give their word that what they think is good is in fact good.' Malmgren, 'Information, expectations and the theory of the firm', *Quarterly Journal of Economics*, 75 (1961), p. 117.

the integrated structure gradually and finances the undertaking out of internal funds, while the second firm perceives the market opportunity later but, to be viable, must move immediately to a comparably integrated structure, the second firm may have to contend with adverse capital market rates.

The learning by doing conditions referred to earlier[45] are also germane to an assessment of the earnings opportunities of an integrated versus nonintegrated new entrant. By assumption, the prospective entrant is well qualified in stage I processes. If learning by doing yields significant cost advantages and if the prospective entrant has no special qualifications in stage II processes, will his incentive to enter be any the less keen if, by reason of the integration of his competitors, he must now come in at both stages? I submit that if the knowledge gleaned from experience is deeply impacted, which is to say that it is not generally known or easily made knowable to those who lack experience, and if it is very costly to hire away the requisite experienced personnel from the integrated firm,[46] the prospective entrant is plainly at a disadvantage. Information impactedness and imperfect labor markets thus combine to explain the cost disadvantage of the otherwise qualified new entrant in relation to the experienced firm. Were the monopolistic stage I producer not to have integrated into stage II, so that the prospective entrant could come in at stage I only and could rely on already experienced stage II firms to acquire the necessary capital to expand appropriately and service his stage II needs, capital costs would be lower and the prospect of entry thereby enhanced.[47]

The problems, moreover, do not vanish if the new entrant comes in at stage I only and relies on independent entry into stage II to occur [condition a(ii)]. Not only is the cost of capital adjusted adversely against potential new processors in stage II, by reason of the lack of experience referred to above, but simultaneous yet independent entry into both stages may be impeded because of 'nonconvergent expectations'[48] such that interdependent decisions between stages will fail to be made in a compatible way. Lack of common information among independent stage I and stage II specialists with respect to the market opportunities which they confront and doubts regarding the true investment intentions and contractual reliability of other parties are the apparent impediments to effective coordination. Ultimately, however, the problems are to be attributed to the human and transactional factors described in section I.

To be sure, the argument has no special significance to analysis of

---

[45] See text accompany footnotes 34 and 36 *supra*.

[46] If the knowledge advantage of the experienced firm is dispersed among a *team* of individuals, negotiations to hire away the team are likely to be prohibitively expensive.

[47] This assumes that the cost of capital varies directly with the perceived risk of the incremental investment, *ceteris paribus*.

[48] Malmgren, *supra* footnote 44, pp. 401, 405.

monopoly power unless the industry in question is already very concentrated[49] or, in less concentrated markets, conditions of effective collusion, which include collective refusal to deal, obtain. In such circumstances, however, interfirm rivalry, by itself, cannot be expected to self-police the market in a way that reliably assures the competitive outcome. Accordingly, potential competition has an important market policing role to play. If potential entrants regard limitation of prevailing vertical structures as contributing importantly to the prospect of successful entry (as they may in highly concentrated industries), vertical restrictions that require funds to be raised by less, rather than more, experienced firms can impede entry.

The financing issue, then, is not that capital markets perversely avoid earnings opportunities, the test proposed by Bork, or that financing cannot be arranged under any terms whatsoever, the condition referred to by Bowman. Rather, the cost of capital is at issue. If a prospective new entrant has the self-financing to come in at one stage (or can raise the capital at reasonable terms, perhaps because of a proven capability at this stage of operations) but lacks the self-financing (and incurs adverse terms should he attempt to raise the capital) to come in at the second stage, the condition of entry can clearly be affected by pre-existing vertical restrictions.[50]

D. CIRCUMVENTING REGULATION

As Ronald Coase[51] and George Stigler[52] have both pointed out, vertical integration is sometimes employed as a device by which to evade sales taxes, quota schemes, and other methods of nonprice rationing. Since such efforts by the government to interfere with the price mechanism typically apply to market-mediated but not to internal transactions, the shift of such transactions from the market to the firm serves to circumvent these regulatory schemes.[53] This is perfectly straightforward and is derived from received microtheory without appeal to transaction cost considerations.

Conventional microtheory can also be made to address the following issue: Can a regulated firm that is permitted only a 'fair' rate of return

---

[49] Provisionally, I define a very concentrated industry to be one where the four-firm concentration ratio exceeds 80 per cent.

[50] Economies of scale at stage II can also serve as an impediment to entry if the monopolist has integrated into stage II. See Williamson, *supra* footnote 42, p. 656.

[51] Coase (1952), pp. 338–9.

[52] Stigler, *supra* footnote 31, pp. 190–1.

[53] For a discussion of private carriage versus ICC regulated motor transport, see L. Schwartz, *Free Enterprise and Economic Organization* 4th edn (1972), St Paul, Minn.; Foundation Press, pp. 359–62.

in supplying a final good or service effectively evade the regulatory restraint by integrating backward into supply of its own equipment? As David Dayan[54] has shown, such backward integration will permit the regulated industry to earn monopoly profits if either equipment transfer prices or the rate of return at the equipment supply stage are unregulated.

While I do not wish to minimize the importance of such considerations in individual industries, I submit that these are rather special cases and that the main incentive for vertical integration is that integration serves to economize on transaction costs and/or is undertaken for the strategic purpose of impeding entry. The types of issues raised in the discussion of the transactional approach in section I and in the earlier parts of this section are the root causes for integration.

E. POLICY IMPLICATIONS

Vertical integration raises serious antitrust issues only in those circumstances where otherwise qualified actual or potential rivals can be said to be disadvantaged by it. The two situations in which disadvantage to rivals may arise are dominant firm (or otherwise very concentrated) industries and moderately concentrated industries where collusion has been successfully effected. For the reasons given in section III, such collusion is usually difficult to achieve. Accordingly, very concentrated industries in which the bulk of production is accounted for by integrated firms constitute the subset of principal interest for antitrust policy.

Even in concentrated industries, vertical integration cannot be held to be objectionable per se. Two cases can be distinguished. The easiest to deal with is the case where, but for vertical integration by the leading firms in stage I of the industry, stage II would be competitively organized. The objection to vertical integration here is twofold. For one thing, the residual (nonintegrated) sector of the stage II market is so reduced that only a few firms of efficient size can service the stage II market. Firms that would otherwise be prepared to enter stage I may therefore be discouraged from coming in by the prospect of having to engage in small numbers bargaining, with all the hazards that this entails, with these few nonintegrated stage II firms. Moreover, integrated entry may be rendered unattractive if prospective stage I entrants lack experience in stage II-related activity, and therefore would incur high capital costs were they to enter both stages themselves. The integration of stages I and II by leading firms is anticompetitive then, in entry aspects at least, if severing the vertical connection would permit competitive (large numbers) stage II activity to develop without loss of scale economies.

[54] Dayan, 'Vertical Integration and Monopoly Regulation', December 1972 (Unpublished Ph D dissertation, Princeton University).

The second case is that where economies of scale at both stages are large in relation to the size of the total (not merely the residual) market. The advantage of severing the vertical connection in these circumstances is that potential entrants into one of the stages will be less deterred from entering that stage, because they will not also have to incur the adverse capital costs attached to entry at the unfamiliar stage. Whether a welfare gain will thereby result depends, however, on offsetting factors of two kinds. First, with only a small number of firms at each stage, frequent haggling over contractual terms, imposing preparatory and negotiating costs on each side, may be expected between stage I and stage II firms. But even if these transaction costs do not obtain, the prospect is that goods and services will not be transferred between the stages at marginal cost prices.[55] Assuming that the technologies in question are of the variable proportions types, inefficient factor utilization results.[56] The question then is whether costs of these two types are more than offset by the gains of facilitating entry accomplished by severing a vertical connection.

Vertical integration in industries with low to moderate degrees of concentration does not, however, pose these same problems. Here a firm entering either stage can expect to strike competitive bargains with firms in the other stage, whether they are integrated or nonintegrated.[57] The reasons are that no single integrated firm enjoys a strategic advantage with respect to such transactions and that collusion by the collection of integrated firms (in supply or demand respects) is difficult to effectuate. Vertical integration rarely poses an antitrust issue, therefore, except when the industry in question is highly concentrated or, in less concentrated industries, collective refusals to deal are observed.[58] But for such circumstances, vertical integration is apt to be of the efficiency promoting kind.[59]

[55] If, however, the condition of entry into the supply stage is easy, small numbers by itself will not occasion monopolistic prices. See Stigler, *supra* footnote 31, p. 188.

[56] McKenzie, *supra* footnote 27.

[57] That a firm can expect to strike competitive bargains does not, of course, guarantee that it will earn 'normal' profits. This depends on supply and demand conditions. In a growing industry, however, the nonintegrated but otherwise qualified entrant should be able to secure a niche for itself without difficulty, although its profit rate may vary over a business cycle more than do the rates of integrated firms.

[58] This assumes that stage II entry is not easy.

[59] Vertical integration *within* a stage, I take it, poses no problems for anyone. The rationale here is that supplied above in the context of the pin-making example. Whether economies of vertical integration are realized *between* stages in what appears to be an unconcentrated industry is apt to turn on product differentiation considerations. Some of the components required by firms producing differentiated products may well be firm-specific, in which event a genuine large numbers supply condition may not be feasible. Where, however, competitive supply terms (both presently and prospectively) can be anticipated, own-supply has little to commend it. (On this, see Williamson, *supra* footnote 15.)

III. Oligopoly

The treatment of oligopoly in this section is less an analysis of oligopoly as such than an explication of why oligopoly can be expected to differ in nontrivial ways from monopoly. Although this difference may seem obvious, it has not always been so; the view that dissolution into oligopoly is no remedy for monopoly is widely held.[60] Don Patinkin contends that unless there are 'enough independent firms resulting from the dissolution to make the operation of competition possible . . . we will replace monopoly with some oligopolistic situation, and it is quite possible that we would be as badly off as under monopoly.'[61]

I take exception to that position here. It fails to make allowance for the advantages of internal organization as compared with contracting in adaptational respects, and it gives insufficient standing to the different incentives, and the related propensity to cheat, that distinguish internal from inter-firm organization.

A. ECONOMIC ANTECEDENTS OF THE TRANSACTIONAL APPROACH[62]

Fellner on Qualified Joint Profit Maximization

William Fellner contends that it is impossible to deduce determinate prices and outputs for oligopoly markets on the basis of demand and supply functions that are derived from technological data and utility functions.[63] Rather, fewness carries with it a range of indeterminacy. Thus, although received price theory is useful for establishing the region of indeterminacy, notions of 'conjectural interdependence' are needed to ascertain how choice is made within these limits. As he sees it, 'all problems of conjectural interdependence are essentially problems of bargaining – provided we interpret bargaining in the broader sense, including the "implicit" variety.'[64]

[60] E.g., J. K. Galbraith, *American Capitalism* (1952), Boston: Houghton Mifflin, p. 58. The view that tight oligopoly and monopoly are equivalent is especially prevalent among nonindustrial organization specialists.

[61] Patinkin, 'Multiple plant firms, cartels, and imperfect competition', *Quarterly Journal of Economics*, 61 (1947), p. 184.

[62] Two important treatments of the oligopoly problem to which I would call attention, but do not discuss here, are L. Telser, *supra* footnote 7 and Shubik, 'Information, duopoly, and competitive markets: A sensitivity analysis, *Kyklos*, 26 (1973), p. 736. Both are somewhat in the spirit of the transactional approach that I propose, and both develop a useful modeling apparatus to help evaluate the issues.

[63] Fellner (1949), pp. 9–11.

[64] Ibid., p. 16.

Within the range of indeterminacy, Fellner identifies four factors which determine relative bargaining power. The first two are concerned with social and political limits on bargaining and need not detain us here. The second two are more situation specific: the ability of the parties to take and to inflict losses during stalemates; and toughness, in the sense of unwillingness to yield.[65]

He notes that quasi-agreements (bargains) will change in response to shifts in relative strength among the parties, and that changing market circumstances make it necessary for oligopolistic rivals to adapt their behavior appropriately.[66] Such quasi-agreements, moreover, 'do not usually handle *all* economic variables entering into the determination of aggregate gains.'[67] Although this is partly because of 'administrative circumstances,' where these are left undefined, 'it is largely a consequence also of uncertainty due to which various persons and organizations discount their own future possibilities. . . . This is especially true of those variables that require skill and ingenuity in handling (such as those directly connected with advertising, product variation, technological change, and so forth).'[68] Later he indicates that the use of strategic variables of these kinds requires inventiveness,[69] and indicates that 'the present value of this future flow of inventiveness cannot be calculated with sufficient accuracy' for the relative strength of the parties to be established.[70] This in turn prevents the corresponding quasi-agreement from being reached. As an industry 'matures,' however, and particularly if new entrants do not appear, the degree of competition with respect to nonprice variables may be attenuated.[71]

Fellner indicates that profit pooling would not be necessary to reach a full-blown joint profit maximization result in those oligopolies where (a) the product is undifferentiated and (b) all firms have identical horizontal cost curves.[72] In these circumstances a simple market sharing agreement will suffice to achieve this result. Such conditions, however, represent a very special case. Even here, moreover, there is the need to reach agreement on what adjustments to make to changing demand conditions: Who decides? How are differences reconciled?

In the more usual case where cost differences and/or product differentiation exist, joint profit maximization requires interfirm cash flows. Complete pooling in these circumstances implies that 'no attention is paid

[65] Ibid., pp. 27–8.
[66] Ibid., p. 34.
[67] Ibid.
[68] Ibid., pp. 34–5.
[69] Ibid., pp. 183–4.
[70] Ibid., p. 185.
[71] Ibid., pp. 188–9.
[72] Ibid., p. 129.

to how much profit each participant earns directly on the market but only to how much the aggregate of the participants earns. Each participant is compensated from the pool of earnings according to his share.'[73] Profit pooling, however, is held to be hazardous both for antitrust reasons and, even more, because some firms will be at a 'substantial disadvantage if the agreement is terminated and aggressive competition is resumed.'[74] Consequently, only qualified joint profit maximization among oligopolists is to be expected.

Stigler on Oligopoly

Stigler takes as given that oligopolists wish, through collusion, to maximize joint profits[75] and attempts to establish the factors which affect the efficacy of such aspirations. While he admits that 'colluding firms must agree upon the price structure appropriate to the transaction classes which they are prepared to recognize,'[76] his analysis is focused entirely on the problem of policing such a collusive agreement. 'A price structure of some complexity,'[77] one which makes 'appropriate' provision for heterogeneity among products and buyers and for the hazard of activating potential entrants, is simply imputed to oligopolists.[78]

Stigler notes that since secret violations of such agreements commonly permit individual members of an oligopoly to gain larger profits[79] than they would gain by strict adherence to the agreement, a mechanism to enforce agreements is needed. Enforcement for Stigler 'consists basically of detecting significant deviations from the agreed-upon prices. Once detected, the deviations will tend to disappear because they are no longer secret and will be matched by fellow conspirators if they are not withdrawn.'[80] Accordingly, a weak conspiracy is one in which 'price cutting is detected only slowly and incompletely'.[81]

Since an audit of transaction prices reported by sellers is unlawful, and in any event may be unreliable,[82] transaction prices paid by buyers are needed to detect secret price cutting. Stigler contends, in this connection, that statistical inference techniques are the usual way in which such price cutting is discovered. In particular, the basic method of detecting a price

[73] Ibid., p. 135.
[74] Ibid., pp. 133, 196.
[75] G. Stigler, 'A theory of oligopoly', *Journal of Political Economy*, 72 (1964), p. 44.
[76] Ibid., p. 45.
[77] Ibid., p. 45.
[78] Stigler simply assumes 'that the collusion has been effected, and a price structure agreed upon.' Ibid., p. 46.
[79] Profits here are expressed as expected, discounted values.
[80] Stigler, *supra* footnote 75, p. 46.
[81] Ibid.
[82] Ibid., p. 47.

cutter is that he is getting business that he would not otherwise obtain.[83] Among the implications of this statistical inference approach to oligopoly are that (a) collusion is more effective in markets where buyers correctly report prices tendered (as in government bidding),[84] (b) collusion is limited if the identity of buyers is continuously changing (as in the construction industries),[85] and (c) elsewhere the efficacy of collusion varies inversely with the number of sellers, the number of buyers, and the proportion of new buyers, but directly with the degree of inequality of firm size among sellers.[86]

B. LEGAL ANTECEDENTS OF TRANSACTIONAL ANALYSIS

Turner on Conscious Parallelism

Donald Turner's basic position on conscious parallelism is that such behavior, by itself, does not imply agreement. It needs to be buttressed by additional evidence that the observed parallelism is not simply 'identical but unrelated responses by a group of similarly situated competitors to the same set of economic facts.'[87] He illustrates the argument by posing an 'extreme hypothetical' in which there are only two or three suppliers – each of identical size, producing an identical product at identical costs – and markets are static.[88] He contends, in these circumstances, that 'the "best" price for each seller would be precisely the same, would be known to be the same by all, and would be charged without hesitation in absolute certainty that the others would price likewise.'[89] Although he is not explicit on this, the price that he appears to have in mind is the joint profit maximizing (monopoly) price.[90]

Turner then goes on to note that the hypothetical is rather unrealistic.

---

[83] Ibid., p. 48.

[84] Ibid.

[85] Ibid.

[86] Ibid., pp. 48–56.

[87] Turner, 'The definition of agreement under the Sherman Act: Conscious parallelism and refusals to deal', *Harvard Law Review*, 75 (1962), pp. 655, 658.

[88] Ibid., p. 663.

[89] Ibid., pp. 663–4.

[90] If this interpretation is correct, Turner does not believe such a price to be collusive. Plainly, however, it is – at least in the sense that it is *not* the price that independently acting Cournot duopolists (or triopolists) would charge. Given linear demands and constant marginal costs, the Cournot equilibrium output (q), for each firm, where price interdependence is not taken into account (i.e., the conjectural variation term is zero), is $q = \left[\dfrac{1}{n+1}\right]\bar{Q}$. where n is the number of firms in the industry and $\bar{Q}$ is the competitive output. The joint profit maximizing output (q^*) for each such firm, by contrast, is $q^* = \dfrac{1}{2n}\bar{Q}$. Plainly, $q^* < q$ for $n > 1$. (For $n = 1$, both formulae yield the monopoly output.)

Products are rarely fully homogeneous, cost differences will ordinarily exist, and adaptations will need to be made to changing market circumstances.[91] He accordingly holds that 'for a pattern of noncompetitive pricing to emerge . . . requires something which we could, not unreasonably, call a "meeting of the minds".'[92] He declines, however, to regard this as unlawful. Absent explicit collusion, this is merely rational price making in the light of all market facts:[93] 'If monopoly and monopoly pricing are not unlawful per se, neither should oligopoly and oligopoly pricing, absent agreement of the usual sort, be unlawful per se.'[94]

Because the behavior in question cannot be rectified by injunction ('What specifically is to be enjoined?'),[95] relief would presumably have to take the form of dissolution or divestiture.[96] This, however, is to admit that the fundamental issue is structure, not remediable conduct. Unless structural monopoly is to be subject to dissolution, structural oligopoly ought presumably to be permitted to stand. Although Turner declined in 1962 to propose a structural remedy for either condition, he has since altered his position on both.[97]

Posner on Oligopoly

Richard Posner takes exception to Turner's position that oligopolistic interdependence of a natural and noncollusive sort explains the price excesses in oligopolistic industries.[98] Rather, a small numbers condition is held to be merely a necessary but not a sufficient condition for such price excesses to appear.[99] Because 'interdependence theory does not explain . . . how oligopolistic sellers establish a supracompetitive price,'[100] including adjustment to changing market conditions, Posner suggests that the study of oligopoly proceed in terms of cartel theory instead.[101]

---

[91] Turner, *supra* footnote 87, p. 664.

[92] Ibid. Note again, as pointed out in footnote 90 *supra*, that independently operating Cournot duopolists do not charge competitive prices yet are not colluding in any usual sense either. Turner seems implicitly to hold that independent pricing will yield the competitive solution. Hence, any price that exceeds the competitive price is regarded as an indication of interdependence realized. Posner appears also to be of this view. See text accompanying footnotes 98–107 *infra*.

[93] Turner, *supra* footnote 87, p. 666.

[94] Ibid., pp. 667–8.

[95] Ibid., p. 669.

[96] Ibid., p. 671.

[97] Turner, 'The scope of antitrust and other economic regulatory policies', *Harvard Law Review*, 82 (1969), p. 207. For a related discussion, see Williamson, 'Dominant firms and the monopoly problem: Market failure considerations,' *Harvard Law Review* 85 (1972), p. 152.

[98] Posner, 'Oligopoly and the antitrust laws: A suggested approach,' *Stanford Law Review*, 21 (1969), p. 1562.

[99] Ibid., p. 1571.

[100] ibid., pp. 1568, 1578.

[101] Ibid., pp. 1568–9.

Posner's basic argument is that 'voluntary actions by the sellers are necessary to translate the rare condition of an oligopoly market into a situation of noncompetitive pricing.'[102] Effective cartel behavior is, moreover, costly to effectuate; costs of bargaining, adaptation, and enforcement must all be incurred.[103] The upshot is that because 'tacit collusion or noncompetitive pricing is *not inherent* in an oligopolistic market structure but, like conventional cartelizing, requires additional, voluntary behavior by sellers,'[104] a conduct remedy under seciton one of the Sherman Act[105] is held to be appropriate.[106] Once the oligopolist is faced with the prospect of severe penalties for collusion, tacit or otherwise, Posner concludes that the rational oligopolist will commonly decide not to collude but will expand his output until competitive returns are realized.[107]

C. THE TRANSACTION COST APPROACH

To focus attention on what I believe to be the critical issues, I will assume, initially, that oligopolistic agreements are lawful, in that there is no legal bar to collusion, but that oligopolists cannot appeal to the courts for assistance in enforcing the terms of an oligopolistic agreement. The oligopolists themselves, however, can take punitive actions to bring deviant members into line, provided that laws such as those prohibiting libel or the destruction of property are respected. Entry is assumed to be difficult; also, I will assume that profit pooling is permitted but that horizontal mergers between the firms are disallowed.[108]

I will argue that oligopolists will commonly have difficulty in reaching, implementing, and enforcing agreements under these circumstances, but this argument does not mean that laws regarding oligopoly are of no account. The stipulations that horizontal mergers are disallowed and that collusive agreements are unenforceable in the courts are both important in this connection. If, however, it can be shown that monopolistic outcomes are difficult to effectuate even when the law permits collusion, then the performance differences between monopolies (dominant firm markets) and oligopolies are not to be attributed principally to the unlawfulness of

---

[102] Ibid., p. 1575.
[103] Ibid., p. 1570.
[104] Ibid., p. 1578 (emphasis added).
[105] 15 USC, section 1 (1970).
[106] Posner, *supra* footnote 98, pp. 1578–93.
[107] Ibid., p. 1591. This conclusion appears, however, to be unwarranted because independently operating Cournot oligopolists do not produce competitive outputs. See footnote 90 *supra*.
[108] Telser, *supra* footnote 7, does not make this last assumption. His analysis differs from mine partly for this reason.

collusion among oligopolists.[109] It follows, of course, that if express and lawful agreements are difficult for oligopolists to reach and implement, tacit agreements are even less reliable instruments for achieving collusion.

An agreement between two or more parties will be attractive in the degree to which (a) the good, service, or behavior in question is amenable to specification in writing; (b) joint gains from collective action are potentially available; (c) implementation in the face of uncertainty does not occasion costly haggling; (d) monitoring the agreement is not costly; and (e) detected noncompliance carries commensurate penalties at low enforcement expense. Consider the application of the transaction cost approach proposed in section I to each of these conditions in an oligopolistic agreement.

Specification of Terms

Recall that oligopolistic collusion is assumed to be lawful. The parties to the collusive arrangement can therefore negotiate openly and express the details of the agreement in writing without exposing themselves to prosecution. The question to be assessed here is whether the latitude thus afforded will permit a comprehensive collusive agreement to be specified.

I submit that, except in rather special and unlikely circumstances, a comprehensive agreement to maximize joint profits (but not entailing merger) will rarely be feasible because of transaction costs. A comprehensive statement of this kind would require an inordinate amount of knowledge about the cost and product characteristics of each firm, the interaction effects between the decision variables within each firm, and the interaction effects of decision variables between firms. Not only is the relevant information costly to come by, to say nothing of digesting it and devising the appropriate adaptation for each of the firms to make, but, if anything approximating a complete agreement is to be written, this information gathering and analysis needs to be done *ex ante* for a whole series of contingent future events, most of which will never materialize.

The point is that joint profit maximization, even as an abstract exercise, is very difficult to accomplish once one departs from the simplest sort of textbook exercise. Homogeneous products, identical linear and horizontal cost curves, and static markets constitute the 'ideal'. Maintaining these product and cost assumptions in the face of changing demand does not greatly complicate the abstract analysis, in that the conditions of joint profit maximization are easy to display, but the operational problems become somewhat more difficult in the face of uncertainty, which will be discussed below.[110]

---

[109] I do not, however, mean to suggest that the antitrust statutes prohibiting collusion are without purpose. They certainly compound the typical oligopolist's problems.

[110] See subsection 'Implementation under Uncertainty'.

In more realistic circumstances, involving differentiated products, product and process innovations, organization form[111] changes, and revisions in selling expense and financial strategies, the resulting complexity becomes impossibly great in relation to the bounded rationality of planners. When, in addition, the optimization problem is cast in a multiperiod framework under conditions of uncertainty, abstract analysis breaks down.[112] One concludes, accordingly, that the absence of legal prohibitions to collusive agreements is not what prevents comprehensive collusion.[113] Rather, it is prevented by elementary considerations of bounded rationality.[114]

Joint Gains

Suppose, arguendo, that it were possible to specify the joint profit maximizing strategy. Would the parties then be prepared to make such an agreement? I submit that, but for the simple textbook cases referred to above, the parties would commonly decline to accept comprehensive joint profit maximization of the profit pooling kind.

Partly disagreement might arise, as Fellner suggests, on account of differences between the parties concerning the appropriate discount rates to be used in evaluating future prospects. Surely more fundamental, however, are the risks and monitoring expenses that profit pooling entails. As Fellner notes, some of the parties must accede to reductions in relative output and to contractions in relative firm size if the joint profit maximizing result is to be realized. This, however, is hazardous. Firms which are authorized to expand relatively as a result of the agreement will be powerfully situated to demand a renegotiated settlement at a later date. Wary of such opportunism, firms for which retrenchment is indicated will

[111] In the sense of Williamson, *supra* footnote 22, pp. 109–81.

[112] For an operational treatment of the problem of joint profit maximization in a multiproduct firm where (a) product lines are *independent*, (b) only *heuristic* rather than full-blown optimization methods are attempted, and (c) only the *financial* decision is considered, see W. Hamilton and M. Moses, 'An optimization model for corporate financial planning', *Operations Research*, 21 (1972), p. 677. Their model contains approximately 1000 variables and 750 constraints, ibid., p. 686, and tests not one but various configurations of the strategic variables. Replicating such an arrangement by interfirm agreement boggles the mind. Complicating the analysis further to include interdependent products (which, of course, is the case in oligopoly) and the full range of decision variables discussed in the text reveals the manifest impossibility of attempting comprehensively to maximize joint profits – even by heuristic simulation methods, much less by determinate written agreements.

[113] Again, however, the view expressed in footnote 109 *supra* applies.

[114] It is possible, of course, that oligopolists could reach agreement on some aspects of the market more easily than on others. Faced with diminishing marginal returns to their efforts to obtain an agreement (transaction costs), they would probably settle on an agreement of less than comprehensive scope. It is also possible, however, that the inability to agree on some matters would frustrate any agreement whatsoever, even on matters which might be settled if they could be considered in isolation.

decline from the outset to accept a full-blown profit pooling arrangement. Moreover, even setting such concerns aside, monitoring the profit pooling agreement will be costly because of the pairing of opportunism with information impactedness. This will be discussed below.[115]

Implementation under Uncertainty[116]

Implementing an agreement under conditions of uncertainty requires that the parties agree, when changes in the environment occur, on what new state of the world obtains. Problems can arise if, for any true description of the state of the world, (a) some parties would realize benefits if a false state were to be declared, and either (b) information regarding the state of the world is dispersed among the parties and must be pooled or (c), despite the possession of identical information by all the parties, definitive agreement must still be reached.

Consider information condition (c). Even though all parties have identical information with respect to the true condition of the environment, they need not agree on what state of the world has actually been realized. Unless the parties have fully stipulated how observations are to be interpreted as state of the world descriptions, differences in opinion can be anticipated. If some parties stand to benefit from having one state declared, but others would benefit if another state were declared, and if each side can make a plausible case for its position, opportunistic representations in support of each outcome can be expected. Costly haggling may then ensue.

To illustrate, suppose that demand on day t is known to be a function only of the mean temperature on day t-1: if the mean temperature on day t-1 exceeds T_o, demand on day t is of type D_1; otherwise it is of type D_2. Suppose also that all firms have free access to temperature readings on day t-1 at 4:00 a.m., 12:00 noon, and 8:00 p.m. If on date t the unit weighted average of the temperatures on the preceeding day is well above or well below T_o, the declaration of demand types is made without difficulty. Suppose however, that the unit weighted average of day t-1 temperatures just slightly exceeds T_o while weights of 0.95, 1.10, and 0.95 would reduce it to below T_o. If some parties benefit if demand is declared to be of type D_2, even though it is actually D_1, they may then assert that 'everyone knows' that the noontime temperature deserves to be assigned a greater weight in computing the daily mean. Protracted haggling could ensue. Moreover, in the usual circumstances where the state of the world

---

[115] See subsection 'Monitoring Execution of the Agreement,' *infra*.
[116] Unlike the preceding and succeeding subsections, the argument here assumes that joint profit maximization is not attempted.

is multidimensional, the occasion for such disputes naturally increases.[117]

The problems are compounded if the (b) condition obtains. Here the necessary information to ascertain the true state of the world is dispersed and pooling of the data is required. An agreement upon how to interpret the data is to little purpose if the parties selectively disclose or distort the information to which they have preferred access. The pairing of opportunism with information impactedness thus poses serious implementation problems to the oligopolists.

Monitoring Execution of the Agreement

As Stigler points out, and as is widely recognized, oligopolists have an incentive to cheat on price fixing agreements if they believe that cheating will go, for a time at least, undetected. Given that information about individual sales is impacted in that the seller knows exactly what the terms were but, given uncertainty, his rivals do not and can establish the terms only at some cost, the individual seller can often cut prices below the agreed level to the disadvantage of the other parties to the conspiracy. The pairing of opportunism (here manifested as cheating) with information impactedness makes oligopolistic agreements difficult to police.

This argument, moreover, applies to oligopolistic collusion with respect to considerations other than price as well. If anything, agreeing to collude with respect to marketing expense, research and development efforts, and similar business practices is even more hazardous than price collusion for nonopportunistic parties who are prepared to abide by the agreements. Although it is easy to establish after the fact that a rival has made significant design changes or introduced a new product in violation of the agreement, such information may come too late. If recovery from a large shift in market share, attributable to, for example, an 'illicit' innovation, is inordinately expensive, the detection of such a violation is to little avail – unless, of course, all firms have maintained a defensive posture against such contingencies, in which case collusion in these nonprice respects can scarcely be said to be operative.

As mentioned above, profit pooling is also subject to problems of monitoring.[118] Even if firms were prepared to enter into agreements in which all profits are pooled and each participant is assigned a share of the total, there is still the problem of determining what the contribution of each firm to the pool should be. Individual firms have an incentive to understate true profits in these circumstances.

---

[117] If the state of the world is described by a vector of n components, each of which can take on only one of two values, the number of possible states is 2^n. For $n = 8$, which hardly constitutes a complex description of the state of the world, the number of possible states is 256, which is impressively large.

[118] See subsection 'Joint Gains', *supra*.

Moreover, merely auditing the earnings of each firm, even to the extent that *all* sources of revenue and cost are fully disclosed, is not sufficient to avoid distortion. An assessment of individual expense items must also be made. The problems facing the auditor here are akin to those facing the defense agencies in monitoring cost-plus (or, more generally, cost-sharing) defense contracts.[119] Unless it can be established that certain types or amounts of actual costs are unwarranted, and hence will be disallowed, each firm has an incentive to incur excessive costs.

Expense excesses can take any of several forms. Perhaps the simplest is to allow some operations to run slack so that the management and workers in the firm take part of their rewards as on-the-job leisure. A second way is to allow emoluments to escalate, in which case corporate personal consumption expenditures exceed levels which, from a profit maximizing standpoint, would be incurred. Third, and most important, firms may incur current costs which place them at a strategic advantage in future periods. Developing new and improved technology or training the work force are examples of this sort of cost. Evaluating individual firm performance in these several respects is at least an order of magnitude more difficult than simple audits of revenue and cost streams. Profit pooling, therefore, poses severe enforcement problems, even assuming that the agreement itself were legal.

Penalizing Violations

Recall that it was assumed that while collusive agreements are not unlawful, the participants in such agreements cannot call upon the courts to help enforce the agreement. Instead, violators must be determined and penalties must be administered by the parties to the contract. Problems of two types arise in connection with penalties. First, do the penalties, if implemented, constitute an effective deterrent to the would-be violator? Second, even if penalties can be devised that would be efficacious, will the parties to the conspiracy be prepared to impose them?

Because the conspirators lack legal standing, conventional penalties such as fines and jail sentences are presumably unavailable. Rather, penalties are exacted in the market place by confronting the violator with unusually adverse circumstances. Price reductions are matched and perhaps even undercut. Normal types of interfirm cooperation (e.g., supply of components) is suspended. Key employees may be raided. Except, however, as deviant firms are highly dependent on rivals for vital supplies, such market reactions may well be ones that the deviant is prepared to risk.

[119] For discussions of defense contracting, see F. Scherer, *The Weapons Acquisition Process* (1964) Boston: Harvard Graduate School of Business and O. E. Williamson, 'The economics of defense contracting: incentives and performance', in *Issues in Defense Economics*, ed. R. McKean, New York: National Bureau of Economic Research, p. 217.

For one thing, the contract violator is not the only firm to be adversely affected by enacting these penalties in the market place. The firms meting out the penalties also incur costs.[120] Second, and related, securing the collective action needed to punish the violator may be difficult. Thus, although all firms may agree both that a violation has taken place and that the violator deserves to be punished, not all may be prepared to participate in administering it. Defectors (e.g., those willing to supply the deviant with the essential component, perhaps at a premium price), which is to say opportunists, who refuse to incur the costs of punishing the violator, naturally reduce the costs of being detected in violation of the agreement. Where such defection is deemed likely, collusive agreements are all the less probable.[121]

D. POLICY IMPLICATIONS: DOMINANT FIRMS VERSUS OLIGOPOLISTIC INTERDEPENDENCE

The monopolist (or dominant firm) enjoys an advantage over oligopolists in adaptational respects because he does not have to write a contract in which future contingencies are identified and appropriate adaptations thereto are devised. Instead, he can face the contingencies when they arise; each bridge can be crossed when it is reached, rather than having to decide *ex ante* how to cross all bridges that one might conceivably face.[122] Put differently, the monopolist can employ an adaptive, sequential decision-making procedure, which greatly economizes on bounded rationality demands, without exposing himself to the risks of contractual incompleteness which confront a group of conspiring oligopolists. Adaptation within a firm (in contrast to that between firms) is also promoted

[120] Punitive market responses require firms to incur short-run profit sacrifices in the hope of discourgaing future chiselers and returning the current chiseler to the fold.

[121] Although the opportunistic behavior described mainly reflects an aggressive effort to realize short-run individual gains, to the disadvantage of the group, firms may also engage in such behavior for defensive reasons. Defensive opportunism reflects a lack of confidence in the trustworthiness of other members of the group and an unwillingness to risk being put to a strategic disadvantage.

While aggressive or assertive opportunism is to be expected whenever the viability of any particular firm is threatened, whatever the degree of 'maturity' of the firms in an industry, defensive opportunism will vary inversely with maturity. Because defensive opportunism, if widely practised, is mutually disadvantageous, and because this is self-evident to the parties, organizational learning is normally to be expected. Among other things, ways of announcing or signaling intentions in ways that will not be misinterpreted as aggressive, when no such intension exists, are apt to develop. Unless, therefore, the industry is one in which new entrants regularly appear, with obviously disruptive consequences for interfirm learning and accommodation, occasions for defensive opportunism are likely to decline as an industry matures.

[122] For a discussion of adaptive, sequential decision making, see H. Chernoff and L. Moses, *Elementary Decision Theory* (1959), New York: Norton, pp. 166–94.

by the more complete development of efficient, albeit often informal, communication codes and an associated trust relationship between the parties.[123] Thus, while I do not mean to suggest that there are no costs whatsover to dissolution,[124] and, accordingly, do not propose it as an automatic remedy, to suggest that oligopolists will be able easily to replicate the (joint) profit maximization strategy of a monopolist is simply unwarranted. Even if cheating on a specific agreement were not a problem, there is still the need among oligopolists to reach the specific agreement. The high cost of exhaustively complete specification of agreements discourages efforts toward comprehensiveness – in which case, because actual oligopolistic contracts are of the incomplete coordination kind, competition of a nonprice sort predictably obtains.

To assume, moreover, that oligopolists will voluntarily adhere to whatever limited agreements they reach is plainly unreasonable. Cheating is a predictable consequence of oligopolistic conspiracy; the record is replete with examples.[125] The pairing of opportunism with information impactedness explains this condition.

The monopolist, by contrast, does not face the same need to attenuate opportunism. Even within the monopoly firm in which self-autonomous operating divisions have been created, with each operated as a profit center, interdivisional cheating on agreements will be less than interfirm cheating because (a) the gains can be less fully appropriated by the defector division, (b) the difficulty of detecting cheating is much less, and (c) the penalties to which internal organization has access (including dismissing opportunist division managers) are more efficacious. Unlike independently owned oligopoly firms, the operating divisions do not have fully pre-emptive claims on their profit streams (so the inclination to cheat is less) and, unlike oligopolies, they are subject to detailed audits, including an assessment of internal efficiency performance. Also, where oligopolists can usually penalize defectors only by incurring losses themselves (e.g., by matching or overmatching price cuts), the monopoly firm has access to a powerful and delicately conceived internal incentive system that does not require it to incur market penalties of a price cutting sort.[126] It can mete out penalties to groups and individuals in the firm in a quasijudicial fashion and in this way it assumes some of the functions of a legal system. Altogeher, the opportunism which threatens agreements among oligopolists is a less severe problem for the dominant firm.

More generally, my argument comes down to this: it is naive to regard

[123] K. Arrow, *On the Limits of Organization* (1974), New York: John Wiley.

[124] See Williamson, *supra* footnote 97, pp. 1528–30.

[125] For some discussions and exmples of cheating and the breakdown of oligopolistic collusion, see Patinkin, *supra* footnote 61, pp. 200–4; Posner, *supra* footnote 98, p. 1570; R. Smith, Corporations in Crisis (1966), New York: Doubleday, pp. 113–66.

[126] See Williamson, *supra* footnote 22, pp. 54–73, 109–19.

oligopolists as shared monopolists *in any comprehensive sense* – especially if they have differentiated products, have different cost experiences, are differently situated with respect to the market by virtue of size, and plainly lack the machinery by which oligopolistic coordination, except of the most primitive variety, is accomplished and enforced. Except, therefore, in highly concentrated industries producing homogeneous products, with nontrivial barriers to entry, and at a mature stage of development oligopoly is unlikely to pose antitrust issues for which dissolution is an appropriate remedy. In the usual oligopoly situation efforts to achieve collusion are unlikely to be successful or, if they are, will require sufficient explicit communication that normal remedies against price fixing, including injunctions not to collude, will suffice.

Where, however, the industry is of the special type just described, recognized interdependency may be sufficiently extensive to permit tacit collusion to succeed. Injunctive remedies, as Turner noted, are unsatisfactory in such circumstances.[127] Accordingly, dissolution ought to be actively considered. The recent case brought by the Antitrust Division against the major firms in the gypsum industry affords a current example of a case in which, assuming the charges can be proved, dissolution would appear to be warranted.[128] By contrast, the cereal case brought by the Federal Trade Commission is not one for which comprehensive collusion seems likely.[129]

This does not, however, imply that the cereal industry poses no public policy problems whatsoever. Simply because the shared monopoly model does not fit well does not mean that public policy concerns vanish. But I would urge that attention be focused on those specific practices in the industry which are thought to be objectionable. If, for example, excessive advertising in the cereal industry can be reasonably established, this can be dealt with directly. Selective attention to specific wasteful practices, rather than grand conspiracy theories, are called for.

A related implication of the argument is that dissolution of dominant firms is not an idle economic exercise, done to reduce large aggregations of corporate power for political or social purposes alone but unlikely to have significant economic performance consequences. For all the reasons developed above, several independent entities cannot realize the same degree of coordination between their policies in price and nonprice respects as can a single firm.[130] Moreover, the price and nonprice

---

[127] Turner, *supra* footnote 95.

[128] *United States* v. *United States Gypsum Co.*, Crim. No. 73–347 (W.D. Pa., filed 27 Dec. 1973); *cf. United States* v. *United States Gypsum Co.*, Crim. No. 1042–73 (DDC, filed 27 Dec., 1973).

[129] In re Kellogg Co., No. 8883 (FTC, filed 24 Jan., 1972).

[130] See footnote 112 *supra*.

differences that predictably arise[131] will typically redound to the consumer's benefit.[132] Accordingly, a more assertive antitrust policy with regard to the dissolution of dominant firms is indicated.[133]

IV. Conglomerate Organization

A. RECEIVED MICROTHEORY VERSUS TRANSACTIONAL INTERPRETATIONS

As the remarks of Bork and Bowman cited earlier make clear,[134] received microtheory is loath to concede that capital markets may fail to operate frictionlessly. Partly for this reason, the fiction that managers operate firms in fully profit maximizing ways is maintained. It is argued that any

[131] Kaysen and Turner (1959), pp. 114–15.

[132] Wasteful selling or product development expenditures among differentiated product oligopolists are sometimes, however, observed. Specific steps might properly be taken to restrict this were a dominant firm to be split into independent, differentiated parts.

[133] See sources cited at footnote 97 *supra*.

The reader may find a summary of the transactional approach and its antecedents useful at this point. The approaches often coincide, but there are many contrasts. The problem of oligopoly under the transaction cost approach, as under Fellner's approach, is treated as a problem of interdependence recognized. Also, as with Fellner, the multidimensional nature of the interdependence issue is emphasized; price coordination is only a part of the problem, especially in industries with differentiated products. But whereas Fellner attributes the problems of interdependence to the complexities of discounting uncertain future values and in pooling risks, I put the issue in terms of 'contracting' about contingent claims. While these approaches are not unrelated, the latter highlights the issues of coming to an agreement and enforcing it which permits us to draw expressly on the transaction cost framework sketched out in section I. A more complete assessment of the problems of oligopolistic collusion is thereby afforded.

Stigler's analysis runs almost entirely in terms of prices. Moreover, he takes the collusive agreement itself as given, focusing attention instead on cheating and on statistical inference techniques for detecting cheaters. While this last is very useful, and calls attention in an interesting way to aspects of the oligopoly problem that others have rather neglected, it is also highly incomplete. The discussion in subsection C reveals that monitoring is only one of a series of steps in the oligopolistic collusion, and not plainly the one that warrants greatest attention.

Both Turner and Posner also give primary attention to prices in their discussions of oligopoly. But their similarity to each other ends there. Whereas Turner emphasizes tacit collusion of the recognized interdependence sort and finds injunctive relief to be inefficacious, Posner regards interdependence theory as unsatisfactory, and discusses oligopoly instead as a cartel problem, concluding that injunctive relief is appropriate.

The spirit of my discussion is somewhat akin to Posner's cartel analysis, but the specifics plainly differ. I restate the problem in terms of what a *lawful* cartel could accomplish. Also, I am much more concerned than Posner with the details of and impediments to successful interfirm agreements. Finally, I agree with Turner that injunctive relief in highly concentrated, homogeneous product, entry-impeded, mature industries is unlikely to be effective. Structural relief is indicated here instead.

[134] Text accompanying footnotes 41–2 *supra*.

attempt by opportunist managers to promote their own goals at the expense of corporate profitability would occasion intervention through the capital market. Effective control of the corporation would be transferred to those parties who perceived the lapse; profit maximizing behavior would then be quickly restored.

Parties responsible for the detection and correction of deviant behavior in the firm would, of course, participate in the greater profits which the reconstituted management would realize. This participation would not, however, be large. One reason is that incumbent managements, by assumption, have little opportunity for inefficiency or malfeasance because any tendency toward waywardness would be quickly detected and costlessly extinguished. Accordingly, the incremental profit gain occasioned by takeover would be small. Moreover, the market for corporate control is presumably one in which large numbers of qualified takeover agents are noncollusively organized. Competitive offers assure that the takeover gains mainly redound to the stockholders.

Shorey Peterson's sanguine views on corporate behavior are roughly of this kind. He characterizes the latitude to disregard the profit goal as 'small'[135] and goes on to observe that '[f]ar from being an ordinary election, a proxy battle is a *catastrophic* event whose mere possibility is a threat, and one not remote when affairs are in *conspicuous* disarray.'[136] Indeed, even 'stockholder suits . . . may be provoked by evidence of *serious* self-dealing.'[137] On the principle that the efficacy of legal prohibitions is to be judged 'not by guilt discovered but by guilt discouraged,' he concludes that such units, albeit rare, may have accomplished much in helping to police the corporate system.[138]

While I do not mean to suggest that such deterrence has not been important, Peterson's observations appear to me to be *consistent* with the proposition that traditional capital markets are beset by serious problems of information impactedness and incur nontrivial displacement costs if the incumbent management is disposed to resist the takeover effort. Why else the reference to catastrophic events, conspicuous disarray, and serious self-dealing? Systems that are described in these terms are not ones for which a delicately conceived control system can be said to be operating. As recent military history makes clear, controls that involve a large and discrete shock to the system are appropriate only when an offense reaches egregious proportions. The scope for opportunism, accordingly, is wider than Peterson seems prepared to concede.

---

[135] Peterson, 'Corporate control and capitalism', *Quarterly Journal of Economics*, 79 (1965), pp. 1, 11.

[136] Ibid., p. 21 (emphasis added).

[137] Ibid. (emphasis added).

[138] Ibid.

The reasons why traditional control of management performance by the capital market is relatively crude are that internal conditions in the firm are not widely known or easy to discover (information impactedness) and that those seeking to gain control of the firm (takeover agents) might well take opportunistic advantage of the shareholders' bounded rationality. Information impactedness means that outsiders cannot make confident judgments that the firm has departed from profit maximizing standards, except with difficulty. The firm is a complex organization and its performance is a joint consequence of exogenous economic events, rival behavior, and internal decisions. Causal inferences are correspondingly difficult to make and, hence, opportunism is costly to detect. Moreover, once detected, convincing interested stockholders that a displacement effort ought to be supported encounters problems. Inasmuch as time and the analytical capacity of stockholders are not free goods (which is to say that the limits imposed by bounded rationality must be respected) the wouldbe takeover agent cannot simply display all of his evidence and expect stockholders to evaluate it and reach the 'appropriate' conclusion. Rather, any appeal to the stockholders must be made in terms of highly digested interpretations of the facts. Although this helps to overcome the stockholder's bounded rationality problem, it poses another: How is the interested stockholder (or his agent) to distinguish between bona fide and opportunistic takeover agents?

The upshot of these remarks is that the transaction costs associated with *traditional* capital market processes for policing management, of the sort described by Peterson, are considerable. Correspondingly, the range of discretionary behavior open to incumbent managements is rather wider than Peterson and other supporters of the fiction of the frictionless capital market concede.[139]

One of the more attractive attributes of the conglomerate forms of organization (of the appropriate kind)[140] is that it serves to overcome certain of these limitations of traditional capital markets. The argument, which I will develop below, essentially reduces to the proposition that conglomerate firms (of the appropriate kind) function as miniature capital

---

[139] Smiley estimates that 'per share transaction costs are approximately 14% of the market value of the shares after a successful [tender] offer' and suggests that such a cost level warrants 'skepticism about the efficacy of the tender offer in constraining managers to act in the best interests of their shareholders.' R. Smiley, 'The Economics of Tender Offers' (July 1973), pp. 124–5. (Unpublished PhD dissertation, Stanford University).

[140] This assumes that the hierarchic structure and internal control processes of the conglomerate satisfy the requirements that I have stipulated elsewhere (Williamson *supra* footnote 22, pp. 120–53). Although there are certainly other types of conglomerates, those which lack for an underlying efficiency rationale (as contrasted with a temporary financial rationale) will presumably be sorted out in the long run. Those which pose financial problems are best dealt with by the SEC. My discussion sidesteps these and focuses on antitrust issues.

markets with consequences for resource allocation which are, on balance, beneficial.

This poses, however, the following paradox: under conventional assumptions that more choices are always preferred to fewer, the banking system ought to have superior resource allocation properties to any miniature imitation thereof. Put differently, why should a miniature capital market ever be preferred to the real thing? As might be anticipated, transaction cost considerations supply the resolution. If decision makers could be easily apprised of an ever wider range of alternatives and choose intelligently among them, there would be no occasion to supplant the traditional market. But it is elementary that, where complex events have to be evaluated, information processing capacities are quickly reached. As a result, expanding the range of choice may not only be without purpose but can have net detrimental effects. A trade-off between breadth of information, in which respect the banking system may be presumed to have the advantage, and depth of information, which is the advantage of the specialized firm,[141] is involved. The conglomerate can be regarded as an intermediate form that, ideally, optimizes with respect to the breadth–depth trade-off.[142] Although the number of alternatives considered by a conglomerate's management is limited, its knowledge (*ex post* and *ex ante*) with respect to each remains relatively deep. Operating as it does as an internal control agent, its auditing powers are more extensive and its control instruments are more selective than an external control agent can employ. Information impactedness is reduced as a result and opportunism is attenuated in the process.

B. OBJECTIONS TO THE CONGLOMERATE

The failure on the part of received microtheory to regard the internal organization of the firm as interesting is, I believe, responsible for what Posner has called 'the puzzle of the conglomerate corporation.'[143] This puzzle has not, however, deterred those who most rely on received microtheory from venturing the opinion that the conglomerate is innocent of anticompetitive purpose or potential and ought not to be an object of

---

[141] Depth of information problems can, however, appear as the specialized firm becomes very large. See O. Williamson, *supra* footnote 22, pp. 14–40.

[142] For a somewhat similar interpretation of the conglomerate, se Alchian and Demsetz (1972), pp. 777–95. For a study of the use of the computer to extend the firm's capacity to deal effectively with a wider set of investment alternatives, see Hamilton & Moses, *supra* footnote 112. For a cross-sectional study of conglomerates (which, however, does not make organization form distinctions), see Weston & Mansinghka, 'Tests of the efficiency performance of conglomerate firms', *J. Finance*, 26 (1971), p. 419.

[143] R. Posner, *Economic Analysis of Law* (1972), Boston: Little, Brown, p. 204.

antitrust prosecution.[144] But an affirmative rationale for the conglomerate, based on received microtheory, has yet to appear.[145]

The populist critics of the conglomerate have not allowed this lapse to go unnoticed. Robert Solo's views are perhaps representative. He contends that 'when faced with a truly dangerous phenomenon, such as the conglomerate mergers of the 1960s, produced by financial manipulators making grist for their security mills, the professional antitrust economists were silent. Like other realities of a modern enterprise, this phenomenon, which will probably subvert management effectiveness and organizational rationale for generations, is outside their conceptual framework.'[146]

Several things should be said in this connection. First, in defense of antitrust economists, I would point out that financial manipulation is not their main concern. This is the principal business of the Securities and Exchange Commission rather than the Antitrust Division. Although Solo might object, with cause, that economists are excessively narrow, nevertheless, as matters are divided up currently, it is the security specialists who are presumably at fault. Second, and more important, Solo's sweeping charges leave the particular dangers of the conglomerate phenomenon completely unspecified. Third, I agree that an understanding of the conglomerate requires an extension of the conventional framework. Nevertheless I think it noteworthy that populist critics of the conglomerate and received microtheorists alike pay little heed to the resource allocation consequences, in the form of capital market substitution effects, of internal organization. Finally, conglomerates come in a variety of forms and have a variety of purposes. Accordingly, any attack on conglomerates should be selective rather than broadside.

Responses to organizational innovations vary. The initial response of rival firms and financial analysts is typically to disregard such changes. Partly this is because 'reorganization' is a common reaction by firms that are experiencing adversity. Discerning whether the response is intended to eliminate accumulated bureaucratic deadwood or to buy time from the stockholders by giving the impression that corrective action has been taken, or whether (instead or in addition) it represents a really fundamental change in structure that warrants more widespread attention is initially

---

[144] For a report that approaches this position, see *US President's Task Force on Productivity and Competition*.

[145] Some contend that reciprocity has attractive efficiency properties, in that it facilitates priceshading in otherwise rigid price circumstances. While I concede that reciprocity can be used in this way, I do not find it an especially compelling economic rationale for the conglomerate. Surely the entire conglomerate movement is not to be explained in these terms. Also, I think it useful to appreciate that reciprocity can have inefficiency consequences. Once begun, perhaps as a price shading technique, it may be continued because it suits the bureaucratic preferences of the sales staff.

[146] R, Solo, 'new maths and old sterilities', *Saturday Review*, 22 Jan. 1972, pp. 47–8.

quite difficult.[147] Expressed in transaction cost terms, the problem is that opportunistic structural changes cannot easily be distinguished from fundamental ones on account of information impactedness and bounded rationality. Given the incapacity (or high cost) of communicating about and abstractly assessing the importance of organizational changes, the tendency is to wait and see how organizational changes manifest themselves in performance consequences. Inasmuch as performance is a function of many factors other than organizational structure alone, sorting out the effect of organizational changes is difficult. Therefore, a long recognition lag between fundamental innovation and widespread imitation is common.[148]

Public policy analysts of populist persuasions are prone to regard organizational innovations as having anticompetitive purposes. Rarely are such innovations thought to have possible efficiency consequences, mainly because efficiency is thought to reside in technological rather than transactional factors. Harlan Blake's widely admired assessment of the conglomerate and its policy implications is in this technological tradition.[149] Like Solo's, his treatment tends to be global rather than selective. References to 'mergers whose anticompetitive potential is so widespread that it might appropriately be described as having an effect upon the economic system as a whole – in every line of commerce in every section of the country'[150] is unguarded. An understanding of the conglomerate phenomenon will be better promoted by delimiting the attack.[151]

For one thing, organization form distinctions, of which Blake makes none, ought to be made. Size considerations aside, he treats all conglomerates as an undifferentiated group. But there are indications that even some courts may be more discriminating than this.[152] More generally, the point is this: just as the structure of markets influences the performance of markets, so likewise ought allowance to be made for the possibility that internal organization influences firm performance.[153]

---

[147] It is interesting in this connection to note that General Motors' executives went to considerable effort in the 1920s to apprise the business community at large of the character and importance of the multidivisional structure which they had devised, but to little avail.

[148] See A. Chandler, *supra* footnote 24.

[149] H. Blake, 'Conglomerate mergers and the antitrust laws', *Columbia Law Review*, 73 (1973), p. 555.

[150] Ibid.

[151] For an attempt to delimit the attack, see the discussion in subsection C *infra*.

[152] Thus the district court in the ITT-Hartford Insurance case was prepared to dismiss reciprocity arguments by the government because of organization form considerations. *United States* v. *International Tel. & Tel. Corp.*, 306 F. Supp. 766, 779, 782–3, 790, 795 (D. Conn. 1969) (hold separate order); *United States* v. *International Tel. & Tel. Corp.*, 324 F. Supp. 19, 45 (D. Conn. 1970) (judgment for defendant).

[153] For an interpretation of the transformation of 'inside contracting,' which was practised by New England manufacturing firms in the late 1900s, to vertical integration for transaction cost reasons, see Williamson, *supra* footnote 2, pp. 322–4.

Although Blake recognizes that the conglomerate may have had invigorating effects on the market for corporate control,[154] he does not regard its ability to reallocate assets internally from lower yield to higher yield uses an affirmative factor. If anything, he seems to suggest that internal resource reallocations are undesirable as compared to reallocations in the capital market.[155] In an economy, however, where returning funds to and reallocating funds by the capital market incurs nontrivial transaction costs and/or where managers of specialized firms have an opportunistic preference to retain earnings, the internal reallocation of resources to uses returning a higher yield is what most commends the conglomerate as compared with similarly constituted specialized firms.[156] The conglomerate in these circumstances assumes miniature capital market responsibilities of an energizing kind. That Blake is unimpressed with such consequences is explained by his assessment (which he shares with conventional microtheory)[157] that only economies having technological origins are deserving of consideration and his conviction that the supplanting of 'competitive market forces,' however feeble these forces may be, by internal organization is anticompetitive.[158]

Blake also finds conglomerates objectionable because of 'hard evidence to support the no longer novel theory – and widely held belief in the business community – that large conglomerates facing each other in several markets tend to be less competitive in price than regional or smaller firms.'[159] There are two problems with the argument. First, I would scarcely characterize the evidence on which Blake relies as 'hard'. Part of the evidence cited by Blake is Scherer's discussion of the 'spheres of

[154] Blake, *supra* footnote 149, pp. 562–3, 572–3.

[155] Ibid., pp. 571–2. Blake observes in this connection that '[O]ne objective of antitrust policy is to preserve a competitive system – a structure of the economy in which all economic units in the unregulated sector are subject to the continuing discipline of competitive market forces. The creation of vast conglomerate enclaves in which decisions with respect to resource use are insulated from these forces is inconsistent with the basic tenets of antitrust policy.' Ibid., p. 574.

I submit that, subject to the condition that the internal resource reallocations result in higher social as well as private yields – which is normally to be expected when investments are shifted from activities with lower to higher marginal profitability, one of the leading objectives of antitrust policy is being served.

[156] For a discussion, see O. Williamson, *supra* footnote 22, pp. 143–4. For a fascinating study of the internal resource allocation process at work in one major corporation, see Hamilton & Moses, *supra* footnote 112. I concede that the system developed for and used by the International Utilities Corporation represents the leading edge of internal resource allocation capabilities in a conglomerate firm, but it is not an isolated instance. Firms such as ITT have had a similar, albeit less formal, approach to the internal resource allocation problem for years. See Address, 'Management Must Manage,' by Harold Geneen, before the Investment Group of Hartford, Conn. 15 Feb, 1968.

[157] Blake, *supra* footnote 149, pp. 566, 578.

[158] Ibid., pp. 574, 579. See footnote 155 *supra*.

[159] Ibid., p. 570.

influence hypothesis.'[160] But Scherer is very careful to characterize the
evidence quite differently, noting that even with respect to the prewar
international chemical industry, which aside from marine cartels is his
only Western example, the evidence is fragmentary. With respect to other
industries he concludes that 'there is a dearth of evidence on spheres of
influence accords.'[161]

Second, the definition of a conglomerate requires attention. Are all
specialized firms (such as National Tea, to which Blake earlier refers)[162]
that operate similar plants or stores in geographically dispersed markets
really to be regarded as conglomerates? Stretching the definition of a
conglomerate to include geographically dispersed, but otherwise specialized, enterprises, shrinks the number of nonconglomerate large firms to
insignificance. If 'conglomerate' is defined in terms of product diversification, Blake (and the Federal Trade Commission) ought to be expected
to generate examples of abuse of conglomerate structure from the universe
of product-diversified firms. If instead all large multimarket firms,
whatever their product specialization ratios, are the objectionable subset,
the suspect firms ought to be expressly identified in this way rather than
by designating them as 'conglomerates.'

Although I share Blake's suspicions with respect to the behavior of
very large product-diversified firms (which is the narrower definition of
the conglomerate), the facts have yet to be assembled. As things
stand now, the price-competitiveness of such firms cannot be adversely
distinguished from that of other large multimarket organizations.

The data are somewhat better with respect to reciprocity. Blake
conjectures in this connection that 'empirical research, if it could be
carried out, would show that reciprocity is as inevitable a result of
widespread conglomerate structure as price rigidity is a consequence of
oligopoly structure'[163] – where, apparently, the latter, and hence the
former, is believed to be extensive. Jesse Markham's recent study of
conglomerates, which was unavailable to Blake, suggests otherwise: 'highly
diversified companies are no more, and may be even less, given to
reciprocity than large corporations generally.'[164]

Blake's principal policy proposal is that conglomerate acquisitions by
firms above a specified size (the subset of firms that are to be restricted
is not explicitly identified, but Blake makes several references to the top

---

[160] Scherer (1970), pp. 278–80.
[161] Ibid., p. 279.
[162] Blake, *supra* footnote 149, p. 557 n. 13.
[163] Ibid., p. 569.
[164] J. Markham, *Conglomerate Enterprise and Public Policy* (1973), Boston: Harvard
Graduate School of Business, p. 176.

200 firms)[165] be accompanied by a spin-off of comparable assets.[166] He further stipulates that no exception be permitted for acquiring a toehold in the new market. His argument against the toehold exception is that small, independent firms are more apt to engage in price competition than large conglomerates – relying a second time on the purportedly 'hard' evidence referred to above – and contents that 'a size based presumption would help restore the idea that internal growth is the normal, and usually the most socially efficient, means of industrial expansion, by making it the only means available to the largest corporations absent a special showing of procompetitive effect or of efficiencies.'[167]

As already indicated, however, the evidence on which Blake relies is rather limited. Moreover, the basis for his refusal to admit a toehold exception is really unclear. By itself the acquisition of a very small firm scarcely contributes much to the growth of the large firm. Correspondingly, requiring the large firm to release assets in an equivalent amount whenever a toehold acquisition is made is scarcely more than a nuisance.[168] Furthermore, toehold acquisitions made for the purpose of securing a position that will subsequently be expanded *is* internal growth of the sort Blake favors. Either there is little point to Blake's toehold argument,[169] or he regards expansion by small firms as socially preferable to similar investments by large firms.

Assuming, arguendo, that the same investments will be made whether the small firm is acquired or not, it is easy to agree with Blake – though I repeat that the evidence on the competitive behavior of small firms, as compared with product divisions in diversified large firms, is scarcely dispositive. But it is doubtful that the same investments will actually occur. This raises transfer process issues.

An examination of these matters suggests that small firms apparently enjoy a comparative advantage at early and developmental stages of the technical innovation process.[170] Large, established firms, by contrast, display comparative advantages at large-scale commercial production and distribution stages.[171] Not only may the management of the small firm

[165] Blake, *supra* footnote 149, pp. 559–69.

[166] Ibid., p. 590.

[167] Ibid., pp. 590–1.

[168] For the purpose of size control, a large firm that engages in a series of toehold acquisitions within a specified time interval might be required to spin off assets comparable to the aggregate of those acquired if some absolute value is exceeded. Even small percentage positions in some industries (e.g., petroleum) can represent quite large absolute asset values. Individual toehold acquisitions in these circumstances might exceed the absolute asset value threshold of, say, $100 million. A spin-off might be indicated.

[169] However, see the qualification in footnote 168 *supra*.

[170] See Turner and Williamson (1971), p. 127.

[171] Though it varies somewhat with organizational structure, projects for which only small-scale commercialization is anticipated are not ones for which large firms are typically well suited. For a novel organizational 'solution', see S. Sabin, 'At Nuclepore they don't work for G.E. anymore,' *Fortune*, 88 Dec. 1973, p. 145.

lack the financial resources to move to the commercial stage in any but a gradualist manner because its credit standing does not permit it to raise significant blocs of capital except at adverse rates,[172] but the management of the small firm may be poorly suited to make the transition. Different management skills and knowledge are required to bring a project successfully to large-scale commercial development than may have been needed at earlier stages. If, because of management experience and team considerations similar to those described in section II above, the talents needed to facilitate internal expansion cannot be costlessly identified and assembled, transferring the project to an established firm that already possesses the requisite talents may be the more economical alternative. Again, it is transactions, not technology, which dictate this result. Put in these terms, it is unclear that the no toehold position survives.

I am nevertheless sympathetic with the proposition that the acquisition of already large firms by other large firms ought to be accompanied by a divestiture of equivalent assets. As Richard Hofstadter has observed, the support for antitrust enforcement rests less on a consensus among economists about its efficiency enhancing properties than it does on a political and moral judgment that power in the American economy should be diffused.[173] The wisdom of such populist social and political attitudes is illustrated by the misadventures of the ITT Corporation in domestic and foreign affairs.[174] Much of Blake's disenchantment with conglomerates appears to be attributable to a concern that giant size and political abuse are positively correlated,[175] and I would urge that the case be made expressly in these terms. If giant firms rather than all conglomerates are what is objectionable, attention ought properly to be restricted to these firms.

A requirement that very large firms divest themselves of equivalent assets when larger than toehold acquisitions are made is also favored by the prospect that this policy will help curb bureaucratic abuses associated with very large size. Although such divestitures sometimes occur voluntarily,[176] such efforts predictably encounter bureaucratic resistance. If,

[172] Moving from a prototype to a commercial stage commonly involves a substantial investment in organizational infrastructure, much of which has no value should the enterprise fail. Lacking a known performance record and tangible assets to secure the investment, lenders are apprehensive to invest except on a sequential basis. The risks of opportunism, given information impactedness, are perceived as too great.

[173] R. Hofstadter, 'What happened to the antitrust movement?' in The Business Establishment ed. E. Cheit (1964), New York: Wiley, p. 113.

[174] See A. Sampson, The Sovereign State of ITT New York: Stein and Day (1973).

[175] Blake, supra footnote 149, pp. 574, 576, 578, 579, and 591. That giant size procures political favors does not imply that atomistic organization (e.g., farmers) is the favored economic alternative. Often with the latter, however, the favors are more likely to be transparent.

[176] See Coase, 'Industrial organization: A proposal for research' in Policy Issues and Research Opportunities in Industrial Organization ed. V. Fuchs (1972), pp. 59, 67.

however, such divestiture commonly has beneficial effects of an organizational self-renewal sort, making divestiture mandatory is scarcely objectionable. It would merely strengthen the hand of those in the firm who are anxious to forestall bureaucratic stagnation. Absent such a rule, internal agreement on divestiture may be difficult to secure; parties with vested interests will make partisan (opportunistic) representations that will be difficult to reject. Given such a rule, however, the general office can simply plead that it has no choice but to divest (assuming that a large acquisition is to be made). The preferences of the general office, reflecting efficiency considerations for the entire conglomerate enterprise, are thus made to prevail more fully.

C. POLICY IMPLICATIONS

A transactional interpretation of the conglomerate, which emphasizes the limitations of capital markets with respect to policing corporate management, reveals that conglomerate firms (of the appropriate kind) are not altogether lacking in social purpose. If maintaining the market for corporate control[177] is thought to be generally beneficial, if reallocating resources away from projects with lower returns to favor those with higher net private returns also generally yields social net benefits as well, and if the antitrust enforcement agencies are to maintain a tough policy with respect to horizontal and vertical mergers, a policy of moderation with respect to conglomerate mergers is in order. In particular, public policy with respect to conglomerate acquisitions should focus on (a) mergers where potential competition is meaningfully impaired, and (b) mergers by giant firms that are not accompanied by a spin-off (or other disposition) of comparable assets. Acquisitions of the second kind have been discussed above.[178] Consider therefore the potential competition issue.

As I have already indicated, Blake's views on potential competition are rather broad.[179] The law, however, appears to be moving in the direction of interpreting the potential competition issue more narrowly. Commissioner Dennison, speaking for a unanimous Commission in the recent FTC decision *Beatrice Foods Co.*, discussed the factual proof required to show that potential competition has been or probably will be reduced:

[177] For a discussion of the market for corporate control, see Manne (1965), p. 110.

[178] Notes 152–9 *supra* and accompanying text. Although I suspect that there is little real cost advantage that an already giant-sized firm can confer on an acquired firm that could not be as (or more) effectively conferred by a somewhat less gargantuan enterprise, it may be useful not to prohibit such acquisitions altogether, so as to preserve the market for corporate control. If requiring the giant-sized firm to divest itself of comparable assets tends to forestall bureaucratic stagnation in the firm and has beneficial political consequences, a reasonable result would seem to have been reached.

[179] See text accompany footnotes 150–7 *supra*.

Complaint Counsel in essence attempt to rest their case on the existence of concentration ratios alone. The test for finding injury due to elimination of a potential competitor is not simple. Additional factors enter into any analysis of the loss of a potential competitor. Among these are: trends toward concentration in the market; extensive entry barriers; high probability that the lost potential competitor would have actually entered the market; whether the lost potential competitor was one of only a few such potential competitors and whether, if he had entered the market, his new competition would have had a significant impact on price and quality. Although the number of competing firms or trends toward concentration may be enough without more to condemn many horizontal mergers between existing rivals in a market, the *condition of entry by new firms as well as these other factors mentioned above must be considered when dealing with elimination of a potential competitor.*[180]

This reference to the condition of entry warrants additional development.

As Turner has argued forcefully, potential competition is apt to be impaired if one of a few most likely potential entrants acquires a firm that exceeds toehold proportions.[181] If the industry in question is highly concentrated, so that, but for the threat of potential competition, competitive results will not reliably obtain, the quality of competition is degraded by the loss of one of a few 'most likely potential entrants.' I would like to urge that the appellation 'most likely potential entrant' has genuine economic significance, as contrasted with transitory business significance, *only* to the extent that nontrivial barriers to entry into the industry in question can be said to exist.

The antitrust distinction to be made is between firms which (for transitory reasons) may have demonstrated an acquisition interest in the industry and firms which, despite entry barriers (nontransitory considerations), are strategically situated to enter. Because the interest of firms of the first kind is unlikely to persist, being dependent on such factors as the current interests of the chief executive, temporary cash balances, and immediate income statement considerations, prohibiting entry by acquisition to such firms is of little affirmative economic purpose. No long-term benefit to potential competition is thereby secured. Rather, the principle effect is to shrink the acquisition market, thereby impairing both the market for corporate control and the incentives for entrepreneurs to invest in new enterprises.

The situation is quite different, however, if the industry in question has nontrivial barriers to entry and the firm evidencing an acquisition interest is one of only a few firms for which de novo or toehold entry would be

---

[180] Beatrice Foods Co., [1970–1973 Transfer Binder] Trade Reg. Rep. paragraph 20,121 at 22,103, 22,109 (emphasis supplied) (FTC 1972).
[181] Turner (1965), p. 1313.

very easy. Consider in this connection the entry barrier conditions identified by Joe Bain, namely, economies of scale that are large in relation to the size of the market, absolute cost advantages, and product differentiation.[182] Although Bain describes these barriers without reference to specific firms, plainly the height of the barrier varies among possible entrants. Thus, though economies of scale may be large in relation to the size of the market, this impediment to entry is apt to be less severe for those few firms which have closely complementary production processes and sales organizations. Similarly, a few firms may be well situated with respect to absolute cost advantages. Although patents may constitute a severe impediment to entry, high-grade ore deposits may be in limited supply, or specialized labor skills may be required, a few firms are apt to stand out from all the rest by reason of a complementary technology, which facilitates inventing around the established patents, because they possess medium-grade ore deposits, or because their labor force has acquired, in a learning-by-doing fashion, the requisite specialized skills. Product differentiation advantages are likewise attenuated for those firms that market related types of consumer goods and themselves enjoy brand recognition. *Ceteris paribus*, those firms for which the barriers are least are the firms that are usefully designated most likely potential entrants.

In circumstances, however, where all such barriers to entry are negligible (economies of scale are not great; patents and specialized or otherwise scarce resources are unimportant; product differentiation is insubstantial), no small subset of firms can be said to enjoy a strategic advantage. In that case, it is fatuous to attempt to identify a group of most likely potential entrants, the loss by acquisition of any of which would significantly impair the quality of potential competition.[183]

V. Concluding Remarks

Received microtheory provides the analyst with some very powerful tools, but it is also incomplete. Among other things, as Peter Diamond has noted, standard 'economic models ...' [treat] individuals as playing a game with fixed rules which they obey. They do not buy more than they know they can pay for, they do not embezzle funds, they do not rob banks.'[184] Expressed in terms of the language introduced in section I,

---

[182] Bain (1956).

[183] One might, however, wish to prevent entry by acquisition by 'dominant firms,' the presence of which discourages rivalry (for deep pocket reasons) and otherwise transforms the market in uncertain ways. The Procter & Gamble acquisition of Clorox has been characterized by Justice Marshall in these terms. *United States* v. *Falstaff Brewing Corp.*, 410 US 526, 558–9 (1973) (Marshall, J., concurring).

[184] P. Diamond, 'Comment', in *Frontiers of Quantitative Economics*, ed. M. Intriligator (1971), Amsterdam: North Holland, pp. 29, 31.

individuals are not opportunists. Standard models also, as Simon has repeatedly emphasized, impute considerable power of computation and analysis to economic actors[185] – which is to say that bounded rationality is rarely thought to pose a problem. The transaction cost approach relaxes both of these behavioral assumptions.

Although there is no necessary connection, those who rely exclusively on the received microtheory model of the firm are prone to express considerable confidence in the efficacy of competition. Problems of small numbers supply and of adapting efficiently to uncertainty are apt to be dismissed or settled in a rather artificial fashion. The upshot is that many of the interesting problems of economic organization are either finessed or dealt with in a dogmatic way.

The transaction cost approach is concerned with the costs of running the economic system, especially the costs of adapting efficiently to uncertainty. It expressly makes allowance for elementary attributes of human decision makers – in particular, bounded rationality and opportunism – and permits the implications of these conditions to be explored in a way that received microtheory does not.

This does not require that received microtheory be rejected, however. Transaction cost analysis is more a complement to than a substitute for received microtheory. It is appropriate for studying the frictions in the system which may prevent the implications of received microtheory from going through. This focus makes it especially well-suited to help delimit the public policy issues with which the antitrust enforcement agencies are concerned. Moreover, transaction cost analysis is comparatively value free: it is biased neither for nor against the modes of organization associated with an unfettered market.

Perhaps the simplest application of the transaction cost approach is to price discrimination. Not only does transaction cost analysis call attention to the fact that price discrimination is costly to effectuate, which has been apparent to any student who has given serious consideration to the issue,[186] but it identifies the reasons for this and permits additional efficiency implications to be derived. The usual proposition that allocative efficiency is improved by fully discriminating monopoly, as compared with uniform price monopoly, is challenged. A private net gain but social net loss can plainly obtain when transaction costs are expressly introduced into the net benefit calculus.

With respect to vertical integration, the transaction cost approach counsels caution. The more strident claims of those who proclaim vertical integration (and, more generally, vertical market restrictions of all kinds)

---

[185] H. Simon, *supra* footnote 14, pp. 198–9.
[186] E.g., A. Pigou, *The Economics of Welfare*, 4th edn (1952), London: Macmillan, pp. 280–2.

to be altogether innocent of anticompetitive potential are shown to be exaggerated. Vertical integration can have entry impeding consequences in highly concentrated industries if capital markets do not operate frictionlessly – which in this context means omnisciently. Where, however, the industry in question is not highly concentrated, this same anticompetitive potential is much less severe. Absent collusion, the presumption that vertical integration is innocent or beneficial is appropriate.

The transaction cost approach also reveals that the oligopoly problem should not be uncritically equated with the dominant firm problem. It is much more difficult to negotiate a comprehensive collusive agreement, and there are many more problems to effecting a joint profit maximizing outcome, than is commonly suggested. Accordingly, theories of 'shared monopoly' ought to be regarded with skepticism. An economically rational antitrust policy would presumably first address the industries with dominant firms and, where feasible, effect dissolution here before going on to attack oligopolies. Contrary to what is sometimes said, there *are* prospective benefits from converting a dominant firm industry into an oligopolistic one.

The broadside attack that some have leveled against conglomerates appears to be overdrawn. Again, frictions in the capital market turn out to be of fundamental importance. Absent capital market frictions impeding takeover or proclivities of incumbent managements to reinvest earnings (or otherwise behave in opportunistic ways), the conglomerate appears to lack compelling economic purpose of a socially redeeming kind. Since enthusiasts of received microtheory have been reluctant to concede that a corporate control problem has even existed, they have had little to offer in the way of a rationale for the conglomerate firm. Once such frictions are admitted, however, there is plainly a case for encouraging, or at least not impeding, organizational innovations which have the potential to attenuate internal organizational distortions of a managerial discretion kind. Subject to the qualifications about organization form, which I have repeatedly emphasized, the conglomerate has attractive properties both because it makes the market for corporate control more credible, thereby inducing self-policing among otherwise opportunistic managements, and because it promotes the reallocation of resources to high yield uses. Except, therefore, among giant-sized firms, where the risk of offsetting political distortions is seriously posed, a more sympathetic posture on the part of the antitrust enforcement agencies toward conglomerates would seem warranted.

Donald Dewey has described the role of economists in antitrust as follows: 'The important issues in the control of monopoly are "economic" in the sense that judges and administrators are compelled to make decisions in the light of what they think the business world is "really" like, and it is the task of economists through research and reflection to provide them with an increasingly accurate picture.'[187] To the consternation of administrators and judges alike, the picture provided by received microtheory is sometimes vague and at other times simplistic. Transaction cost analysis is intended to supplement received microtheory in such circumstances.

[187] D. Dewey, *Monopoly in Economics and Law* (1959), Chicago: Rand McNally, i.

6

Assessing Vertical Market Restrictions: Antitrust Ramifications of the Transaction Cost Approach

Whether troublesome antitrust issues are posed when vertical restraints are placed on distributors by manufacturers has long been disputed. Although economic analysis is needed to assess the ramifications of such restraints, this analysis comes in a variety of forms and does not speak with one voice to these issues. Defective economic reasoning predictably leads to results that are inimical to economic efficiency and sound public policy. Such was the case when franchise restrictions were held anticompetitive in *United States* v. *Arnold, Schwinn & Co.*[1]

This chapter develops the argument that failure to make express allowances for transaction cost considerations is responsible for mistaken public policy in this area.[2] The transaction cost approach applies symmetrically both to an assessment of the efficiency gains, if any, arising from vertical restraints and to an evaluation of the strategic purposes and effects, if any, that accompany such restraints. After developing the justifications for, and occasional anticompetitive effects of, vertical market restrictions, I will suggest guidelines for federal antitrust policy. Part I outlines the general transaction cost approach and concludes that antitrust enforcement agencies and the courts should assume that vertical market

The chapter benefited from support by the Center for Advanced Study in the Behavioral Sciences, a fellowship from the Guggenheim Foundation, and support from the National Science Foundation. Comments by Eitan Muller, Chester Spatt, and David Teece are gratefully acknowledged. Reprinted from *University of Pennsylvania Law Review*, 127 (April 1979), pp. 953–93. © Copyright 1979 by the University of Pennsylvania Press.

   [1] 388 US 365 (1967).

   [2] For a discussion of the transaction cost approach, see footnote 5 *infra*. The transaction cost approach is especially helpful in the context of vertical market relations. See Phillips, Schwinn 'Rules and the "New Economics" of vertical relations,' *Antitrust Law Journal* (1975), p. 573 (transaction cost theory is the 'new economics' of vertical market relations).

restrictions are efficiency enhancing unless certain structural conditions exist within the industry. Part II discusses strategic behavior and the structural characteristics of industries needed to support strategic outcomes. Vertical restraints pose troublesome antitrust issues only when these conditions exist. Part III examines the development of American distribution systems late in the nineteenth century and concludes that efforts to economize on transaction costs played a central role in the forward integration of certain manufacturers into distribution. Part IV applies my economic analysis to the facts and law of *Schwinn* and concludes that failure to recognize and make allowances for transaction costs is what led to public policy error. Part V contrasts the premises of alternative approaches to vertical restrictions with those of the transaction cost approach. The legal principles derivable from the transaction cost approach are summarized in part VI. When evaluated in light of these proposed legal principles, the Supreme Court's recent decision in *Continental T.V., Inc.* v. *GTE Sylvania Inc.*[3] can be seen to rest on much sounder ground than did the *Schwinn* decision.

I. Economizing on Transaction Costs

A. BACKGROUND

The relevant unit of economic analysis differs, depending upon the behavior under examination. When the purpose is to explain alternative modes of organization, the fundamental unit of analysis is the transaction.[4] Such an approach recognizes that neither firms nor markets come in predetermined shapes. Rather, both evolve in active juxtaposition to one another. Strategic purposes aside, the object of that evolution is to reach a complementary configuration that economizes on transaction costs.[5] This elementary way of studying economic practices and institutions has only recently been introduced into antitrust economics.[6] Both major and minor errors of enforcement can be attributed to its previous neglect. Its neglect has had especially serious consequences in the area of vertical market relations.

[3] 433 US 36 (1977).

[4] See R. Commons, 'Institutional economics,' *American Economic Review*, 21 (1931), p. 648.

[5] See O. E. Williamson, 'Economies as an antitrust defense revisited,' *University of Pennsylvania Law Review*, 125 (1977) pp. 690. 723 (hereinafter cited as 'Economies defense'). This oversimplifies somewhat, in that it takes technology as given. Strategic purposes aside, the more general purpose of economic organization is to devise arrangements that economize on the sum of production and transaction costs.

The basic tenets of the transaction cost approach are stated succinctly in chapter 5.

[6] Chapter 5.

I have examined the vertical integration of successive production stages from a transaction perspective elsewhere.[7] The argument may be summarized in the following conclusions: (a) vertical integration in production is explained primarily by transaction cost considerations rather than technological determinacy;[8] (b) although vertical integration commonly yields transaction cost savings, strategic consequences that pose antitrust concerns occasionally arise;[9] (c) antitrust enforcement ought to be more discriminating and restrict its attention to cases in which strategic effects arguably appear;[10] and (d) although vertical integration serves to overcome some of the disabilities to which interfirm trading is subject, the successive integration of additional transactions eventually engenders operating limitations of its own.[11]

This chapter deals with vertical market relations between the production and distribution stages. Each of the conclusions reached in my study of the vertical integration of production holds true when the production–distribution nexus is assessed. Some specific differences should be recognized, however, and it is instructive to examine the interface between production and distribution on its own terms. Two novel problems, neither of which is present when integration occurs in intermediate product markets, arise when a firm considers forward integration into distribution.

First, final consumers are ordinarily much less well informed than industrial buyers. Specific efforts to 'assist' consumers, sometimes taking the form of product differentiation, may be warranted and observed on this account. Second, but for vertical restrictions, distributors' efforts to promote local profitability objectives can sometimes impair the integrity of the distributorship system. This is often subsumed under the heading of 'free rider' effects,[12] but the more general phenomenon is that of subgoal pursuit[13] with adverse systems consequences.

To be sure, subgoal pursuit is responsible for the 'ideal' outcomes attributed to competitive markets. The independent pursuit of profit by each of the parties is what the proverbial invisible hand is all about. How is it that competition between a group of distributors handling a common brand is any less valued than competition between autonomous firms selling rival brands? If competition yields social benefits in one context,

---

[7] See Williamson (1975), pp. 82–131; Chapter 2.

[8] See Williamson, *supra* footnote 7, pp. 82–105; Williamson, *supra* footnote 7, pp. 112–17.

[9] See Williamson, *supra* footnote 7, pp. 106–16; Williamson, *supra* footnote 7, pp. 117–19.

[10] See Williamson, *supra* footnote 7, pp. 115–16.

[11] Ibid., pp. 117–31.

[12] See footnote 26 *infra*.

[13] By 'subgoal pursuit' I refer to efforts to promote local or individual goals to the possible detriment of global or system objectives.

why not in the other? The uncritical extension of competitive reasoning from the inter-firm context to the manufacturer–distributor nexus is doubtlessly responsible for much of the confusion in the vertical restraints arena.

After setting out the principal behavioral assumptions upon which the transaction cost approach is based, I advance the argument below that organizational innovations normally indicate attempts to realize efficiency gains. This, however, is merely a presumption: it can be rebutted in individual instances when certain strategic conditions are shown.[14]

B. BOUNDED RATIONALITY AND OPPORTUNISM

Bounded rationality and opportunism are the central behavioral assumptions upon which the transaction cost approach is based. Bounded rationality, which should not be confused with irrationality, refers to a condition in which human agents are '*intendedly* rational, but only *limitedly* so.'[15] Put differently, it refers to rationality in the ordinary, dictionary sense of the term – agreeable to reason; not absurd, preposterous, extravagant, foolish, fanciful, or the like; intelligent, sensible'[16] – rather than in the hyperrational sense in which it is commonly used in microeconomics textbooks.[17] Thus, economic agents who are boundedly rational are able to receive, store, retrieve, and process only a limited amount of information. Such agents are routinely overwhelmed by the amount of information supplied to them in relation to their capacity to use it effectively. Accordingly, the economics of attention is an important but generally neglected item on the research agenda.[18]

[14] See text accompanying footnotes 27–31 *infra*.

[15] H. Simon, *Administrative Behavior*, New York: Macmillan 2nd edn (1961), p. xxiv.

[16] *Webster's New International Dictionary of the English Language*, 2nd edn (1959), p. 2066.

[17] See H. Simon, 'Rationality as process and as product of thought,' *American Economic Review*, May 1978, pp. 1, 2–3.

[18] See ibid., p. 13. Simon argues that attention, i.e., our capacity for considering and processing a given piece of information, is the scarce resource, not information. Calling for procedural means of focusing attention in a rational and productive way, he notes that '[i]n a world where attention is a major scarce resource, information may be an expensive luxury, for it may turn our attention from what is important to what is unimportant.' Ibid. Bounded rationality should also be distinguished from the 'least reasonable man' approach, which some marketing specialists associate with the Federal Trade Commission's approach to advertising. See R. Cunningham and L. L. Cunningham, 'Standards for advertising regulation,' *Journal of Marketing* (October 1977), p. 92. The focus of that approach is on "the public – that vast multitude which includes the ignorant, the unthinking, and the credulous, who in making purchases, do not stop to analyze, but are governed by appearances and general impressions".' Ibid [quoting *Florence Mfg. Co.* v. *J.C. Dowd & Co.*, 178 F. 73, 75 (2d Cir. 1910)]; see *Charles of the Ritz Distribs. Corp.* v. *FTC*, 143 F.2d 676, 679 (2d Cir. 1944). To be sure, when the hazards are severe and communication difficult, a cautious standard such as this has merit. Presumably, however, these are the exceptions rather than the rule: a reasonable-man standard normally ought to apply.

Opportunism extends the usual motivational assumption of self-interest to make allowance for self-interest with guile. Thus, whereas bounded rationality suggests decision making less complex than the usual assumption of hyperrationality, opportunism suggests calculating behavior more sophisticated than the usual assumption of simple self-interest. Opportunism refers to 'making false or empty, that is, self-disbelieved threats or promises,'[19] cutting corners for undisclosed personal advantage, covering up tracks, and the like. Although it is a central assumption, it is not essential that all economic agents behave this way. What is crucial, however, is that *some* agents behave in this fashion and that it is costly to sort out those who are opportunistic from those who are not.

It has long been recognized that opportunism poses economic problems in the context of public goods,[20] in the trading of information,[21] and in insurance markets.[22] But recognition that opportunism is a pervasive economic problem has taken much longer to develop. Peter Diamond observed just seven years ago that the usual assumption is that economic agents do not lie, cheat, or steal. Instead, their actions are overt and agreements are binding.[23] Reliance upon simple self-interest, however, has been changing. More recently, Jack Hirshleifer observed that the key question 'for the viability of a pattern of exchange ... is control of cheating.'[24] and Steven Salop characterizes the Rational Economic Man as one who 'choose[s] to tell the truth or misrepresent according to the relative profits of the two strategies, unencumbered by any moral bounds.'[25] This is a remarkable transformation in the brief span of seven years.

Given both bounded rationality and opportunism, the following organizational design problem must be faced by the firm and recognized by society: the need to organize transactions in such a way as to economize on bounded rationality while simultaneously safeguarding the transactions in question against opportunism. What is especially interesting about the

[19] E. Goffman, *Strategic Interaction* (1969), Philadelpia, University of Pennsylvania Press, p. 105.

[20] See e.g. P. Samuelson, 'The pure theory of public expenditure', *Review of Economics and Statistics*, 36 (1954), p. 387.

[21] See e.g., K.J. Arrow, 'Economic welfare and the allocation of resources for invention,' *National Bureau of Economic Research, The Rate and Direction of Inventive Activity: Economic and Social Factors* (1962), Princeton: Princeton University Press, pp. 609, 614–16.

[22] K. J. Arrow, *Essays in the Theory of Risk-Bearing* (1971), Chicago: Markham, p. 142.

[23] P. Diamond, 'Comments,' *Frontiers of Quantitative Economics*, ed. (1971), M. Intriligator, Amsterdam: North Holland, pp. 29, 31.

[24] J. Hirshleifer, 'Economics from a biological standpoint,' *Journal of Law and Economics*, 20 (1977), p. 1, 27.

[25] S. Salop, 'Parables of Information Transmission in Markets 6–7' (April 1978) (Unpublished discussion paper no. 21, Center for the Study of Organizational Innovation, University of Pennsylvania).

production–distribution interface is that the manufacturer is concerned not only with the bounded rationality of the immediate parties, but with that of the ultimate consumer as well. Devising transactions that economize on the information needs of consumers is thus a major consideration. Opportunism is also of concern in two respects. The manufacturer is concerned both that the integrity of the distribution system be protected against free riders[26] and that the quality of his product not be debased. Although these are commonly interrelated, it is useful to address each separately. If hazards of either kind are observed, vertical market restrictions may be warranted.

C. THE PRESUMPTION THAT VERTICAL MARKET RESTRICTIONS NORMALLY ENHANCE EFFICIENCY

A transaction cost analysis applies at each separate stage of activity in the production and distribution of a good or service. Whether each separate stage is autonomous or not is unimportant. In principle, each could be and market contracts could be used to bring activity at successive interfaces into adjustment. Such a proliferation of contracts can be costly, however. The basic presumption of the transaction cost approach is that successive interfaces are organized in a manner that economizes on transaction costs. Such an approach is consistent with the common law tradition for assessing economic activity.[27]

Antitrust doctrine typically maintains a more skeptical posture. Given the legal system's reliance on the adversary process, it is not surprising that a former chief of the Antitrust Division of the Justice Department should observe, 'I approach territorial and customer restrictions not hospitably in the common law tradition, but inhospitably in the tradition of antitrust law.'[28] The major problem with this orientation, which has

---

[26] An example of a free rider is a retailer who sells a product promoted by one of his competitors. He benefits from the promotion, but because it has cost him nothing, he can sell the product at a lower price than the competitor who promotes it. Territorial restrictions imposed by the manufacturer may prevent this free riding, thus encouraging retailers to push the manufacturer's product. For a discussion of the free rider phenomenon in the context of resale price maintenance, see R. Posner, *Antitrust Law: An Economic Perspective* (1976), pp. 149–50, 160, 185; L. Telser, 'Why should manufacturers want fair trade', *Journal of Law and Economics*, 3 (1960), p. 86.

[27] For some recent views on the presumption of efficiency in the common law, see L. Rubin, 'Why is the common law efficient?' (1977), *Journal of Legal Studies*, 6 p. 51; Priest, 'The common law process and the selection of efficient rules,' *Journal of Legal Studies*, 6 (1977), p. 65. Richard Posner consistently emphasizes efficiency in his wide-ranging and influential studies of the law. See e.g., R. Posner, *Economic Analysis of Law* (1972).

[28] The quotation is attributed to Donald Turner (at a time when he was assistant attorney general in charge of the antitrust division) by Stanley Robinson. *1968 N.Y. St B. Assn, Antitrust Law Symposium*, 29.

been the prevailing one, is that the contestants have played the enforcement game entirely on the inhospitability tradition's turf.[29] Rather than affirmatively arguing the case in terms of transaction cost economies, defendants have mainly argued that there are no ill effects.[30] As a consequence of this preoccupation with (real or imagined) anticompetitive effects, the affirmative defenses based on the transaction cost economies underlying many vertical market restrictions have gone undeveloped. *United States* v. *Arnold, Schwinn & Co.*[31] is an example.

I believe that the common law tradition is based on sound premises and that, confronted with a novel organizational arrangement, the immediate reaction of antitrust enforcement agencies and the courts should not be to attribute anticompetitive purpose and intent.[32] Instead, they should inquire whether efficiency gains can plausibly be associated with the arrangement under consideration. Only when this exercise has been completed should the issue of anticompetitive abuse be raised.

The principal reason for maintaining an efficiency presumption is that this presumption accords with reality. As set out in the following section, anticompetitive effects can appear only if rather special structural conditions exist. When these are present, vigilance is warranted. Maintaining a general attitude of inhospitability, however, encourages the enforcement agencies to behave in a counterfactual way and interpret innocent and beneficial developments in a suspect and even hostile manner.

An efficiency presumption is needed to remedy the distortions that earlier traditions have introduced into the enforcement process. However, although presumptions reflect central tendencies and provide framework,

---

[29] Robert Bork makes a similar point, noting the significance of a recent shift in the Supreme Court's orientation in *Continental TV Inc.* v. *GTE–Sylvania Inc.*, 433 US 36 (1977): 'The present misshapen look of antitrust doctrine is due in large measure to the Supreme Court's habit of regarding business efficiency as either irrelevant or harmful ... The point is that insufficient regard for efficient methods of production and distribution meant that hardly any business practice challenged could survive. The sole benefit the practice might confer was ruled out of court, and only possible dangers were considered.
. . .

The Court's *Sylvania* opinion not only counted efficiencies in favor of a challenged business practice but did so in a sophisticated way ... This approach – concern for consumer welfare and an intelligent inquiry into the efficiency potential of challenged business practices – is capable of altering the entire corus of antitrust jurisprudence, which now stands in considerable need of repair.'
Bork, 'Vertical restraints: Schwinn overruled,' *1977 Sup. Ct. Rev.* (1978), pp. 171, 172.

[30] E.g., *United States* v. *Arnold, Schwinn & Co.*, 388 US 365 (1967).

[31] 388 US 365 (1967).

[32] An extreme example of this inventive proclivity to emphasize anticompetitive effects, even to the extent of regarding simple efficiency as an anticmpetitive advantage, is the argument of the Federal Trade Commission in *Foremost Dairies Inc.*, 60 FTC 944, 1084 (1962).

they are also subject to challenge. This brings us to matters of strategic purpose and oligopolistic relations.

II. Possible Anticompetitive Effects: Strategic Behavior and Oligopolistic Interdependence

Practices that ordinarily are unobjectionable and indeed arguably are efficient should under some sets of circumstances come under further scrutiny and perhaps be proscribed. Specifically, vigilance is warranted in situations in which the behavior in question promotes strategic purposes or oligopolistic interdependence. The distinction between these two effects is this: activities of a strategic kind serve to disadvantge small rivals and potential entrants in circumstances in which actual competition is attenuated; the creation of oligopolistic interdependence, by contrast, entails efforts to maintain compliance and avoid mutually disadvantageous interfirm rivalry among estabished oligopolists. Thus, whereas strategic behavior is directed outward, to discipline actual and potential rivals, oligopolistic interdependence focuses inward, the concern being rivalry among major, established firms.

A. STRATEGIC BEHAVIOR AND IMPEDIMENTS TO ENTRY

My discussion of strategic behavior is selective rather than comprehensive. It deals only with circumstances in which vertical restrictions can serve as impediments to entry. Predatory pricing, pre-emptive investment, strategic research and development, and other types of strategic behavior are neglected – although these are all members of the same family.[33]

The Views of Bork and Posner

Robert Bork contends, and I agree, that much antitrust mischief has resulted from loose use of the phrase 'barriers to entry.'[34] In order to avoid continuing abuse, Bork suggests that business practices hereafter be classified as efficiency enhancing or predatory.[35] Provided that allowance is made for the possibility that behavior that is efficient in one context can be exclusionary when used by firms with large market shares, I am prepared to accept this approach. Inasmuch as Bork expressly acknowledges that exclusionary behavior should be examined in contingent

---

[33] See S. Salop, 'Strategic entry deterrence,' *American Economic Review*, 69 (1979); A. M. Spence, 'Entry, capacity, investment and oligopolistic pricing,' *Bell Journal of Economics*, 8 p. 534 (1977); Williamson, 'Predatory pricing: A strategic and welfare analysis,' *Yale Law Journal*, 87 (1977), p. 284.

[34] Bork (1978), p. 310.

[35] Ibid., pp. 160, 329.

terms,[36] there would appear to be no serious conceptual differences between us. Our views do diverge, however, due to the narrowness with which he defines exclusionary practices.

Although Bork at one point concedes that a dominant firm can disadvantage a rival by disrupting optimal distribution patterns,[37] he develops the case in rather circumscribed terms and thereafter argues that there is 'nothing to the notion that an established firm might integrate vertically in order deliberately to raise the capital requirements of entry.'[38] The 'instances of deliberate predation'[39] that expressly concern him are boycotts,[40] individual refusals to deal,[41] and predation through government processes.[42] He believes that all vertical restraints are unqualifiedly lawful.[43]

Richard Posner also cautions against excessive concern with entry barrier claims. Thus he counsels that '[a] barrier to entry is commonly used ... to mean anything which a new entrant must overcome in order to gain a foothold in the market, such as the capital costs of entering the market on an efficient scale. This is ... meaningless ... since it is obvious that a new entrant must incur costs to enter the market, *just as his predecessors ... did previously.*'[44]

A Different View

For the reasons set out below, I am not persuaded that capital market impediments cannot arise because of vertical restraints or that the cost conditions facing early and later entrants are equal. I should make clear, however, that my differences with Bork and Posner arise only in dominant firm industries and, possibly, in collusive oligopolies. In other circumstances, efforts to behave strategically will be self-defeating. Accordingly, concern over strategic behavior vanishes in industries characterized by neither dominant firms nor tight oligopolies.

To illustrate that a capital market impediment can arise as a result of vertical integration, posit an industry with two stages, a production stage

---

[36] Ibid., pp. 156–7. Bork cites the exclusive deawling agreement as an example of a practice that manifests a very weak possibility of predation and a very strong probability of efficiency. Although his view of the lawfulness of the practice is clear, it implicitly recognizes the possibility of exceptions. '[T]he law cannot properly see predatory behavior in *all* unilaterally enforced changes in patterns of distribution.' Ibid., p. 156 (emphasis added).

[37] Ibid., pp. 156–8.

[38] Ibid., p. 323.

[39] Ibid., p. 329.

[40] Ibid., pp. 330–44.

[41] Ibid., pp. 344–6.

[42] Ibid., pp. 347–64.

[43] Ibid., p. 288; Bork, *supra* footnote 29, pp. 173–80, 181–2.

[44] Posner, *supra* footnote 26, p. 59 (emphasis added).

and a distribution stage. Assume that the industry is equally efficient whether or not these stages are integrated.[45] In addition, assume that manufacturing (stage I) is monopolized and that the monopolist has integrated forward into distribution (stage II). Finally, assume that a potential entrant with experience is manufacturing, but none in distribution, subsequently develops a rival product that it can manufacture at a competitive cost. The question to be addressed is whether this rival is disadvanaged by the monopolist's earlier decision to integrate.

Assessing this will be facilitated by comparing the conditions facing the potential entrant under the following nonintegrated and integrated alternatives:

(1) [T]he monopolistic stage I producer is not integrated, in which case the prospective new entrant can enter at stage I only and utilize the facilities of stage II producers ... (suitably expanded if necessary), [or] ... (2) the monopolistic stage I producer is integrated into stage II so that either (a) the new entrant himself comes in at both stages or (b) independent new entrants appear simultaneously at both stages. If Bork ... [is] correct, the cost of capital ought to be independent of these conditions.

To contend that the terms of finance are the same under 2(a) as they are under 1 implies that the capital market has equal confidence in the new entrant's qualifications to perform stage II activities as it does in firms that are already experienced in the business. Except in circumstances where experienced firms are plainly inept, this is tantamount to saying that experience counts for nought. This, however, is implausible for transactions that involve large, discrete rather than small, but recurring commitments of funds. Although transactions of the latter type can be monitored reasonable effectively, on the basis of ex post experience, this is much less easy for transactions of the large, discrete variety – which are the kind under consideration here. Reputation, which is to say prior experience, is of special importance in establishing the terms of finance for transactions that involve large, discrete commitments of funds.[46]

The problems are worse, moreover, if the 2(b) scenario unfolds. As compared with condition 1, would-be stage II entrants are presumably penalized both for lack of experience and because nonconvergent expec-

---

[45] It should be noted that vertical integration could be a less efficient mode of structuring transactions but might be adopted nonetheless because of strategic incentives.
[46] Williamson, *supra* footnote 7, p. 111.

tations[47] pose more serious problems in the 2(b) context. The latter argument is that the flexible or expanded capacity of existing stage II processors can accommodate new entry at stage I much more easily than if simultaneous new entry by independent distributors at stage II is required. Problems with interdependent investments by new independent entities arise because of differing perceptions of the market, incentive differences, and because interfirm intentions may be difficult to signal. These hazards are presumably reflected in the cost of capital. As a consequence, neither of the type 2 scenarios is on a parity with the type 1 condition. Bork's unrestricted claim that vertical integration cannot influence the cost of capital, and hence the conditions to entry, is evidently overstated.[48]

Consider now the cost issue that Posner addresses. As he puts it, the issue appears to be whether early entrants are somehow able to avoid costs that later entrants incur. He claims they are not, with which contention I agree. But this does not reach the question whether timing differences can give rise to differential cost-bearing consequences. This is related to, but goes beyond, the matter of differential capital costs discussed above.

Whether potential entrants will be disadvantaged by prior integration depends on (a) the importance of learning-by-doing, (b) the degree to which learning-by-doing economies are shared by employer and employee, (c) the ease with which specialized human assets can be bid away, and (d) the degree to which prices track costs.[49] Assuming that prices track the current costs of the least-cost supplier in a fairly regular way and that it is difficult to bid specialized human assets away from current employers in effective team configurations, potential entrants will be more severely disadvantaged by prior integration the more important that learning-by-doing economies are and the less completely these learning economies are appropriated by employees.

The upshot is that decisions to integrate into activities that require investments in idiosyncratic human or physical assets can affect the subsequent ease of entry. Whether the argument has antitrust significance, however, depends on the circumstances. For one thing, the conditions of

---

[47] Firms' expectations converge, creating equilibrium in a market as a whole, when every firm bases its expectations on the same set of events and signals, and comes to the same conclusions. Whether or not such market equilibrium can be achieved depends on several factors, among them the degree of interdependence among the firms, the level of certainty about the future, the number of variables to be considered, the capacity of firms to adapt to change, and the amount of information available to the firms. See Malmgren, *Quarterly Journal of Economics*, 75 (1961), pp. 399, 405–11; Williamson, *supra* footnote 7, p. 120.

[48] See Caves and Porter (1977), pp. 241, 246–7 (vertical integration may raise the capital-cost entry barrier).

[49] See Williamson, *supra* footnote 7, pp. 216–17.

entry are relatively unimportant if actual competition is already effective. Even where this is problematical, an additional entry impediment because of integration can be said to exist only to the extent that access through established distribution channels is impracticable. This, in turn, depends on the size of the residual (nonintegrated) market and on whether sales through the distribution channels of integrated firms are realistic. The subset of industries warranting close antitrust scrutiny, from both actual competition and market access points of view, reduces to industries characterized by dominant firms and tight oligopolies that have comprehensively integrated into distribution.

Even here, the question whether forward integration or vertical restrictions yield net benefits should be addressed. Are the benefits great or slight in relation to the anticompetitive consequences? The results of this inquiry can vary depending on the industry's stage of development. Thus, economic benefits realized immediately after the restraint has been effected may not continue indefinitely. Put differently, although 'administered distribution' may be needed to ensure viability at an early stage in an industry's development, a more mature industry may be able to support the requisite distribution system without the same need for restraints on forward integration. Thus, although forward integration may represent an effort to realize private gains with resulting economies at one stage, it may constitute an unneeded restraint at a later stage and indeed may serve strategically to disadvantage rivals if it is continued.

Although the above argument is primarily couched in terms of vertical integration, I also refer to vertical restrictions. The scope of the latter term should be qualified. Among exclusive dealing, territorial restrictions, and customer restrictions, only the first of these vertical restrictions constitutes a possible entry impediment, and this only under the special circumstances of structural dominance or tight oligopoly.[50]

More generally, except as oligopolistic interdependence is promoted,[51] I am persuaded by Bork's arguments that territorial and customer restraints should not be proscribed.[52] Manufacturers will introduce these only as they are expected to attenuate subgoal pursuit and promote efficiency.[53]

[50] I have defined a dominant firm industry as one in which the market share of the largest firm is at least 60% and entry into the market is not easy. Tight oligopoly is less easy to characterize. It is mainly apt to appear in mature, highly concentrated industries producing homogeneous products under uniform cost conditions and having significant barriers to entry. The reasons why oligopolistic interdependence is difficult to sustain in other circumstances is traceable to the transaction costs of reaching and policing collusive agreements. See generally Williamson, *supra* footnote 7, pp. 234–47.

[51] See text accompanying footnotes 57–62 *infra*.

[52] See footnote 40 *supra*.

[53] L. Preston observes that 'customer-territorial restrictions considered alone . . . do not contribute to the weakening of the interbrand competition in final markets or serve as barriers to entry.' Preston, 'Restrictive distribution arrangements: economic analysis and public policy standards, *L. & Contemp. Prob.*, 30 (1965), pp. 506, 520. Furthermore, '[t]he

But what of the possibility that exclusive dealing has objectionable effects other than that of impeding entry? If it does, under what circumstances do these effects occur and what are the ramifications for antitrust enforcement?

Suppose that entry is unaffected but that exclusive dealing benefits some customers (for example, by permitting a product to be effectively differentiated) but simultaneously disadvantages others. For instance, comparison shopping is often facilitated by side-by-side examination; exclusive dealing precludes this. Marginal customers who wish to establish whether differentiation warrants a price premium will, if confronted by exclusive dealing, be less able to make informed judgments easily. How should this be evaluated?

Or suppose that, although the restraint itself negligibly affects the condition of entry, other factors impede entry and widespread use of the restraint effectively precludes customers who *know* that they place little value on the additional services (which are not offered separately under exclusive dealing restrictions) from obtaining the product without services included.

Bork meets these types of objections with the argument that when 'the technology of distribution ... [does] not allow the preferences of both groups of customers to be met, ... the manufacturer will choose to satisfy the larger number,' which he regards as the efficient thing to do.[54] Actually, I would expect that manufacturers would service the more profitable subset – which recent scholarship discloses commonly will be, but need not be, the larger market.[55] More troublesome is the possibility that the use of a profitability calculus to decide what mix of products to offer may be at variance with welfare gains, even when the decision is to service the larger market.

However, inasmuch as such defects in the product mix calculus are difficult to ascertain in practice and since exclusive dealing does not obviously bias such choices adversely, it seems prudent to separate exclusive dealing restraints from the product variety issue. Accordingly, except as entry impediments result, a policy of permissiveness with respect to exclusive dealing restraints would normally appear to be warranted.[56]

case against customer-territorial restrictions where suppliers are profitable or relatively large appears to rest on an association between these restrictions and parallel limitations on the range of products marketed by a distributor, i.e., exclusive dealing.' Ibid., pp. 520–1 (footnote omitted).

[54] Bork, *supra* footnote 29, p. 181.

[55] See A. Dixit and J. Stiglitz, 'Monopolistic competition and optimum product diversity,' *American Economic Review*, 67 (1977), p. 297; A. M. Spence, 'Product differentiation and welfare,' *American Economic Review*, 66 (1976), p. 407.

[56] Note that, directly or indirectly, all of the above issues depend on transaction-cost considerations. Thus, investors demand a premium to invest in new enterprises because (a) it is costly to assess the merits of the investment proposal (the relevant data cannot be

B. OLIGOPOLISTIC INTERDEPENDENCE AND THE REGULARIZATION OF PRICE

Although Posner is unconcerned with strategic (outward-directed) uses of vertical restrictions, he argues that such restrictions can be used to strengthen a dealer cartel.[57] This is worrisome, however, only when a 'manufacturer ha[s] a very large market share or ... [when] all or most of the manufacturers in the market imposed uniform restrictions on their dealers so that (in either case) the dealers had a monopoly position in a genuine economic market.'[58] In all other circumstances, vertical restrictions evidently pose no antitrust concerns.

Although I agree that the issue of dealer cartels warrants antitrust scrutiny, the possibility that vertical restrictions can be used to consolidate a *manufacturer* cartel is to me more troublesome. Thus, even if, contrary to Bork, dealer cartels are not easy antitrust enforcement targets,[59] I question whether dealers are often in a position to impose restrictive terms on unwilling manufacturers. When they are not, we can be confident that manufacturers will not knowingly adopt strategies the effect of which is to transfer money from their pockets to those of their retailers.[60] Observed restrictions can thus be assumed to promote manufacturer interests.

The more troublesome possibility to which I refer – that vertical restrictions can be used to support manufacturer cartels – hinges on the proposition that regularizing exchange commonly serves to stabilize frangible associations. A crucial operating concern of a manufacturers' cartel is to devise signals whereby adherence to the cartel policy can be inferred with confidence. The elimination of false moves or ambiguous

---

displayed and evaluated costlessly) and (b) there are hazards of opportunism. The idiosyncrasies of human assets also reflect a condition of information impactedness in which inexperienced firms are disadvantaged. Comparison shopping has advantages because the characteristics of rival products cannot be described adequately in objective terms to allow abstract comparisons to be made. This is a reflection of bounded rationality. And nonseparable offers of product and service are made because manufacturers are unable to price-discriminate fully and cannot rely on customers to reveal true preferences accurately – manifestations of bounded rationality and opportunism, respectively.

[57] Posner, 'The rule of reason and the economic approach: reflections on the *Sylvania* decision,' *U. Chi. L. Rev.*, 45 (1977), pp. 1, 17.

[58] Ibid. Posner would use a 'rule of reason' approach 'to isolate, and condemn, restrictions that are imposed nominally by the manufacturer but are in fact desired for monopolistic purposes by dealers using the manufacturer as their enforcement agent.'

[59] Bork, *supra* footnote 34, pp. 292–3. In disposing of the 'dealer cartel objection' to his proposal that all vertical restraints be held lawful, Bork argues not only that dealer cartels are not difficult to uncover, but also that manufacturer-imposed restraints, affecting only intrabrand competition, are of limited, if any, use to a dealer cartel.

[60] See Bork, *supra* footnote 29, p. 188.

actions which, if misinterpreted, would cause the cartel to unravel, is of special importance.

The avoidance of pricing ambiguity is especially critical. When retail outlets are owned or extensively controlled by manufacturers, retail price changes can normally be assumed to reflect manufacturers' intent. By contrast, the responsibility for pricing changes is less clear where dealers are fully autonomous agents. To the extent that pricing latitude among such dealers makes it more difficult for manufacturers to reach cartel agreements because *ex ante* confidence in the subsequent execution of agreements is lacking, efforts to remove 'unwanted' degrees of freedom can be anticipated. The same is true when, despite agreement, price variability creates suspicion that cartel members are defecting, which in turn may cause the cartel to unravel.

Bork argues that the manufacturer cartel objection to vertical restrictions is 'insubstantial' and 'applies only to resale price maintenance.'[61] I would characterize it somewhat differently. Although I agree that regularizing price is the main antitrust concern, vertical restraints other than resale price maintenance can be used to promote pricing discipline. The use of vertical restrictions to tighten oligopolistic interdependence is likely to be attractive, however, only in industries with homogeneous products.[62] It is noteworthy, moreover, than an economies justification for such restrictions is difficult to provide in homogeneous product markets. Accordingly, the burden of justifying vertical restrictions in homogeneous, oligopolistic industries rests heavily on the firms employing them. The normal efficiency presumption is unwarranted in such circumstances.

III. Aspects of the Historical Development of American Distribution Systems

Alfred Chandler, Jr.'s recent monograph[63] describing marketing developments during the late nineteenth century provides strong support for the proposition that transaction costs are sufficiently significant to affect the structure of industries, sometimes motivating firms to integrate forward from manufacturing into the retail stage. In the following subsections Chandler's findings concerning efficiency-enhancing and strategic behavior will first be described, then analyzed from a transaction cost perspective.

---

[61] Bork, *supra* footnote 34, p. 294.

[62] See P. Newman, 'Strategic groups and the structure–performance relationship,' *Review of Economics and Statistics*, 60 (1978), p. 417. For a discussion of the problems associated with effecting tight interdependence in oligopoly, see Williamson, *supra* footnote 7, pp. 234–47.

[63] A. Chandler, *The Visible Hand: The Managerial Revolution in American Business* (1977). Cambridge: Harvard University Press.

A. EFFICIENCY AND FORWARD INTEGRATION

Chandler's Findings

Chandler's description of forward integration into distribution by American manufacturers distinguishes between the developments of infrastructure and the induced distributional response. The appearance of the railroads and the telegraph and telephone systems in the latter part of the nineteenth century permitted wider geographic areas to be served in a reliable and timely way. The 'reliability and speed of the new transportation and communication' permitted greater economies of scale to be realized in factory organization.[64] These economies of scale at the factory level were latent – in the sense that the technology was there waiting to be exploited. Because it is not manufacturing cost but delivered cost that matters, however, it became profitable to realize these scale economies only when a low-cost distribution system appeared. That is, so long as transportation expenses were great, the most efficient way to serve markets was by dispersing factories.

Once the new transportation and communication infrastructure was in place, the stage was set for the distributional response. A crucial question was how to devise a coordinated manufacturing–distribution response. In principle, both stages could have remained autonomous: manufacturers could have remained specialized and built larger scale plants while specialized distributors could have responded simultaneously, either on their own initiative or by contract, by assembling the requisite distribution network. In many industries, however, 'existing marketers were unable to sell and distribute products in the volume they were produced. . . . Once the inadequacies of existing marketers became clear, manufacturers integrated forward into marketing.'[65] An administrative override was evidently needed.[66]

Not all industries integrated forward, however, and those that did integrate forward did not do so to the same extent. Some industries linked manufacturing only with advertising and wholesaling; retail integration was not attempted. Nondurable industries that had recently adopted continuous process machinery – cigarettes, matches, cereals, and canned goods are examples – were in this category.[67] More ambitious and

[64] Ibid., p. 245.

[65] Ibid., p. 287.

[66] For an interesting treatment of vertical integration forward into distribution in the sale of gasoline, see D. Teece, *Vertical Integration and Vertical Divestiture in the US Oil Industry* (1976), Washington: American Enterprise Institute, pp. 40–4.

[67] 'Such entrepreneurs found that the existing marketers were unable to move their goods quickly enough or to advertise them effectively enough to keep their high-volume production facilities operating steadily.' Chandler, *supra* footnote 63, p. 287.

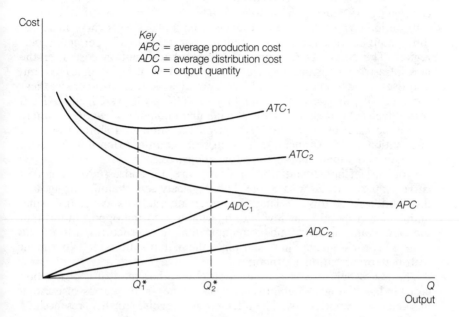

Figure 6.1

interesting were producer and consumer durables that required 'specialized marketing services – demonstration, installation, consumer credit, after-sales service and repair,' services that existing middlemen 'had neither the interest nor facilities to provide.'[68] Examples here included sewing machines, farm machinery, office machines, and heavy electrical equipment.

A Transaction Cost Interpretation

The new transportation and communication infrastructure permitted manufacturers to serve larger markets in a low-cost way. The ramifications of these infrastructural developments on plant size are displayed in figure 6.1.[69]

The *APC* curve shows the average cost of production as plant size

[68] Ibid., p. 288.

[69] F. Scherer, A. Beckenstein, E. Kaufer, and R. Murphy, *The Economics of Multiplant Operation: An International Comparison Study* (1975). Cambridge: Harvard University Press.

increases. These average costs decrease over a wide range due to assumed economies of scale. The curve ADC_1 shows othe original average distribution cost of delivering products from a plant. This curve increases throughout because greater sales require marketing to a larger geographic region. The curve ADC_2 shows the average distribution cost after the new infrastructure is put in place. It is everywhere lower than ADC_1, but also rises throughout. ATC_1 and ATC_2 are average total cost curves: these are given by the vertical summation of APC with ADC_1 and ADC_2, respectively. Average total costs reach a minimum at Q_1^* and Q_2^*, where Q_2^* is necessarily larger the Q_1^*, given the stipulated shift in average distribution costs. An increase in plant scale and the extension of service to larger geographic markets are thus indicated.

Problems of implementation, however, are not addressed by this cost curve apparatus. How are the linkages between manufacturing and distribution to be forged? They are not created automatically. If existing middlemen respond in a slow and faltering way to the opportunities that the new transportation and communication infrastructures afford, the stage is set for someone, in this instance the manufacturers, to experiment with new organizational structures.

The issues here are of a transaction cost rather than of a production cost kind. Although a definitive analysis of the 'inadequacies of existing marketers'[70] reported by Chandler would require further research, I conjecture that these distributional difficulties are due to a failure of 'convergent expectations'[71] coupled with the hazards posed by small numbers supply relations between autonomous parties.[72] Convergent expectations problems are mainly attributable to bounded rationality. It was difficult for marketers who were accustomed to operating in a local market regime to perceive the opportunities that awaited them. And there was no obvious way to signal these opportunities by relying upon decentralized pricing.[73] Moreover, even if manufacturers and distributors had both perceived the opportunities that the new transportation and communication infrastructure afforded, and if each responded independently in reliance upon the other, problems of divergence would arise if each recorded or interpreted the data differently. Such divergent expectations would exist, moreover, at both an aggregate and a disaggregate level.

In principle, manufacturers could have taken the initiative and effected convergent expectations by contract. Coordination by contract is costly,

[70] Chandler, *supra* footnote 63, p. 287.

[71] See Malmgren, *supra* footnote 47, pp. 405–11.

[72] For a discussion of these transaction cost issues, see Williamson, *supra* footnote 7, pp. 86–95.

[73] See Malmgren, *supra* footnote 47.

however, where the two parties are bargaining in an unfamiliar situation and the hazards of contracting are great. The hazards to which I refer have been discussed elsewhere in the context of idiosyncratic exchange.[74] Such problems arise when investments in specialized human and/or physical assets are required in order that the transaction be completed in an economical way. With respect to the issues of concern to Chandler, the problems were especially severe when the mass production and sale of consumer or producer durables was contemplated. Distributors here would have to be induced to make specialized (product- and brand-specific) investments and, once made, manufacturers and distributors would thereafter often be dealing with each other in what, essentially, was a bilateral exchange arrangement.[75] Given the hazards of opportunism that arise in such circumstances, both parties were reluctant to rely on autonomous contracting to accomplish the investments and govern a continuing exchange relation.

Forward integration by manufacturers into distribution was the organizational response to these contracting difficulties. Not only were profits realized in the process, but social cost savings resulted. Absent reasons to believe otherwise, net social as well as net private gains accrue when such organizational innovations appear.

B. STRATEGIC BEHAVIOR AND FORWARD INTEGRATION

Chandler's Findings

Chandler assigns long-lasting entry consequences to the forward integration decisions of American manufacturers described above. Thus he observes:

The administrative networks built to integrate the new processes of production and distribution gave the pioneering enterprises their greatest competitive advantage. Although capital intensive in terms of the ratio of capital to labor inputs, the new machinery was not that expensive. The absolute cost of entry [into manufacturing] was not high, nor in most industries were patents a barrier to entry....

The most imposing barrier to entry in these industries was the organization the pioneers had built to market and distribute their newly mass-produced products. A competitor who acquired the technology had to create a national and often a global organization of managers, buyers, and salesmen if he was to get the business away from the one or two enterprises that already stood astride the major marketing channels. Moreover, where the pioneer could finance the building of

---

[74] Williamson, *supra* footnote 7, pp. 60–4; Wachter and Williamson (1978), pp. 549, 556–7.
[75] See Williamson, *supra* footnote 7, pp. 89–95.

the first of these organizations out of cash flow, generated by high volume, the newcomer had to set up a competing network before high-volume output reduced unit costs and created a sizeable cash flow.[76]

A Transaction Cost Interpretation

Four things are noteworthy about Chandler's conclusions. First, entry barriers of the conventional kinds were not, in his judgment, significant. Second, the main barriers were attributable to the linking of manufacturing with distribution. Third, late entrants were at a disadvantage with respect to early entrants not because the latter were able to avoid costs but because of the differential cost-bearing consequences of later entry. This is precisely the matter of temporal cost differences discussed above.[77] Finally, although the linking of manufacturing and distribution arguably had strategic consequences, the original decisions to integrate were not motivated by a strategic purpose. Rather, the resulting entry effects appear to be unintended spillovers.

Such unintended spillovers should be contrasted with predatory pricing or predatory investment, in which a punitive or pre-emptive purpose is clear and an antitrust issue is sharply posed. Should the consequences of benign historical decisions also come under antitrust scrutiny? In addition, should antitrust law attempt to effect remedies for such consequences?

As to the first question, it seems clear that any development, historical or otherwise, that contributes significantly to the creation of durable dominant firms or collusive oligopolies should be identified and analyzed – lest it be unnecessarily repeated. But whether the law should attempt to undo unwanted outcomes that are attributable to once-lawful responses to business opportunities is a more difficult matter. This problem involves a tension between two fundamental values.

The affirmative case for legal intervention is based on the premise that, except when lawful patents are involved or when intervention would result in diseconomies, durable monopoly power of any kind results in direct and indirect economic losses. The direct losses include simple allocative efficiency decrements, due to the excesses of prices over costs, and the reduced vigor of intraindustry rivalry (which may impair both process and product innovation). Indirect losses are of an intergenerational kind, in which later generations find that opportunity sets are sharply circumscribed by earlier events.

---

[76] Chandler, *supra* footnote 63, pp. 298–9.
[77] See text accompanying footnotes 34–56 *supra*.

The essence of Chandler's argument is that a 'first mover' advantage can affect the conditions of entrance later faced by others. A general discussion of this phenomenon can be found in my book 'Markets and hierarchies: Analysis and antitrust implications,' Williamson, *supra* footnote 7, pp. 34–5.

The opposing argument is that penalizing winners is contrary to the spirit of an enterprise system and will impair incentives to innovate. Presumably, however, the strength of these arguments weakens as the period over which monopolistic results remain unchallenged lengthens. Whether the gains from intervention exceed the losses after only five years of uncontested dominance is perhaps doubtful. But indefinite insularity is not obviously optimal. Twelve to fifteen years of unchallenged dominance might well be reasonable,[78] though even this is subject to dispute. Dominant firm outcomes simply pose an unhappy public policy dilemma – a dilemma is made more actue when such outcomes are attributable to pre-emptive signaling and investment.[79]

IV.   A Transaction Cost Critique of the *Schwinn* Decision

The law of vertical restrictions appears to be tentative and unsettled.[80] Its protean character is apparent in the Supreme Court's inconsistent application of legal principles and standards in three cases: *White Motor Co.* v. *United States*,[81] *United States* v. *Arnold, Schwinn & Co.*,[82] and *Continental TV Inc.* v. *GTE–Sylvania Inc.*[83] Of these, *Schwinn* best reflects the hazards of grounding legal decisions in defective economic reasoning. Although *Sylvania* made progress toward remedying some of the mischief created by *Schwinn*, I believe further progress can be made if the transaction cost attributes of vertical restriction cases are developed. The transaction cost approach to antitrust issues applies broadly,[84] and powerfully illuminates matters relating to vertical integration and vertical

[78] At a discount rate of 15%, the discounted values of a dollar earned 12 or 15 years in the future are 19 and 12 cents, respectively. At a 20% discount rate, the corresponding present values drop to 11 and 7 cents. The present value of a project that earns K dollars per year in perpetuity is $7.1K$ if discounted at 15% and $5.5K$ if discounted at 20%. Eighty per cent of these values are realized during the first $11\frac{1}{2}$ and 9 years, respectively. Claims that investment incentives are sharply curtailed if monopoly outcomes are, at some point, subject to challenge should come to terms with this arithmetic.

[79] See Spence, 'Investment strategy and growth in a new market,' *Bell Journal of Economics*, 10 (1979).

[80] See Bork, *supra* footnote 29, p. 171; V. Goldberg, 'The law and economics of vertical restrictions: A relational perspective' (1978) (Unpublished paper on file with the University of Pennsylvania Law Review).

[81] 372 US 253 (1963).

[82] 388 US 253 (1967).

[83] 433 US 36 (1977).

[84] See 'Transaction cost considerations,' *supra* footnote 5, p. 1439.

restraints.[85] With the expectation that systematic criticism of past mistakes aids the process of creating better antitrust law, in this section I will discuss the efficiency and strategic aspects of vertical restraints like those found in *Schwinn*. One of the reasons why inhospitable economic reasoning of the kind that prevailed in *Schwinn* has since been discredited is the growing realization that transaction cost issues that were suppressed then are central – both to *Schwinn* and to a broader understanding of economic organization.

A. TRANSACTION COST EFFICIENCIES

Suppose that a producer has a distinctive good or service and perceives that the public, or some part thereof, will be prepared to purchase it, possibly by paying a premium above the price of substitutes, if the producer can (a) create recognition for the attributes that distinguish the item, (b) maintain quality control with respect to these attributes, and (c) maintain cost control such that the price at which the product will recover its full costs is not prohibitive. Specifically, assume that the distinctive item in question is a bicycle, that distinctiveness takes the form of quality and service, and that the brand name of the bicycle is Schwinn.

If customers were fully knowledgeable or could be apprised without cost of all relevant attributes of all products, Schwinn could simply announce that it was supplying a bicycle that had these properties, the announcement would be registered among potential buyers, customers could verify that these conditions existed (though verification is a redundant operation in a world of complete knowledge), and those who valued the attributes could judge whether the premium was justified. Product differentiation in a world of unbounded rationality would thus proceed in a smooth and faultless manner.

Consumers, however, do not have these high-powered attributes: their capacity to receive, store, recover, and process information is limited. In the light of these limitations, not only does Schwinn face the problem of transmitting its distinctive qualities, but it faces the problem of having its image believed. Thus, if consumers are occasionally misled, in that they are sometimes told one thing and learn to their dismay that it is incorrect, and if instances of fraud or deception are not known without cost to other potential buyers, so that reputations are not instantly and accurately

---

[85] Teece, *supra* footnote 66, pp. 7–25; W. C. Liebeler, 'Integration and competition,' in *Vertical Integration in the Oil Industry*, ed. E. Mitchell (1976) Washington: American Enterprise Institute; Phillips, *supra* footnote 2. Phenomena that other approaches regard with puzzlement, or even hostility, fall naturally into place when vertical relations issues are cast in contracting terms and the properties of alternative contracting modes are examined with rsepect to their transaction cost attributes.

updated, consumers will be wary when sellers apprise them that their brand has 'superior' qualities.

In a market of boundedly rational consumers, Schwinn is faced with three interrelated information problems. First, it needs to bring to the attention of consumers the distinctive attributes that it purports to supply. Second, it needs to provide an institutional infrastructure that will prevent these attributes from being degraded. Third, it needs to accomplish both of these goals in an economical fashion.

Assume that it is uneconomical for Schwinn to mount a massive advertising campaign in which to proclaim the superiority of its product. In addition, assume that, because quality and service are related attributes, Schwinn determines that the most effective way to accomplish its product differentiation objectives is to distribute through authorized dealers who agree, as a condition of franchising, to provide specified minimum services (advertising, assembly, maintaining a stock of bicycles and replacement parts, providing qualified repair personnel, and the like). Inasmuch as these services are costly to provide, Schwinn bicycles sold and serviced by authorized dealers will be priced at a premium, other things being equal.[86] Assume further that Schwinn's product differentiation efforts will be vitiated if this set of minimum services is not reliably provided.[87] Assume finally that Schwinn's franchise program is successful in that, with appropriate franchisee constraints, the image appeals to a sufficient number of customers to make it viable.

Several economic questions now arise. First, which customers will be attracted by such an image? Second, why might Schwinn want to prevent nonfranchised sales? Third, will Schwinn integrate forward into retailing if vertical restraints are not permitted? Each of these poses transaction cost issues.

With respect to customer appeal, the buyers that will be attracted by Schwinn will presumably be those for whom the opportunity cost of time is great or who are relatively inept at self-assembly and service. Thus, high-priced lawyers and other consultants who bill clients on an hourly basis will pay several times the going rate for a haircut, by patronizing barber shops that cut hair by appointment, rather than joining the queue at a wait-your-turn establishment.[88] The argument generalizes to the procurement of consumer durables. Time is economized if the customer does not have to search for a brand possessing the requisite properties and is easily able to locate and visit an outlet where the brand is stocked.

---

[86] Furthermore, the premium will also increase to the extent that Schwinn incurs additional expense at the manufacturing stage in order to accomplish its quality objectives.

[87] Possible causes of this problem are discussed below.

[88] See G. S. Becker, 'A theory of the allocation of time,' *Economics Journal*, 75 (1965), p. 493.

And additional time is saved if the item comes pre-assembled, is reasonably trouble-free, and is reliably serviced at convenient outlets.

Such a brand of bicycle will also be attractive to customers who, though their unit opportunity cost of time may be below average, are particularly inept at self-assembly and repairs. In this situation, despite low unit costs, the total opportunity cost is great – because this is the product of unit cost and time expended. Thus, two classes of customers will respond positively to the Schwinn image: those who are inept and those who, although capable, have a high per-unit opportunity cost of time.

This merely establishes, however, that franchised sales of Schwinn bicycles will appeal to some customers. It does not reach the question whether Schwinn should sell to all comers, allowing dealers to determine whether or not to offer the set of services that would qualify them as franchisees. Were Schwinn to do this, customers who have the above-described attributes would presumably go to the franchised outlet; those who do not could go elsewhere. Because in a world of unbounded rationality, more degrees of freedom – in this instance, more methods of merchandising – are necessarily better than less, the natural policy inclination would be to let consumers decide the question for themselves.

Several justifications, however, can be articulated in support of franchise restrictions: first, the Schwinn quality image may be debased without sales restraints; second, even if quality images are not impaired, the viability of franchises may hinge on sales restraints; third, the costs of enforcing the distribution contracts are increased in a mixed distribution system.[89] The quality image of Schwinn turns partly on objective considerations: Schwinn bicycles bought from authorized dealers come with an assured set of sales and service attributes. But the image may also be affected by information exchanged by word of mouth. If potential customers are told, 'I bought a Schwinn bike and it was a lemon,' but are not advised that the bicycle was bought from a discount house and was misassembled, and that Schwinn's guarantees were thereby vitiated, customer confidence in Schwinn is easily impaired. Put differently, quality reputation may be preserved only if goods and services are sold under conditions of constraint.[90] Note in this connection that the incentive to invest in

[89] Although arguably not applicable to the *Schwinn* case, a fourth justification can be based on unfair allocation of demonstration costs: customers might shop for Schwinn bicycles at the franchised dealer – deciding on what model, features, etc., to buy – and then make their purchase at the discount house, where the costs of demonstration are largely avoided. This may be a more serious concern when more expensive items, such as automobiles, are being marketed.

[90] The fact that 20% of Schwinn's authorized sales were made by outlets – B. F. Goodrich, hardware and department stores – which did not provide service might be taken as 'proof' that the above hazard is insubstantial. See Brief for the United States at 43–4, *United States* v. *Arnold, Schwinn & Co.*, 388 US 365 (1967). But there are three mitigating considerations: (a) while 20% nonserviced sales may be permissible, 40% may not be; (b) the outlets described have reputation attributes rather different from discount houses, and hence may

commercial reputation, by surrounding transactions with institutional infrastructure, occurs only in a world of bounded rationality.[91]

Even if the quality image of franchise sales is unimpaired by nonfranchise selling, the commercial viability of franchisees, which hinges on volume considerations, should be examined. Suppose that it is determined that a franchised dealer needs to sell a minimum number of bicycles in order to break even. Suppose further that Schwinn carefully locates its franchisees cognizant of these break-even needs.[92] Finally, suppose that the system is initially viable but that discount sales subsequently appear. Marginal franchise operators shortly thereafter become nonviable. As a consequence, the assurance of convenient Schwinn service outlets is jeopardized. Customer interest declines and other viable franchisees become marginal. This deterioration, taken together with the impaired quality image described above, creates the risk that the franchise mode will become nonviable, and customers for whom such differentiation yields net gains will be able to deal only in the undifferentiated market.

The third justification for franchise restrictions involves policing costs. The argument here is that it is less costly to police simple systems than it is to police more complicated ones. Causality (responsibility) is difficult to trace (attribute) in complex systems. If few 'excuses' can be offered, fewer veracity checks have to be made. Although I do not suggest that this was a major consideration for Schwinn, it could be relevant to the design of other marketing systems. Again this is a problem only in a world of bounded rationality, because frictionless systems are self-policing.

Consider finally whether Schwinn will integrate forward into retailing if restrictions on sales to nonfranchised outlets are prohibited. If Schwinn's costs of integrated sales were identical with those of its franchisees, this presumably would occur. There are several reasons, however, to believe the case to be otherwise. First, franchised dealers were not exclusively engaged in the sales and service of Schwinn bicycles; other brands were also handled.[93] Also, many franchisees engaged in nonbicycle sales. Assuming that multiple brand and multiple product sales are necessary

---

'stand behind' sales more completely; and (c) business judgment on such matters is entitled to a certain degree of undisputed respect.

[91] True attributes are presumably known or can be ascertained without cost in a world of unbounded rationality. If this boggles the mind, the reader is encouraged to examine the once-for-all time-cum-environmental bidding procedures in J. E. Meade's *The Controlled Economy* (1971), London: Allen & Unwin.

[92] This is altogether to be expected. Franchisors will ordinarily auction off franchise locations where greater than competitive returns are expected unless such auctions are costly to run.

[93] Schwinn required its franchisees to display Schwinn bicycles 'with position equal to and as prominent as that of any competitive bicycle.' Brief for Arnold, Schwinn & Co., Appendix 1, at 57 n.89, *United States* v. *Arnold, Schwinn & Co.*, 388 US 365 (1967).

for distributors to break even, forward integration would require Schwinn to engage in unwanted and possibly unavailable sales activities.[94] Diversification into other products with which Schwinn had no expertise or familiarity is the unwanted activity. Stocking other brands, moreover, might pose difficulties of availability, as other bicycle manufacturers might suspect, with cause, that their brands would be slighted and demeaned if sold by Schwinn employees.

Furthermore, even if disabilities of these kinds did not exist, the question still remains whether Schwinn could provide incentives for managers of integrated sales outlets that prompt performance equal to that when franchising is used. Both carrot and stick considerations must be addressed. The incentive disabilities associated with bureaucratic modes of organization[95] stand as a further impediment to forward integration by Schwinn.

The upshot is that if the worst consequences obtain (namely that the franchise system collapses, Schwinn is unable to integrate forward economically, and the Schwinn brand image vanishes), prohibiting franchise restraints gives rise to real economic losses of the kind shown in figure 6.2. The demand curve for Schwinn bicycles is here given by $p_2 = g(q_2; \bar{p}_1)$, where $\bar{p}_1$ is the price at which other bicycles sell (which is taken as given). The curve AC_2^f is the average cost of sales and service for franchised outlets. As drawn, franchising just breaks even (covers all of its costs, including a fair rate of return) at a price and quantity of p_2^*, q_2^*, respectively. Assuming that the costs of supplying nondifferentiated bicycles are not increased by Schwinn franchising, the net welfare gains (losses) realized by offering (withdrawing) the Schwinn brand will be given by the shaded consumer surplus region.

B. THE ABSENCE OF STRATEGIC EFFECTS

Having established the transaction cost efficiencies that may be derived from a restrictive franchise arrangement, the next step of the analysis invovles an inquiry into whether the franchise system promotes anticompetitive effects. Specifically the question is whether Schwinn, by itself or in conjunction with other large bicycle manufacturers, introduced vertical

---

[94] Alternatively, Schwinn could run the distribution stage at a loss. However, it is doubtful that profits from manufacturing would be sufficient to cover these losses. See text accompanying footnotes 15–26 *supra*. For a discussion of the disincentives to integrate forward into distribution, see Preston, 'Restrictive distribution arrangements: Economic analysis and public policy standards,' *Law and Contemporary Problems*, 30 (1965), pp. 506, 512.

[95] See Williamson, *supra* footnote 7, pp. 118–29.

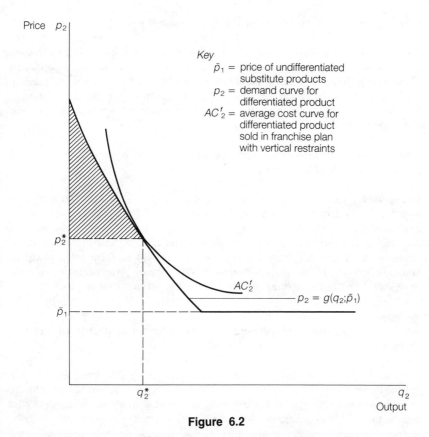

Figure 6.2

restraints that placed rivals or customers at a strategic disadvantage.[96] The Government plainly regarded these restraints as anticompetitive and its jurisdictional statement advanced the following theory of the case:

> In industries in which products are highly differentiated, a particular brand – like Schwinn bicycles – often has a market of its own, within which [intrabrand] competition is highly important to the consumer and should be preserved.... Schwinn's strenuous efforts to exclude unauthorized retailers from selling its bicycles suggest that, absent these restraints, there would be a broader retail distribution of these goods with the resulting public benefits (including lower price) of retail competition.[97]

[96] The Supreme Court recognized the relevancy of such an inquiry in *White Motor Co.* v. *United States*, 372 U 253, 263 (1963) ('economic and business stuff' out of which restraints arose and their 'actual impact' are relevant to determining the existence of an antitrust violation).

[97] Jurisdictional Statement for the United States at 14, *United States* v. *Arnold, Schwinn & Co.*, 388 US 365 (1967).

Similar views were repeated in the Government's brief:

The premise of the Schwinn franchising program is that Schwinn is a distinctive brand which commands a premium price – that it enjoys, in other words, a margin of protection from the competition of other brands. To the extent that this premise is sound, it is clear that the only fully effective control upon the retail price of Schwinn bicycles is that imposed by competition among Schwinn dealers and distributors.[98]

The government also disclosed the animosity with which it regarded product differentiation:

Either the Schwinn bicycle is in fact a superior product for which the consumer would willingly pay more, in which event it should be unnecessary to create a quality image by the artificial device of discouraging competition in the price of distributing the product; or it is not of premium quality, and the consumer is being deceived into believing that it is by its high and uniform retail price. In neither event would the manufacturer's private interest in maintaining a high-price image justify the serious impairment on competition that results.[99]

And the Government expressed its view about the merits of vertical integration as compared with vertical restraints:

Even if the threat to integrate were not wholly lacking in credibility in the circumstances of this case, we would urge that it was not a proper defense to the restraint of trade charge. In the first place, a rule that treats manufacturers who assume the distribution function themselves more leniently than those who impose restraints on independent distributors merely reflects the fact that, although integration in distribution may sometimes benefit the economy by leading to cost savings, agreements to maintain resale prices or to impose territorial restrictions of unlimited duration or outlet limitations of the type involved here have never been shown to produce comparable economies.[100]

The Government's views on product differentiation and franchise restraints thus can be reduced to the following three propositions: (a) differentiated products can be classed as those for which a price premium is warranted and those for which such a premium is not; (b) whether differentiation is real or contrived, intrabrand price competition is essential

---

[98] Brief for the United States at 26, *United States* v. *Arnold, Schwinn & Co.*, 388 US 365 (1967).
[99] Ibid., p. 47.
[100] Ibid., p. 50.

to the protection of consumer interests; and (c) although vertical integration sometimes yields economies, the same cannot be said for vertical restraints. Each of these premises is significantly flawed and for that reason the government's anticompetitive effect argument should have failed.[101]

The Government's first premise, that it is 'unnecessary to create quality images' for products that are objectively superior to those of rivals, depends upon an assumption of unbounded rationality. Plainly, however, customers are not endowed with perfect cognitive processes. Accordingly, efforts to 'assist' customers and thereby economize on bounded rationality, have merit. Reliability images serve this purpose. Inasmuch as the Schwinn franchising program did not entail exclusive dealing, neither actual rivals nor potential rivals could be said to have experienced any adverse effects. Suppose, however, for purposes of argument, that exclusivity had been involved. The matter of anticompetitive effect then turns on Schwinn's market share and the conditions of entry. The Government's brief, however, is devoid of any attention to market structure.

The simple facts are these: Schwinn's market share, which had been 22 per cent in 1951, the year before it introduced its disputed marketing program, fell steadily in the decade that followed, dropping to 13 per cent in 1961.[102] Schwinn plainly was not a dominant firm at any time during this interval.

[101] Posner, who 'briefed and argued the *Schwinn* case for the government,' contends that his analysis of the issues at that time 'reflected the then prevailing thinking of the economics profession on restricted distribution.' Posner, *supra* footnote 57, p. 3. Although I agree that there was (and is) economic thinking congenial to the views set out in the *Schwinn* brief, I would hesitate to characterize it as that of the economics profession. Inasmuch as the brief is inexplicit about the sources of its economic reasoning (Preston's is the only economics article dealing with vertical restraints that is cited in the brief. Brief for the United States at 49, *United States* v. *Arnold, Schwinn & Co.*, 388 US 365 (1967), and Preston expressly discusses a series of legitimate economic purposes that can be served by vertical restraints, see Preston, *supra* footnote 53, pp. 507–19), because Telser's work on the rationality of restraints was in the public domain at that time, see Telser, *supra* footnote 26; Telser, 'Abusive trade practices: An economic analysis,' *Law and Contemporary Problems*, 30 (1965), p. 488, and because I expressly took exception with the brief while it was in preparation, Posner's attribution may sweep too broadly.

[102] The following table shows the market shares of the four largest firms and of foreign imports in the bicycle industry during the period of 1951 to 1961:

Market shares of four largest domestic producers and of foreign imports, 1951–1961

	Four largest domestic producers %	Foreign imports %
1951	63	8
1953	52	22
1955	34	40
1957	46	28
1959	49	28
1961	49	30

Source: Brief for Arnold, Schwinn & Co., Appendix 1, at 8, n.21, *United States* v. *Arnold, Schwinn & Co.*, 388 US 365 (1967).

What then of the possible existence of a tight oligopoly in which the main firms all employed exclusive franchising? Although concentration in the bicycle industry was in the high–moderate range in 1951, the four-firm concentration ratio then being 63 per cent, the decade following was one of intense competition. Foreign imports, which accounted for 8 per cent of the market in 1951, rose to a high 40 per cent in 1955. The escape clause to the GATT agreements was invoked in August, 1955,[103] and bicycle imports thereafter dropped – remaining in the neighborhood of 30 per cent in the years that followed.[104]

Not only did the market share of the four largest firms fall sharply over this interval, but there was considerable shifting of market shares among them. Schwinn, which was the largest firm with 22 per cent of the market in 1951, dropped to second place with 13 per cent of the market in 1961. AMF, the second-place firm in 1951 with 16 per cent of the market, dropped to third with 8 per cent of the market in 1961. The third-place firm in 1951, Columbia, dropped to fifth place in 1961, the respective market shares being 12 and 5 per cent. However, Murray, the fourth-place firm in 1951, jumped from a 12 per cent position to a 22 per cent position in 1961, taking over first place in the process.[105] Four established bicycle producers were acquired during the decade, two of them by AMF, a large, diversified producer of consumer and industrial products.[106] The record thus discloses active competition among extant domestic producers and with foreign rivals.

Finally, the Government's third premise that intrafirm restraints (vertical integration) are less objectionable than interfirm restraints, because vertical integration often yields offsetting economies that do not accrue when interfirm relations are restrained, is simply naive. As developed above,[107] vertical market restrictions in this and other markets can often yield economies. Furthermore, vertical integration is not a cost panacea.[108] The hostility of the Government to interfirm trading restrictions reflects a bias in favor of bureaucratic, as opposed to market, modes of organization

---

[103] General Agreement on Tariffs and Trade, 30 Oct. 1947, art. XIX, 61 Stat. pts. 5 & 6, TIAS No. 1700. The escape clause was invoked by the United States on 19 August 1955, to raise the rate of duties on bicycles imported into the United States. GATT Doc. L/433 (1955), reported in *General Agreement on Tariffs and Trade, Analytical Index*, 2d rev. (1966), p. 104.

[104] Brief for Arnold, Schwinn & Co., at 5 n.15, *United States v. Arnold, Schwinn & Co.*, 388 US 365 (1967).

[105] See footnote 102 *supra*.

[106] Brief for Arnold, Schwinn & Co., at 2 n.5, *United States v. Arnold, Schwinn & Co.*, 388 US 365 (1967).

[107] See text accompanying footnotes 12–30 & 86–94 *supra*.

[108] See Williamson, *supra* footnote 7, pp. 82–131.

that it not only unwarranted but inimical to social welfare.

In summary, the franchise restrictions which Schwinn introduced not only had a plausible efficiency justification, but, in addition, no anticompetitive effects could possibly be attributed to them. They were not part of an exclusive dealing program; Schwinn's market share was too small, by itself, to warrant antitrust concern even if exclusivity had been involved; rivals did not engage in franchising, much less exclusive dealing; and the bicycle market was characterized by active competition. Where actual competition is, and arguably will continue to be, effective, concern over potential competition is misplaced. The Government's case against Schwinn was wholly fanciful.

V. Approaches Alternative to the Transaction Cost Approach

With the exception of the inhospitability tradition referred to above, the leading alternatives to the transaction cost approach are partly or mainly complementary to it. None, however, deals as comprehensively with the central issues posed by vertical restrictions, and hence none is an adequate substitute.

A. THE INHOSPITABILITY TRADITION

Proponents of the inhospitability tradition eschew reliance on common law reasoning and emphasize real or imagined effects instead.[109] Not only is there no presumption that business practices are ordinarily motivated by efficiency purposes, but this possibility is not even actively considered. Instead, attention is focused on the possibility that some anticompetitive effect, however remote, might be connected with the practice in question. This type of orientation and reasoning is hostile to an enterprise mode of organization and commonly results in bad public policy arguments and outcomes.[110]

B. THE POPULIST APPROACH

The populist approach favors attention to fairness and relies little on economic analysis. Some of those who advocate the populist approach seem to regard economic analysis as not merely unhelpful but ill-advised. Thus the populist approach has been characterized by Professor Sullivan as one that regards allocative efficiency as 'useless as a guide to antitrust

---

[109] See text accompanying footnote 28 *supra*.
[110] See, e.g., *United States* v. *Arnold, Schwinn & Co.*, 388 US 365 (1967); *Brown Shoe Co.* v. *United States*, 270 US 294 (1962).

policy.'[111] Values other than efficiency are instead assigned a decisive role:

During the eighty-odd years that antitrust has been with us, there have been ebbs and flows of interest in enforcement, all correlated with other developments in national life. The values which, until very recently, have shown themselves most strongly in the expression of policy have been populist in origin, and have had such aims as the transfer of wealth and power from industrial interests to agrarian ones, the decentralization and dispersion of economic and related political power, the preservation of a commerce and industry open to entry by small entrepreneurs, the reduction of prices, and the prohibition of unfair competitive tactics.[112]

Sullivan's argument against the use of partial equilibrium welfare economics is that considerations of 'second best' demonstrate that efficiency claims are pointless.[113] The reduction of price distortions in one sector when they remain in others is 'just as likely to ... make allocations worse – or to leave allocations as bad as they are' as it is to yield an efficiency gain.[114]

Although this is a common interpretation of the second best literature,[115] it is not a correct one. To demonstrate that a local correction can yield a global loss in the face of distortions elsewhere in an existence argument.

[111] Sullivan, Book Review, *Columbia Law Review*, 75 (1975), p. 1214.
[112] Ibid.
[113] Sullivan's premise is that '[t]he standard theoretical demonstration of the allocative efficiency of a competitive market as contrasted to a monopolized market ... has no welfare implications except as part of a general equilibrium analysis.' Sullivan, *supra* footnote 111, p. 1219 (footnote omitted). Thus, '[t]he theoretical conclusion that consumer welfare (as measured by the aggregate amounts consumers will pay for goods and services) will be improved when a monopoly market is converted (without loss of scale economies) into a competitive one is warranted only if it is presupposed, first, that all other industries are already competitively organized, and, second, that there exist no other deviations from optimality....' Ibid., p. 1219. From this premise Sullivan reasons that '[a]bsent the simultaneous fulfillment of all conditions of optimum allocation ... *economic theory tells us nothing about how to improve resources allocations....* Economics simply provides no basis on which to say, for example, that ending monopoly in the shoe industry or ending a price cartel in the electrical equipment industry (or doing both of these things) will improve resource allocations and increase aggregate welfare. Given the persistence of other deviations (other monopolies, cartels, tariffs, and distorting taxes), there is no basis for assuming that doing away with any one or more deviations from optimality would improve efficiency at all.' Ibid., p. 1220 (emphasis in original).
[114] Sullivan, *supra* footnote 111, p. 1220 (emphasis added).
[115] As Bork notes, the theory of second best 'does not address itself to the probability of the bad result, but merely states it as a possible outcome.' Bork, *supra* footnote 34, p. 113. Consequently, to take the 'possibility of second best as destroying the rationality of the consumer welfare basis of the law (which it does not) and therefore freeing the courts to evolve new rules on other social and political values ... is little short of preposterous.' Ibid., p. 114.

It says nothing about likelihood, which is a much stronger statement. Sullivan's leap from an existence to a likelihood claim is unwarranted. As Baumol points out, the policy importance of second best qualifications turns on the strength of interdependence: '[A] great many interrelationships within the economy are weak enough to be ignored. Thus, for all practical purposes, the demand for most goods is likely to be dependent only on the demands for a few other items. . . . It may, then, be possible to partition the economy more effectively than some might have suspected.'[116] Strong interaction effects then can be taken expressly into account, and elsewhere the second best qualification deserves the weight that lawyers label 'de minimis.'

Additionally, Sullivan's comments appear to be restricted entirely to price distortions (due to 'monopolies, cartels, tariffs, asnd distorting taxes'[117]). But allocative inefficiency is more apt to arise with respect to cost concerns, such as diseconomies of scale, failure to operate assets in a least cost way, and the incurring of significant transaction costs. Organizational changes that give rise to cost savings in any of these respects will, if not accompanied by offsetting price distortions, invariably yield social gains. Thus Sullivan both overstates the weight to be assigned to second best arguments in evaluating relative price distortions and makes no allowance for allocative efficiency analysis in the matter of cost savings.

A further problem with this approach is that it easily links up with the inhospitability tradition, in which anticompetitive purpose is found lurking behind every business initiative. The populist approach has the advantage, however, of calling attention to the merits of process in a way that other approaches do not. Although this last is often disregarded, it is the distinctive strength of the populist orientation. As Richard Zeckhauser observes in his discussion of 'The Importance of Process,' '[m]any analysts dismiss too quickly the significance of having an equitable and widely accepted process.'[118] For many societal decisions, 'the procedure by which the decision is made may be as important as the actual dollar numbers employed. . . . [Consequently] monies available for other goods may give a wholly unrealistic impression of welfare. How people feel about the society in which they are living matters a tremendous amount.'[119]

To be sure, process values are not easily quantified and even the qualitative aspect may be disputed. When one is close to the margin, however, process considerations can frequently be used to break ties. Moreover, in circumstances in which fairness is thought to be a central

---

[116] W. J. Baumol, 'Informed judgment, rigorous theory and public policy,' *S. Econ. J.*, 32 (1965), pp. 137, 144.
[117] R. Zeckhauser, 'Procedures for valuing lives,' *Pub. Pol'y* 23 (1975), pp. 419, 446.
[118] Ibid.
[119] Ibid., p. 459.

issue, process values ought to be assigned even greater weight. Lest arguments in favor of dispersed economic power be used or manipulated irresponsibly, however, claims of this kind ought to be reserved for circumstances in which they are plainly important. Again, *Brown Shoe Co.* v. *United States* illustrates the hazards of relying on such arguments when the facts of a case are inapposite.[120]

C. THE STRUCTURE–CONDUCT–PERFORMANCE APPROACH

The structure–conduct–performance approach also complements the transaction cost approach. Recall that although the transaction cost approach employs an efficiency presumption, this can be rebutted by a showing of strategic purpose and effect.[121] The latter showing requires a demonstration that the industry in question is characterized by a dominant firm or collusive oligopoly. This entails an examination of conventional structure and conduct relations.

The preoccupation of the structure–conduct–performance paradigm with technological features, however, has been self-limiting. Vertical integration, which is principally a transaction cost phenomenon, remained a puzzle for so long precisely because of this technological orientation.[122] For this reason, the structure–conduct–performance paradigm served to reinforce the orientation of the inhospitability tradition – because if transaction cost economies are unimportant, the suspicion that novel business practices are motivated by anticompetitive purposes is easy, indeed natural, to entertain. Recent contributions to this approach,[123] however, have moved away from this technological orientation.

D. NEW MODELING APPROACHES

Opportunism was, until recently,[124] mainly disregarded in formal models of economic processes, but this has been changing. A convergence between the transaction cost issues that I emphasize and formal strategic analysis seems to be developing. How far this convergence will go remains to be seen. My sense accords with Simon, who argues that 'qualitative institutional analysis, in which discrete structural alternatives are compared' can frequently proceed by relying on 'only rather modest and simple applications of mathematical analysis.'[125] At the same time, however, I am both encouraged and greatly impressed by the quality of rigorous

---

[120] 370 US 294 (1962).
[121] See text accompanying footnotes 27 and 28 *supra*.
[122] See Liebeler, *supra* footnote 85.
[123] See, e.g., Caves and Porter, *supra* footnote 48.
[124] See text accompanying footnote 19 *supra*.
[125] Simon, *supra* footnote 17, pp. 6–7.

modeling that is being done on the matter of strategic behavior. Even if formal analysis merely confirms qualitative institutional arguments, it is useful to express the same arguments in different languages. And frequently I expect that formal models will yield sharper and sometimes additional implications.[126]

E. THE NONSTRATEGIC TRADITION

What I refer to as the nonstrategic tradition is the important stream of antitrust research that traces its origins to Aaron Director's teaching and research at the University of Chicago. Prominent examples are Bork and Bowman and, more recently, Posner. As I have indicated elsewhere, antitrust specialists in law and economics owe an everlasting debt to this tradition, which has insisted that complex policy matters be assessed in a tough-minded economic fashion in which the rudimentary issues are stated in stark microeconomic terms. Logical errors of less rigorous antitrust reasoning have been exposed in the process and a deeper appreciation for the economic benefits of purportedly anticompetitive practices has been manifested.

The principal problems that I find in this approach are that its proponents often disregard transaction costs and rarely concede that strategic considerations sometimes operate. These are clearly interrelated: if transaction costs are zero or negligible, strategic intentions are beside the point, because they can have no effect, and the simple microtheory model applies. Examples of this 'friction-free' approach are Bowman's views on price discrimination[127] and Bork's views on vertical market restrictions.[128]

With respect to price discrimination, the friction-free view is that, perverse elasticity conditions excepted, allocative efficiency gains will result if a monopolist is permitted to price discriminate.[129] The argument depends on the assumption that discrimination, in whatever degree attempted, is costless to effectuate. Once allowance is made for the transaction costs of discovering differential valuations among customers and enforcing restrictions against resale (so that there can be no arbitrage), however, this allocative efficiency claim is much more problematical.[130] Simple sensitivity to bounded rationality (which explains the inability of

---

[126] See, e.g., Dixit and Norman, 'Advertising and welfare,' *Bell Journal of Economics*, 9 (1978), p. 1; Nelson and Winter, 'Forces generating and limiting concentration under Schumpeterian competition,' *Bell Journal of Economics*, 9 (1978), p. 524; Schmalensee (1978), p. 305.

[127] See generally W. Bowman, *Patents and Antitrust Law: A Legal and Economic Appraisal* (1973) Chicago: University of Chicago Press.

[128] R. Bork, *supra* footnote 34, pp. 280–98.

[129] See W. Bowman, *supra* footnote 127, pp. 111–13.

[130] For an elaboration, see Williamson, *supra* footnote 7, p. 113.

the monopolist to assess differing customer valuations without cost) and the hazards of opportunism (whence the need to police against resale) are the missing ingredients in the friction-free tradition.

The possibility that vertical restraints and strategic objectives are linked is also resisted by the nonstrategic tradition.[131] Although Bork acknowledges that exclusionary purposes occasionally operate, his discussion of these matters reduces them to insignificance.[132] A broader view in which transaction costs are expressly acknowledged demonstrates that strategic behavior may occur in a wider range of circumstances than his discussion discloses. If the logic of this broader view is adopted – under which the possibilities of human asset and capital market frictions of the kinds that I decribe are admitted – the question then is whether Bork's position on the lawfulness of vertical restrictions ought to prevail because the frictions that I describe are quantitatively unimportant and too insubstantial to influence the enforcement of the law on vertical restrictions. My response to this is as follows: (a) I have attempted to delimit the objectionable subset of restrictive practices more carefully than had been done previously; (b) as a consequence, Bork and I differ in a serious way only with respect to the use of exclusive dealing in dominant firm industries; (c) I am not persuaded that the effects of the frictions that I discuss are insubstantial in this context, and Chandler's historical survey suggests otherwise; and (d) until the transaction cost attributes of these markets are studied more fully and the basis for my concerns and Chandler's are expressly allayed, the discriminating application of the law along the lines that I propose is the prudent posture to take.

VI. Conclusion

Antitrust is an interdisciplinary field that is best served by acknowledging that a deeper understanding of the issues will result by addressing the subject from several points of view. The economic approach that I favor, especially for dealing with vertical market relations, is the transaction cost approach. The principal points of this chapter and the legal principles that result from the systematic application of transaction cost analysis to vertical restraints are summarized below.

A. ECONOMIC IMPLICATIONS OF THE TRANSACTION COST APPROACH

1   As with the integration of successive intermediate product market

---

[131] See text accompanying footnotes 34–44 *supra*.
[132] Bork, *supra* footnote 34, pp. 320–4.

stages, vertical restrictions between manufacturing and distribution are primarily to be understood in transaction cost terms.

2 Despite striking similarities, there are also important differences between these two types of vertical relationships. The differences arise because the interests of final consumers as well as those of distributors have to be considered in designing the interface between manufacturing and distribution.

3 Contrary to the inhospitability tradition, contractual constraints can and often do serve legitimate economic purposes. Specifically, vertical constraints may be needed lest subgoal pursuit by the individual parts destroy the viability of the system.

4 Contrary to the inhospitability tradition, product differentiation can and often does promote consumer welfare. The feasibility of differentiation, moreover, may depend on the use of constraints at the manufacturer–distributor nexus.

5 The principal hazard that should concern the antitrust enforcement agencies in enforcing the law on vertical restrictions is if restraints are introduced with the strategic purpose and effect of disadvantaging rivals. Exclusive dealing restraints by dominant firms or tight oligopolies can have this effect.

6 Economies defenses should be entertained before exclusive dealing restrictions are prohibited.

7 Whether one is interested in assessing the vertical relations that govern a specific interface, as in *Schwinn*, or in understanding the historical evolution of vertical relations, such as the transformation that occurred in response to infrastructural changes late in the nineteenth century, the same microanalytic approach in which transaction costs are featured should apply.

That the errors that appeared in the Government's jurisdictional statement and brief in *Schwinn* are not repeated today suggests to me that antitrust law has made real progress. I submit, moreover, that this is partly because there is now a greater sensitivity to transaction cost considerations.[133]

[133] Turner and Posner were both instrumental in persuading the Supreme Court to reverse itself in *Continental TV, Inc.* v. *GTE–Sylvania Inc.*, 433 US 36 (1977). Posner's reservations with the *Schwinn* doctrine appeared in 1977. See Posner, *supra* footnote 57. Turner participated in an amicus brief with attorneys for the Motor Vehicle Manufacturers Assocation. The brief argues, among other things, that 'the "new economics of vertical relations" is increasingly illuminating the economies that can be achieved by manufacturer influence on dealer practices.' Motion for Leave to File Brief and Brief for Motor Vehicle Manufacturers Association as Amicus Curiae, at 24, *Continental TV, Inc.* v. *GTE–Sylvania Inc.*, 433 US 36 (1977) (quoting Philips, *supra* footnote 2, p. 574) (footnote omitted).

B. LEGAL IMPLICATIONS OF THE TRANSACTION COST APPROACH

Federal agencies charged with enforcing antitrust law should rely on the foregoing economic principles when implementing enforcement policy. Vertical market restrictions should be assumed to be efficiency enhancing unless specific structural characteristics exist within the industry. Exclusive dealing is the only vertical restraint posing the threat of strategic hazards. Absent the existence of a dominant firm or a tight oligopoly within an industry,[134] vertical restrictions of all kinds, exclusive dealing included, should be assumed to promote transaction costs economies.

When the industry is characterized by a dominant firm or tight oligopoly, antitrust agencies and courts should subject exclusive dealing constraints, but not other vertical restrictions, to close scrutiny to ascertain whether they create barriers to entry. A firm in such a situation should not be charged with nor found to have committed an antitrust violation if it can affirmatively show that nontrivial transaction cost economies are created by the vertical restraint under scrutiny.[135]

Finally, uniform reliance on vertical restrictions of any kind – on price, territories, customers, or exclusive dealing – in industries marked by tight oligopolies should be subject to close scrutiny to determine whether the restriction regularizes trade and promotes greater interdependence. Again, firms in such a situation should not be charged with nor found to have committed an antitrust violation if they can affirmatively demonstrate that nontrivial transaction cost economies are achieved by the vertical restraint under scrutiny.

---

[134] See footnote 50 *supra*.

[135] A rigorous demonstration of these economies is not apt to be feasible. But more than a showing that some economies are plausibly realized should be required. For a discussion of economies as an antitrust defense, see generally Williamson, 'Economies defense,' *supra* footnote 5.

Note that Posner proposes an output test – 'did the manufacturers' output increase or decrease after imposing the restriction?' – to get at these issues. Posner, *supra* footnote 57, p. 19. (An equivalent test would be to examine the effect on price.) Ordinarily, however, I would expect that output and price effects would be distributed over time and confounded by many other factors. The elaborate econometric investigation that Posner contemplates to sort these out does not appear to me to be feasible.

The basic issues, if exclusive dealing is to be prohibited, are what transaction cost economies does exclusive dealing promote and whether the sacrifice of these will be significant. These matters ought ordinarily to be amenable to examination in qualitative and crude quantitative terms.

7

Assessing Contract

A general framework for assessing contract is herein proposed and applied to contractual puzzles of two kinds. What factors are responsible for vertical restrictions and related restraints on trade that are of concern to antitrust? When ought 'impossibility' and related contrat doctrines be grounds for discharging a contract?

What Ronald Coase (1972) characterized as the applied price theory approach to industrial organization maintained that restraints on trade had monopoly origins. As discussed below, this was not a wholly unified perspective; there were and are several monopoly variants within this tradition. Differences among them notwithstanding, all were informed by the then prevailing (and still robust) firm-as-production-function orientation. Technolology was thus held to be largely determinative of firm and market organization.

Contract doctrines that permit excuse from strict performance were originally explained by reference to fairness. As Karl Llewellyn (1931) put it, 'When we approach constructive conditions bottomed on the unforeseen, not agreement, but fairness is the goal of the inquiry. This holds of impossibility, and of frustration; it holds of mistake' (p. 746). More recently, however, impossibility and related doctrines have been interpreted with reference to efficient risk bearing.

Dismay is sometimes registered over the readiness with which economists have invoked monopoly to explain restrictive trade practices: 'If an economist finds something – a business practice of one sort or another – that he does not understand, he looks for a monopoly explanation' (Coase, 1972, p. 67). Not only was this too easy – since any inventive economist could always discover some monopoly purpose, however remote or insubstantial, lurking somewhere – but it discouraged efforts to investigate whether the business practice in question had other origins (as well or instead).

The chapter was presented and benefited from the ensuing discussion at the Conference of Law, Economics, and Organization at Yale University in October 1984. Support from the Sloan Foundation is gratefully acknowledged.
Journal of Law, Economics, and Organization, vol. 1 (1) (Fall 1985).

The same is true of the readiness with which efficient risk-bearing arguments are invoked. To be sure, important features of economic organization are unarguably crafted in response to differential risk aversion and capacities to bear risk. But if there is a good deal more to economic organization than this, then when an economist finds somethings – a business or legal practice of one sort or another – that he does not understand, he ought not to rest content with an efficient risk-bearing explanation.

The possibility that nonstandard business practices often arise in the service of efficiency – specifically, of economizing on transaction costs – was the neglected alternative to which Coase (1972) called attention. The intervening years have witnessed successive efforts to operationalize this approach by ascertaining the factors that are responsible for the previously neglected 'costs of running the economic system.'[1] I submit, moreover, that this approach has relevance not merely to restrictive trade practices but applies to the study of economic organization overall. The possibility that excuse from strict enforcement is warranted because of 'contractual failures' that have transaction cost origins thus warants scrutiny.

This chapter attempts to set out the rudiments of the transaction cost economics approach to contract; to compare related approaches to contract in which some but not all of the key features of the transaction cost economics approach are preserved; to display the main differences within and between alternative monopoly and efficiency approaches to restrictive trade practices in a single contractual framework; and to assess contractual doctrines relating to excuse (for which the aforementioned efficient risk-bearing treatments have already been advanced) from a transaction cost economics point of view.

I. Transaction Cost Economics

A variety of economic lenses can be and have been applied to the study of contract. The Chicago School has relied extensively on the lens of price theory (Posner, 1979). The lens of property rights affords another illuminating perspective. I address issues of contract mainly through the lens of transaction cost economics. Such an approach to the study of economic organization was urged by Ronald Coase in his classic 1937 paper, 'On the nature of the firm.' Although Coase lamented, 35 years later, that this approach had not taken root (Coase, 1972), Vernon Smith was persuaded that economic orthodoxy was spent and boldly predicted that a new microtheory would appear which 'will, and should, deal with the foundations of organization and institution, and this will require us

---

[1] The phrase originates with Kenneth Arrow (1969, p. 48).

to have an economics of information and a more sophisticated treatment of the technology of transacting' (1974, p. 321).

Implementing such a program can take a variety of forms. What I refer to here as transaction cost economics adopts John R. Commons's proposal that the transaction be made the basic unit of analysis. Attention is focused on economizing efforts that attend the organization of transactions – where a transaction occurs when a good or service is transferred across a technologically separable interface. One stage of activity terminates and another begins. With a well-working interface, as with a well-working machine, these transfers occur smoothly. In mechanical systems we look for frictions: do the gears mesh, are the parts lubricated, is there needless slippage or other loss of energy? The economic counterpart of friction is transaction cost: do the parties to the exchange operate harmoniously, or are there frequent misunderstandings and conflicts that lead to delays, breakdowns, and other malfunctions? Transation cost analysis supplants the usual preoccupation with technology and steady-state production (or distribution) expenses with an examination of the comparative costs of planning, adapting, and monitoring task completion under alternative governance structures.

As compared with other approaches to the study of economic organization, transaction cost economics: (a) is more microanalytic; (b) is more self-conscious about its behavioral assumptions; (c) introduces and develops the economic importance of asset specificity; (d) relies more on comparative institutional analysis; (e) regards the business firm as a governance structure rather than a production function; and (f) places greater weight on the *ex post* institutions of contract, with special emphasis on private ordering (as compared with court ordering). The underlying viewpoint which informs the comparative study of issues of economic organization is this: transaction costs are economized by assigning transactions (which differ in their attributes) to governance structures (the adaptive capacities and associated costs of which differ) in a discriminating way.

A. BEHAVIORAL ASSUMPTIONS

Behavioral assumptions are often regarded casually, almost a matter of convenience. This is sometimes justified by the view that social scientists who play hardball will emphasize what really counts – which, after all, are the refutable implications (Friedman; Baiman). This orientation has been variously disputed, but none more effectively than Nicholas Georgescu-Roegen's prescription for serious science. He contends that 'the purpose of science in general is not prediction, but knowledge for its own sake' (1971, p. 37). He nevertheless insists that prediction 'is the touchstone of scientific knowledge' (p. 37). Lest reasoning become speculative and undisciplined, prediction necessarily plays a central role. But greater respect for behavioral assumptions is introduced if knowledge rather than prediction drives scientific inquiry.

Much of Frank Knight's work on economic organization is in this spirit. He argued that the study of organization needed to be informed by an appreciation for 'human nature as we know it' (1965, p. 270), with special reference to the condition of 'moral hazard' (p. 260). And Percy Bridgeman reminded social scientists that 'the principal problem in understanding the actions of men is to understand how they think – 'how their minds work' (1955, p. 450). Coase more recently remarks that 'modern institutional economics should start with real institutions. Let us also start with man as he is' (1984; p. 231). Coase urges in this connection that the view of man as a 'rational utility maximizer' should be abandoned (1984, p. 231), but the salient attributes of 'man as he is' otherwise remain undescribed.

I have previously argued that contracting man is distinguished from the orthodox conception of maximizing man in two respects. First, his ability to receive, store, retrieve, and process information is strictly limited. Second, contracting man is given to self-interest seeking of a deeper and more troublesome kind than his economic man predecessor.

Although it is sometimes believed that Herbert Simon's notion of bounded rationality is alien to the rationality tradition in economics. Simon actually enlarges rather than reduces the scope for rationality analysis. Thus the economic actors with whom Simon is concerned are '*intendedly* rational, but only *limitedly* so' (1961, p. xxiv). Both parts of the definition warrant respect. An economizing orientation is elicited by the intended rationality part of the definition, while the study of institutions is encouraged by acknowledging that cognitive competence is limited: 'It is only because individual human beings are limited in knowledge, foresight, skill, and time that organizations are useful investments for the achievement of human purpose' (Simon, 1957, p. 199).

It is sometimes argued that bounded rationality is merely a convoluted way of stating that information is costly. Once this has been acknowledged, maximizing modes of analysis can deal with all of the issues with which bounded rationality is concerned. There is something to be said for this: as Simon observes, a large 'plot of common ground is shared by optimizing and satisficing analysis' (1978, p. 8, n. 6). Although one might, on grounds of parsimony, recommend that 'we prefer the postulate that men are reasonable to the postulate that they are supremely rational when either one of these assumptions will do' (Simon, 1978; p. 8), it is easy to understand how others can decide differently. Working within an extended neoclassical framework is not a benefit that will be sacrificed lightly.

As Richard Nelson and Sidney Winter (1982) argue, however, fundamental tensions remain:

There is ... a fundamental difference between a situation in which a decision maker is uncertain about the state X and a situation in which the decision maker has not given any thought to whether X matters or not, between a situation in which a prethought event judged of low probability occurs and a situation in which something occurs that never has been thought about.... Most complex models of maximizing choice do not come to grips with the problem of bounded rationality. Only metaphorically can a limited information model be regarded as a model of decision with limited cognitive abilities. (pp. 66–7)

Maximizing analysis can deal with much, but not with the entire landscape with which bounded rationality is concerned.[2]

Transaction cost economics pairs the assumption of bounded rationality with a self-interest seeking assumption that makes allowance for self-interest seeking with guile. This allows economic agents to disclose information in a selective and distorted manner. Calculated efforts to mislead, disguise, obfuscate, and confuse are thus admitted. This self-interest seeking attribute is variously described as opportunism, moral hazard, and agency. As discussed below, problems of contract and, more generally, of economic organization are vastly complicated by this condition.

B. DIMENSIONS

Having adopted the transaction as the basic unit of analysis, the question is, what are the principal dimensions with respect to which transactions differ? If some transactions are organized in one way and other transactions are organized in another, underlying differences in the attributes of transactions are presumably contributing factors.

The principal dimensions on which transaction cost economics presently relies for purposes of describing transactions are (a) the frequency with which they recur; (b) the degree of uncertainty to which they are subject; and (c) the condition of asset specificity (Williamson, 1979, 1985). The latter two are of special importance for the purposes of this chapter.

As discussed elsewhere (Williamson, 1985), different kinds of uncertainty need to be distinguished. Suffice it to say here that all long-term contracts are necessarily incomplete (fail to make express provision for all future contingencies) if human agents are subject to bounded rationality and if contracts are executed under conditions of uncertainty. The central

---

[2] A further point which deserves mention is the temptation – to which maximizing analysis sometimes yields – of dealing with toy problems. This is not a necessary consequence. It is nevertheless common, upon acknowledging that information is costly, to press ahead with the formal analysis rather than examine the factors that are responsible for this condition. Especially for an understanding of contract, the underlying costliness conditions are often the key features.

problem with which transaction cost economics is concerned is thus posed: How, in the face of *ex ante* contractual incompleteness, are effective adaptations to changing circumstances to be implemented?

The condition of asset specificity has reference to what, in the legal literature, is often referred to as reliance investments. These are investments in which the full productive values are realized only in the context of an ongoing relation between the original parties to a transaction. Put differently, such assets cannot be transferred to alternative uses or users without loss of productive value (Klein et al., 1978). Parties who are engaged in a trade that is supproted by nontrivial investments in transaction-specific assets are effectively operating in a bilateral trading relation with one another. Harmonizing the contractual interface that joins the parties, thereby effecting adaptability and promoting continuity, becomes the source of real economic value.

II. Contractual Schematics

My examination of contract in this section proceeds in two parts. The first contrasts alternative conceptions of the process of contract and relates these to the two behavioral attributes and to the condition of asset specificity discussed above. The second describes a general schema for examining contract in which interactions between technology, prices, and governance are all joined.

A. CONTRACT AS PROCESS

The world of contract is variously described as one of planning, promise, competition, and governance (or private ordering). Which of these descriptions is most applicable depends on the behavioral assumptions which pertain to an exchange and on the economic attributes of the good or service in question.

Thus assume that uncertainty is present in nontrivial degree and consider the ramifications for contract of differences in bounded rationality, opportunism, and asset specificity. Assume, in particular, that each of these conditions can take on either of two values: either it is present in significant degree (denoted +) or it is presumed to be absent (denoted 0). Consider the three cases in which only one of these factors is presumed to be absent and then that in which all three are joined. Table 7.1 shows the four conditions to be compared and the contracting model that is associated with each.

The case where parties are opportunistic and assets are specific but economic agents have unrestricted cognitive competence essentially describes the mechanism design literature (Hurwicz, 1972, 1973; Myerson,

Table 7.1 Contracting models

Behavioral Assumption		Asset specificity	Implied contracting process
Bounded rationality	Opportunism		
0	+	+	Planning
+	0	+	Promise
+	+	0	Competition
+	+	+	Governance

+   Present in significant degree
0   Presumed to be absent

1979; Harris and Townsend, 1981). Although the condition of opportunism requires that contracts be written in such a way as to respect private information, whence complex incentive alignment issues are posed, all of the relevant issues of contract are settled at the *ex ante* bargaining stage. Given unbounded rationality, a comprehensive bargain is struck at the outset, according to which appropriate adaptations to subsequent (publicly observable) contingent events are fully described. Contract execution problems thus never arise – or defection from such agreements is deterred because court adjudication of all disputes is assumed to be efficacious (Baiman, 1982; p. 168). Contract, in the context of unbounded rationality, is therefore described as a world of planning.

Consider alternatively the situation where agents are subject to bounded rationality and transactions are supported by specific assets, but the condition of opportunism is assumed to be absent. This last implies that the word of an agent is as good as his bond. Thus although gaps will appear in these contracts, because of bounded rationality, these do not pose execution hazards if the parties take recourse to a self-enforcing general clause. Each party to the contract simply pledges at the outset to execute the contract efficiently (in a joint profit-maximizing manner) and to seek only fair returns at contract renewal intervals. Strategic behavior is thereby denied. Parties to a contract thus extract all such advantages as their endowments entitle them when the initial bargain is struck. Thereafter, contract execution goes efficiently to completion because promises of the kind described above are, in the absence of opportunism, self-enforcing. Contract, in this context, reduces to a world of promise.

Consider then the situation where agents are subject to bounded rationality and are given to opportunism, but asset specificity is presumed to be absent. Parties to such contracts have no continuing interests in the identity of one another. This describes the world where discrete market contracting is efficacious, where markets are fully contestable,[3] where franchise bidding for natural monopoly goes through. Inasmuch as fraud and egregious contract deceits are deterred by court ordering,[4] contract, in this context, is described by a world of competition.

Each of these conceptions fails when bounded rationality, opportunism, and asset specificity are joined. Planning here is necessarily incomplete (because of bounded rationality), unguarded promise predictably breaks down (because of opportunism), and the pair-wise identity of the parties now matters (because of asset specificity). This is the world of governance. Since the efficacy of court ordering is problematic, contract execution falls heavily on the institutions of private ordering (Kronman, 1985). This is the world with which transaction cost economics is concerned. The organizational imperative that emerges in the circumstances is this: organize transactions so as to economize on bounded rationality while simultaneously safeguarding them against the hazards of opportunism. Such a statement supports a different and larger conception of the economic problem than does the imperative 'maximize profits!'

B. A SIMPLE CONTRACTING SCHEMA

I take as given that the parties to a contract are subject both to bounded rationality and to opportunism. Accordingly, concepts of contract as either planning or promise are disallowed. The condition of asset specificity, however, is regarded as variable. It will be useful for this purpose to expand the concept of governance to include competition as one of the possible alternatives. In particular, competition is the appropriate governance structure for the case where assets are fully redeployable ($k = 0$).

The object of the exercise in this subsection is to display the systematic relations that obtain between technology, governance, and the price under which product is supplied. Albeit rudimentary, failure to acknowledge the interactive nature of these three features has been responsible for

---

[3] Differences between transaction cost economics and 'contestability theory' (Baumol, Panzer and Willig, 1982) in asset specificity respects are noteworthy. Both approaches to the study of economic organization acknowledge the importance of asset specificity, but they view it from opposite ends of the telescope. Thus contestability theory reduces asset specificity to insignificance, whence hit-and-run entry is easy. Transaction cost economics, by contrast, magnifies the condition of asset specificity. It maintains that durable, firm-specific assets are widespread, in which case hit-and-run entry is often not feasible. For recent assessments of contestability theory, see Michael Spence (1983) and W. G. Shepherd (1984).

[4] The assumption that court ordering is efficacious in a regime of bounded rationality, and opportunism is plainly gratuitous, but it is the maintained assumption nonetheless.

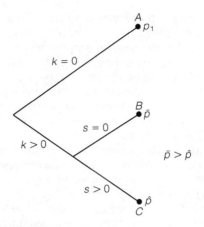

Figure 7.1 A simple contracting schema

repeated confusion in earlier treatments of contract where these are treated in a piecemal way.[5]

Assume that a good or service can be supplied by either of two alternative technologies. One is a general purpose technology; the other is a special purpose technology. The special purpose technology requires greater investment in transaction-specific durable assets and is more efficient for serving steady-state demands.

Using k as a measure of transaction-specific assets, transactions that use the general purpose technology are ones for which $k = 0$. When transactions use the special purpose technology, by contrast, a $k > 0$ condition obtains. Assets here are specialized to the particular needs of the parties. Productive values would therefore be sacrificed if transactions of this kind were to be prematurely terminated. The bilateral monopoly condition described above and elaborated elsewhere applies to these.

Whereas classical market contracting – the discrete contracting ideal – suffices for transactions of the $k = 0$ kind, unassisted market governance poses hazards whenever nontrivial transaction-specific assets are placed at risk. Parties have an incentive to devise safeguards to protect investments in transactions of the latter kind. Let s denote the magnitude of any such safeguards. An $s = 0$ condition is one in which no safeguards are provided; a decision to provide safeguards is reflected by an $s > 0$ result.

Figure 7.1 displays the three contracting outcomes corresponding to this description. Associated with each node is a price. To facilitate comparison between nodes, assume that suppliers are risk neutral, are

---

[5] See my discussions of the confusions that arise upon failure to assess contracts in their entirety (Williamson, 1983).

prepared to supply under either technology, and will accept any safeguard condition whatsoever so long as an expected breakeven result can be projected. Thus node A is the general purpose technology ($k = 0$) supply relation for which a breakeven price of p_1 is projected. The node B contract is supported by transaction-specific assets ($k > 0$) for which no safeguard is offered ($s = 0$). The expected breakeven price here is $\bar{p}$. The node C contract also employs the special purpose technology. But a safeguard is employed in this instance ($s > 0$), whence the breakeven price, $\hat{p}$, at node C is less than $\bar{p}$.

The protective safeguards to which I refer nromally take on one or more of three forms. The first is to realign incentives, which commonly involves some type of severance payment or penalty for premature termination. A second is to create and employ a specialized governance structure for referring and resolving disputes. The use of arbitration, rather than litigation in the courts, is thus characteristic of node C governance. A third is to introduce trading regularities which support and signal continuity intentions. Expanding a trading relation from unilateral to bilateral exchange – through the concerted use, for example, of reciprocity – thereby to effect an equilibration of trading hazards is an example of this last. If, despite best efforts, nonstandard contracting still experiences great governance strains, market contracting may eventually be supplanted by unified ownership (vertical integration). Transaction cost economics thus maintains the premise that 'in the beginning there were markets' and that internal organization is adopted not immediately but only when contracts (comparatively) fail.[6]

This simple contracting schema applies to a wide variety of contracting issues. It facilitates comparative institutional analysis by emphasizing that technology (k), contractual governance/safeguards (s), and price (p) are fully interactive and are determined simultaneously. Vertical integration,[7]

---

[6] This market-favoring presumption is a device by which to set comparative analysis in motion. Since transactions need to be located somewhere, why not start in markets and, if problems develop, see what can be done to mitigate the difficulties and keep them there. To be sure, one could start instead with internal organization and ask what disabilities it experiences. Transaction could then be moved into markets because of the (comparative) failures of internal organization. Originating transactions in markets comes more naturally to economists and is favored by the differential development of the market failure in relation to the bureaucratic failure literature. For efforts to treat the latter, see Williamson (1975, chapter 7; 1985, chapter 6).

[7] My first efforts to address these matters were in the context of vertical integration (Williamson, 1971). For a related discussion, see Klein, et al. (1978). John Stuckey's examination of joint ventures and vertical integration in the aluminum industry demonstrates the merits of the microanalytic approach. Also see studies by Monteverde and Teece (1982) and by Masten (1984). Although many students of economic organization have only limited interest in vertical integration, it turns out to be a paradigm problem.

labor market organization,[8] regulation,[9] corporate governance,[10] reciprocity and vertical restraints on trade,[11] and even family organization[12] turn out to be variations on a theme. As Friedrich Hayek observed, 'Whenever the capacity of recognizing an abstract rule which the arrangement of these attributes follows has been acquired in one field, the same master mould will apply when the signs for those abstract attributes are evoked by altogether different elements' (1967, p. 50).

By the way of summary, the nodes A, B, and C in the contractual schema set out in figure 7.1 have the following properties:

1   Transactions that are efficiently supported by general purpose assets ($k = 0$) are located at node A and do not need protective governance structures. Discrete market contracting suffices. The world of competition obtains.

2   Transactions that involve significant investments of a transaction-specific kind ($k > 0$) are ones for which the parties are effectively engaged in bilateral trade.

3   Transactions located at node B enjoy no safeguards ($s = 0$), on which account the projected breakeven supply price is great ($\bar{p} > \hat{p}$). Such transactions are apt to be unstable contractually. They may revert to node A [in which event the special purpose technology would be replaced by the general purpose ($k = 0$) technology] or be relocated to node C (by introducing contractual safeguards that would encourage the continued us of the $k > 0$ technology).

4   Tranactions located at node C incorporate safeguards ($s > 0$) and thus are protected against expropriation hazards.

5   Inasmuch as price and governance are linked, parties to a contract should not expect to have their cake (low price) and eat it too (no safeguard). More generally, it is important to study contracting in its entirety. Both the *ex ante* terms and the manner in which contracts are thereafter executed vary with the investment characteristics and the associated governance structures within which transactions are embedded.

---

[8] See Williamson, Wachter, and Harris (1975); Wachter and Williamson (1978); and Williamson (1984a).
[9] See Williamson (1976); Goldberg (1976); Joskow and Schmalensee (1983); and Palay (1985).
[10] See Fama and Jensen (1983); Williamson (1984b); and FitzRoy and Mueller (1985).
[11] See Williamson (1979); Goldberg (1980); Klein and Leffler (1981); Williamson (1983); and Kenney and Klein (1983).
[12] See Ben-Porath (1980); Pollak (1983).

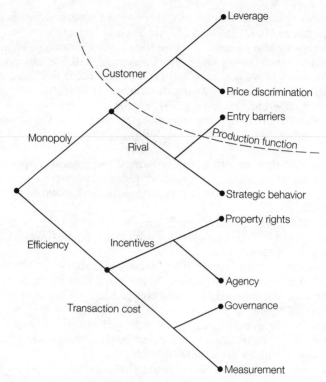

Figure 7.2 Cognitive map of contract

III. Restrictive Trade Practices: Monopoly and Efficiency
Approaches to Contract

The field of specialization with which transaction cost economics is most
closely associated is that of industrial organization. A number of the
leading approaches to the study of industrial organization and the relation
that transaction cost economics bears to them are examined here.

Industrial organization examines contract in terms of the purposes
served. What are the parties trying to accomplish? Nonstandard forms of
contracting – customer and territorial restrictions, tie-ins, block booking,
franchise restrictions, resale price maintenance, exclusive dealing, and the
like – are of special interest. Here as elsewhere in industrial organization,
monopoly and efficiency purposes are usefully distinguished. The partition-
ing shown in figure 7.2 begins with this distinction.

A. THE MONOPOLY BRANCH

All of the approaches to contract shown in figure 7.2, monopoly and efficiency alike, are concerned with the same puzzle: What purpsoes are served by supplanting classical market exchange – whereby product is sold at a uniform price to all comers without restriction – by more complex forms of contracting (including nonmarket modes of economic organization)? The monopoly approaches ascribe departures from the classical norm to monopoly purpose. The efficiency approaches hold that these departures serve economizing purposes instead.

The four monopoly approaches to contract are grouped under two headings. The first examines the uses of contractual restraints in relation to buyers. The second is concerned with the impact of such practices on rivals.

The leverage theory of contract and the price discrimination interpretation of nonstandard contracting both focus on buyers. Richard Posner (1979) associates leverage theory with the (earlier) Harvard School and price discrimination with the Chicago School approaches to antitrust economics. Leverage theory maintains that original monopoly power can be extended and that nonstandard contracting practices accomplish this. Although leverage theory is largely discredited among economists, it maintains an appeal to many lawyers[13] and continues to find its way into legal briefs[14] and court opinions.[15]

The price discrimination approach to nonstandard contracting maintains that original monopoly power is unchanged. Price discrimination is merely a means by which latent monopoly power is actualized. This interpretation of nonstandard contracting has been advanced by Aaron Director and Edward Levi (1956) in conjunction with tie-in sales and by George Stigler (1963) in relation to block booking. Tie-in sales and block booking are purportedly devices by which sellers are able to discover underlying product valuation differences among consumers and monetize consumers' surplus.

The other two monopoly approaches examine nonstandard contracting

---

[13] Louis Kaplow's recent effort to resuscitate it locates leverage theory in an intertemporal context. This is more promising, but it is not the applied price theory context in which it was originally presented. Kaplow's leverage arguments are more usefully regarded as part of the developing literature on strategic behavior – on which I have little to say here but regard as much more instructive than the earlier monopoly traditions. For a discussion, see Williamson (1982).

[14] See, for example, the Amicus brief prepared by Lawrence A. Sullivan in support of the respondent in *Monsanto Company* v. *Spray-Rite Service Corporation*.

[15] Although the majority opinion in *Jefferson Parish Hosp. Dist. No.2* v. *Hyde* (44CCH S. Ct. Bull., P.) reaches the correct result, it also muddies the opinion by passing reference to leverage theory.

practices in relation to rivals. These are expressly concerned with the enlargement of monopoly power by large established firms in relation to smaller actual or potential rivals. The barriers to entry literature, which is prominently associated with the work of Joe Bain (1956), is in this tradition. The early work in this area has come under considerable criticism, much of it originating with the Chicago School. The main problems with the early work are that it was static and did not carefully identify the essential preconditions for entry barrier arguments to go through. The more recent literature on strategic behavior relieves many of the objections.[16] Investment and information asymmetries are expressly introduced. Intertemporal attributes are recognized and reputation effect features are developed. The use of nonstandard contracting as a means of 'raising rivals' costs' (Salop and Scheffman, 1983) is an especially intriguing possibility.

The recent strategic behavior literature excepted, all of the monopoly approaches to contract work within the neoclassical framework, in which the firm is regarded as a production function. Inasmuch as the natural boundaries of the firm are therein defined by technology, any effort by the firm to extend its reach by recourse to nonstandard contracting was presumed to have monopoly purpose and effect.[17] This 'applied price theory' approach to industrial organization was the prevailing postwar orientation. As Coase observed (1972, p. 61), it informed both of the leading industrial organization texts – the one by Joe Bain (1958) and the other by George Stigler (1968). Public policy toward business was massively influenced by this approach. Examples here are legion. None, however, displays the pervasive influence of production thinking better than the Government's confusion over the merits of vertical restraints as compared with vertical integration, as expressed in *Schwinn*:[18]

Even if the threat to integrate were not wholly lacking credibility in the circumstances of this case, we would urge that it was not a proper defense to the restraint of trade charge. ... A rule that treats manufacturers who assume the distribution function themselves more leniently than those who impose restraints on independent distributors merely reflects the fact that, although integration in distribution may sometimes lead to cost savings, agreement to maintain resale prices or to impose territorial restrictions of unlimited duration or outlet limitations

---

[16] These matters are surveyed in Williamson (1982).

[17] To be sure, it can be argued that price discrimination is efficient, which it ordinarily is if it can be effected at zero transaction cost and if income distribution effects wash out. The zero transaction cost assumption is rarely warranted, however. Private and social valuations of price discrimination can yield contradictory results for this reason (Williamson, 1975, pp. 11–13).

[18] Brief for the United States at 50, *United States* v. *Arnold, Schwinn & Co.*, 388 US 365 (1967).

of the type involved here have never been shown to produce comparable economies.

Evidently those who briefed the Government's case[19] were persuaded that economies of a production function kind (economies of scale, economies of scope) were real but that to exercise control over distributors through contractual restraints could only have pernicious monopoly purpose and effect. The predisposition to favor monopoly explanations, which Coase had attributed to economists, was thus shared by antitrust enforcement officials as well. The production function conception of the firm, which held that the natural boundaries between firms and markets were a parameter (defined mainly by technology) – hence did not need to be assessed or derived – was virtually determinative of this result.

Much of the strategic behavior literature, by contrast, is more closely associated with the governance structure conception of the enterprise. To highlight this important monopoly distinction, the dashed curve (denoted *PF*) in figure 7.2 separates the earlier production function approaches from the more recent strategic conception of contract.

B. THE EFFICIENCY BRANCH

Most of what may be referred to as the new institutional economics is located on the efficiency branch of contract. The efficiency branch of contract distinguishes between those approaches in which incentive alignments are emphasized and those which feature economies of trans-action costs. The incentive alignment literature focused on the *ex ante* side of contract. New forms of property rights and complex contracting are thus interpreted as efforts to overcome the incentive deficiencies of simpler property rights and contracting traditions. Ronald Coase (1960), Armen Alchian (1961, 1965), and Harold Demsetz (1966, 1969) are prominently associated with the property rights literature.[20] Leo Hurwicz (1972; 1973); Michael Spence and Richard Zeckhauser (1971); Stephen Ross (1973); Michael Jensen and William Meckling (1976); and James Mirrlees (1976) opened up the agency approach.[21]

The property rights literature emphasized that ownership matters, where the rights of ownership of an asset take three parts: the right to use the asset; the right to appropriate returns from the asset; and the right to change the form and/or substance of an asset (Furubotn and Pejovich; 1974, p. 4). Upon getting the property rights straight, it is commonly

---

[19] The principal architects of the Government's brief were highly sophisticated antitrust specialists, Richard posner and Donald Turner. Each has since changed his position.
[20] For a recent survey, see Louis DeAlessi (1983). For an earlier survey, see Eirik Furubotn and Svetozar Pejovich (1974).
[21] For a recent survey, see Stanley Baiman (1982).

assumed (often implicitly; sometimes explicitly) that asset utilization will thereafter track the purposes of its owners. This will obtain if (a) the legally sanctioned structure of property rights is respected, and (b) human agents discharge their jobs in accordance with instructions.[22]

Thus, whereas the monopoly branch of contract interprets nonstandard forms of exchange as having monopoly purpose and effect, the property rights literature would inquire whether mistaken property rights assignments were responsible for resource misallocations. Redescribing property rights, possibly in complex (nonstandard) ways, is what explains contractual irregularities. In other words, discrete market contracting is supplanted by more complex forms of contracting because this is the way residual rights to control can be placed in the hands of those who can use these rights most productively.

The agency literature, particularly the early agency literature, emphasizes that principals contract in full awareness of the hazard that contract execution by agents poses. Although the separation of ownership from control attenuates profit incentives, this is anticipated at the time that separation occurs and is fully reflected in the price of new shares (Jensen and Meckling, 1976). The future therefore holds no surprises; all of the relevant contracting action is packed into *ex ante* incentive alignments.

Actually, as Michael Jensen's influential survey points out (1983), this literature has actually developed in two parts. He refers to the one branch as the positive theory of agency. Here, capital intensity, degree of specialization of assets, information costs, capital markets, and internal and external labor markets are examples of factors in the contracting environment that interact with the costs of various monitoring and bonding practices to determine the contractual forms' (Jensen, 1983, pp. 334–5). Thus described, numerous commonalities appear between this branch of the agency literature and the governance branch of transaction costs described below. Jensen refers to the second type of agency literature as that of 'principal-agent' (1983, p. 334). This relatively mathematical literature features *ex ante* incentive alignments in superlative degree. It has come to be known more recently as the mechanism design approach. This line of research is akin to the earlier contingent claims contracting

---

[22] The recent treatment of vertical integration by Sanford Grossman and Oliver Hart (1984) illustrates both of these propositions. Thus they view asset ownership as control over residual rights: 'Each asset will have a single owner and that owner has the right to control the asset in the case of a missing [contractual] provision' (p. 7). They further contend that the owner of physical assets 'can order plant employees' to utilize these assets in accordance with his directions (p. 17). Differences between market organization and vertical integration are thus entirely attributed to the asset ownership differences which distinguish them.

literature[23] but moves beyond it by admitting contracting complications in the form of private information. Complex problems of incentive alignment are posed (which the contingent claims contracting literature had ignored) if full and candid disclosure of private information cannot be assumed. In other respects, however, the mechanism design and contingent claims contracting literature are very similar: both resolve all of the relevant contracting issues in a comprehensive *ex ante* bargain,[24] and both assume that court ordering is efficacious.[25] Again, efficiency rather than monopoly purposes drive the argument.

The transaction cost literature also maintains the rebuttable presumption that nonstandard forms of contracting have efficiency purposes. Greater attention is shifted, however, to the contract execution stage. As shown in figure 7.2, the transaction cost approach is split into a governance branch and a measurement branch. Both are important and, in fact, are interdependent.

In common with the property rights literature, transaction cost economics agrees that ownership matters. It furthermore acknowledges that *ex ante* incentive alignments matter. But whereas the property rights and mechanism design approaches operate within the tradition of legal centralism, transaction cost economics disputes that court ordering is efficacious. Attention is shifted instead to private ordering. What institutions are created with what adaptive, sequential decision-making and dispute settlement properties? To ownership and incentive alignment, therefore, transaction cost economics adds the proposition that the *ex post* support *institutions* of contract matter.

James Buchanan has argued that 'economics comes closer to being a "science of contract" than a "science of choice" ... [on which account] the maximizer must be replaced by the arbitrator, the outsider who tries to work out compromises among conflicting claims' (1975, p. 229). The

---

[23] Mervyn King characterizes the Arrow-Debreu model as follows: 'Commodities are distinguished not only by physical and spatial characteristics, and by the date at which the commodity is made available, but also by the "state of the world" in which it is delivered. A "state of the world" is defined by assigning values to all the uncertain variables which are relevant to the economy ... and comprises a complete list of all these variables. These states of the world are mutually exclusive, and together form an exhaustive set .... Commodities are now defined as contingent on the occurrence of certain events, and the market system comprises markets in all these contingent commodities' (p. 128).

[24] The mechanism design literature assumes that the parties to a contract have the cognitive competence to craft contracts of unrestricted complexity. In effect, the parties to a contract have unbounded rationality (see Bengt Holmstrom, 1983). By contrast with the property rights literature, the mechanism design approach holds that 'since each party's obligation to the other is completely specified for every state of nature, there are no residual rights of control over assets to be allocated' (Grossman and Hart, 1984, p. 7). Complex contracts are not concerned therefore with residual rights but with getting the obligations defined at the outset – due provision for private information having been acknowledged.

[25] See Baiman (1982, p. 168).

governance approach adopts the science of contract orientation but joins the arbitrator with an institutional design specialist. The object is not merely to resolve conflict in progress but also to recognize potential conflict in advance and devise governance structures which forestall or attenuate it.

Transaction cost economics maintains that it is impossible to concentrate all of the relevant bargaining action at the *ex ante* contracting stage. Instead, bargaining is pervasive – in which case the institutions of private ordering and the study of contracting in its entirety take on critical economic significance. The behavioral attributes of human agents, whereby conditions of bounded rationality and opportunism are joined, and the complex attributes of transaction (with special reference to the condition of asset specificity) are responsible for this condition.

The measurement branch of transaction cost economics is concerned with performance or attribute ambiguities that are associated with the supply of a good or service. The Alchian–Demsetz (1972) treatment of technological nonseparabilities (team organization) is an example. The issues have since been addressed by William Ouchi (1980), with respect to the organization of markets. A recent interesting application is the study of Roy Kenney and Benjamin Klein (1983) of what they refer to as 'oversearching.' They take exception to Stigler's view that block booking has monopoly (price discrimination) purposes and argue instead that it serves to economize on measurement costs.

Breaking out of the production function framework as it does, the transaction cost approach leads to a very different interpretation of the contractual restrictions to which the Government objected in *Schwinn*. Indeed, since the strategic hazards in *Schwinn* were negligible (market shares were too small to effect foreclosure; there was no collective action), and since the restrictions arguably contributed to the integrity of the franchise mode of distribution (an $s > 0$ result), the Government's arguments were wholly inapposite.[26] Attributing monopoly purpose where there could be none and disregarding possible transaction cost benefits were to be expected of antitrust contract analysis, however, so long as the monopoly predisposition ruled.

More recent assessments of restraints on trade acknowledge that both monopoly and efficiency are sometimes served. The easy cases, of course, are those where one of these purposes predominates. Identifying the pre-conditions that most favor monopoly in relation to efficiency (or the reverse) is now feasible and will permit the polar cases to be distinguished. Considering the primitive state of our knowledge, however, mixed cases will sometimes arise for which an unambiguous net assessment will sometimes be impossible. Candid ambiguity is nonetheless to be preferred

---

[26] For an elaboration, see Williamson (1979).

to the mistaken clarity of the monopoly era.

IV.   Commercial Impossibility[27]

Contract doctrines of commercial impossibility have been interpreted from both fairness and efficiency points of view. Llewellyn's views on fairness were cited at the outset. Richard Posner and Andrew Rosenfield appeal not to fairness but to efficient risk bearing in their examination of this doctrine. They observe that whereas the law could treat each failure to perform 'by reason of an unforeseeen or at least unprovided-for event' as a breach of contract, thereby assigning the risk to the promisor, it could also excuse the failure and 'discharge the contract, thereby in effect assigning the risk to the promisee' (1977, p. 83). Efficient discharge, they contend, 'should be allowed where the promisee is the superior risk bearer; if the promisor is the superior risk bearer, nonperformance should be treated as a breach of contract' (p. 84).

The analysis here also adopts an efficiency orientation. The emphasis, however, is not on a firm-to-firm comparison of risk bearing but on the transaction cost ramifications of contract doctrines which permit discharge. Also, whereas the examples discussed by Posner and Rosenfield mainly have reference to one-time events, those with which I am concerned involve significant investments in durable transaction-specific assets. Continuity of the relation is valued for this class of transactions. These are the same transactions that are of concern to Richard Speidel in his recent examination of court-ordered contract adjustment.

The mine-mouth coal contracts to which Joskow (1985) refers, which have a typical duration of 25 to 50 years, are plainly of this kind. The long-term contract between Alcoa and Essex Wire, whereby Alcoa agreed to supply molten aluminum ingot to a plant that Essex Wire located near an Alcoa facility, is another illustration (Speidel). The Westinghouse agreements to supply uranium fuel to a large number of electric utilities is a third example (Joskow, 1977).[28] How does transaction cost economics have a bearing on the choice between strict enforcement and court-ordered adjustment when unanticipated circumstances intrude that place one of the parties (usually the seller) to such contract under severe stress – in the *Westinghouse* case amounting to billions of dollars?

My treatment of these issues is comparative and does not pretend to

---

[27] The discussion of commercial impossibility in this section is related to and relies upon earlier treatments of these matters by Paul Joskow (1977) and Richard Speidel (1981).

[28] The asset specificity in the mine-mouth and aluminum supply contracts involved site specificity. The investments for uranium supply are of the dedicated-asset kind. For discussion of asset specificity in its various forms, see Williamson (1983; p. 526; 1985, chapter 4).

be dispositive. As discussed earlier, the transaction cost approach to economic organization always proceeds in comparative terms. Choices are made among alternatives, all of which are 'defective' if judged with reference to a frictionless ideal. My purpose here is merely to ascertain whether previously neglected transaction cost features should be taken into account in shaping public policy in this area.

The argument is in five parts. I begin with a precontract analysis of alternative modes of economic organization. I then examine the ramifications of long-term contracting in a regime of strict enforcement whereby parties are relieved under claims of impracticability only if they have made contractual provision for it. The use of contract doctrine to permit excuse is then considered. Enforcement problems of effecting adjustment under both strict and excuse regimes are addressed next. An overview of the argument is then attempted.

A. PRECONTRACT ANALYSIS OF ALTERNATIVE MODELS OF ECONOMIC ORGANIZATION

The comparative institutional approach to economic organization regards both the mode of organization and the choice of technology as decision variables. By contrast, noncomparative analysis typically takes both as given. If, however, one mode/technology pair for accomplishing a task experiences severe difficulties, a superior result can often be realized by making changes in one or both.

Thus suppose that long-term contracts for a good or service that are supported by significant investments in transaction-specific assets are thought to pose severe hazards. What are the main alternatives for getting the job done?

One possibility is to preserve the technology and shift to a governance structure that is believed to be less hazardous. Vertical integration is often adopted for this reason. An electric generating plant, for example, could integrate backward into mine-mouth coal supply. Such backward integration is not always feasible, however.[29] Even where feasible, moreover, the adaptive benefits of vertical integration must be weighed against its incentive disabilities.[30]

Another alternative is to sacrifice the transaction-specific technology in favor of a more general purpose technology. This corresponds to a shift from the $k > 0$ to the $k = 0$ branch on the contractual schema in figure

---

[29] Backward integraton by electric utilities into the supply of uranium fuel would not be economical unless first the electric utilities were reorganized, possibly through a gigantic horizontal merger – which poses problems of its own.

[30] The issues here are rather involved. I have addressed them elsewhere (Williamson, 1985, chapter 6).

7.1. For example, rather than use mine-mouth coal, which poses the aforementioned contracting costs (or is subject to the incentive limits of vertical integration), the electric utility could use petroleum fuel as its thermal source. Inasmuch as little transaction-specific investment is required to supply refined petroleum, a bilateral dependency between buyer and supplier would not develop. Large numbers of suppliers being available both at the outset and at the contract renewal interval (which interval can now be short), adaptive, sequential decisions can be made here under the aegises of competition.

The first lesson of transaction cost economics for the study of contract doctrine, therefore, is that it does not suffice to show that one doctrine is superior to another in a context where technology and governance structures are regarded as parametric. Doctrines that encourage parties to employ inferior (but less hazardous) technologies or to abandon markets in favor of hierarchies come at a high cost.

A comprehensive assessment of these matters is enormously ambitious, however. Except for brief remarks later, it will simplify matters to assume that technology is given and that market organization will be employed and to focus on previously unremarked transaction cost consequences of the contract doctrines relating to commercial impossibility.

B. STRICT ENFORCEMENT

The main trade-off with which economic organization is beset is that incentives for cost economizing or demand enhancement can often be intensified only at the sacrifice of adaptability features of the relation. Cost plus contracting, which is highly adaptable but has weak incentive properties, is an example. To be sure, inferior modes of organization can sometimes be identified for which improvements in both respects can be realized. The move from the functional to the multidivisional form of organization was arguably of this kind (Chandler, 1966; Williamson, 1975; chapter 8). Limits, however, are eventually reached. The use of high-powered incentives (such as strict transfer pricing rules) in the multidivisional enterprise, for example, can limit adaptability.

Suppose, for the purposes of this subsection, that contracts will be strictly enforced at the insistence of either party. Since long-term contracts are unavoidably incomplete, how will the parties deal with unanticipated contingencies? One possibility is to make no adaptation whatsoever. Despite misalignment, business is continued as usual. A second is to accommodate to the needs of one another in an informal, uncontested reciprocal manner. But what if the shock to the system is really great? If one party asks to be relieved from 'business as usual' and the other party refuses to accommodate, what then?

The obvious way to deal with such an impasse is to recognize the potential in advance and create a machinery to deal with it. An agreement to submit such disputes to an arbitrator is an illustration. Certainly this weakens incentives. But presumably the parties regard the adaptability gains as more than offsetting.

Suppose, however, that the parties consciously refuse to create an arbitration machinery. Evidently the contingencies which would warrant such relief are thought to be too remote, or the costs of arbitration too great, or the incentive impairments too severe. Strict enforcement, despite its adaptive limitations, may nevertheless survive a comparative institutional test. For contract doctrine to declare otherwise and permit adjustment in these circumstances undermines both the integrity of contract and the purposes of the parties.

This is plainly a reasonable view of contract. It suffers, however, from three unremarked disabilities: gambling incentives, possible information disparities, and unintended cost escalation. Enforcement ramifications also warrant remark. Consider these seriatim.

The gambling incentives of a regime of strict enforcement can be addressed in two parts. The first is that a decision not to attenuate outliers by contract may sometimes reflect a preference for gambling. The issue here is whether the game of commerce should be available to play for such purposes. The second and more troublesome part is that those who make the decision to gamble may be gambling with other peoples' resources. Suppose, for example, that firm-specific skills of workers are placed in jeopardy because the management has agreed to a contract that does not permit adjustment when severe adversity eventuates. If these workers are not appraised of this risk and do not have the opportunity to realign their own contractual relation to the firm to reflect this condition, the presumption that the labor agreement reflects responsible risk bearing breaks down.

Consider next the possibility that the contracting parties have differential knowledge or sophistication. If the more knowledgeable party, recognizing that outliers are skewed to the disadvantage of the other, is silent or crafts terms that afford it but not the other with ample protection, the presumption that the agreement reflects intended and intelligent risk bearing is again problematic. Successive generations of commercially able but contractually unsophisticated small firms may find that business risks are needlessly great in such a milieu.[31]

The possibility that contracting costs are unavoidably increased when more legalistic approaches to contract are adopted is suggested by the following observation by Stewart Macaulay: 'Detailed negotiated contracts can get in the way.... If one side insists on a detailed plan there will be

---

[31] The implicit assumption here is that new entrants are unable to craft contracting language that puts them on a parity with more established firms.

a delay while letters are exchanged as the parties try to agree on what should happen if a remote and unlikely contingency occurs' (1963, p. 64). Some agreements may not be reached at all, while in others 'one gets performance only to the letter of the contract' (p. 64).

More generally, highly legalistic approaches toward contracting (hard bargains, strictly enforced) operate to the advantage of those whose calculative instincts are greater. Possibly that is a desirable outcome, but different societies may assess the benefits of intensifying calculativeness differently. Those that wish to attenuate calculativeness will be more apt to adopt contract doctrines which permit contract adjustment when outliers occur.

Consider finally the enforcement of general clauses that have been crafted by the parties to permit adjustment should unanticipated events place one of the parties at an extreme disadvantage. Whether private ordering efforts to deal with surprise have enforcement advantages over court ordering turns on the following comparative issues: (a) the ease of determining whether the preconditions for surprise are satisfied; (b) the efficacy of the adjustment; and (c) the costs of reaching an accommodation. As discussed in section D below, there are reasons to believe that court ordering is at a disadvantage in all three of these enforcement respects.

C. DOCTRINAL EXCUSE

The use of contract doctrine which permits excuse for commercial impracticability does not, of course, preclude private efforts to address these matters in the context of the contract: 'If prospective contracting parties do not like the terms supplied by contract law, normally they are free to supplant them with their own express terms' (Kronman and Posner, 1979, p. 6). What it does is provide blanket language to deal with surprise in the event that the contract is silent on these matters: 'Many substantive rules of contract law are simply specifications of the consequences of some contingency for which the contract makes no provision' (p. 4). But contract doctrines that relate to commercial impossibility should also be evaluated in relation to the aforementioned disabilities of strict enforcement. Thus consider whether doctrinal provision for discharge in the event of surprise relieves the gambling features, the hazards of information asymmetry, and the cost escalation conditions discussed in section B.

It plainly relieves the first of these. In particular, it limits the degree to which managers are able to expose suppliers of firm-specific inputs to unwanted and unbargained-for hazards. It is useful for this purpose to think of the firm as a 'nexus of contracts' (Jensen and Meckling, 1976) but a nexus that is subject to possible distortion by reason of the strategic relation of the management to the contracting process.

Thus whereas each constituent part of the enterprise strikes a bilateral deal with the firm (along the lines set out in Williamson, 1984), the management has knowledge of and is implicated in all of the contracts. Consider, for example, the contracts that are struck between the firm and each of the following: labor, management, and the firm's customers.

Assume, arguendo, that labor is asked to make firm-specific investments in human capital. Assume further that, expressed with reference to the contractual schema in figure 7.1, a node C bargain (with wage $\hat{w}$ and safeguards s) is struck between firm and labor. This bargain is reached on the assumption that the commercial hazards to which the firm is subject can be inferred from a simple extrapolation of the recent past. An employment agreement between the firm and the management also needs to be reached. Assume that this agreement provides for extensive profitsharing. Finally, a contract between the firm and its customers needs to be negotiated. Suppose, with respect to this last, that the buyer is prepared to pay a price of $\bar{p}$ if the contract does not permit adjustment in the event of unanticipated cost increases and $\hat{p}$ if adjustment is permitted (where $\bar{p} > \hat{p}$). If a contract of the $\bar{p}$ kind is struck and if the unanticipated does not eventuate, the seller will show a large profit when the contract is completed. If, however, a $\bar{p}$ agreement is reached and the unanticipated does occur, then the seller will bear the full costs of adversity. If the management of the selling firm appropriates the benefits in the first instance and, because of lock-in effects, is able to shift the burdens of adversity to the suppliers of specific inputs in the second (for example, by asking for give-backs), then a remediable failure in the private ordering contracting process (one for which contract doctrine that permits *ex post* adjustment in the event of adversity afford partial relief) may be said to exist.[32]

Suppose these matters are set aside. Consider whether contract doctrine that permits discharge helps to mitigate *ex ante* information asymmetries between a supplier and a buyer. The concern here is that one of the parties is more knowledgeable or sophisticated than the other and that asymmetric provision for contractual hazards is the result. Two cases are usefully distinguished: the contract is silent with respect to all such contingencies; and the contract makes selective provision for some but not all of the hazards.

Contract doctrine that permits discharge is easier to justify in the first case than the second. The difference is that the disadvantaged party is alerted to the possibility of unforeseen (and possibly unforeseeable)

---

[32] I do not mean to suggest that the contract that joins the firm-specific inputs to the firm is defective except in this one respect. To the contrary, I assume that the labor contract accurately reflects the main governance needs of the firm-to-labor interface. But it does not provide for review by labor of other contracts made by the firm which potentially place firm-specific labor inputs at hazard.

hazards as soon as the more knowledgeable party makes selective provision for any of them. If, being alerted, it makes no effort to broaden the protection, it is more reasonable to infer that the incentive-adaptability trade-off was expressly faced and resolved in favor of maintaining high-powered (unattenuated) incentives.

Consider finally whether a contract doctrine that admits to surprise and *ex post* contract adjustment has a bearing on the cost escalation consequences that Macaulay ascribes to more legalistic styles of contracting. Conceivably it does, but this depends on the way in which the parties attempt to deal with remote contingencies. One way is to identify and stipulate appropriate adaptations to such contingencies very carefully in advance. The second is to provide for such contingencies through a general arbitration clause.[33] Contract doctrine that admits to surprise may be a real benefit in the first instance, in that it relieves the parties of the need to deal with remote contingencies and permits them to focus on the main contingencies and central tendencies. This more affirmative orientation not only saves contracting costs but carries over to the manner in which contracts are executed as well. Getting the job done, rather than preoccupation with legal rules is more apt to be the prevailing orientation.[34] The same benefits cannot, however, be claimed in the case where the parties eschew comprehensive contracting in favor of a general purpose arbitration clause.

The upshot is that between the three transaction cost benefits that might be ascribed to the contract doctrine of commercial impossibility – attenuating gambling hazards, compensating for information asymmetries,

---

[33] Consider the following 'general clause' that appears in the 32-year coal supply agreement between the Nevada Power Company and the Northwest Trading Company: 'It is the intent of the Parties hereto that this Agreement, as a whole and in all of its parts, shall be equitable to both Parties throughout its term. The Parties recognize that omissions or defects in the Agreement beyond control of the Parties or not apparent at the time of its execution may create inequities or hardships during the term of the Agreement, and further, that supervening conditions, circumstances or events beyond the reasonable and practicable control of the Parties, may from time to time give rise to inequities which impose economic or other hardships upon one or both of the Parties. In the event an inequitable condition occurs which adversely affects one Party, it shall be the joint and equal responsibility of both Parties to act promptly and in good faith to determine the action required to cure or adjust for the inequity and effectively to implement such action. Upon written claim of inequity served by one Party upon the other, the Parties shall act jointly to reach an agreement concerning the claimed inequity within sixty (60) days of the date of such written claim. An adjusted base coal price that differs from market price by more than ten percent (10%) shall constitute a hardship. The Party claiming inequity shall include in its claim such information and data as may be reasonably necessary to substantiate the claim and shall freely and without delay furnish such other information and data as the other Party reasonably may deem relevant and necessary. If the Parties cannot reach agreement within sixty (60) days the matter shall be submitted to arbitration' (1980, pp. 11–12).

[34] Karl Llewellyn's distinctions between contract as legal rules and contract as framework are apposite (1931, p. 737).

reducing contracting costs – the benefits are most evident for the first of these and obtain only with qualifications for the latter two. The transaction cost case for the doctrine of commercial impossibility is thus real but limited. It is even weaker when enforcement considerations are taken into account.

D. CONTRACT ENFORCEMENT

In consideration of the advantages of having contract doctrine that admits to surprise and permits adjustments to be made in such instances, are there any disabilities? As discussed above, private ordering and court ordering need to be compared in the following enforcement respects: (a) ascertaining whether a state of the world realization qualifies as an exception; (b) the efficacy of the resulting adjustment; and (c) the cost of reaching agreement on the adjustment.

Court ordering is arguably inferior to private ordering on all three criteria. To be sure, both methods will experience difficulty in ascertaining whether a contingency qualifies as an outlier. Many remote contingencies will be so idiosyncratic as to defy *ex ante* description. To list 'wars, embargoes, changes in government rules and regulations, destruction of key supply facilities, hyperinflation, etc.' (Joskow, 1977, p. 154), to which 'acts of God' and other open-ended categories can be added, does not delimit matters in any very useful way. Judgment based on detailed *ex post* knowledge of the particulars, including an examination of the magnitude of the profitability consequences that accrue, will often be the only way to ascertain whether an adjustment is warranted. If both private and public ordering must go through substantially the same exercise, the advantage accrues to the mechanism which is more knowledgeable, or can be more easily apprised, of the particulars.

Arbitration has an advantage over the courts in this respect. For one thing, arbitrators can be prsumed to have superior *ex ante* knowledge of the industry and even of the firms. For another, there are important procedural differences between arbitration and litigation:

There are open to the arbitrator .... quick methods of education not open to the courts. An arbitrator will frequently interrupt the examination of witnesses with a request that the parties educate him to the point where he can understand the testimony being received. The education can proceed informally, with frequent interruptions by the arbitrators, and by informed persons on either side, when a point needs clarification. Sometimes there will be arguments across the table, occasionally even within reach of the separate camps. The end result will usually be a clarification that will enable everyone to proceed more intelligently with the case. (Fuller, 1963, pp. 11–12).

Not only are the costs of litigation relatively great for these reasons, but they are furthermore partly socialized – in that the parties do not bear the full costs of court ordering. Arbitration thus offers the prospect of superior adjustments, often at a lesser social cost.[35]

E. RECAPITULATION

A transaction cost approach to commercial impracticability discloses that hitherto neglected benefits can be attributed to such a doctrine under the special circumstances where parties to a contract are operating in a long-term bilateral relation to each other. Speidel has already made this argument in general terms. I address the issues at a somewhat more microanalytic level and attempt to identify the particular form these benefits might take. An even more narrowly circumscribed case for such a doctrine than Speidel advances is the result.

To be sure, there is more to the study of contract than transaction cost economizing. The other two leading candidates upon which to justify *ex post* adjustment of contract are to effect a more efficient assignment of risks and to promote fairness. The conditions that would warrant adjustment for the first of these reasons are very special (Posner and Rosenfield, 1977). If, therefore, a broader case for commercial impossibility is to be made, either an additional justification needs to be advanced or fairness must bear the burden.

The problem with the fairness doctrine, as it stands now, is that it lacks a cutting edge. It does not clearly distinguish between those cases which qualify for *ex post* adjustment and those which do not. Although one can agree that 'all promises [are not] enforceable [because] the people and the courts have too much sense' (Llewellyn, 1931, p. 738), the intuitive appeal of this remark must be given operational content, lest the doctrine be invoked uncritically. Absent an effort to delimit the applications, changes away from or around contract, of the comparative institutional kinds discussed in section A, will be provoked.[36]

---

[35] Note, however, that the courts have displayed considerable ingenuity in dealing with cases in which court-ordered adjustment is requested. Speidel's description of the role of the court in *Westinghouse* is especially instructive (1981, pp. 413–14).

[36] Joskow observes that courts have been unwilling to allow excuse merely because a contract has become unprofitable: 'It appears ... that moderate increases in cost of up to 100 per cent do not satisfy the requirement, while extreme increases of 1000 per cent or more do. This leaves a considerable area for controversy' in judging whether a contract has become impracticable (Joskow, 1977, p. 360). The 100 to 1000% range applicable to court-ordered adjustment is usefully contrasted with the 10% range referred to in the arbitration agreement in footnote 33 above.

V. Concluding Remarks

The study of economic organization is an enormously complex undertaking. Such a complex subject matter is usefully viewed from several perspectives. The most seasoned and leading perspective is that of neoclassical economics. But several other approaches have recently been proposed in which the production function theory of the firm has been supplanted by a more microanalytic, contract-based orientation. The concept of the firm as governance structure and/or nexus of contracts informs these alternative perspectives.

Transaction cost economics is one of these alternatives and is the one that is emphasized here. Upon setting out the rudiments of the transaction cost economics approach, I thereafter contrast this with other approaches to contract – with special emphasis on differences between the transaction cost and neoclassical orientation.

Neoclassical treatments of contract deal with contract proscriptions (restraints on trade) and facilitative practices (contract doctrine) rather differently. Monopoly purposes are said to be mainly responsible for those restraints on trade with which antitrust has been traditionally concerned – customer and territorial restrictions, tie-ins, block booking, exclusive dealing, vertical integration, and the like. By contrast, efficient risk bearing is invoked to ascertain when impossibility and related contract doctrines which permit discharge from contract should be permitted.

Transaction cost economics acknowledges merit in both monopoly and efficient risk-bearing approaches to contract. It insists, however, that efficiency purposes are sometimes served by restraints on trade. Furthermore, if the requisite preconditions are satisfied, excuse may sometimes be warranted for reasons that are unrelated to differential risk aversion.

Examination of the underlying attributes of transactions discloses that restraints on trade can help to safeguard the integrity of transactions when firm-specific investments are at hazard. A presumption of monopoly (in any of its forms – leverage, price discrimination, barriers to entry, and combinations thereof) is thus unwarranted where restraints on trade observed to occur in conjunction with, and possibly in support of, a condition of asset specificity. A more even-handed assessment in which both monopoly and efficiency purposes are admitted is needed.

Fewer applications of transaction cost reasoning to contract doctrine have been attempted. It is nevertheless noteworthy that the behavioral assumptions that inform contract doctrine and transaction cost economics are substantially identical. What, if not the conjunction of opportunism and bounded rationality, are manipulative interpretation, capacity, fraud

– to name a few – all about?[37] But the more fruitful use of transaction cost economics to contract doctrine will involve applications of more microanalytic kinds.

The effort to assess the doctrine of commercial impracticability in transaction cost terms discloses that such a doctrine should be invoked (for transaction cost reasons) only in carefully delimited circumstances. The threshhold question is whether the transactions in question are supported by nontrivial investments in transaction-specific assets. Absent this condition, continuity of the exchange relation is not greatly valued – whence a case for *ex post* adjustment for transaction cost reasons is not evident. Even, moreover, if this threshhold test is satisfied, the reason why the contract did not provide for adjustment through arbitration, or some other informal dispute resolution mechanism, must be asked (Speidel, 1981, p. 422). If a contractual failure occurred, wherein does it originate? Of the various possibilities, the strongest transaction cost rationale for *ex post* adjustment obtains if the management has struck a deal that exposes the specific assets of workers (or other suppliers) to risk of contractual catastrophe without having received their express (bargained-for) consent.

[37] Significant headway has been made by Kenneth Clarkson et al. (1978) and by Timothy Muris (1981) in developing the ramifications of opportunism for the law of contracts.

Part III
Strategic Behavior

A difficult condition of entry into an industry is neither here nor there *unless entry can be made easier with net social gains*. Antitrust enforcement was long informed by a different conception of entry barriers, however. This is because a noncomparative standard was employed. Any barrier, remediable or not, was held to be objectionable. Since excesses of price over minimum average cost can always be attributed to entry barriers, and since such excesses violate neoclassical tests for efficiency (and are also believed to have adverse income distribution effects), entry barriers were always and everywhere held to be contrary to the public interest. The deprecation of scale economies to which I earlier referred (see my Introduction to the essays in section 1 and the text in chapters 1 and 13) had these origins. This same attitude spilled over to include deep suspicion if not hostility toward product differentiation, local resource advantages, differential learning curve advantages, and the like. In short, anything that favored large, established firms in relation to smaller potential entrants was objectionable.

Entry barrier arguments were quickly embraced by and became enormously powerful instruments in the hands of the antitrust enforcement agencies. Upside-down economic arguments carried the day. Defendants, in a desperate effort to save themselves from the ruling excesses of entry barrier reasoning, asked the Supreme Court to *reject* claims by the Government that a merger would result in economies.

That entry barrier arguments were taken to excess does not, however, mean that the entire approach lacked merit. Rather, what was needed was an effort to identify the circumstances whereby entry barriers (a) had contrived origins and (b) could be remedied with prospective net social gains. Much of the recent literature on strategic behavior has these twin purposes.

The first essay in this section is an early effort to examine what Steven Salop and David Scheffman (1983) have since referred to as 'raising rivals' costs.' Whether such behavior is a widespread condition or not is hotly disputed. Even where it occurs, remedies with net social gains are often difficult to fashion. My treatment of wage rates as a barrier to entry plainly represents a rather special condition – even in the industry (bituminous coal) and the period (the 1950s) when it was alleged to have occurred. (International competition has since made such behavior all the more problematic since.) That there are circumstances that will support contrived barriers to entry against which effective relief can be fashioned is nevertheless suggested by the theory and evidence developed in this chapter.

The second essay deals with predatory pricing, which is the leading exemplar of strategic behavior. Volumes have since been written on this subject without reaching a definitive conclusion. Although I am less convinced now than when I wrote the predatory pricing chapter that my proposed criterion is workable, the essay nevertheless discloses (a) that predatory pricing is fundamentally an intertemporal problem, whence static treatments fail to go to core issues, (b) that established firms will preposition themselves in relation to any legal rule on predation, and (c) that partial equilibrium welfare economics helps to inform the issues.

The last essay in this section illustrates excesses of entry barrier reasoning in a predatory pricing context. My concern is that the antitrust enforcement process will be abused by those who allege predation when, in fact, the behavior in question is merely a manifestation of hard-ball competition. Rudimentary tests of plausibility can be used to check protectionist abuses. This chapter employs tests of 'incentive logic' and decision process as screens against reckless claims of predation.

8

Wage Rates as a Barrier to Entry: The Pennington Case in Perspective

The question of what types of conditions would most effectively support the manipulation of wage rates by one group of firms to bar entry or disadvantage a second group of firms is sufficiently interesting in itself to deserve theoretical analysis. The recent Supreme Court decision in *United Mine Workers* v. *Pennington*[1] permits us to claim more than mere theoretical interest for such an investigation, however. In that decision the Court indicated that a labor union will be found in violation of antitrust laws where it can be shown that the union has conspired with one group of employers to impose wage rates that disadvantage a second group of employers. More precisely, Justice White, in delivering the majority opinion for the Court, ruled that although 'a union may make wage agreements with a multi-employer bargaining unit and may in pursuance of its own union interests seek to obtain the same terms from other employers, ... [the] union forfeits its exemption from the antitrust laws when it is clearly shown that it has agreed with one set of employers to impose a certain wage scale on other bargaining units.'[2] In a vigorous minority opinion, Justice Goldberg, in one of his last appearances as an Associate Justice, took exception to the majority position.[3] After an extended review of the application of the antitrust laws to labor unions and of the subsequent exemptions from antitrust provided to unions by Congress, he argued that the opinion of the Court in *Pennington* was

I would like to acknowledge the helpful comments of Thomas Asher, Edwin Mansfield, Almarin Phillips, Jonathan Rose, and the referee on an earlier version of this chapter. Research on this chapter was supported by a grant to the author from the National Science Foundation. Originally published in *The Quarterly Journal of Economics*, LXXXII (Feb. 1968) pp. 85–116. © Copyright, 1968, by the President and Fellows of Harvard College. Reprinted with permission of John Wiley & Sons, Inc.

[1] *United Mine Workers* v. *Pennington* 85 S. Ct. 1585 (1965).
[2] Ibid., p. 1591.
[3] *United Mine Workers* v. *Pennington* 85 S. Ct. 1607 (1965). He was joined by Justices Harlan and Stewart.

contrary to congressional intent and that the implicit economic model which the Court relied upon was incorrect. Whether congressional intent was abrogated is not something that we will be concerned with here. It is nevertheless relevant to inquire in what circumstances (if any) agreements between one group of employers and a union to impose uniform wage rates throughout an industry could be used to establish a barrier to entry or (as alleged in the present case) force small rivals to abandon the industry. Whether the economic reasoning of the Supreme Court is correct or not turns on (a) a theoretical demonstration that wage rates can be used as a barrier to entry, and, assuming that this can be shown, (b) the correct application of the theory to the particular circumstances at hand.

Where the tools of economic analysis can be effectively brought to bear on a question before the courts, it is surely incumbent on the profession to respond. Indeed, the circumstances provided by the *Pennington* decision appear to be precisely of the type that Kaysen and Grether had in mind in their 1958 report to the Antitrust Division of the Department of Justice when they wrote:

Economic 'evidence,' strictly speaking is not enough. Economic argument is also required. The 'facts' must be placed in a conceptual framework provided by economic conceptions – theory, if you will. In trying an ordinary private-law case, the court has a whole conceptual apparatus, which it shares with the bar – reasonable men, necessary and probable courses of action, etc. – by means of which the 'facts' in evidence are organized. In antitrust cases neither the courts nor the bar are in this position; thus some care in placing economic facts *in an appropriate frame of economic argument is of the highest importance*.[4]

Although a formal economic model in which wage rates operate as a barrier to entry was unavailable to the Court, we will argue that the majority opinion was substantially correct in holding that, in principle, serious product market effects *can* result where wage rates are negotiated with the purpose of barring entry. At the same time it would appear that precisely because of the absence of an appropriate economic frame of reference, parts of Justice Goldberg's dissent went wrong. Had the relevant economic model been available to the Court, the dispute over the *existence* of possible product market effects could be dispelled at the outset and attention turned instead to questions of specifying criteria for detecting collusion and (if it could be shown that wage rates were used for the purposes claimed) of the probable *magnitude* of the product market effects, given the structural conditions prevailing in the bituminous coal industry.

[4] Cited in E. T. Grether, 'Economic analysis in antitrust enforcement,' *Antitrust Bulletin*, 4 (1959), p. 70, (emphasis added).

The most ambitious objective of an attempt at using wage rates to eliminate rivals and bar entry would be one of throughgoing joint profit maximization among the favored members of the industry. For all the reasons given by Fellner in his classic analysis of the economics of joint profit maximization, this objective is unlikely to be realized in any but the most exceptional circumstances.[5] More to the point is the amount of deviation from the joint profit maximization objective to be expected. In general, the degree of adherence to a qualified joint profit maximization agreement will depend on the structure of the (reconstituted) industry and the condition of the environment.[6] A strategy of distributing market demand among the membership of the industry on a pro-rata market share basis probably represents the upper bound on enforceable quasi-agreement. The lower bound would be a simple rationalization of the industry in which disadvantaged rivals are forced out but essentially competitive relations prevail among the survivors.

A brief statement of the causes of damages as claimed by Pennington and of Justice Goldberg's economic reasoning (as contrasted with his social and political arguments, which deserve attention on their own merits) is given in section I. The economic model required in order to place the 'economic facts in an appropriate frame of economic argument' is developed in section II. The basic data necessary to determine whether differences in technology between large and small firms in bituminous coal would support the use of wage rates as a barrier to entry are developed in section III. The structural conditions which influence the degree of adherence to a qualified joint profit maximization objective are examined in section IV. Our conclusions follow in section V. It may be useful to stress at the outset that use of the term 'barrier to entry' (both here and in the entry literature generally) refers not mainly to effects on firms which, intrinsically, are operating at the margin, but to a broad class of firms which, except for the barrier, would otherwise be viable. Entry analysis is thus concerned with identifying conditions under which quantitatively significant entry effects will predictably obtain.

I. The Allegations

It should be pointed out that the Supreme Court did not rule on the sufficiency of the evidence presented in the case. For technical reasons that need not detain us here, they held that the lower court failed to instruct the jury correctly and the case was remanded for further

---

[5] Fellner (1949, pp. 198–9).
[6] O. E. Williamson, 'A dynamic theory of interfirm behavior,' *Quarterly Journal of Economics*, LXXIX (1965), pp. 579–607.

proceedings. The Court, did, however, indicate that the union would be found in violation of the antitrust laws and subject thereby to triple damages if the allegations of wage conspiracy could be supported. Thus, although on remand the District Court found the evidence insufficient to sustain the conspiracy charge,[7] the Supreme Court in *Pennington* nevertheless established the legal basis for a wage barrier violation.

The action began as a suit by the trustees of the United Mine Workers against James M. Pennington, et al., individually and as owners of the Phillips Brothers Coal Company to recover royalty payments alleged to be due the UMW as of 31 December, 1958, the date on which the company terminated its business. Phillips filed a cross claim in which they alleged that the National Bituminous Coal Wage Agreement of 1950, which marked an end to a long period of strife between the industry and the union, and subsequent amendments to it represented a collusive arrangement by which large coal operators joined with the union in stabilizing the industry and forcing small, marginal producers to abandon their operations. The Supreme Court summarized the principal allegations (as they relate to the wage rates as a barrier to entry argument) as follows:

Allegedly the [UMW and large operators] considered over-production to be the critical problem of the coal industry. The *agreed* solution was to be the elimination of the smaller companies, the larger companies thereby controlling the market. More specifically, the union abandoned its efforts to control the working time of the miners, agreed not to oppose the rapid mechanization of the miners which would substantially reduce mine employment, agreed to help finance such mechanization and *agreed to impose the terms of the 1950 agreement on all operators* without regard for their ability to pay. The benefit to the union was to be increased wages as productivity increases with mechanization, these increases [also] to be *demanded of the smaller companies whether mechanized or not.*[8]

The Court then went on to indicate that if such allegations could be proved, then the union would be in violation of the antitrust laws. 'One group of employers may not conspire to eliminate competitors from the industry and the union is liable with the employers if it becomes a party to the conspiracy. This is true even though the unions' part in the scheme is an undertaking to secure the same wages, hours or other conditions of employment from the remaining employers in the industry.'[9] More generally, it would appear to be the opinion of the Court that it is illegal for unions to conspire with any group of employers to limit

---

[7] *Lewis* v. *Pennington,* 257 F. Supp. 815 (1966).
[8] *United Mine Workers* v. *Pennington* 85 S. Ct. 1585, 1588 (1965) (emphasis added).
[9] Ibid., p. 1591.

competition by using wage rates as a barrier to entry.[10]

Justice Goldberg took issue with the view that such wage agreements could have anticompetitive product market effects and argued that 'where there is an "agreement" to seek uniform wages in an industry, in what item is competition restrained? The answer to this question can *only* be that competition is restrained in employee wage standards.'[11] Since labor is expressly exempted from the antitrust laws on the grounds that the 'labor of a human being is not a commodity or article of commerce,'[12] he argued that uniform wage agreements cannot possibly constitute grounds for antitrust violation. Later he relaxes this position to admit the possibility of product market effects, but he continues to insist that these are hardly of an anticompetitive nature:

The kind of competition that is suppressed by employer–employee agreement on uniform wages can only be competition between unions to see which union will agree to supply labor at a lower rate, or competition between employers in the sale of their products based on differences in labor cost. Neither type of 'suppression' ... can be supported as a restraint of trade condemned by the antitrust laws.[13]

---

[10] The existence of a conspiracy is quite critical. Thus Justice White went on to observe in a footnote that 'Unilaterally, and without agreement with any employer group to do so, a union may adopt a uniform wage policy and seek vigorously to implement it even though it may suspect that some employers cannot effectively compete if they are required to pay the wage scale demanded by the union. The union need not gear its wage demands to those which the weakest units in the industry can afford to pay. Such union conduct is not alone sufficient evidence to maintain a union–employer conspiracy charge under the Sherman Act. There must be additional direct or indirect evidence of the conspiracy.' *United Mine Workers* v. *Pennington*, 85 S. Ct. 1585, 1591, n. 2 (1965).

Elsewhere in the opinion, however, White appears to suggest that extra-unit bargaining agreements, with or without conspiracy, conflict with antitrust policy: 'From the viewpoint of antitrust policy, ... all such agreements between a group of employers and a union that the union will seek specified labor standards outside the bargaining unit suffer from a more basic defect, without regard to predatory intention or effect in the particular case. ... Prior to the agreement the union might seek uniform standards in its own self-interest but would be required to assess in each case the [net gains]. ... After the agreement the union's interest would be bound in each case to that of the favored employer group. It is just such restraints upon the freedom of economic units to act according to their own choice and discretion that run counter to antitrust policy.' *United Mine Workers* v. *Pennington*, 85 S. Ct. 1585, 1592 (1965).

Bernard Meltzer argues that this is inconsistent with national labor policy 'It is ... not clear why a union is able lawfully to surrender its freedom of action by consenting to an industry-wide bargaining unit and yet is subject to an automatic loss of exemption if it enters into an extra-unit agreement.' ['Labor unions, collective bargaining, and the antitrust laws,' *Journal of Law and Economics*, VI (1963), p. 208.] He fails, however, to detect what may frequently be an important difference between industry-wide and extra-unit agreements: it may be possible to extract from a subset terms to which the whole set would not consent.

[11] *United Mine Workers* v. *Pennington* 85 S. Ct. 1607, 1621 (1965) (emphasis added).

[12] Section 6 of the Clayton Act, Sec. 17, Title 15 United States Code.

[13] *United Mine Workers* v. *Pennington* 85 S. Ct. 1607, 1622 (1965).

As we show in section II, however, the product market effects need not be so innocent as he is suggesting. Under the 'right' circumstances, there exist very real opportunities for large firms to conspire with labor unions to use wage rates as a barrier to entry. A good part of our analysis will be directed at discovering precisely what these circumstances are. Given that the essential conditions for using wage rates as a barrier to entry are satisfied and that a conspiracy between large employers and a union to impose uniformly high wages on other firms in an industry exists, significant anticompetitive effects that violate the spirit of the Sherman Act can easily result.

II. The Model

The theoretical basis for using wage rates as a barrier to entry is developed in four parts. First the assumptions of our model are specified and the expressions for the optimal wage premium and the corresponding optimal (entry-preventing) price are derived. Next, we examine the comparative static properties of the resulting solution and provide a summary statement to the question posed at the outset of this chapter: What types of conditions would most effectively support the use of wage rates as a barrier to entry? An operationally more convenient expression for estimating the wage premium follows. A digression on the dynamics of entry problems concludes this section.

A. OPTIMALITY RELATIONS

The necessary condition for wage rates to act as a barrier to entry is that an increase in wages must produce a differential shift in the level of average costs to the relative disadvantage of small-scale firms. And for this to occur, systematic differences in technology between successive scales of operation must exist.[14] In particular, consider an industry with the following attributes:

1   There are two scales of operation.
2   Within each scale:
    (a)   factors are used in fixed proportions;
    (b)   there are constant returns to scale.

[14] In a footnote to his study of the way in which scale economies may confer barriers to entry, Modigliani observes that 'It may ... be profitable for existing firms to tolerate high wages as long as these are enforced by a trade union strong enough to impose the same wage scale on any potential entrant.' Franco Modigliani (1958, p. 228, n. 21). He relates the argument only to demand elasticities, however, and makes no mention of the possible influence of different technologies which occupy a central role in *Pennington* and in our analysis.

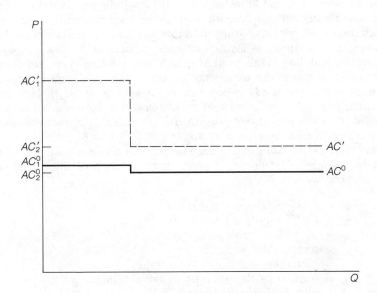

Figure 8.1

3   The labor/capital ratio is higher for the smaller scale operators.
4   Average cost at competitive factors prices in the large-scale firms is less than or equal to the average cost experienced by small-scale firms.
5   An agreement exists between the principal large-scale firms in the industry and the union to impose a uniform wage on all firms in the industry independent of ability to pay. Alternatively, if an agreement is lacking and the union would prefer to discriminate in pricing labor to firms of different size, an increase in the wage rate negotiated with the large firms makes it politically expedient to increase the wage to smaller rivals by substantially the same absolute amount.

The question then is: In what sense can the principal firms, with or without the conscious collaboration of the union, use wage rates to impose a barrier to entry? The way in which such a barrier would operate is shown in figure 8.1.

The level of average costs at competitive wage rates for the two scales of operation is shown by the solid line. The maximum price that large-scale firms could charge without attracting small-scale entrants is thus given by AC^0_1. If, however, supercompetitive wage rates are negotiated with the union with the knowledge that these will be imposed on all firms extant and potential, a differential shift in the level of average cost curves which disadvantages small-scale operators will occur. The shift in the level of average cost curves as a result of such an increase in wages is shown by the dashed line. Due to the greater labor intensity of small-scale operations, average costs experienced by the small-scale firms increase by more than those of the large-scale firms $[\Delta(AC_1) > \Delta(AC_2)]$. Hence the principal firms may well find that an increase in wages which raises the level of the entry preventing price to AC_1' is relatively attractive, despite an increase in own average costs to AC_2'.

Whether and to what extent such a shift will prove advantageous can best be shown by developing a more formal version of the model. For this purpose we let:

$$\alpha_i = L_i/K_i = \text{labor/capital ratio}$$
$$\beta_i = Q_i/L_i = \text{output/labor ratio}$$
$$\omega = \omega_o + \delta = \text{negotiated wage}$$
$$\omega_o = \text{competitive wage}$$
$$\delta = \text{premium over competitive wage}$$
$$\gamma_i = \text{fraction of the wage premium transmitted to scale } i$$
$$r = \text{competitive interest rate}$$
$$L_i = \text{labor input}$$
$$K_i = \text{capital input}$$
$$Q_i = \text{output}$$
$$\pi_i = R_i - C_i = \text{net revenue}$$
$$R_i = \text{gross revenue}$$
$$C_i = \text{total cost}$$
$$AC_i = \text{average cost}$$

and the subscript i refers to the ith scale of operation, an increase in scale being denoted by an integer increase in the value of the subscript.

In terms of these relations we can now restate assumptions 2 through 5 as follows:

A2 Within each scale,
   $Q_i = \beta_i L_i$.
A3 Between scales,
   $a_i > a_{i+1}$.
A4 Between scales,
   $AC_i \geq AC_{i+1}$.
   at competitive factor prices.
A5 $\gamma_i = 1$ with collusion;
   γ_i is less than but nevertheless close to unity if discrimination is possible but politically difficult to sustain.

And from assumptions A2–A4 it necessarily follows that:

$$\beta_{i+1} > \beta_i.^{15} \tag{8.1}$$

Letting $i = m$ be the subscript for the largest firms among which a joint profit maximization objective is assumed to prevail and $i = 1$ be the supscript for the smallest relevant scale against which an entry barrier is maintained, we can express the objective of the largest firms as

maximize: $\pi_m = R_m - C_m$ $\qquad\qquad$ (8.2)
subject to: $P_m \leq AC_1$,

where $P_m = P_m(Q_m)$, $\dfrac{\partial P_m}{\partial Q_m} < 0$, and $R_m = P_m Q_m$.

By definition, we have

$$C_i = w_i L_i + rK_i \tag{8.3}$$

$$= [(w_0 + \gamma_i\delta)\,a_i + r]K_i.$$

Now

$Q_i = \beta_i L_i = a_i\beta_i\,K_i$, so that C_i is given by:

$$C_i = \frac{[(w_0 + \gamma_i\delta)\,a_i + r]\,Q_i}{a_i\,\beta_i} \tag{8.4}$$

and AC_i can be expressed as

$$AC_i = \frac{[(w_0 + \gamma_i\delta)\,a_i + r]}{a_i\,\beta_i}. \tag{8.5}$$

---

[15] This can be shown as follows:

By definition: $AC_i = \dfrac{wL_1 + rK_i}{Q_i}$

$$= \frac{(wa_i + r)K_i}{a_i\beta_i K_i}.$$

By assumption: $AC_{i+1}^o \leq AC_i^p$
Hence,

$$\frac{w_0 a_{i+1} + r}{a_{i+1} + \beta_{i+1}} \leq \frac{w_0 a_i + r}{a_i B_i}$$

or, rearranging, we have:

$$\frac{\beta_i}{\beta_{i+1}} \leq \frac{a_i w_0 a_{i+1} + ra_{i+1}}{a_i w_0 a_{i+1} + ra_i}.$$

Since $a_{i+1} < a_i$, the right-hand side of the inequality is less than one. Hence, $\beta_i < \beta_{i+1}$, QED.

The analysis will be faciliated by observing that the constraint will be binding whenever a positive wage premium (δ) is charged. That is, if the optimal wage premium were zero, the cost advantage of the large firms would be sufficiently great that entry by the smaller scale operators would be unattractive at competitive factor prices even when product price was set at the monopoly level. In the language of entry analysis, this corresponds to a condition of 'blockaded entry'[16] and represents a limiting case which is not of principal concern to us here. We therefore set the problem up as a Lagrangian in which the constraint is binding. We also set $\gamma_m = 1$ since the full wage premium is paid at the largest scale. Letting λ be the Lagrange multiplier, equation (8.2) can be expressed as:

$$\text{maximize } V(Q_m, \delta, \lambda) = P_m Q_m - [(w_0 + \delta)a_m + r]\frac{Q_m}{a_m \beta_m} \qquad (8.6)$$
$$- \lambda \left[P_m - \frac{(w_0 + \gamma_1 \delta) a_1 + r}{a_1 \beta_1} \right].$$

Setting the first derivatives of V with respect to each of its arguments equal to zero we obtain as first-order conditions for a maximum:

$$\frac{\partial V}{\partial Q_m} = \frac{\partial P_m}{\partial Q_m} Q_m + P_m - \frac{1}{a_m \beta_m}[(w_0 + \delta)a_m + r] \qquad (8.7)$$
$$- \lambda \frac{\partial P_m}{\partial Q_m} = 0$$

$$\frac{\partial V}{\partial \delta} = -\frac{Q_m}{\beta_m} + \frac{\lambda \gamma_1}{\beta_1} = 0 \qquad (8.8)$$

$$\frac{\partial V}{\partial \lambda} = P_m - \frac{(w_0 + \gamma_1 \delta) a_1 + r}{a_1 \beta_1} = 0 . \qquad (8.9)$$

Letting E be the price elasticity of demand, we can replace

$$\frac{\partial P_m}{\partial Q_m}$$

by

$$- \frac{1}{E} \cdot \frac{P_m}{Q_m}.$$

Making this substitution and solving equations (8.7)–(8.9) for the optimal

[16] The term is due to Bain (1956, p. 22). Technically it amounts to a case of a redundant constraint. O. E. Williamson, 'Selling expense as a barrier to entry,' *Quarterly Journal of Economics*, LXXVII (1963), pp. 122–3.

(entry preventing) price (P_m^*) and the optimal wage premium (δ^*) we obtain:

$$P^* = \frac{(w_0 + \gamma_1\delta^*)\, a_1 + r}{a_1\beta_1} \tag{8.10}$$

$$\delta^* = \frac{\left(1 - \dfrac{a_m}{a_1\gamma_1}\right) r + a_m\left(1 - \dfrac{1}{\gamma_1}\right) w_0}{a_m\left(1 - \dfrac{1}{E}\right)\left(\dfrac{\gamma_1\beta_m}{\beta_1} - 1\right)} - \frac{w_0}{\gamma_1} - \frac{r}{a_1\gamma_1}. \tag{8.11}$$

Letting AC_1^0 be the average costs experienced by scale 1 firms when the wage premium is zero, equation (8.10) can be rewritten as:

$$P^*_m = AC_1^0 + \frac{\gamma_1\delta^*}{\beta_1}. \tag{8.10'}$$

If the transmission ratio (γ_1) is unity, in which case the full amount of the wage premium would be extracted from scale 1 size firms, equation (8.11) simplifies to:

$$\delta^* = \frac{\left(1 - \dfrac{a_m}{a_1}\right) r}{a_m\left(1 - \dfrac{1}{E}\right)\left(\dfrac{\beta_m}{\beta_1} - 1\right)} - \frac{r}{a_1} - w_0, \tag{8.11'}$$

where all terms in the numerator and denominator of this expression are positive.

Since it is somewhat easier to establish the properties of our model by treating the case where the transmission ratio is unity, and as probably this is the most common case, the subsequent analysis will be mainly concerned with this condition. It is, however, important to note that we encounter no problem in principle in comprehending the condition where γ_1 is less than unity. (And to the degree of course that γ_1 is less than unity, the incentive to use wage premiums as a barrier to entry is correspondingly attenuated.)

B. COMPARATIVE STATIC PROPERTIES

Equations (8.10') and (8.11') can now be used to derive directly the comparative static rseponses shown in table 8.1. The direction of adjustment in the optimum price or wage premium to a displacement from equilibrium caused by an *increase* in any particular parameter is found by referring to the row and column entry corresponding to the variable–parameter pair.

Table 8.1

Variable	α_i	α_m	E	w_o	β_i	β_m	r
			Parameter				
P^*	+	−	−	0	+	−	+
δ^*	+	−	−	−	+	−	+

Interpreting these results will be made easier by referring to the geometric relations shown in figure 8.2. The monopoly output at competitive factor prices is given by the intersection of the marginal revenue curve with the marginal cost curve (MC_m) of the large-scale

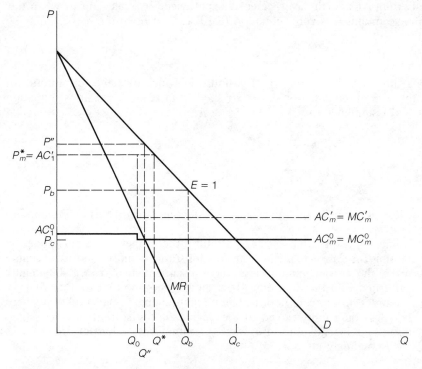

Figure 8.2

firms, namely Q''. The corresponding monopoly price is P''. But should the large-scale firms attempt to charge this price and supply this output, new entry would quickly occur and the price could not be sustained. The ideal or competitive output is given by Q_c, where MC_m intersects the demand curve. The corresponding price in these circumstances is P_c. Yet, although the large firms cannot safely charge the monopoly price, neither is it necessary for them to drop the price to P_c to prevent entry; small-scale firms will find it unattractive to enter at competitive factor prices if the product price is AC^o_1.

The question now is how high above AC^o_1 will the larger firms choose to push the entry preventing price by using wage premiums as a barrier to entry?

Since increasing the wage premium increases the level of average costs to the small-scale operators more than it does to the large operators, clearly the premium will be increased until the industry is operating in the elastic region of the demand curve. Thus the point on our linear demand schedule where elasticity is unity, namely (Q_b, P_b), provides a lower bound to the value of P^*_m; below this point increases in the wage premium which increase P^*_m will necessarily increase the net revenue of the large-scale firms. Once the elastic portion of the demand curve is reached, however, increasing the price reduces total revenue to the industry and the trade-off between cost and revenue must be explicitly calculated. We have nevertheless been successful in bounding the value of P^*_m from below by P_b, and on the upper side we would not expect P^*_m to exceed the monopoly price P'' (as calculated at competitive factor prices), but this latter is only an approximate and not a firm upper bound.[17]

With this background in mind, we consider now the verbal restatement and interpretation of our comparative static results. *Ceteris paribus*, we have:

1 Large firms adjust to an increase in the labor/capital ratio of the small-scale firms (a_1) by increasing the wage premium (δ) and, as a result, the entry preventing price (P_m).
2 An increase in the labor/capital ratio of the larger firms (a_m) has precisely the opposite effect. Thus it is in circumstances where the ratio a_1/a_m is relatively large – that is, where the technology of the smaller firms is significantly more labor intensive than that of the larger firms – that a large wage premium can be expected.
3 As demand becomes more elastic (E increases), the wage premium and the entry preventing price are both reduced. This effect of demand elasticity on price is a standard result from conventional monopoly theory and agrees with Modigliani's analysis of entry conditions.[18]
   18
4 An increase in the competitive wage (w_o) has no effect on the entry

---

[17] That it is not true upper bound results from the fact that the intersection of marginal costs with the marginal revenue curve shifts to the left somewhat as the wage premium is increased.

[18] Modigliani (1958), p. 220.

preventing price but permits the wage premium to be lowered. That this is correct can be seen as follows. Let w_1 be the optimal wage rate, w_o be the prevailing competitive wage, and δ_1 be the optimal wage premium. Then $w_1 = w_o + \delta_1$. Now let w_o increase to w'_o, where $w'_o < w_1$. Obviously the level of the optimal wage rate is unaffected by such a change, and with w_1 constant, the optimal price remains constant. The optimal wage premium, however, is now given by $\delta'_1 = \delta_1 - (w'_o - w_o)$, and with $w'_o > w_o$, δ'_1 is necessarily less than δ_1.

5   The ratio β_m/β_1 can be viewed as a 'magnification ratio.' Since an increase in δ increases AC_1 by $\Delta\delta/\beta_1$ and AC_m by $\Delta\delta/\beta_m$, the increase in the average costs of small-scale firms exceeds that of large-scale firms by the multiple β_m/β_1. Thus the larger the value of β_m/β_1, the smaller the wage premium needed to disadvantage small rivals. Hence the value of the optimal wage premium decreases as the magnification ratio increases. The directional adjustment in the value of the optimal entry preventing price is identical to that of the wage premium.

6   An increase in the competitive interest rate (r) reduces the relative cost advantage experienced by the capital-intensive (large) firms. The wage premium is therefore increased to restore the cost advantage and an increase in the entry preventing price occurs as a result.

By way of summary, the *sine qua non* for wage premiums even to be seriously contemplated is that differences in technology between large- and small-scale firms must be of the sort described above. Most important, the labor/capital ratio must be larger for the small-scale operators. If differences in the labor/capital ratio between scales are insignificant, the incentives to influence the condition of entry through the use of wage premiums are correspondingly attenuated. Given, however, that the indicated labor/capital differences exist and that (approximate) cost parity at competitive factor prices prevails, it follows that the output/labor ratio must be lower in the small scale. In addition to these production function relations, either agreement with the union to impose the full amount of the wage premium on small rivals is required, or the natural pressures for wage uniformity must be substantial. Finally, although a discussion of industry structure is deferred to section IV, this also has an important influence on both the attractiveness of a wage barrier policy and the way in which it can be implemented.

C. THE WAGE PREMIUM AS A FUNCTION OF w_o

Although equation (11') is adequate for examining the qualitative properties of the model, it is not expressed in a form convenient for estimating the value of δ^*. For this purpose we observe that, by assumption $A4$, $AC^o_1 = \theta\, AC^o_m$ where $\theta \geqslant 1$, and superscript zero denotes competitive factor prices. Solving for the value of r in terms of w_o and substituting into (11'), the following expression is obtained:

$$\delta^* = \frac{(1 - \frac{\alpha_m}{\alpha_1})\,[\frac{\beta_m}{\beta_1}(1 - \theta) + \frac{1}{E}(\frac{\beta_m}{\beta_1} - 1)\,\theta]}{(\theta - \frac{\alpha_m\,\beta_m}{\alpha_1\,\beta_1})\,(1 - \frac{1}{E})\,(\frac{\beta_m}{\beta_1} - 1)}\; w_o\,. \tag{8.12}$$

If θ is equal to unity, in which case the large firms enjoy no cost advantage at competitive factor prices, equation (8.12) reduces to:

$$\delta^* = \frac{(1 - \frac{\alpha_m}{\alpha_1})}{(E - 1)\,(1 - \frac{\alpha_m\beta_m}{\alpha_1\beta_1})}\; w_o\,. \tag{8.12'}$$

D. A DIGRESSION ON DYNAMICS

Two standard assumptions in the analysis of entry conditions are (a) that there is a critical entry preventing price above which value entry will surely occur and at or below which entry will be successfully forestalled,[19] and (b) the output response by potential rivals should price exceed the critical value is both large and immediate. As I have argued elsewhere, the dichotomy posed by this first assumption is unnecessarily extreme.[20] Rather, if the probability of entry can be assumed to increase monotonically with the value of the market price, the problem can be formulated probabilistically with the expected value of discounted profits being maximized. This shift to a probabilistic, multiperiod analysis gains something in the way of realism but fails to change significantly the general qualitative properties of the deterministic, single-period solution.[21]

Bain has considered briefly the question of lagged responses and argues that the effect of any 'given condition of entry on market behavior will ... be likely to vary with the entry lags which accompany it.'[22] He considers this a rather subordinate issue, however, and rather than complicate the analysis of entry conditions by including it as an integral part of the

[19] Both Bain (1956), p. 9 and Modigliani (1958), p. 217 emphasize a critical price-to-cost gap.

[20] Williamson, 'Selling expense as a barrier to entry' (1963), pp. 124–7.

[21] It has the advantage of removing the constraint from the objective function and treats the probability of entry as a decision variable. By increasing price in the current period the firm can realize larger current period profits but only reducing expected future period profits. Ibid., p. 126.

[22] Bain (1956), p. 11.

analysis, he instead studies the entry relation without regard for lags and then qualifies the analysis to the extent that this appears necessary by later adjustment for lags as an auxiliary operation. Since entry analysis is concerned with devising strategies with fundamental, long-term consequences, while 'gaming' the lag in response is a distinctly short-run operation, to include lags as a part of the basic model may have the effect of diverting attention from the issues that are of principal concern. Where lag considerations are believed to be important, *ad hoc* adjustments can usually be made[23] – although a stochastic sequential decision analysis may occasionally be necessary for an adequate treatment of this problem.

One further issue of a dynamic variety that is particularly relevant to the analysis of wage rates as a barrier to entry involves the question of the time-pattern of demands. Where demand is highly unstable, labor-intensive operations that avoid heavy fixed costs will tend to be preferred. Stated in *ceteris paribus* terms, the greater the variability in demand the more attractive do operations become in which the proportion of variable costs is high. This is shown graphically in figure 8.3 where the short-run total cost curves for a capital-intensive (TC_{k2}) and a labor-intensive (TC_{k1}) type of operation are drawn. The capacity of both plants is identical, namely Q'', and at the capacity output the lowest cost is realized with the capital-intensive plant. Plant is assumed to be fully divisible for operating purposes (although discrete for capital investment purposes) so that the output/labor ratio is constant over the output range 0 to Q''. However, the output/labor ratio is higher for the capital-intensive plan and hence the total cost curve TC_{k2} is flatter than TC_{k1}. As a result, at output levels below the intersection of TC_{k2} with TC_{k1} (namely Q'), the labor-intensive plant realizes lower total costs. If demand is highly variable so that output below Q' occurs frequently, the labor-intensive form of organization may well be preferred over the capital-intensive form which minimizes total costs at Q''.

The implication of this for our model is that where demand is highly variable, the management in large-scale plants may forego the choice of technologies which have very low labor/capital ratios despite the fact that these yield steady-state cost advantages and enhance the steady-state incentive to use wage rates as a barrier to entry. This does not, however, alter the *qualitative properties* of our model. Rather, we accommodate this condition within the framework of our model by indicating that the incentive to use wage rates as a barrier to entry is weakened where demand is highly variable; capital-intensive forms of organization are less attractive to the large-scale firm in these circumstances. More precisely, this implies an

[23] Lags in response in both exit and entry would, for example, be increasing functions of the ratio of fixed to total costs and decreasing functions of the difference between product price and AC_1.

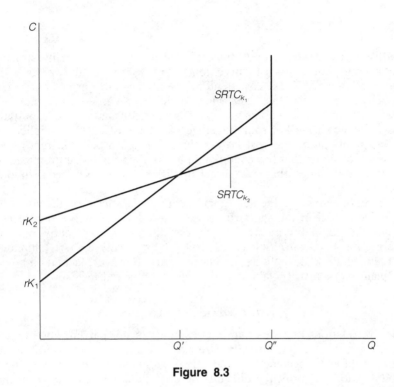

Figure 8.3

increase in the labor/capital ratio (a_m) and a reduction in the output/labor ratio (β_m) at the large scale occur in response to increases in the variability of demand, *ceteris paribus*.

III. Wage Barrier Parameters in the Bituminous Coal Industry

Our objective in this section is to examine the gross characteristics of the bituminous coal industry to determine the extent to which our model is applicable. We consider first the shapes of average variable cost curves and demand elasticities. Next we examine the output/labor and labor/ capital ratios beween large and small firms. Finally, we look at the relations between the large operators and the UMW as these affect the transmission ratio.

A. COST AND DEMAND

Both Moyer and Baratz report that, for a given mine and fixed investment, the average variable cost curve tends to be horizontal over a wide operating range.[24] These costs tend to rise at very low outputs and when capacity is reached, but over what might be regarded as a 'normal' operating range, the average variable costs are constant. Since at outputs less than capacity a horizontal average variable cost curve is implied by the assumptions of the cost curves shown in figure 8.3, the reports of Moyer and Baratz that this condition holds to a reasonable approximation gives us confidence that the model applies to bituminous coal in this aspect.

There is general agreement that the price elasticity of demand for bituminous coal in the short run is quite low.[25] Considering the degree of interfuel competition between coal, gas, oil, and more recently, nuclear energy, the long-run elasticity is, surely, substantially higher. Estimates of the magnitude of the long-run elasticity are, however, lacking; a range of 'plausible' elasticity values are therefore employed instead.

B. LABOR, CAPITAL, AND PRODUCTIVITY

The two relations that we attempt to estimate in this part are the output/labor and labor/capital ratios by size class. A pure measure of either of these is difficult to come by, and this is particularly true of the labor/capital ratio. The principal difficulty here is obtaining an estimate of the capital stock.

Maddala similarly finds estimating the capital stock to be the 'main problem' in his recent study of productivity in the bituminous coal industry, and he had only to determine total capital stock by states not by size classes of firms.[26] He chose finally to use the horsepower-rating of power equipment as a proxy. Inasmuch as this is not reported by size class, however, we are forced to adopt a somewhat more roundabout procedure. One possible alternative would be to develop our estimate of the capital stock from the *Statistics of Income* as compiled from corporate income tax reports. Such a procedure has several disadvantages, however. First, the size classes employed in the *Statistics of Income* are asset categories

[24] Reed Moyer, *Competition in the Midwestern Coal Industry* (Harvard University Press, Cambridge, Mass., 1961), pp. 99–100; M. S. Baratz, *The Union and the Coal Industry* (Yale University Press, New Haven, 1955), pp. 14–17.

[25] There is virtually unanimity on this. See Moyer (1961) p. 61; Baratz (1955), p. 19; J. B. Hendry, 'The bituminous coal industry,' in *The Structure of American Industry*, ed. Walter Adams (3rd edn, Macmillan, New York 1961), pp. 98, 100.

[26] G. S. Maddala, 'Productivity and technological change in the bituminous coal industry, 1919–54,' *Journal of Political Economy*, LXXIII (1965), p. 354.

and no precise matching with our employment categories is possible. As a result it would be impossible to compute capital/labor ratios for identical subsets of firms, and a possibly serious measurement error would necessarily result. Second, variation in the age of capital equipment and in accounting conventions between firms introduces an additional source of measurement error. Third, noncorporate assets are not reported in the *Statistics of Income*, and surely the noncorporate form is common, and perhaps even prevailing, among the smaller coal operators. If, therefore, an alternative measure of capital can be devised that does not suffer from these shortcomings, such a measure might well be preferable.

Before attempting an alternative measure of the capital stock, we note first the importance of studying underground mines separately from strip mines. During the decade of the 1950s, strip mines accounted for between 22 and 29 per cent of total bituminous coal production, the proportion increasing to 31 per cent in 1963.[27] Strip mines are hardly an insignificant fraction of the total, therefore, and it is not for this reason that we wish to exclude them. Rather, the technology employed in strip mining is sufficiently different from that of underground mining that to include all mines without regard for type would be to contaminate the data seriously. In addition, as will be clear shortly, it is mainly against the small underground mines that the tactic of using wage rates as a barrier to entry could be used effectively. We attempt, therefore, to study underground mines separately wherever the data permit.

As it turns out, one possible basis for distinguishing between large and small underground mines is a capital measure. Thus a simple separation of underground mines into those which have mechanical loading and those that do not serves as a crude but effective basis for assigning mines to large and small categories. Since, *ceteris paribus*, mechanical loading operations are more capital-intensive than hand loading, this provides us with our first qualitative estimate of the differences in capital intensity between size classes.[28] The data required to make this judgment are presented in table 8.2.

Several things should be noted in examining the data in table 8.2. First, the hand-loading mines vastly exceed in number the mechanical loading mines, the ratio running over four to one. Second, despite this numerical advantage, the hand-loading mines account for only 11 per cent of the output. Assuming that operating rates are approximately the same in both

---

[27] US Bureau of Mines, *Minerals Yearbook 1963* (Washington, DC, 1964), p. 59.

[28] The most important change in underground coal mining technology since 1940 has been in the mechanical loading of coal, the most advanced form of this development being the continuous mining machine which both mechanically removes the coal from the face and loads it onto hauling equipment. C. L. Christenson, *Economic Redevelopment in Bituminous Coal: The Special Case of Technological Advance in United States Coal Mines, 1930–1960* (Harvard University Press, Cambridge, Mass., 1962), p. 144.

Table 8.2 Mechanical loading and mine size for five states, underground mining, 1955

| State | Hand loading | | Mechanical loading | | |
	Number of mines	Average annual tonnage/ mine (000)	Number of mines	Average annual tonnage/ mine (000)	Per cent of underground tonnage mechanically loaded
Pennsylvania	319	27	214	274	91
West Virginia	938	16	372	306	89
Kentucky	1974	7	153	257	73
Ohio	345	8	48	233	81
Illinois	47	6	55	475	99
Total	3623	11	842	299	89

Source: C. L. Christenson (1962) table 29, p. 147.

large and small mines, it follows directly that the hand-loading mines are the small mines. As the data show, annual tonnage in the hand-loading mines averages only about 4 per cent of the output of the larger mechanical loading operations. Finally, these relations hold in every state for which data were available. Granting that the hand loading versus mechanical loading distinction provides us with a crude proxy of the labor/capital ratio, it follows that the ratio is clearly higher in the smaller mines as required by our model.

Additional support for the proposition that the small mines tend generally to be unmechanized is provided by *Ramsey* v. *United Mine Workers*, a case involving wage conspiracy claims that relies on *Pennington*, argued recently before the United States District Court of Eastern Tennessee. The court's opinion includes a review of the characteristic size and extent of mechanization among the several plaintiffs. As the model requires, most of these are found to be small hand-loading operations.[29] (The court goes on to offer the observation that the failure or inability of the small mines to mechanize explains much of the difficulty that they have experienced.)[30]

A somewhat more specific measure is obtained by correlating average

[29] *Ramsey* v. *United Mine Workers*, 1967 CCH Trade Cases, para. 72,051 (E.D. Tenn., S.D., 1967).
[30] Ibid. Similar observations also appear in the District Court's opinion in the remand of *Pennington*, 257 F. Supp. 815, 832–33 (1966).

mine size to horsepower per production worker, both measured on a statewide basis (which is the only basis for which the horsepower per production worker data are available). Here we obtain a rank correlation of 0.83, significant at a 0.01 level.[31] Although the statewide data are perhaps too crude to support more than a rank correlation meaningfully, the linear regression of horsepower per production worker (H) on average mine size (S), as given by average number of workers of all types per mine, at the very least permits us to make a rough judgment as to whether the size differences give rise to quantitatively significant differences in the labor/capital ratio. The least squares linear regression based on these statewide statistics is $H = 10 + \underset{(0.04\ )}{0.24S}$, the coefficient of determination being 0.79. This implies that small mines with 20 or fewer employees have capital/labor ratios about half as large as in mines with 100 employees. Whichever measure we use, therefore, we obtain broadly the same estimate of the difference in the labor/capital ratio (the inverse of the capital/labor ratio) between small and large underground mines: it is always higher among the smaller mines.

We consider next the output/labor ratio between large and small mines. Here the opinion of the court in *Ramsey* is more precise. The mines in the southeastern Tennessee coal field tend to be small and, over time, have fallen progressively behind in productivity.

Whereas productivity in Tennessee was about in line with productivity throughout the nation for underground mines in 1950, since that time productivity of underground mines elsewhere has steadily risen while ... [productivity in Tennessee has] tended to remain constant or [has risen] to a smaller degree. Whereas productivity in underground mines was at a level of approximately $5\frac{1}{2}$ to $5\frac{3}{4}$ tons per man-day in 1950, both in Tennessee mines and in underground mines throughout the nation, by 1960 national productivity had risen to 10.64 tons, whereas Tennessee mines advanced only to 6.70 tons. By 1963 the gap had further widened with national productivity rising to 12.78 tons but with Tennessee mines advancing only to 7.80 tons per man-day.[32]

Since it is principally these small Tennessee mines that appear to have fallen on hard times as a result of wgae changes during the period since 1950, the data cited above are especially relevant for judging output/labor

---

[31] Identical size rankings are obtained whether average mine size is measured as value added per mine, average production workers per mine, or average total workers per mine. The statewide averages used in the correlation were computed from data reported in table 4B, *1954 Census of Mineral Industries*.

[32] *Ramsey* v. *United Mine Workers*, 1967 CCH Trade Cases, para. 72,051 (E.D. Tenn., S.D. 1967).

Table 8.3 Output labor ratios and average employment, underground mines without cleaning plant, 1954 and 1958

Output/ labor ratio (short tons of coal per man-hour)	1954*		1958*	
	Number of establish-ments	Average number of employees	Number of establish-ments	Average number of employees
Less than 0.20	24	.7.5	88	4.4
0.20–0.39	166	9.6	115 (118)	10.4 (10.3)
0.40–0.59	430	22.9	210 (268)	9.8 (14.0)
0.60–0.79	488	35.2	333 (403)	14.8 (17.8)
0.80–0.99	365	35.9	292 (354)	15.0 (22.9)
1.00–1.19	183	43.4	329 (377)	15.2 (18.4)
1.20–1.39	105	54.4	213 (251)	10.0 (18.3)
1.40–1.59	72	87.5	182 (202)	21.9 (23.8)
1.60–1.79	33	61.2	130 (149)	17.0 (20.6)
1.80–1.99	22	60.8	81 (93)	37.9 (39.2)
2.00 and over	34	86.8	393 (444)	15.7 (19.0)

Source: 1954 Census of Mineral Industries, Vol. I, p. 12A–64, table 8.
           1958 Census of Mineral Industries, Vol. I, p. 12A–50, table 8A.
* The 1954 figures, and the 1958 figures in parentheses, include mines with mechanical crushing, screening,m and sizing.

ratio differences. A more general comparison is nevertheless available in table 8.3, where output/labor ratios and mine size (measured by average employment) for underground mines without cleaning plants are listed.[33] Again a strong positive association between the output/labor ratio and mine size is evident from the data.

[33] The elimination of cleaning plants from the comparison tends to screen out large mines, but to include these leads to ambiguous output labor and size measures since cleaning is an additional operation. Among mines with cleaning plants, a positive association between the output/labor ratio and average employment continues to hold.

C. THE TRANSMISSION RATIO

The basic document which has guided wage negotiations since 1950 is the National Bituminous Coal Wage Agreement of 1950. Principal among the provisions of the agreement was the statement that, 'All mine workers, whether employed by the month, day, or tonnage, yardwork, deadwork, or footage rate, shall receive four dollars and seventy-five cents [\$4.75] per day in addition to that provided for in the contract which expired March 31, 1946.'[34] That is, the differentials prevailing as of 31 December, 1946 were taken as the base and to this base was added the amount of \$4.75 per day for every worker independent of his base pay. Successive additions to the wage payment have taken precisely this same form and have been regarded as mere amendments to the basic agreement. Through 1 April 1959 the cumulative additions came to \$14.25 per day, the effect being to raise the estimated Appalachian union minimum hourly rates from \$1.807 in March 1950 to \$3.05 in April 1959.[35] As Christenson puts it, 'these cumulative additions have effected a progressive transformation in the wage structure from one that involved detailed occupational classification and a mixture of hourly with tonnage rates, to one consisting of a simple, almost single, hourly rate pattern.'[36] The court in *Ramsey*, in evaluating changes in the differential once favoring the southeastern Tennessee coal field, reached an identical conclusion.[37]

The question naturally arises as to why the small operators have failed to adapt successfully to the steady elimination of the productivity related differentials that existed in 1946. The answer, not surprisingly, turns on the existence of indivisibility. Mechanical loading is well suited to seam thicknesses of four or more feet, but seams of less than four feet are generally hand loaded.[38] Indeed, the correlation between mechanical loading and seam thickness is quite striking. The linear correlation between per cent of coal mechanically loaded (M) and per cent of tonnage from seam thicknesses of four or more feet (T) using statewide averages for nine states in 1955, was
$$M = 17 + 0.89T$$
$$(0.15)$$
, the coefficient of determination being 0.81.[39] Unable to employ the large-firm technology in the narrow seams where the small mines tend predominantly to be located,[40] the

---

[34] Cited by Christenson (1962), p. 206.
[35] Ibid., p. 47.
[36] Ibid., p. 206.
[37] *Ramsey* v. *United Mine Workers*, 1967 CCH Trade Cases, para. 72,051 (E.D. Tenn., S.D. 1967).
[38] Christenson (1962), pp. 144–5.
[39] Data for the correlation were obtained from Christenson (1962), tables 27 and 28.
[40] Ibid., p. 148.

option of mechanization is thus effectively out of reach. Elimination of wage differentials therefore has placed the small operators at both an initial and a continuing disadvantage.

D. ESTIMATED VALUE OF δ^*

The foregoing can be used to estimate the optimal value of δ. Two things should, however, be noted in this connection. First, the fact that the bituminous coal industry would, structurally, support the use of wage premiums to bar entry to (or induce the exit of) small-scale firms does not establish that such wage premiums exist. Second, even if they have been used for this purpose, the actual value of the wage premium may, for any number of reasons, differ from the optimum value that we estimate. Thus, although the small, southeastern Tennessee mines appear to have been seriously disadvantaged by the wage policy of the UMW, this is only a small segment of the total small-mine population; the optimum value of δ taking the industry as a whole may therefore differ from that estimated from Tennessee data. The value of δ^* estimated below should be interpreted with these qualifications in mind.

Between 1950 and 1960 the output/labor ratio in all mines nationally relative to the small mines in Tennessee appears to have increased from 1:1 to, approximately, 3:2. Using horsepower per production worker as a proxy for the capital/labor ratio, the large mines appear possibly to stand in a 2:1 ratio relative to the small mines. (Since the model uses the reciprocal of the capital/labor ratio, the relevant ratio in labor/capital terms is 1:2.) Assuming that the value of θ in equation (8.12) is 1.05, the optimum value of δ is given by $(0.525 - 0.075 E) w_o / (0.30)(E - 1)$. If the relevant demand elasticity is 3, the value of δ^* is $w_o/2$. This seems somewhat high and is at best merely suggestive; but a better estimate obviously requires more precise knowledge of the relevant parameters than we have been able to develop here.

IV. Industry Structure

Two additional factors essential to an understanding of wage premiums as a barrier to entry are the size distributions of firms in an industry and the ease with which entry at the large scale can occur.[41] With respect to

[41] Other factors that may also be important, but which I am inclined to subordinate at this time, are the economic age of an industry and the degree of product differentiation. The concept of economic age, although intuitively meaningful, has never been specified operationally. Presumably if an industry is sufficiently sophisticated to employ wage rates as a barrier to entry it would be regarded as reasonably mature, but this is judging structure from behavior whereas the objective is to predict behavior from structure.

Product differentiation is a more 'familiar' measure, but it too is difficult to specify quantitatively. Estimates of its importance in any particular market tend to vary, sometimes significantly, between investigators. Perhaps the most satisfactory way of treating it at this

the latter, it is essential either that existing large firms control a scarce resource which prevents potential rivals from entering at the large scale, or the additional output placed on the market by entry at the large scale must itself be significant relative to the size of the market.

Entry foreclosure at the large (capital-intensive) scale is, of course, assured if existing large firms have pre-empted a scarce resource vital to large-scale operations. Where control over a scarce resource is missing, the size of firm relative to the size of market issue becomes relevant. This question has been examined previously by Bain[42] and Sylos-Labini[43] and developed somewhat more formally by Modigliani.[44] As Modigliani shows, if the size of firm at which minimum average costs are reached represents only a small fraction of the market, the opportunity for large firms to charge a price that exceeds minimum average costs is sharply circumscribed. To set the price significantly above minimum average costs would signal profit opportunities to potential entrants, and the price could not be sustained. Put in terms of our diagram in figure 8.2, the critical issue is how large is Q_o relative to the size of the market (Q_c). If Q_o is relatively large our preceding analysis goes through unchanged. If, however, Q_o is relatively small, the fact that wage premiums can be used effectively to bar small-scale operators is of limited consequence. For if a price that exceeds AC_m is charged, potential entrants will come in – not at the small scale but at the large scale – without individually affecting significantly the market price. The cumulative effect of such entry, of course, would lower market price and thereby reduce whatever monopoly advantage large firms realized initially.

The number and size distribution of firms in an industry are also critical. Thus, given only that the natural pressures for wage uniformity are substantial, which is probably typical in industries of small numbers, large firms in concentrated industries may use wage premiums to eliminate small rivals on their own initiative. Specific agreements in which wage uniformity and implementation terms are spelled out may be inessential in industries of small numbers; perceptiveness among the large firms together with natural pressures for wage uniformity may be sufficient. Such an occurrence would merely be another manifestation of the familiar but difficult problems that oligopoly presents for antitrust policy where

time is as an *ad hoc* amendment to the basic wage barrier theory developed in the text. The relevant *ceteris paribus* proposition would be: the greater the degree of product differentiation, the more difficult it becomes to reach a satisfactory quasi-agreement and the less likely that wage premiums will be used in a calculated way to bar entry.

[42] Bain (1956).

[43] Paolo Sylos Labini, *Oligopoly and Technical Progress* (Harvard University Press, Cambridge, Mass., 1961).

[44] Modigliani (1958), pp. 215–32.

concerted action exists, but for which the element of explicit collusion is missing.

Conditions of large numbers, by contrast, ordinarily prevent effective quasi-agreements from being reached; unassisted concerted action is here quite infeasible. Thus to observe that effective concerted action has developed in an atomistic industry would suggest the existence of what Fellner classifies as 'Case 3 oligopoly'; namely, those that 'require the active aid of an outside agency, which in turn means that some compromise must be reached between the interests of the atomistic group in question and the organizing agency.'[45]

Consider now the structural characteristics of the bituminous coal industry on these size distribution and entry dimension.

A. NUMBER AND SIZE DISTRIBUTION OF FIRMS

The size distribution of operating groups and companies in the bituminous coal industry for the years 1946, 1954, and 1962 is shown in table 8.4 (An operating group is a collection of companies that are interrelated by one form or another of joint ownership.[46] Associations of companies into operating groups are common among the larger companies, but such arrangements occur progressively less frequently as size class decreases.) The three striking features that emerge from an examination of the size distribution statistics reported in table 8.4 are: (a) the very large number of firms in the industry; (b) the extreme inequality in firm size (as revealed, e.g., in the Gini coefficients) that prevails among them; but (c) the very low degree of output concentration that exists in the industry. The concentration ratio for the four largest operating groups in 1962 was only 22 per cent, and it required over 400 operating groups to account for 86 per cent of industry production. Based on national concentration ratios, this is clearly an unconcentrated industry according to any accepted standard. Even regional refinements of the data, which may be appropriate for studying some aspects of the behavior of this industry, are unlikely to upset this gross judgment.[47]

In view of these large numbers conditions, any use of wage premiums to bar entry would, presumably, fall within Fellner's 'Case 3 oligopoly' classification. Thus the aid of an outside agency and specificity in the

[45] Fellner (1965), p. 47.
[46] Christenson (1962), p. 41.
[47] Moyer argues that the midwestern coal market should be regarded as oligopolistic (1961, p. 68). But operationally the actual and potential coal shipments into this region from other areas would appear to prevent most midwestern mines from enjoying any but a local, limited variety of price insularity. Moreover, even if insularity in the midwestern market were substantial, the fact that this is a much more concentrated region than most makes it the exception rather than the rule, and thus has limited relevance for our analysis.

Table 8.4 Size distribution of operating groups and companies, bituminous coal, 1946, 1954, 1962

	1946	1954	1962
Total number of companies in the industry	7198	5000	7000
% of production accounted for by four largest operating groups	NA	21	22
Gini coefficient			
By operating group	0.82	0.81	0.84
By company	0.78	0.78	0.83
Operating groups with over 3,000,000 ton production			
Number of groups	28	22	26
Number of companies included	83	65	58
% of total production	34	36	50
Operating groups with over 100,000 ton production			
Number of groups	688	379	405
Number of companies included	908	563	503
% of total production	86	85	86

Source: Derived from *Keystone Coal Mine Directory* 1946, 1954, 1962.

wage agreement with respect both to uniformity objectives and procedures for securing implementation could be expected. The UMW clearly qualifies as an outside agency potentially able to supply the necessary assistance, the 1950 Wage Agreement includes an explicit statement of wage uniformity objectives,[48] and the 1958 Protective Wage Clause amendment can be interpreted as a means of implementing the agreement.[49] This

---

[48] See section III, part 3.

[49] The 1958 Protective Wage Clause amendment was designed to deny access to the processing and marketing facilities of the large firms the coal produced by mines in which the full terms of the 1950 agreement and subsequent amendments were not observed. The Protective Wage Clause thus provided that all signatory companies 'would not buy or process coal from nonunion mines, and neither would they lease any coal lands to operators who failed to observe the full terms of the union agreement including welfare fund payments' Christenson (1962), p. 268.

does not, of course, establish that an agreement was reached with these wage barrier objectives in mind, but the conspicuous evidence scarcely permits its dismissal either.

B. THE CONDITION OF ENTRY

Although the inequality in firm size within the bituminous coal industry is extreme, so that the size of the large firms vastly exceeds that of the small, output concentration is quite low and thus entry at the large scale could occur without the entering firm adding significantly to total industry output. Thus economies of large-scale production cannot be regarded as barriers to entry. Neither can capital requirements in bituminous coal be considered a serious limitation to entry.[50] Thus if entry at the large scale is to be restricted, the absolute cost advantages of extant mines must be responsible for this result.

The absolute cost advantage in bituminous coal takes the form of a geological constraint imposed by the scarcity of wide-seam deposits. Given the state of technology prevailing in the 1950s only the wide-seam deposits were well-suited to mechanical loading, and access to these had been pre-empted. For this reason Christenson takes the position that 'it is preposterous to say, "There is no barrier to the entrance of new concerns and the development of new properties." The barriers are clear and easily identified; they grow out of the character of the geological foundations upon which the industry rests.'[51] And he argues later that 'the real foundation for the output rate is the nature of the coal bed. ... [S]mall mines have to function without large amounts of capital equipment because they operate on a natural resource base which does not encourage its use.'[52] Moyer likewise finds that the large operators have secured control over the premium reserves in the midwestern coal market,[53] and goes on to observe that although the untapped reserves of coal are staggering, only the high-grade reserves will currently support mining operations. Negative rents would have to be imputed to the inferior reserves to bring them into production at the current state of technology.[54]

---

[50] Baratz reports that 'the intended output and degree of permanence of a coal mine determines its initial investment cost, beginning at perhaps $1,000 for a punch mine, and from $10,000 for a strip mine up to $1,000,000 for a permanent large-scale strip-mining tract. For deep mine producing high-quality washed coal, initial capital requirements run between $1,000,000 and $2,500,000' (1955, p. 3). Although $2,500,000 is not a trivial sum, it hardly constitutes a serious impediment to entry.

[51] Christenson (1962, p. 115). Christenson's position sharply contradicts that taken by Baratz, who argues that the 'principal obstacle to entry is the initial investment outlay' (1955, p. 2). We find Baratz unconvincing and side with Christenson on this issue.

[52] Ibid., p. 199.

[53] Moyer (1961), p. 126.

[54] Ibid., pp. 127–8.

Resource conditions thus protect large firms against entry at the large scale. Hence, although the large numbers condition prevents monopolistic pricing schemes from being enforced, the combination of wage premiums and resource control would provide the large operators with circumstances in which the relatively modest but possibly attractive objective of permanently eliminating the marginal operators could potentially be realized. If the 'compromise' referred to by Fellner were to include an implicit agreement by the union not to resist mechanization in exchange for an implicit agreement by the large operators to share productivity gains, a rational basis for using wage rates as a barrier to entry might well exist between them.

V. Conclusions

That economic theory fails to play a more important role in the formulation and enforcement of antitrust policy is at least partly the responsibility of the economics profession. Too often the relevant economic theory has not been provided. Where it has been, it is often nonoperational. The pressing necessity for the courts to render judgments on the cases brought before them nevertheless requires that problems of economic consequence be decided. If occasionally economists believe these decisions to be economically unsound, it is germane to enquire whether an operational statement of the relevant theory has been available to the courts before expressing discontent.

The issues raised in the *Pennington* case illustrate these difficulties. Questions of theoretical significance did exist and, in some implicit sense at least, were both recognized and actively disputed. The principal economic issue on which Justice Goldberg (joined by Justices Harlan and Stewart) and the Supreme Court differed involved the product market effects of wage agreements collusively negotiated and uniformly enforced. The majority took the position that uniform wage agreements could have anticompetitive product market effects and, if the collusive use of wage premiums could be established, would constitute a violation of the Sherman Act. Although their arguments were somewhat imprecise, they were not nearly so obscure as those of the minority. But lacking the relevant economic theory, lucidity from either is hardly to be expected. As it was, the implicit model employed by the majority led them to a position which our analysis supports, but this scarcely justifies complacency. Another time and the decision could go differently.

As we have shown in section II, the relevant economic theory can be provided for the circumstances under dispute in *Pennington*, and indeed we provide a quite unambiguous verdict: where the assumptions of our model are fulfilled, wage premiums *can* be used to erect a barrier to entry, and thus the uniform wage agreement may indeed be a device by which monopoly advantage is secured. This is not to condemn uniform wage agreements per se; as pointed out earlier, the Supreme Court took deliberate care to make clear that an act of conspiracy must be present before such agreements would be declared illegal. The virtue of our model is that not only does it show the possible economic effects of wage conspiracy, but it also identifies the circumstances in which such a conspiracy is most likely to be successful. It thus permits the antitrust authorities to focus on that subset of industries in which the incentives for wage conspiracy are greatest. And it permits the courts to determine whether complaints of wage conspiracy should be seriously entertained.

The law may, however, experience difficulties in highly concentrated industries. Given that the assumptions of the model are fulfilled, effective concurrence among the largest firms supported by natural pressures for wage uniformity in the union would be sufficient, without agreement, for wage premiums to be used with entry barrier effects. Alternatively, if the unions in oligopolistic industries key their wage demands to the profit performance of the largest firms and insist on substantially identical terms from all members of the industry, wage barrier effects which reinforce the oligopolistic structure of the industry can result. In neither case need the element of conspiracy exist. This serves to point up the fact that conspiracy is a requirement of the law rather than the model. Given the value of the transmission ratio, the economic effects, with or without conspiracy, will be the same. Wage barrier theory thus provides still another example of the fundamental tension between the concept of monopoly in law and economics.[55]

With respect to industries of large numbers, failure to fulfill the conditions of the model would render claims of wage conspiracy suspect. Therefore, both in industries of large and small numbers, the fears of Goldfinger and St Antoine, who expressed concern that for the Supreme Court to uphold the circuit court opinion in *Pennington* 'could have a shattering impact . . . on the labor movement,'[56] seem at least exaggerated. In large numbers industries, the plausibility of a claim of wage conspiracy is fundamentally impaired if the industry in question fails to satisfy the conditions of the model. Thus the model performs the useful function of providing protection against conspiracy charges in unconcentrated indus-

---

[55] The distinction is discussed in E. S. Mason, 'Monopoly in law and economics,' *Yale Law Journal*, XLVII (1937), pp. 34–54. A general discussion of the anticompetitive incentives that collective bargaining sets up is provided by Ralph K. Winter, Jr., 'Collective bargaining and competition: The application of antitrust standards to union activities,' *Yale Law Journal*, LXXIII (1963), pp. 14–73.

[56] Nat Goldfinger and Theodore J. St Antoine, 'A view from labor,' in *Perspectives on Antitrust Policy*, ed. Almarin Phillips, Princeton University Press, Princeton, New Jersey, 1965, p. 406, n. 32.

tries where the relevant parameters deviate substantially from those required by the model. Hence the model makes it possible to avoid uncritical application of the *Pennington* decision. In concentrated industries, by contrast, conspiracy may be inessential to the achievement of wage barrier effects; a threat to the labor movement under existing law is here not even posed.

The failure of the court on remand to find the evidence sufficient to support a charge of wage conspiracy disposes of the antitrust question in *Pennington* from the standpoint of the law. But since the industry is one in which the basic wage parameter conditions are fulfilled, we can still express an interest in the case from the standpoint of economics. What are the predictable economic results? What advantages might the large operators expect to realize? In our opinion, the most the large operators might succeed in doing is discourage small-scale entry and hasten the exit of small operators. Their numbers are simply too great to permit them to realize the benefits of monopoly profits that potentially inhere in such a situation. If stability rather than profits were the principal objective of the large operators, this might be achieved. The more ambitious objective of monopoly profits requires interfirm collusion with respect to output restriction of a much more extensive sort. One should not, however, conclude from the fact that large operators fail to realize monopoly prices that the welfare effects of a wage barrier policy are negligible.

The welfare effects of wage premiums (if they exist) on economic performance in bituminous coal are separable into four types: static inefficiencies, displacement losses, progressiveness effects, and labor peace. Static inefficiencies refer to the welfare effects associated with a simple distortion in factor prices. As a result, factors will be inefficiently employed in equilibrium relative to the social optimum.[57] Probably more important, however, are the displacement losses that movement to the new equilibrium entails. Since the opportunity costs of small-mine labor and capital may be substantially zero, the displacement of these factors from what had been productive uses in the mining of bituminous coal may result in significant economic losses. An offsetting consideration in all of this is the strong possibility that the introduction of mechanized methods into the industry was conditional on reaching an agreement between the large mines and the UMW – one which provided for sharing the gains in a way which a wage premium policy would effect. Also, there is Justice Goldberg's argument that the labor peace which resulted from the formation of the bituminous coal employer's association in 1950 is to be valued.[58]

[57] This is, of course, subject to the usual 'second-best' qualifications. For a general discussion, see Albert Fishlow and Paul David, 'Optimal resource allocation in an imperfect market setting,' *Journal of Political Economy*, LXIX (1961), pp. 529–46.
[58] *United Mine Workers* v. *Pennington*, 85 S. Ct. 1607, 1626 (1965).

Whereas the welfare consequences of static inefficiencies and displacement losses are both negative, it is not obvious that a net negative welfare result obtains when mechanization and labor peace consequences are taken into account – especially if these could not easily be had otherwise. This raises the question of whether a rule of reason or per se standard is more appropriate in dealing with wage premium issues. Inasmuch as *Pennington* may not be wholly representative, a broader frame of reference in making this judgment is probably required. Also relevant in making this decision is whether the tools for assessing net effects are or will be adequate. The dependence of the courts on assistance from the economics profession is again evident.

9

Predatory Pricing: A Strategic and Welfare Analysis

Until recently predatory pricing[1] has been a relatively vague concept in antitrust law. This may be because emotive terms, such as predatory pricing, do not invite and sometimes defy analysis. But the lack of precision may also reflect a sense that the familiar tools of static economic analysis are ill-suited to cope with the issues posed by predatory pricing. As developed in this chapter, predatory pricing involves strategic behavior in which intertemporal considerations are central. Static economic models that fail to capture these attributes miss crucial features of the predatory pricing issue.

Recently a remarkable degree of consensus in favor of cost-based rules

Research on this chapter was supported by the Center for the Study of Organizational Innovation at the University of Pennsylvania and by a grant from the National Science Foundation. Work on the final version of the chapter was completed while I was a Fellow at the Center for Advanced Study in the Behavioral Sciences, Stanford, California. Comments by Paul Joskow, Richard Posner, and Donald Turner on earlier versions of the chapter are gratefully acknowledged, as are comments by Industrial Organization Workshop participants at the University of Pennsylvania and the University of Chicago. Economists and lawyers in the Antitrust Division of the United States Department of Justice also commented usefully on an oral presentation of the penultimate version of this chapter. Reprinted by permission of The Yale Law Journal Company and Fred B. Rothman & Company from the *Yale Law Journal*, 87, pp. 284–340.

[1] Section 2 of the Sherman Act, 15 USC (Supp. V 1975), proscribes predatory pricing as an act of monopolization or an attempt to monopolize. See e.g., *United States* v. *American Tobacco Co.*, 221 US 106, 182 (1911); *Standard Oil Co.* v. *United States*, 221 USI, 43 (1910), Clayton Act section 2, as amended by the Robinson-Patman Act, 15 USC section 13 (1970), and Robinston-Patman Act, section 3, ibid., section 13a, also proscribe predatory pricing. The issues are the same under all three provisions.

has appeared in court opinions dealing with predatory pricing.[2] This judicial consensus may be a response to a series of articles addressed to predatory pricing issues, the most significant being commentary by Edward Cooper and studies by Richard Posner and by Philip Areeda and Donald Turner.[3] Posner and Areeda–Turner brought the tools of static economic analysis to bear on the problem and produced a set of cost-based tests for evaluating allegations of predatory pricing.[4] The Areeda–Turner rules have not only been embraced by the courts, but have also influenced a Justice Department decision to withdraw a suit in progress.[5]

Though the Areeda–Turner and Posner studies are important contributions, I nonetheless have serious reservations about them. Both studies fail to account for two major intertemporal attributes of predatory pricing. First, although static welfare economics may be adequate to evaluate a market where there is a shift from one steady level of supplying a good or service to a second steady level, the same model can be misleading if the shift in question is temporary or contingent and arguably has the purpose of deterring future rivalry. Second, and perhaps somewhat more subtle, firms have incentives to adapt to rules of law. These adaptations must expressly be taken into account in an evaluation of the economic consequences of a legal rule. When allowance is made for these dynamic effects, the Areeda–Turner rules can be shown to have inferior efficiency properties as compared with the alternative set of rules proposed in this chapter. In addition, the alternative rules are more easily enforced and

---

[2] See *Pacific Eng'r & Prod. Co.* v. *Kerr-McGee Corp.*, 551 F.2d 790, 797 (10th Cir. 1977), petition for cert. filed, 46 USL W 3141 (US 19 Sept. 1977); *Hanson* v. *Shell Oil Co.*, 541 F.2d 1352, 1358 (9th Cir. 1976), cert. denied, 97 S. Ct. 813 (1977); *National Ass'n of Regulatory Util. Comm'rs* v. *FCC*, 525 US 630, 637–38 & n.34 (D.C. Cir. 1976), cert. denied, 425 US 992 (1976); *International Air Indus.* v. *American Excelsior Co.* 517 F.2d 714, 723–5 (5th Cir. 1975), cert. denied, 424 US 943 (1976); *Weber* v. *Wynne Trade Reg. Rep.*, (CCH) (1977–1 Trade Cas.) paragraph 61,315 (D.N.J. 1977); *Inter City Oil Co.* v. *Murphy Oil Co.* [1976–1] Trade Cas. paragraph 60,948, at 69,176 (D. Minn. 1976).

[3] R. Posner, *Antitrust Law; An Economic Perspective (1976, pp. 184–96); Areeda and Turner (1975) p. 697; Cooper, 'Attempts and Monopolization: A mildly expansionary answer to the prophylactic riddle of section two, Michigan Law Review*, 72 (1974), pp. 373, 435–40.

[4] Important differences should, however, be noted. Areeda and Turner favor a short-run marginal cost rule while Posner proposes long-run marginal cost as the test criterion. Compare Posner, *supra*, footnote 3, pp. 191–3 with Areeda and Turner, *supra* footnote 3, pp. 732–3.

[5] Former Assistant Attorney General Thomas E. Kauper explained the Antitrust Division's decision to dismiss the Government's antitrust case against two major tire companies partly on the ground that '[i]t is now clear that any theory of Section 2 liability upon which we could rely in these cases cannot rest upon traditional predatory conduct, because we cannot demonstrate that the defendant in either case set prices below marginal or average variable costs.' Memorandum for Attorney General Edward Levi. 23 February 1976, reprinted in *Trade Reg. Rep.*, 5 CCH paragraph 50,259 (1976) [in relation to *United States* v. *Firestone Tire and Rubber Co.*, Civ. No. C-73-836, and *United States* v. *Goodyear Tire & Rubber Co.*, Civ. No. C-73-835 (N.D. Ohio 1976)].

explicitly recognize the differences between competition among a group of established oligopolists and the rivalry that occurs between a dominant firm and new entrants.

Part I begins by providing background on predatory pricing and gives reasons to be skeptical about the properties of the rules favored by Areeda and Turner. The efficiency benefits of their marginal cost pricing rules are questioned on the ground that they may not yield the immediate social welfare gains that Areeda and Turner attribute to them and, more importantly, because their proposed rules make no allowance for strategic behavior by dominant firms.[6] An attempt is then made to remedy the latter shortcoming by developing a model in which the strategic motivations of firms engaging in predatory behavior are expressly acknowledged. The model focuses on predatory pricing to deter entry into the dominant firm's market, and investigates the effects of three alternative predatory pricing rules on prices and output before (*ex ante* consequences) and after (*ex post* consequences) entry (or, more generally, rivalous investment) occurs. Part II examines the welfare properties of these three alternative rules.

Part III extends the basic model, which assumes that goods and services are supplied on a continuing basis, to cover equipment that undergoes significant design changes between successive production runs ('generational equipment'). A third case, which should be distinguished from both of these entry variants, is predatory pricing among established firms. This case is treated in part IV.

Part V applies the analysis to recent antitrust cases, and part VI expressly sets out the proposed rules of law. The chapter concludes with a brief examination of the relation between predatory pricing rules and notions of industrial fairness.

I. Predatory Pricing, Efficiency, and Strategic Modeling

A. THE ISSUES

The existence of predatory pricing has long been regarded with skepticism by many economists and some lawyers. Without objective standards defining predatory pricing, allegations of predatory pricing are easy to level but difficult to evaluate. Further, pricing 'below cost' (variously defined) has been difficult to show empirically.[7] Perhaps most persuasively, predatory pricing is held to be 'irrational' since economic analysis suggests

---

[6] Strategic behavior, in the context of predatory pricing, involves not merely prepositioning, which is standard to entry barrier analysis, but also contingent responses to entry. Both need to be examined in an integrated way.

[7] See Areeda and Turner, *supra* footnote 3, pp. 699 and n. 7; R. Koller, 'The myth of predatory pricing: An empirical study.' *Antitrust Law and Economic Review* (Summer 1971), p. 105.

that it is always cheaper for a firm to acquire rather than to undersell a competitor.[8]

These arguments, however, are unpersuasive. As Professor Posner observes, the irrationality position 'is convincing only if mergers are assumed to be legal, and . . . the illegality of mergers to create a monopoly has been clear for a long time now.'[9] If predatory pricing, though also unlawful, is more difficult to detect than merger, 'predation may in fact be a cheaper mode of monopolization than acquisition.'[10] Predatory pricing may also be used to influence the terms under which an acquisition is made[11] and may be directed less at destroying extant rivals than at discouraging prospective rivals.[12] The latter point is especially significant. The simple net benefit calculus upon which the irrationality argument rests can easily be upset if aggressive responses to entry in one market can have entry-deterring effects in other markets. If by responding aggressively to a current threat of entry a dominant firm can give a 'signal' that it intends to react vigorously to entry in later time periods or different geographical regions, discounted future gains may more than offset sacrifices of current profit. Signaling, whether intertemporal or interspatial, is plainly strategic behavior. Areeda and Turner nevertheless model the predatory pricing issue mainly in static terms.[13]

B. THE EFFICIENCY CRITERION

Lest the antitrust laws be invoked as a means to discourage legitimate rivalry, often as a shelter against inefficiency, workable criteria are sorely needed for distinguishing between meritorious and defective predatory pricing claims. Areeda and Turner reject 'such empty formulae as "below cost" pricing, ruinous competition, or predatory intent,' and instead 'attempt to formulate meaningful and workable tests for distinguishing between predatory and competitive pricing by examining the relation

---

[8] The standard reference on the purported irrationality of predatory pricing is J. S. McGee, 'Predatory price cutting: The standard Oil (N.J.) case,' *Journal of Law and Economics (1958)*, p. 137. For a commentary, see B. Yamey, 'Predatory price cutting: Notes and comments,' *Journal of Law and Economics*, 5 (1972), p. 129.

[9] Posner, *supra* footnote 3, p. 185.

[10] Cooper makes a similar argument. Cooper, *supra* footnote 3, p. 436 n. 228.

[11] Yamey, *supra* footnote 8, pp. 130–1.

[12] Posner, *supra* footnote 3, pp. 185–6; Note, *Telex* v. *IBM*: 'Monopoly pricing under section 2 of the Sherman Act,' *Yale Law Journal*, 84 (1975), pp. 558, 564, n. 27.

[13] Occasional quasi-dynamic elements do appear, as in their treatment of promotional pricing. Areeda and Turner, *supra* footnote 3, pp. 713–15. But the central argument and the main rules are developed in a static framework.

between a firm's costs and its prices.'[14] Posner likewise eschews reliance on intent in evaluating claims of predatory behavior; he argues that intent is an unreliable indicator of market behavior.[15] Without considerable confidence that a manifestly anti-competitive marketing plan is disclosed by the documents, and that the evidence is not just sales executive puffery, an enforcement effort based on intent is apt to be unrewarding.[16]

[14] Areeda and Turner, *supra* footnote 3, pp. 699–700. Areeda and Turner also 'suggest that extreme care be taken in formulating [predatory pricing] rules, lest the threat of litigation, particularly by private parties, materially deter legitimate, competitive pricing.' Ibid., p. 699.

[15] Posner, *supra* footnote 3, pp. 189–90:
A firm with executives sensitized to antitrust problems will not leave any documentary trail of improper intent; one whose executives lack this sensitivity will often create rich evidence of such intent simply by the clumsy choice of words to describe innocent behavior. Especially misleading here is the inveterate tendency of sales executives to brag to their superiors about their competitive prowess, often using metaphors of coercion that are compelling evidence of predatory intent to the naive. Any doctrine that relies upon proof of intent is going to be applied erratically at best.

[16] Professor Scherer, in responding to Areeda and Turner, argues that cost-based approaches are simplistic and that a comprehensive appraisal of a complex set of economic facts together with an inquiry into the monopolist's intent is needed to reach a correct predatory pricing verdict. F. M. Scherer, 'Predatory pricing and the Sherman Act: A comment,' *Harvard Law Review*, 89 (1976), pp. 869, 890. Depending on the particulars, Scherer's 'comprehensive reappraisal shows that long-term economic welfare is maximized in some cases when the monopolist's price exceeds its marginal cost and in other cases when marginal cost is undercut.' Ibid. The particulars involve a determination of the relative cost positions of the monopolist and fringe firms, the scale of entry required to secure minimum costs, whether fringe firms are driven out entirely or merely suppressed, whether the monopolist expands its output to replace the output of excluded rivals or restricts supply again when the rivals withdraw, and whether any long-run compensatory expansion by the monopolist entails investment in scale economy-embodying new plant.
Ibid. (footnote omitted). Scherer concludes that 'I do not know how these variables can be assessed properly without a thorough examination of the factual circumstances accompanying the monopolist's alleged predatory behavior, how the monopolist's officials perceived the probable effects of its behavior (i.e., intent), and the structural consequences actually flowing from the behavior.'
    Although I also urge that greater knowledge of the circumstances is needed than uniform application of a cost-based standard admits, I am persuaded by Areeda and Turner's rebuttal that Scherer's approach relies on 'long-run possibilities [that] are intrinsically speculative and indeterminate.' Areeda and Turner, 'Scherer on predatory pricing: A reply,' *Harvard Law Review*, 89 (1976), pp. 891, 897 (footnote omitted). Scherer evidently would supplant antitrust enforcement with a price commission. Findings of illegality would turn on a study of full fact situations, including an examination of whether entrants are efficient or not. Where they are, the dominant firm would be constrained to charge a higher price than where they are not.
    The exercise is troublesome on several accounts. Whether a price cut is predatory turns on whether or not entrants are efficient. (And if they are not, it is an easy step to extend the argument to consider the possibility that, given a 'fair chance,' they will be.) How the dominant firm is to be so apprised is not disclosed. Secondly, whether or not a price cut is predatory turns on whether it is subsequently reversed. But this involves monitoring for an indeterminate period. Among other things, it would be necessary to investigate whether a price is reversed or has been adjusted to meet new circumstances (for example, higher input

Both Areeda–Turner and Posner repeatedly assert that the 'predatory impact' of a price reduction by a dominant firm must be judged by whether such a reduction will exclude an equally efficient rival. They presume that competition is running a beneficial course if the price cut excludes only firms that are less efficient than the dominant firm. To be sure, the demise of any firm has painful consequences for the affected employees and investors. Seen in a broader context, however, the elimination of inefficiency is a leading benefit of competition. It is crucial to make the distinction between protecting competitors and protecting competition. Sentiment is a cruel hoax if it leads to protecting competitors, since the consumer is invariably the loser when such rules are introduced. An appreciation for the long-run efficiency benefits of competition is essential if the uncertainty that surrounds the law on predatory pricing is to be removed and useful rules are to be developed.[17]

Predatory pricing should thus be evaluated in efficiency terms. But whereas Areeda–Turner and Posner invoke static economic analysis to argue that marginal cost pricing promotes efficiency, this chapter formulates the problem in a more general way that makes express allowance for strategic considerations. The basic static economic proposition to which Areeda–Turner and Posner appeal is that, second-best[18] and strategic considerations aside, allocative efficiency is promoted by setting price equal to marginal cost. The underlying argument is that net social benefits are maximized when marginal social benefits (as reflected by price) are set equal to marginal social costs. Areeda–Turner invoke both this condition and the less efficient rival criterion in arguing for a short-run marginal cost pricing test.[19]

There are technical problems with the less efficient rival claim and substantive problems with the allocative efficiency aspect of this two-part

---

costs or EPA restrictions). Dominant firm industries are easily converted to quasi-regulation in the process. But surely the record on price regulation counsels caution. Rather than slip inadvertently into a regulatory posture – which, experience discloses, is typcially hostile toward competition – antitrust is better advised to seek simple rules enforceable in court.

[17] These uncertainties can be a major concern. '[U]ncertainties surrounding the process and criteria of judicial evaluation may deter much competitive activity that even courts would have found desirable.' Cooper, *supra* footnote 3, p. 435.

[18] Second best refers to the proposition that partial equilibrium analysis (which focuses on local conditions – e.g., a particular industry, rather than the whole economy) may be an unreliable indicator of overall welfare effects if sectors other than those being expressly investigated experience distortions. Though occasionally important, second-best arguments are rarely operational and are commonly set aside. They are ignored in the remainder of this chapter.

[19] They argue that '[i]f a monopolist produces at a point where price equals marginal cost, only less efficient firms will suffer larger losses per unit of output,' and that if a firm is forced to charge a price greater than marginal cost, '[o]utput that could be produced at a lower cost than its value to consumers would be eliminated.' Areeda and Turner, *supra* footnote 3, p. 711.

argument. The problem with the first part is that marginal costs are sometimes a poor indicator of total, and hence unit, costs.[20] The second part of the argument raises a more serious problem. Their allocative efficiency claims do not distinguish between marginal cost pricing of a continuing kind and temporary cutting of prices to marginal cost levels for strategic purposes. Marginal cost pricing on a continuing basis has the optimality properties to which Areeda and Turner refer. Moreover, temporary price cuts to marginal cost levels may be warranted by business exigencies other than strategic responses to entry. As Professor Cooper remarks, '[a]ny sale that returns a margin above the added cost of making that sale is unimpeachably sound business practice if it is the best available opportunity.'[21] Both of these practices, however, must be distinguished from the temporary cutting of prices to marginal cost levels for the *strategic* purpose of deterring entry. Although Areeda and Turner recognize that price reductions by the dominant firm may be rescinded when the entry threat vanishes, and express a clear preference for continuous marginal cost pricing, the only difference in the social benefits that they impute to permanent and temporary reductions is one of duration.[22]

An example may help to illustrate the problematic nature of the optimality properties associated with marginal cost pricing of an occasional, strategic kind. Consider a regulated public utility for which the regulatory authority, at periodic intervals, examines price-to-cost relations for the utility to ascertain whether the monopoly franchise should be renewed. Suppose that marginal cost pricing is favorably regarded by the authority and that the utility, recognizing this, adopts marginal cost pricing prior to each franchise review, but reverts to monopoly pricing as soon as the renewal is issued. How should these temporary price cuts be interpreted? The immediate benefit of such temporary price cuts will likely be negligible. Moreover, whatever the immediate benefits, long-run resource misallocations arguably result when the utility reverts to monopolistic pricing following each franchise renewal.

The insignificance of the immediate efficiency gains can be demonstrated by considering three cases: (a) the product or service is nonstorable and consumers recognize that the price cut is merely temporary; (b) the

---

[20] The types of problems that can arise here have been examined by Rosalind Seneca in the context of competition between alternative transportation modes. As she observes and demonstrates, '[a]llocating traffic to the mode with the lowest long-run [or short-run] marginal cost will not *necessarily* minimize the total cost of providing the service.' Seneca, 'Inherent advantage, costs, and resource allocation in the transportation industry,' *American Economic Review*, 63 (1973) pp. 945–946 (emphasis in original). To be sure, these problems may occur infrequently. Nevertheless, the contention that marginal cost prices accurately reflect relative efficiency is in trouble from the outset.

[21] Cooper, *supra* foonote 3, p. 437.

[22] Areeda and Turner, *supra* footnote 3, pp. 706–11.

product is storable but the monopolist is unable to satisfy the demand for the product caused by the influx of orders from consumers attempting to increase their inventories; and (c) consumers mistakenly believe that the price cut will be permanent and adapt their investments accordingly.

There is little incentive to alter consumption practices under case (a) because consumers correctly perceive the temporary nature of the price cut and are unable to accumulate inventories. Here a temporary price cut mainly causes a transfer of income from the monopolist to consumers. Allocative efficiency is little affected.

Under case (b) consumers have an incentive to build up inventories in response to temporary price cuts. But the monopolist can satisfy these demands only if it has considerable excess capacity. Lacking excess capacity, a temporary low price can be sustained only by resorting to nonprice rationing – and hence inventory accumulation demands will go unfulfilled and the allocative effects will again be negligible.

The worst case is (c). If the price cut is thought to be permanent, when in fact it is temporary, consumers will be misled if they significantly alter their consumption practices. Negative net benefits can easily result if consumers incur significant fixed costs in adapting to what were thought to be permanent, but turn out to be temporary, changes in relative prices. Whatever the immediate responses to the price cut, in this example it is obvious that the price cut is merely a strategem. The regulatory authority is extremely myopic if it renews the monopoly franchise because prices are equal to marginal costs at the review interval, especially since more permanent price reductions could have been made a condition for franchise renewal.

To be sure, most of the dominant firms that are of concern here are not regulated industries.[23] But the example is instructive nonetheless. The argument that temporary price cuts, whatever their motivation, yield negligible social benefits applies to regulated and unregulated firms alike. Areeda and Turner's appeal to social optimality as support for temporary marginal cost pricing is thus suspect. Furthermore, putting aside the differences between regulation and antitrust, there is a striking strategic similarity: the temporary price cut is designed in both instances to maintain a monopoly.[24]

[23] Charges of sales below cost do, however, arise between unregulated and regulated firms in the communications industry. The famous *Telpak* case was of this kind. American Tel. & Tel. Co. (Telpak), 37 FCC 1111 (1964); 38 FCC 370 (1964). See also Note, 'Competition in the telephone industry: Beyond Telerent,' *Yale Law Journal*, 86 (1977), p. 538 (examining Bell System's potential for subsidization of competitive services with monopoly revenues).

[24] The example, however, breaks down thereafter. Thus the regulatory agency in the example is empowered to reassign the franchise itself, while a new entrant into an unregulated industry is not awarded a market share but makes inroads by actively contesting for sales. Furthermore, regulatory agencies are frequently able to reach and monitor price agreements on a continuing basis, while antitrust relies on the competitive process to perform this policing function.

Faced with strategic behavior of this kind, the basic question is whether antitrust should tolerate or acquiesce in responsive pricing by dominant firms confronted by the prospect or fact of new entry, subject only to the condition that prices exceed marginal cost. I am inclined to regard price and output responses of a contingent kind – now it's there, now it isn't, depending on whether an entrant has appeared or vanished – as inherently suspect. At the very least, it would seem judicious to examine the properties of alternative predatory pricing rules before concluding that the allocative efficiency properties of marginal cost pricing on a contingent basis are beneficial.

C. STRATEGIC BEHAVIOR

The analysis will be limited to firms that have a clear incentive to behave in a strategic way toward existing and potential rivals. Firms in competitively organized industries are exempted because the incentives are lacking. There is no purpose in sacrificing current profits unless offsetting gains in other geographical markets or in later periods are likely, and firms in competitive industries cannot reap these gains.[25] Only in dominant firm and collusive oligopoly industries do firms have a clear incentive to exclude or eliminate rivals. Although behavior akin to predatory pricing can appear in loose oligopolies or even in competitively organized industries, such behavior is caused by breakdowns in pricing discipline or by personal animus and must be distinguished from the strategic efforts to acquire long-term market power that characterize predatory behavior by dominant firms and collusive oligopolies.

The analysis will be principally concerned with the response of dominant firms and collusive oligopolies to new entry.[26] A dominant-firm industry can be defined as one in which the largest firm has a market share of at least 60 per cent and entry into the market is not easy.[27] Although only

[25] Areeda and Turner expressly recognize this and accordingly rely on the monopoly model to characterize demand and cost conditions. See Areeda and Turner, *supra* footnote 3, pp. 698–9. Areeda and Turner make frequent references to 'the monopolist' on the one hand and 'new entrants and small firms' on the other.

[26] Although the model applies to dominant firms and collusive oligopolists alike, for convenience dominant firm terminology is used throughout the chapter. The particular entry barrier employed is a variant of the entry barrier analysis of Joe Bain and Franco Modigliani. See Bain (1956); Modigliani (1958), p. 215. I am concerned with new investment, whether it is made by new entrants or fringe firms, rather than de novo entry per se. Again, however, it will be convenient to refer to new investment in new entry terms.

[27] See Williamson (1975), pp. 208–33. Although the 60% figure is not etched in stone, in defining dominant firms it must be recognized that disciplining rivals is costly. Only firms with a strong interest in the future configuration of an industry will be prepared to act *unilaterally* to influence such conditions.

a few industries satisfy this definition for a national market,[28] many more industries satisfy the conditions in geographic markets. In collusive oligopolies, firms are able to maintain an effective concurrence of market action. This is not, however, nearly so widespread a condition as is sometimes alleged,[29] but occurs mainly in mature, highly concentrated industries producing homogeneous products under uniform cost conditions and having significant barriers to entry.[30] Again, a consideration of geographic markets increases the number of markets that qualify as collusive oligopolies.

Since the welfare attributes of marginal cost pricing rules cannot be established abstractly, evaluation requires well-specified, operational, alternative rules. Three propositions guide this evaluation. First, post-entry welfare differences aside, rules that invite greater pre-entry output restriction and higher cost supply are plainly less favored. Second, for any given level of post-entry supply, social gains are realized whenever product is supplied at lower cost. Additionally, though less important and more difficult to characterize with the welfare economics apparatus used here, rules that require prospective entrants to have greater knowledge or to bear greater uncertainty are disfavored, *ceteris paribus*.

These propositions contemplate two kinds of strategic behavior. Temporary price cutting to marginal cost levels is transparently a stratagem calculated to discourage current and future entry. This involves reactive (post-entry) behavior. But strategic considerations arise at the pre-entry stage as well. Each predatory pricing rule gives rise to pre-entry price, output, and investment adjustments on the part of dominant firms whose markets are subject to encroachment. To neglect the incentives of rules whereby dominant firms make *pre-entry adaptive responses of a strategic kind* necessarily misses an important part of the problem.[31] Prior treatments are incomplete in that pre-entry effects are ignored, significant alternatives to marginal cost pricing rules are bypassed, and welfare effects are dealt with in a limited and overly sanguine fashion.

[28] See W. Shepherd, *Market Power and Economic Welfare* (1970), New York: Random House, pp. 151–3.

[29] As the postwar Japanese and German experiences suggest, oligopolies behave rather differently from both the prewar holding companies (*Zaibatsus*) in Japan and the government-sanctioned cartel operations in Germany. J. Montias, *The Structure of Economic Systems* (1976), New Haven, Conn.: Yale University Press, pp. 187–90.

[30] Williamson, *supra* footnote 27, pp. 234–47.

[31] I decided to formulate the problem in this way after reading a prepublication draft of A. Michael Spence's interesting paper, 'Entry, capacity, investment and oligopolistic pricing,' *Bell Journal of Economics*, 8 (1977), p. 534 in which he investigates the use of capital investments as a barrier to entry.

D. MODELING ASSUMPTIONS

Dominant firms are assumed to be influenced by predatory pricing rules in the following way:[32] whatever rule is in effect, dominant firms will invest in plant and equipment in an amount and kind such that the profits of any entrant, were one to appear, would be reduced to zero if the dominant firm responded to entry in the most aggressive manner allowed by the prevailing rule.[33] An aggressive (as opposed to a conciliatory) response involves producing the maximum output consistent with the prevailing rule. Given that investment is determined with this strategic objective in mind, the dominant firm behaves in all pre-entry periods by maximizing short-run profits. Pre-entry investment and post-entry pricing behavior are thus both conditional on the specification of the predatory behavior rule.

The strategic model assumes that potential entrants are aware of and understand the economic consequences of entry responses by dominant firms under whatever rule is in effect. As in most entry models, potential entrants are assumed to assess their entry opportunities with respect to a residual demand curve, which shows how much market demand remains to be satisfied at every price given the dominant firm's contingent response to entry.[34] The location of the dominant firm's response curve depends

[32] Alternative behavioral assumptions that involve no strategic prepositioning (myopic profit maximization) and sophisticated prepositioning of a probabilistic kind are examined later in the chapter, and footnote 33 *infra*. As indicated there, few dominant firms are ignorant of the strategic relation they bear to the industry of which they are a part, which casts doubt on the assumption of myopia. Expected profit maximization in which probabilities are taken into account is more plausible. The model in the text easily generalizes to deal with this condition. The same qualitative arguments apply.

[33] The analysis assumes that whenever a predatory behavior rule is specified the dominant firm will 'locate' so that it can act within the law and still render entry unattractive.

The dominant firm faces the strategic problem of maximizing expected profits, recognizing that for each predatory pricing rule there is no unique price at or above which entry will surely occur and below which entry will never occur. Rather, the probability of entry varies directly with the price established by the dominant firm. Kamien and Schwartz, 'Limit pricing and uncertain entry,' *Econometrica* 39 (1971) p. 441; Williamson, 'Selling expense as a barrier to entry' (1963) p. 112. The analysis, however, is not greatly changed on this account. All that need be done is to recognize that a family of residual demand curves will be associated with each predatory pricing rule and a probability of entry attached to each. The dominant firm will then proceed to maximize expected profits by reference to these probabilistic demand curves. The same qualitative results characterizing rule differences, see sections E and F *infra*, can be expected.

[34] George Stigler, among others, has expressed serious reservations about limit pricing entry barrier analysis. As he puts it, the 'ability of the oligopolist to agree upon and police the limit price is apparently independent of the sizes and numbers of oligopolists,' whereupon the difficult issues of oligopoly theory are assumed away. Stigler (1968), p. 21. But the analysis presented in this chapter is expressly restricted to dominant firms and collusive oligopolists, as defined above. Oligopolistic industries not satisfying the delimiting conditions given in text are arguably unable to engage in collective prepositioning and mutual policing as assumed in a strategic reaction curve model.

on the dominant firm's pre-entry investment, and its shape depends on the prevailing predatory pricing rule.[35]

It will facilitate the analysis to make simplifying assumptions of three kinds. First, it will be assumed that, whatever rule is in effect, the dominant firm always chooses a plant design consistent with operating on the long-run average cost curve to which it has access. This assures that the plant design chosen satisfies rudimentary efficiency tests. Second, it is assumed that entrants have access to the same long-run cost curves as established firms.[36] Third, it is assumed that the long-run average cost curve falls in steps rather than continuously. As will be shown in section B of part II, relaxing these assumptions mainly buttresses the argument.[37]

E. ALTERNATIVE RULES

Three rules for restraining dominant firms in the post-entry period will be investigated. The first rule is designated $Q \leqslant \bar{Q}$, where $\bar{Q}$ is the dominant firm's pre-entry level of output and Q is the post-entry level of

---

If dominant firms and collusive oligopolies are the relevant subset, then the basic issue is whether predatory pricing rules are appropriately described in terms of strategic response functions. If so, residual demand curves for potential entrants may be obtained in the manner described below. Academic differences about entry models and their limited applicability to certain types of oligopoly thus miss the point. What matters is whether the strategic considerations are critical and, if they are, if they are adeqately reflected in the modeling apparatus employed.

[35] For the purposes of this chapter, I will assume that the shape of the dominant firm's response curve is fully determined by the prevailing predatory pricing rule. Thus, if a marginal cost pricing rule were adopted, the response curve would be the dominant firm's marginal cost curve. Actually, legal rules place an outer bound on admissible responses rather than uniquely determine them. The qualitative results obtained below stand up provided that legal rules have the general effects attributed to them.

[36] This ignores a strategic asymmetry between established firms and potential entrants. However qualified the latter may be, they have not made the investment in fixed plant and operating infrastructure that estabished firms have. Accordingly, new entrants have to persuade investors to make funds available while established firms are not required to make similar appeals. Threats by established firms to contest entry vigorously can thus affect the terms on which capital becomes available to the potential entrant, while the potential entrant is not able to impose similar costs on the established firm.

Once entry has occurred, entrant and established firm are more on a parity in this respect – unless entry has occurred in a tentative way, (e.g., the entrant has leased general purpose equipment rather than bought special purpose equipment). The incentives for the dominant firm to engage in short-run predatory behavior are especially strong where entry is plainly tentative.

[37] I also assume that effective entry can rarely be assured by resorting to long-term contracting. The dominant firm can be expected to contest pre-entry sales just as it contests post-entry sales. Also, prospective customers would be reluctant to jeopardize a known source of supply before the entrant has irreversibly committed himself by incurring fixed costs. Finally, long-term contracts are both costly and hazardous. See Williamson, *supra* footnote 27, pp. 82–105.

output. This rule, called the 'output restriction rule,' stipulates that in the period after entry occurs the dominant firm cannot increase output above the pre-entry level. It is essential to specify the time period over which the output restriction rule holds. Unless predatory responses to new entry quickly threaten the viabiilty of the new entrant, such responses are unlikely to be effective. As discussed below, the cost disadvantages of new entrants decrease as they accumulate experience and demonstrate their viability. Ordinarily an initial restraint period of 12 to 18 months is sufficient to allow the entrant to realize cost economies and establish a market identity.[38] A shorter period would permit the dominant firm to hold excess capacity as a strategic reserve to be unleashed at the end of the grace period, and a longer period would pose severe administrative problems and weaken the incentives of new entrants quickly to achieve cost parity with the dominant firm.

The second rule, designated $P \geq SRMC$ (where P is price and $SRMC$ is short-run marginal cost), permits the dominant firm to increase output in the post-entry period subject to the condition that price not fall below short-run marginal cost. This is called the 'marginal cost rule.' The third rule, designated $P \geq SRAC$ (where $SRAC$ is short-run average cost), permits output expansion if the resulting price exceeds short-run average cost. This is called the 'average cost rule.'[39]

Consider first the price and output of a monopolist not threatened by entry. These are shown in figure 9.1 as P^* and Q^*, respectively, and represent the short-term profit-maximizing position. This is the price and output at which marginal revenue (denoted MR in the figure) is just offset by, and is thus equal to, the marginal cost of the last unit sold. Consider now how price and output are affected if dominant firms are concerned with entry and a predatory pricing rule is in effect. The three alternative rules and their effect on entry will be considered in turn.

The Output Restriction Rule, $Q \leq \mathbf{Q}$

The basic rule allows the dominant firm to operate at $Q = \mathbf{Q}$, but the rule must be qualified by a requirement that the resulting price exceed

---

[38] Moreover, the recent entrant is not defenseless but enjoys the protection of the law, albeit in the capacity of an 'established' firm, once the initial period has expired. The rules appropriate for evaluating predatory pricing among established firms are set out earlier.

[39] These rules are not exhaustive. The most conspicuous omission is the proposal that dominant firms faced with new entry must maintain price until the entrant has had an opportunity to become established. Such a rule requires dominant firms to hold up a 'price umbrella,' which implies an output reduction by dominant firms and is an invitation for inefficient firms to enter. The inferior welfare properties of a rule having these implications are, I believe, obvious. See footnote 109 *infra*, and accompanying text.

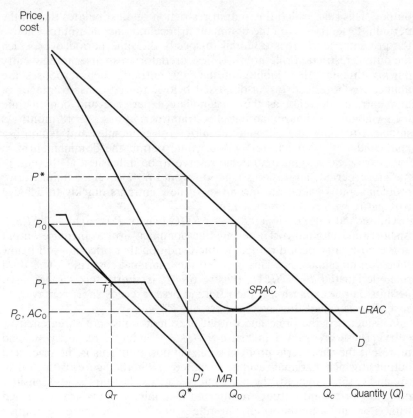

Figure 9.1

average variable costs when output is held unchanged.[40] This qualification
will normally be satisfied.[41]

1 $Q = Q$. The behavioral assumption on which most entry barrier
analysis is based is that 'potential entrants behave as though they expected
existing firms to adopt the policy most unfavorable to them, namely, the

---

[40] The operational import of this qualification is slight, however. It mainly allows for
remote contingencies and tidies up the model.

[41] Indeed, earlier entry barrier models have ignored altogether the remote possibility that
the post-entry price would fail to cover the dominant firm's average total cost. Inasmuch
as $ATC > AVC$ when the dominant firm is operating at Q_0, see figure 9.1 and footnote
122 *infra*, the AVC constraint is even less likely to be violated if the dominant firm holds
its output unchanged.

policy of maintaining output while reducing the price (or accepting reductions) to the extent required to enforce such an output policy.'[42] The basic model is shown in figure 9.1. The curve D is the industry demand curve and $LRAC$ is the long-run average cost curve accessible to existing firms and potential entrants.[43] The curve D' is the residual demand curve, which shows the amount of demand remaining when the dominant firm holds its output unchanged. Taking Q_o as the dominant firm's pre-entry output, so that the firm may not supply more than Q_o in the immediate post-entry period (12 to 18 months), residual demand is that part of the demand curve to the right of Q_o. The curve labeled D' represents the horizontal displacement of this residual demand curve to the origin.

Given that the dominant firm chooses investment such that the prospective entrant can at best earn zero profits on the residual demand curve, the dominant firm's object is to select Q_o such that D' is just tangent to (never exceeds in value) the long-run average cost curve. This tangency occurs at the point denoted by T in the figure. Were the dominant firm to supply less than Q_o in the pre-entry period, D' would be shifted to the right and the new entrant could earn positive profits under the output restriction rule. If, however, the monopolist charges the price P_o and produces Q_o, the best that a potential entrant could hope for under the output restriction rule is to break even by constructing a plant and producing an output of size Q_τ. Any entering firm that produces an output larger or smaller than Q_τ will not be able to cover its costs, since the residual demand curve lies below the $LRAC$ curve at all other points.

The dominant firm's pre-entry output and price (Q_o and P_o, respectively) differ from the unconstrained profit-maximizing position (Q^*, P^*) due to the threat of entry. But for the threat of entry, the monopolist would set marginal revenue (MR in the diagram) equal to marginal cost[44] by producing an amount Q^*, which is less than Q_o. The price at which the quantity Q^* clears the market exceeds the market-clearing price for the quantity Q_o so that $P^* > P_o$.

Even though potential competition serves to restrict the monopolist's profit margins, pre-entry operation at the limit price (P_o, Q_o) nevertheless yields supracompetitive profits. Only if the monopolist were to expand pre-entry output to the level Q_c, where price is equal to long-run average

---

[42] Modigliani, *supra* footnote 26, p. 217.

[43] If potential entrants have to incur set-up costs, allowance must be made to recover these during the anticipated production interval.

[44] Note that short-run and long-run marginal costs are equal when plant size is adjusted optimally to produce the amount Q^*.

cost,[45] would his economic profits vanish. Although output at the level Q_c is socially preferred to output at Q_0, the former is unattainable short of regulation – which, by assumption, is disallowed.[46]

If entry occurs and additional supplies of amount Q_T are brought onto the market, the resulting market price (P_T) still exceeds the monopolist's costs of production (at Q_0). Thus, although the new entrant just breaks even at the point (P_T, Q_T), the dominant firm continues to realize positive, albeit reduced, post-entry profits. Differential profits between large and small firms in concentrated industries are thus a predictable consequence of the entry barriers model.[47]

2 $Q < Q$. In the unlikely event that the new entrant brings onto the market a quantity of output so large that, if the dominant firm holds its output unchanged, price is driven below the dominant firm's average variable costs, the dominant firm (and entrant, if the entrant is selling below its average variable costs) should be required to reduce output until a $P \geqslant AVC$ result is realized.[48] Absent this stipulation, dominant firms that held output unchanged irrespective of entry might occasionally drive prices below remunerative levels in the immediate post-entry period. The $P \geqslant AVC$ requirement forestalls this possibility.

The Short-run Marginal Cost Rule, $P \geqslant SRMC$

Suppose instead that the monopolist is permitted to expand output when confronted with entry, and that his only restriction is that price should not be reduced below short-run marginal cost. Assume, for purposes of evaluating this possibility, that in response to entry the monopolist chooses to expand output until price precisely equals marginal cost. What are the entry and output implications of contingent output responses of this kind?

Figure 9.2 depicts the relationships with the marginal cost rule in effect. Since the monopolist is permitted under this rule to respond to new entry by expanding output,[49] he can safely reduce pre-entry output below Q_0

---

[45] It is assumed that the demand curve intersects the long-run average cost curve in the region where $LRAC$ is flat. This seems reasonable for most industries in a large economy such as the United States.

[46] Regulation is beset with numerous difficulties of its own. Where competition can be made to work reasonably well, it is usually to be preferred.

[47] The evidence is consistent with this prediction. See Demsetz, 'Two systems of belief about monopoly,' in *Industrial Concentration: The New Learning*, eds H. Goldschmidt, H. Mann and J. Weston (1974), p. 164.

[48] See, however, 'Promotional Pricing' later in chapter for the qualifications that allow entrants to engage in promotional pricing of short duration for consumer nondurables. Although entrants might price below average variable costs temporarily under this exception, no massive market dislocations would be permitted.

[49] Plainly the output unchanged rule is not the 'most unfavorable' behavior that an entrant could impute to existing firms in the industry; output expansion as a reply to entry is more adverse.

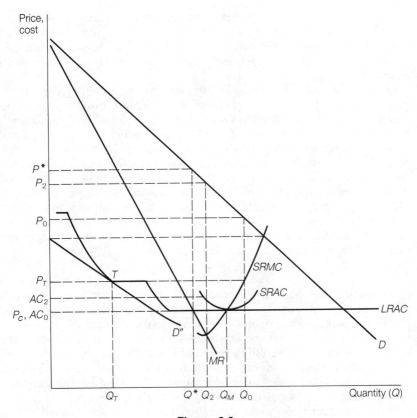

Figure 9.2

without inducing entry. The optimum level of investment is again determined by the residual demand curve. But whereas previously the residual demand curve was given by $D - Q_0$, now it is given by $D - SRMC$, since the monopolist can expand output as long as price remains above short-run marginal cost. The optimal scale can be obtained graphically by considering the family of plant scales consistent with operating on the long-run average cost curve[50] and finding the horizontal difference between the corresponding short-run marginal cost curve of each such plant and the demand curve, D. The plant scale for which there

---

[50] For a discussion of long-run cost curves and their relationship to short-run cost curves, see Viner, 'Cost curves and supply curves,' *Zeitschrift für Nationalökonomie* (1931), reprinted in *Readings in Price Theory*, eds K. Boulding and G. Stigler, Homewood, Ill.: Richard D. Irwin (1952).

is a point of tangency between the residual demand curve, thus defined, and the long-run average cost curve ($LRAC$) is then the optimal plant scale for the dominant firm. As shown in figure 9.2, the plant scale with $SRMC$ curve yielding this tangency has minimum short-run average costs at output Q_M.

Once a plant of this scale is put in place in the pre-entry period, the monopolist will choose the output that maximizes his profits. This entails equating industry marginal revenue with the short-run marginal costs corresponding to plant scale Q_M. The monopolist thus produces the amount Q_2 (which is less than Q_0-) and charges the price P_2 (which exceeds P_0-). Were entry to occur, however, the monopolist would respond by operating where price equals marginal costs. This would involve a movement along his $SRMC$ curve until he reaches the output Q_0[51] The prospective entrant, in anticipation of this output response, will not enter unless price exceeds P_2.[52] Thus a prospective entrant will enter only if the monopolist has chosen too small a plant, so that his short-run marginal costs exceed P_T at output Q_0.

The Short-run Average Cost Rule, P $\geqslant$ SRAC

A similar investigation can be made of the average cost rule. Inasmuch as the average cost curve is flatter than the marginal cost curve, the residual demand curve (given by the horizontal difference $D - SRAC$)[53] is likewise flatter. It will be convenient to assume, however, that the tangency between the resulting residual demand curve and the long-run average cost curve remains at the point T, where the cost curve is kinked. The optimum plant scale is thus that plant scale for which the short-run average cost curve passes through the point (P_T, Q_0).

Optimum plant scale under the $SRAC$ rule is necessarily smaller than Q_M.[54] Accordingly, the output at which the dominant firm's short-run

[51] Market price is determined by aggregate supply. Given that the entrant supplies Q_T, the ruling market price will be P_T if the dominant firm supplies Q_0. The dominant firm's short-run marginal cost of supplying Q_0 is P_T by construction (otherwise the residual demand curve would be differently located).

[52] The prospective entrant assumes that the dominant firm maximizes profits given its plant scale in the pre-entry period. Given this assumption, if the dominant firm's pre-entry price exceeds P_2, the dominant firm that responds along its short-run marginal cost curve will be unable to eliminate positive profits for an entrant that accurately perceives the industry opportunities.

[53] The residual demand curve is here given by the difference $D - SRAC$ because at any price, P, the most that the dominant firm can supply without violating the average-cost rule is the quantity where $P = SRAC$. Hence the entrant is assured that at any price the amount $D - SRAC$ will be the minimum demand left unfilled by the dominant firm.

[54] This follows because the response curve of the dominant firm under the $SRAC$ rule is the curve $SRAC$, which is flatter than $SRMC$ and thus allows the dominant firm to respond to entry by bringing greater post-entry product onto the market than would be the case if an $SRMC$ rule were in effect, *ceteris paribus.*

marginal cost is equal to industry marginal revenue will be less than Q_2. Pre-entry price will thus exceed P_2.

F. INNOCENT PROFIT MAXIMIZATION

Thus far the analysis of the three predatory pricing rules has assumed that dominant firms position themselves so that they can exclude potential entrants without violating the predatory pricing rule. But what if dominant firms do not follow this strategy? Will a change in strategy call for a different predatory pricing rule? Suppose, arguendo, that the dominant firm is myopic and simply maximizes profit in every period without regard to strategic pre-entry positioning or post-entry extinction of its rival. Is the output restriction rule apt to preclude simple nonstrategic responses of this kind? If so, should it be abandoned from the outset?

The answer is that nonstrategic or myopic responses by dominant firms will, under plausible assumptions about the behavior of entrants, normally lead to an output reduction (which is a conciliatory response) by dominant firms, in which case the output restraint will be satisfied. Thus, consider three scenarios. Although the dominant firm is assumed to maximize profits with respect to its residual demand curve under each scenario, the behavior imputed to entrants is assumed to vary.

In the first scenario, the new entrant is assumed to maintain output unchanged in the immediate post-entry period: it enters at Q_r and continues to supply Q_r during the post-entry interval. The residual demand curve of the dominant firm is thus the horizontal difference between the industry demand curve and Q_r. The dominant firm that maximizes profits by setting marginal cost equal to the corresponding (residual) marginal revenue curve will, under this scenario, always reduce output below what it had supplied in the pre-entry period.

Suppose, alternatively, that the new entrant and dominant firm behave symmetrically in that each assumes that its rival will supply an amount of product in the next period identical to the amount that the rival supplied in the current period. The corresponding residual demand curve of each will then be given by the industry demand curve less the recent output of its rival. Firms behaving in this myopic fashion will converge to a solution that implies an output reduction for the dominant firm.[55] Again, the output restraint is redundant.

Suppose, thirdly, that the new entrant treats market price as a parameter and adjusts output so as to supply at every price the amount of product that equates price with short-run marginal cost. Suppose, further, that the dominant firm accurately perceives that the new entrant responds to

---

[55] This is the normal Cournot solution. See F. Scherer, *Industrial Market Structure and Economic Performance* (1971), Chicago: Rand McNally, p. 132.

price changes in this way. The residual demand curve to which the dominant firm now refers is the horizontal difference between the market demand curve and the marginal cost curve of the new entrant. The output supplied by the dominant firm after entry then becomes a function both of the entrant's marginal cost curve and its own marginal cost curve. The shapes of both marginal cost curves thus jointly determine whether the dominant firm will supply more or less product following entry. It is conceivable under these circumstances that a strategy of equating marginal cost to marginal revenue on the residual demand curve would lead to an output increase by the dominant firm.[56] This is, however, merely a hypothetical possibility. Operationally it seems unlikely. Not only must the short-run marginal cost curve of the entrant be of a special kind, but the immediate post-entry behavior imputed to the new entrant is myopic and implausible.

It is important to recognize that the current costs of new entrants normally exceed the costs that the entrant will incur in later periods, due to the benefits that accrue to experience. Inexperienced but otherwise qualified firms are often at a disadvantage to established firms in two respects: they do not have an experienced work force[57] and they may be perceived as high-risk ventures.[58] Post-entry competition commonly serves to mitigate both of these conditions. Learning-by-doing economies accrue to the labor force and experience is often the least expensive method by which the entrant can convince investors that it possesses the requisite management talent and perseverance to compete effectively. Unless,

[56] The qualitative output response of the dominant firm in these circumstances is indeterminate. It depends on the position and relative slopes of the dominant firm's and entrant's marginal cost curves and on the industry demand curve.

[57] If workers appropriate all of the benefits of idiosyncratic training and experience, so that productivity differences between experienced and inexperienced work forces would be fully reflected by wage differentials, the labor force disadvantage of new entrants would vanish. Alternatively, if wages did not fully reflect the increased productivity of experienced workers, but the new entrant could raid the dominant firm and hire talent away easily, the work force disability would vanish. If, however, neither of these conditions were satisfied – which is to say that idiosyncratic advantages are incompletely appropriated by workers and wage premiums have to be offered to bring talent from the established firm to the new entrant – the new entrant would suffer a work force disadvantage. As I have argued elsewhere, the incomplete appropriation and wage premium conditions are common. Williamson, *supra* footnote 27, pp. 72–8, 216–17. The new entrant thus often suffers a temporary cost disadvantage until learning-by-doing brings the entrant's labor force to a level of experience and productivity comparable to the dominant firm's.

[58] New entrants may be perceived as high-risk ventures because they are relatively risky according to an objective standard or because, though they possess the requisite management and other talents to compete effectively, it is very costly to disclose their competitiveness in a compelling way to potential investors. Ibid., pp. 110–13. An entrant can make a more compelling case for its competitiveness by presenting evidence of demonstrated ability to achieve cost control and a demonstrated commitment to persevere under difficult circumstances than it can using *ex ante* representations on these matters.

therefore, a dominant firm can arrest and reverse an entry incursion quickly, the relative costs of continuing a predatory campaign shift to the dominant firm's disadvantage and the prospects of successful entry improve.

Given the advantages of perseverance, it seems unlikely that a new entrant would curb output in order to behave in the manner described by the third scenario. Rather, the new entrant will maintain or increase its supply in the immediate post-entry period, as assumed by the myopic dominant firm in the first two scenarios. The myopic dominant firm (seeking continuously to equate marginal revenue to marginal cost) thus arguably refers to a residual demand curve that calls for a post-entry output reduction. The output restriction rule is therefore redundant if nonstrategic profit maximization is practised by the dominant firm.[59]

G. DIFFERENTIAL ENFORCEABILITY

In choosing among predatory pricing rules, an important consideration is the relative difficulty of enforcing the rules. An output rule should be

---

[59] A variant of the innocent profit maximization argument is that dominant firms maximize profits at the point (P^*, Q^*) in the pre-entry period heedless of the threat of entry and heedless of whatever predatory pricing rules are declared. Accordingly, pre-entry price and output are identical for all of the predatory pricing rules. To the extent that setting price equal to marginal cost in the post-entry period maximizes welfare, the $P > MC$ rule is arguably superior and should be approved.

The argument is troublesome on several counts. For one thing, it assumes that dominant firms are massively unsophisticated. A more plausible proposition is that persistent dominance is a prima facie indicator that the dominant firm in question has keenly appreciated the strategic relation it bears to its industry. Dominant firms that price heedless of entry will rarely maintain their market positions.

It has been suggested that the Spence model demonstrates that setting marginal revenue equal to marginal cost in the pre-entry period and price equal to marginal cost in the post-entry period is the 'rational' strategy and that this is exactly what the Areeda–Turner rules permit. See Spence, *supra* footnote 31. The correspondence exists, but the Spence model *assumes* that price will be set equal to marginal cost in the post-entry period rather than demonstrates that this is the unique profit maximizing strategy.

One of the arguments that Spence invokes in support of the assumption that $P = MC$ post-entry is that the appearance of a new entrant causes the pre-entry condition of oligopolistic collusion to break down. Although loose oligopolies may well revert to marginal cost pricing when entry occurs, the Nash logic upon which Spence relies applies neither to dominant firms nor collusive oligopolies (of the special kind described in the text). Restricting attention to these, a post-entry response function of the $P = MC$ kind can be asserted but it cannot be said to hold uniquely by reason of necessity or competitive self-interest.

Additionally, for the reasons set out above, temporary marginal cost pricing yields negligible immediate welfare benefits. If alternative rules of a nonprotectionist kind can be devised which less severely deter entry (in other geographic regions or in later periods) than does temporary marginal cost pricing, net negative welfare consequences may well be associated with reaction functions of the marginal cost kind – *even if* dominant firms have made no effort to position themselves strategically in the pre-entry period.

easier to enforce than a marginal cost rule. The ease with which theoretical cost functions can be used to secure analytical insights should not obscure the very real difficulties encountered in any attempt to make precise empirical studies of these functions. Standard accounting costs rarely bear a close relation to an economist's conception of cost, especially when marginal cost estimates are required.

Since estimates of short-run marginal cost involve an enormous amount of judgement, a marginal cost test would be a defendant's paradise. The time period across which costs are to be allocated is disputable, as is any decision about which costs to include. Allocations of overhead, especially in a multiproduct enterprise, can be juggled, and inventories can be valued differently under different rules. Either a standard or an actual cost argument can be made, depending on which suits the litigant's purposes. The list goes on, as different cost variances can be treated differently, with each estimate supported by a plausible, though *ad hoc*, rationale. The upshot is that estimation of short-run marginal costs is a mare's nest. It is unrealistic to expect a judge or jury to sort out the various representations.

To be sure, establishing the admissible level of output (Q) entails a demand forecast rather than simple reference to pre-entry period production. Except, however, for products where period-by-period demand is subject to severe stochastic disturbancs, this should not pose a serious problem. The test is especially simple for products that are sold in many separate geographic markets. Since only one or a few of these submarkets are apt to occasion claims of predation, the test is whether output in the suspect markets has increased disproportionately. In other circumstances a simple trended average of recent sales will give an estimate accurate to within five per cent of realized demands. A ten per cent allowance over the trended projection will be adequate for most cases,[60] and such an allowance will scarcely permit the dominant firm to effect a massive market dislocation of the kind a marginal cost rule would often permit. Business planning records and industry forecasts can be examined for corroboration of the trended estimates, and more sophisticated demand projection tools are available if needed. Thus the output rule, although not problem free, is eminently more enforceable than the marginal cost rule (or even the average variable cost surrogate) favored by Areeda and Turner.[61]

---

[60] Special circumstances can be imagined where appropriate demand adjustments would be difficult to make. For example, an oil embargo may give rise to a temporary spurt in natural gas sales. I am unaware of predatory pricing claims in such circumstances and have no reason to believe that such claims typically have arisen or will arise in circumstances involving an unusual demand shift.

[61] The argument has been made that it is optimal to require the dominant firm to hold output unchanged in the event of entry. The question arises whether it is optimal to place

II. Welfare Evaluation of Predatory Pricing Rules

As is characteristic of most applied welfare economics studies, the analysis in this part focuses entirely on a local condition – in this case, on the industry in which a risk of predation is believed to exist. Second-order interactions between this industry and other parts of the economy are ignored. The object of the inquiry is to ascertain differential welfare effects attributable to the three alternative predatory behavior rules set out in part I. Social benefits will be taken to be the area under the demand curve between the origin and the quantity of goods that is sold. This area represents the gross gain that consumers receive from the product. Social costs will be interpreted in terms of opportunity costs: costs are defined as the value in their best alternative employments of the resources used to supply the product. It will simplify the analysis, and will have no effect whatsoever on the qualitative nature of the results, to assume that social costs are accurately reflected by the pecuniary costs

---

the same restriction on the dominant firm's other activities, such as selling expense or research and development. The answer is no, though for somewhat different reasons.

The output restriction rule has the twofold purpose of giving new entrants a threshold opportunity to become established and of discouraging dominant firms from ominously holding excess capacity in reserve. Dominant firms may hold up the introduction of technological developments for strategic purposes, but the risks of holding completed developments off the market for very long are severe. Since trade secrets are fugitive and rivals are apt to market a similar product before the dominant firm, this contingency does not appear to be very serious. In any event, technological developments held in reserve would be difficult for courts to evaluate and control. Moreover, research and development spending in response to new entry will rarely pose an immediate threat to the viability of new rivals. Rather, research and development responses should be interpreted mainly in the context of long-run rivalry, in which case it seems reasonable to exempt research and development and other long-run manifestations of rivalry from antitrust control over predatory behavior – subject only to the usual long-run cost recovery stipulation. (The usual controls on patent infringements, trade secret pirating, etc., would, however, continue.)

Selling expense, on the other hand, arguably does have short-run impact. Should it be regarded symmetrically with output, adding a constraint $S \leqslant S$ (where S is selling expense and S is the level of selling expense in the pre-entry period) to the $Q \leqslant Q$ rule? Although this proposal has superficial appeal, the purported symmetry between selling expense and output is mistaken, since selling expense is really an alternative to price reductions as a means of influencing post-entry sales. The dominant firm would be permitted to choose any combination of price and selling expense consistent with the condition that price exceeds short-run marginal costs when output remains in the $Q \leqslant Q$ range.

A possible exception might be warranted where selling expense is thought to have pernicious social effects. This is, however, more difficult to ascertain than is commonly believed. Indeed, such products will presumably be subject to special controls prior to any effort to enter, in which case additional entry restraints are not needed. Note, moreover, that selling expense is simply an unproductive way by which to discourage entry in most homogeneous product and/or producer good industries. Except for consumer good industries where products are heavily promoted to emphasize real or imagined differences, selling expense vanishes as a predatory technique.

incurred by the dominant firm and new entrants to the industry.[62]

A. Application

Two kinds of effects of predatory pricing rules must be examined. First, what is the effect of each rule on pre-entry welfare? This aspect of the problem has previously been neglected. Second, how do the rules affect post-entry supply? Although prior treatments have dealt with this second question, the issues have not been developed expressly in terms of the differential effects of proposed rules on the cost of post-entry supply.

Pre-entry Welfare

The pre-entry welfare differences among rules can be examined in two parts: an output effect (will more or less output be supplied if a rule change is made?); and the cost of supply (do the average costs of supplying product differ under alternative rules?).

It will be convenient to use the output restriction rule as the standard by which to evaluate the welfare effects of adopting different rules. With the output restriction rule in effect, pre-entry supply will be Q_0, and the corresponding average costs will be AC_0. As discussed earlier,[63] permitting firms to respond to entry under the marginal cost rule induces the dominant firm to reduce pre-entry supply from Q_0 to Q_2, whereupon price increases from P_0 to P_2. But the costs of supply also change. Pre-entry product is supplied at an average cost of AC_2 under the marginal cost rule, and AC_2 exceeds AC_0.

The pre-entry welfare losses of shifting from the output restriction rule to the marginal cost rule are shown in figure 9.3. The area A_1 is the loss resulting from output reduction: the area A_2 is the loss attributable to the higher average cost. Plainly, the output restriction rule is superior to the marginal cost rule in terms of pre-entry welfare.

The average cost rule can be evaluated in the same way. The rule causes further output reductions in the pre-entry period, and the average cost of supplying the reduced amount of product will exceed AC_0. The

---

[62] No corrections (by reason of externalities, factor rents, or the like) to the cost curves shown in the preceding section are thus required for social cost accounting. To be sure, this is a simple apparatus and a variety of refinements can be introduced. See A. Harberger, 'Three basic postulates for applied welfare economics: An interpretive essay.' (9) *J. Econ. Literature* (1971), p. 785. It is noteworthy, however, that defects in the apparatus are more severe if measures of total welfare are attempted (e.g., should the product be supplied at all) rather than, as here, with an examination of the marginal welfare differences attributable to rule changes. Differential welfare effects are much less affected by measuring rod defects when the welfare measures of interest involve evaluating the incremental effects of rule changes on prices and quantities within a local region.

[63] pp. 233–234 *supra*.

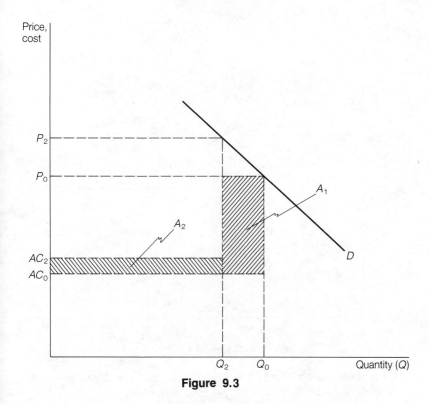

Figure 9.3

average cost of supplying product in the pre-entry period under the average cost rule may or may not exceed AC_2. If the average costs do not exceed AC_2,[64] the average cost rule may or may not be inferior to the marginal cost rule in pre-entry welfare loss respects. It is plainly inferior, however, to the output restriction rule.

Post-entry Welfare

Recall that the product supplied by the dominant firm in the post-entry period is Q_0 under each of the rules. Also recall that the entrant supplies Q_T in the post-entry period under each rule. Total post-entry product (Q_0

---

[64] If the *SRAC* curve for the small plant scale that obtains under the average cost rule is merely a horizontal displacement to the left of the *SRAC* curve that obtains under the marginal cost rule, average costs will be lower than under the marginal cost rule since marginal cost under the marginal cost rule will intersect marginal revenue at a value that is closer to the minimum point on the *SRAC* curve.

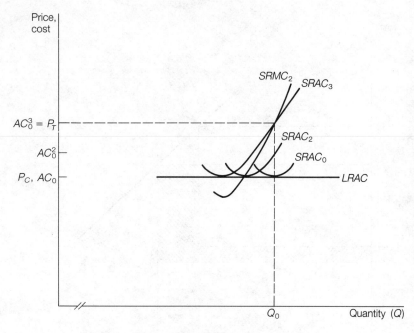

Figure 9.4

$+ Q_T)$ is thus identical under all rules.[65] The welfare differences among the rules turn entirely, therefore, on cost differences.

Since the entrant's costs of supply are identical for all three rules (namely $AC_T = P_T$) the cost differences among the rules depend entirely on the costs incurred by the dominant firm in supplying Q_0. The relevant cost relations are shown in figure 9.4. The average cost of supplying Q_0 under the output restriction rule is AC_0. When the marginal cost rule is in effect, average cost will be AC_0^2, which exceeds AC_0 but is less than P_T. When the average cost rule is in effect, the average cost of supplying Q_0 will be AC_0^3, which is equal to P_T.[66] Since $AC_0 < AC_0^2 < AC_0^3$,

[65] It will be shown that this is an artifact of the stepwise long-run average cost curve that has been constructed.

[66] A rough interpretation can be made of these post-entry costs of supply. Entry, if it occurs at all, involves supplying incremental product in the amount of Q_T under each of the rules (given the assumptions of the model). The object of the dominant firm in each case is to react to entry in such a way that the entrant's profits are reduced to zero. This will occur if post-entry market price is driven down to P_T, which requires that aggregate post-entry product in the amount $Q_0 + Q_T$ be supplied. The dominant firm thus supplies post-entry product of Q_0, whichever rule is in effect. The reference coordinates (P_T, Q_0) are therefore identical for each predatory pricing rule (in the sense that the curves $Q = Q$, $SRMC_3$ and $SRAC_1$ all must pass through this point). Given this common reference point, the relations among the cost curves all follow by construction.

there is a clear post-entry welfare ordering of rules, whereby the output restriction rule is superior to the marginal cost rule, which in turn is superior to the average cost rule. Moreover, a rank ordering of rules according to the average variable cost of supplying Q_0 in the post-entry period – which arguably is the better measure of social cost[67] – will normally yield an identical result.

Conclusion

The output restriction rule is thus superior to the alternative rules with respect to both pre-entry and post-entry welfare. The marginal cost rule is probably superior to the average cost rule in its effect on pre-entry welfare and is clearly superior in its effect on post-entry welfare. The partial equilibrium welfare analysis thus yields the following rank ordering of rules: the output restriction rule is best; the marginal cost rule is probably second; and the average cost rule is probably third.

B. EXTENSIONS

The partial equilibrium analysis in the preceding section has, necessarily, been based on numerous assumptions. Although all possible complications cannot be considered, this section will discuss three issues: the welfare implications of Areeda and Turner's average variable cost formulation of the marginal cost rule; the effects of information needs and uncertainty on the ordering of the rules; and the welfare effects of relaxing the three simplifying assumptions made in part I.

Average Variable Cost

In view of the difficulties in measuring marginal cost. Areeda and Turner suggest the substitution of average variable cost as a surrogate for marginal cost.[68] Average variable cost is everywhere lower than average total cost. Hence, if the average variable cost rule were adopted the response function of the dominant firm would be flatter than under the avergae cost rule. Pre-entry output would be lower (hence pre-entry price would be higher) under the average variable cost rule. The average variable cost curve that passes through (P_T, Q_0) corresponds to a smaller plant scale and higher average total costs (evaluated at Q_0) than is shown by the

---

[67] The social costs of supplying Q_0 are the real costs incurred in the process. These include user costs of capital, but exclude depreciation of plant and equipment that is independent of utilization rates. Average costs include capital charges of both kinds, but average variable costs include only the former.

[68] Areeda and Turner, *supra* footnote 3, pp. 716–18, 733.

curve $SRAC_3$.[69] Hence, if the dominant firm chooses a plant that allows it to charge P_T (and thus deter entry) while still meeting a test that price exceed average variable costs, the firm will produce less in the pre-entry period and its cost will be higher in the post-entry period than under the other three rules. Altogether, the average variable cost rule, plausible though it appears, has the worst welfare properties of all.

Information and Uncertainty

The prospective entrant can form expectations relatively easily when the output restriction rule is in effect. The dominant firm may reduce output in response to entry. But the 'worst' that it will do is hold output

---

[69] These cost relations can be shown graphically as follows:

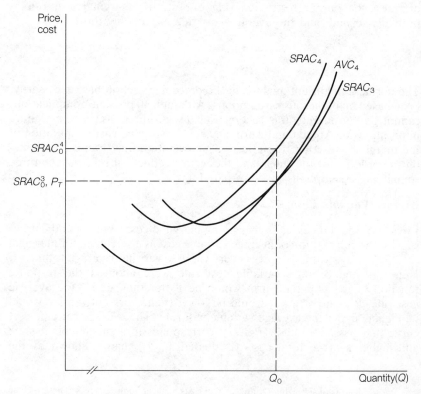

Note that for AVC_4 to pass through the point (P_T, Q_0), as required, the corresponding short-run average cost curve ($SRAC_4$) is displaced to the left of $SRAC_3$. Accordingly, the cost of supplying Q_0 if the cost curve is of type 4 exceeds that of supplying Q_0 if the cost curve is of type 3 instead.

unchanged. Even recognizing that the rule allows for a trend adjustment of the maximum output, Q, which will be necessary in a growing market, the maximum output allowed the firm will be relatively easy to establish.

Where either a marginal cost or average cost rule is in effect, however, the prospective entrant also needs to know the dominant firm's response curve (*SRMC* or *SRAC* as the case may be). This is a much more demanding knowledge requirement and, since such cost curves can only be approximated, an additional estimating error appears in the prospective entrant's calculations, adding a further source of risk. These same cost estimation difficulties, moreover, complicate litigation and increase uncertainty if either of the cost-based rules is in effect because the court must ask whether lower bound cost conditions were really violated. This can be very difficult to establish – as Cooper remarks[70] and as both Areeda–Turner[71] and Posner[72] concede.

Finally, even if a potential entrant knew with certainty the dominant firm's response curve, the curve merely reflects a constraint. The constraint places a limit on the dominant firm's post-entry behavior, but does not uniquely determine it. Under the output restriction rule, the output of the dominant firm will either be reduced or remain unchanged. With either of the cost-based rules in effect, output may increase, decrease, or remain unchanged. The greater latitude for dominant firm reaction permitted by the cost-based rules introduces greater uncertainty for the potential entrant.

Simplifying Assumptions

Recall that three simplifying assumptions were introduced to facilitate modeling: the potential entrant and dominant firm were assumed to have access to the same long-run average cost curve; the dominant firm was assumed to choose a technology consistent with the long-run average cost curve; and the long-run average cost curve was assumed to be a step function. This section considers the welfare ramifications of relaxing these three assumptions.

The assumption of identical cost curves was a modeling convenience but may be at variance with the facts. To the extent that learning-by-doing yields operating cost savings or differential risks give rise to capital cost differences between new entrant and established firm,[73] the new entrant will not have immediate access to the identical cost function as the dominant firm. So long, however, as these cost differences are no greater when the output restriction rule is in effect than under either of

---

[70] Cooper, *supra* footnote 3, p. 438.
[71] Areeda and Turner, *supra* footnote 3, pp. 716–18, 733.
[72] Posner, *supra* footnote 3, pp. 189–91.
[73] pp. 244–5 and footnotes 57 and 59 *supra*.

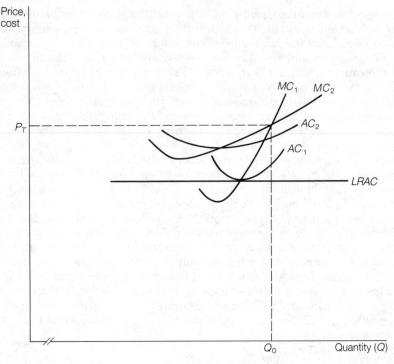

Figure 9.5

the cost-based rules, the ordering of rules will be unaffected. And arguably cost differences will be less under the output restriction rule since entry risk is greater under cost-based rules.

The assumption that the dominant firm chooses a technology consistent with the long-run average cost curve favors the cost-based rules. Suppose that the dominant firm is governed by the marginal cost predatory pricing rule. The issue that was suppressed is whether the dominant firm might select an inferior technology if this gives it access to a more 'advantageous' response curve (in the sense that the result is higher pre-entry profits). The dominant firm's problem can be formulated as follows: from among the family of plant designs with short-run marginal cost curves passing through the coordinates (P_T, Q_0), choose the plant design that maximizes pre-entry profits. As shown in figure 9.5, in these circumstances a plant design with a relatively flat average cost curve (AC_2) may be preferred to the efficient plant design with a more steeply sloped cost curve (AC_1).[74]

[74] For an early treatment of these types of cost curve choices in terms of risk and plant flexibility, see J. Stigler, 'Production and distribution in the short run,' *Journal of Political Economy* (1939), p. 305, Philadelphia: Blakiston reprinted in *Readings in the Theory of Income Distribution*, eds W. Fellner and B. Haley (1951), p. 119.

Given the greater flexibility to respond to entry afforded by the flat average cost curve, the dominant firm may realize greater profit in the pre-entry period by restricting output more than it otherwise would.[75] Pre-entry output is smaller, and social welfare is reduced, if plant of type 2 rather than plant of type 1 were to be constructed.

Plainly, however, this is a rather risky strategy. Should an entrant appear with requisite capacity at an efficient scale, the monopolist would find that his inefficient plant placed him at a competitive disadvantage. Accordingly, strategic selection of plant designs in which plants off of the long-run average cost curve are actively considered has been ignored. The trade-off between pre-entry profits and post-entry hazards was settled decisively by sacrificing the former in favor of strict avoidance of the latter. This is an arbitrary assumption. To the extent that dominant firms are prepared to run such risks, the welfare effects need to be taken into account. But the incentives to select inferior technologies, which plainly exist when cost-based rules are in effect, vanish if the output restriction rule is in effect.[76] An inferior technology is attractive only if post-entry output expansion is permitted; the output restriction rule disallows this. The welfare advantages associated with the output restriction rule are thus reinforced when the assumption that dominant firms must choose plants on the long-run average cost curve is relaxed.

Consider finally the effect of relaxing the assumption that the long-run average cost curve is a step function. The step function assumption is attractive because it is realistic[77] and because it facilitates the analysis. The analytical advantage is that the residual demand curves, which vary with the predatory behavior rule in effect, have a common tangency at the point (P_T, Q_r) under this assumption.[78] Were the long-run average cost curve to decline smoothly throughout, the tangency would vary, there would no longer be a common dominant firm post-entry output of Q_0, and welfare effects would be more complicated to evaluate.

[75] As is evident from the discussion of residual demand curves, a flatter cost curve always permits the dominant firm to make a greater post-entry output response if cost-based rules are in effect, *ceteris paribus*. But flatter (more flexible) cost curves can be realized only by sacrificing plant specialization. Inasmuch as a more specialized plant affords lower costs when the plant is operated at design capacity, the revenue benefits attributable to the greater pre-entry output reduction permitted by a more flexible plant are eventually offset by the greater costs implied by an unspecialized plant.

[76] Conceivably the dominant firm will select a 'flexible' plant for the reasons given by Stigler, *supra* footnote 74. But there are no response function incentives for the firm to do so under the output restriction rule.

[77] The step function reflects the fact that discrete technologies become available at higher levels of output that are infeasible at all lower levels. Changes in kind cause discontinuities in long-run average cost curves, thus turning the continuous curve into a step function.

[78] This is obviously arbitrary. For a large enough shift in the residual demand curve, tangency might not occur at the point (P_T, Q_r), and a new technology would be adopted.

Given a smoothly declining average total cost curve, rules that cause flatter residual demand curves (as the cost-based rules do) will be tangent to the long-run average cost curve at a lower price and larger output. The pre-entry output of the dominant firm will be further reduced for cost-based rules than for the output restriction rule. Post-entry output (of dominant firm and new entrant taken together), however, will be greater under the cost-based rules.

Although the pre-entry welfare advantages of the output restriction rule are unambiguously greater when the tangency point varies among the rules, the post-entry welfare effects may (but need not) favor the output restriction rule. A weighted average of these two effects wuld probably preserve the rule ordering, however, since entry (and hence post-entry adaptations) is presumably the exception in industries given to the type of strategic behavior investigated here. Thus the pre-entry effects are likely to dominate.

III.   Entry into Generational Equipment Industries

The discussion has assumed that the commodity is in continuous production and that improvements in product and process are introduced gradually. The changes resulting from these improvements are assumed to be of degree rather than kind. Although some sales of the improved product will be to new customers, most of the sales will be to current users – to renew intermediate product inventories, to replace damaged or worn-out durable items, or to continue consuming nondurables.

Yet there are a few products for which simple renewal or replacement sales rarely occur. This is the case where new product embodies significant technological improvements. Existing product is displaced by the superior technology; successor generations of product render the earlier model obsolete.

Consider in particular the case where the dominant firm introduces a new line of equipment and completes its production run before rivals imitate the line and offer substitute products. Assume that the product is durable and has several years of useful life before being displaced by a successor generation of equipment that embodies superior technology. Also assume that the product is initially leased rather than sold. What marketing behavior by the dominant firm shall be regarded as nonpredatory during the period between termination of production and the appearance of the new technology?

A. MARKET CLEARING AT $Q + \Delta$

Let the stock of equipment produced by the dominant firm be Q. Assume that the costs of leasing and servicing this stock are negligible and that the dominant firm is prepared to sell the entire stock at whatever nondiscriminatory price the market will bring. If no additional product appears, market price, denoted $P(Q)$, is then $P(Q)$, which corresponds to the intersection of the demand curve and the quantity Q. Suppose, moreover, that the dominant firm places its entire stock on the market whatever the state of the market.[79] The dominant firm effectively becomes a price taker. If demand is unchanged and new entrants bring incremental output of an amount Δ onto the market, market price will be given by $P(Q + \Delta)$, which is less than $P(Q)$.

When new entrants anticipate that the dominant firm will not take product off the market in the face of entry, entrants will have access only to the residual demand curve to the right of Q. Additional product can be sold only by attracting new customers and selling more product to existing customers, the demands for both of which are represented by the portion of the demand curve to the right of Q. Moreover, entrants' output decisions effectively determine price. The amount of product that they place on the market determines aggregate supply and hence market price. Entrants will presumably supply the amount of additional product that maximizes their profits given that they are optimizing with respect to the residual demand curve.

In figure 9.6, if the industry demand curve is D_1, then D'_1 will be the residual demand curve and the entrant (or firm 'imitating' the dominant firm's new generation of equipment) will be indifferent between producing zero output and producing Q_T. There is, however, a welfare gain, shown by the shaded region, if the imitator produces Q_r under these circumstances. The market price, to both dominant firm and imitator, will be P_T. If instead the market demand curve is D_2 and the dominant firm has discontinued production after the stock Q has been completed, the residual demand curve will be D'_2 and the entrant can earn positive profits by producing Q_E,[80] in which case the price falls from P_2 to P_E. Special rules that prevent the dominant firm from selling Q on whatever terms the market will bear have significant welfare implications if, as is commonly true of specialized equipment, the value of the dominant firm's stock of product is negligible in its best alternative use. Any rule requiring

---

[79] That is, the entire stock is put on the market despite shifts in demand, new product supplied by entrants, or other factors.

[80] Q_E is assumed to be the profit maximizing output for the imitating firm. The entrant will earn positive profits on any output within the region where the residual demand curve, D'_2, exceeds the long-run average cost curve.

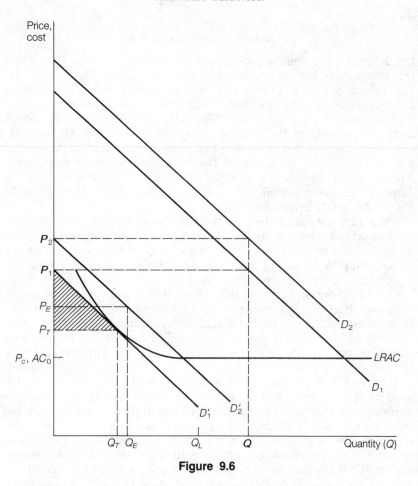

Figure 9.6

the dominant firm to maintain its price at pre-entry levels prevents utilization of product that can be used at zero social cost. Although price maintenance rules yield private gains to new entrants, social losses result.

Suppose, however, that a price maintenance rule is in effect and that the demand curve is D_2. Before entry the market-clearing price for the stock Q is P_2. The relevant demand curve for the new entrant is then a kinked demand curve that is horizontal at P_2 between O and Q and follows D_2 thereafter. The corresponding marginal revenue curve will have a discontinuity at Q. Suppose, moreover, that the new entrant is not able to maximize its profits by equating marginal revenue and marginal cost because it has a capacity limit of Q_L, (where $Q_E < Q_L < Q$). If the new entrant then offers product at a price $P_2 - \epsilon$, where ϵ is a small number, while the dominant firm is constrained to offer product at the price P_2, the entrant will sell Q_L of product at an average social cost of AC_0 while the dominant firm will sell approximately $Q - Q_L$ of the product at a social cost of zero. Essentially no additional product is sold, even though the aggregate stock of product available for sale is increased by Q_L, since the dominant firm retires stock in an amount Q_L as a result of the price maintenance rule.

Absent a special justification for such a price maintenance rule, a waste of valuable resources plainly results, since without the price maintenance rule the dominant firm would sell its entire stock, Q, at zero social cost, and additional product in the amount Q_E would come onto the market bringing incremental welfare gains.[81] More generally, any rule, price maintenance or otherwise, that prevents the dominant firm from selling Q at the prevailing market price is tantamount to a rule stipulating that some part of Q be placed on the shelf or scrapped. Such rules waste goods having social value.

B. POSSIBLE EXCEPTIONS

Might there be countervailing considerations not yet taken into account that would justify a policy of forced retirement of assets? Two appear plausible. First, a dominant firm confronted with a price maintenance rule might be induced to produce and offer more product for sale in the pre-entry period.[82] Pre-entry social gains would thereby result, although this assumes that the dominant firm will still find it attractive to develop and produce a new generation of equipment under a $P = P$ rule. This last assumption is problematic. The magnitude of pre-entry gains must in any event be weighed against the previously described losses entailed by a post-entry price maintenance rule.

A second possible justification is the 'infant firm' argument. The general infant firm argument would presumably take the following form: preventing the dominant firm from selling Q at the market price (for example, permitting it to sell only $Q - \delta$) when new entry appears will permit entry to occur on a larger scale than would otherwise be feasible; entry at this larger scale is needed for the new entrant to become a qualified innovator (or earlier imitator) of original equipment; future period gains on successor generations of equipment would thus be realized if the dominant firm is

---

[81] The incremental welfare gains are given by the area under the residual demand curve between the origin and Q_E less the costs of supplying Q_E.

[82] The dominant firm must form expectations about how much product new entrants will bring onto the market as a function of the pre-entry stock in order to optimize production. Presumably the amount of product supplied by entrants varies inversely with the stock of product supplied by the dominant firm.

constrained to hold its price at or near the pre-entry level (which effectively requires it to retire product). This is a rather bold argument that entrants may invoke in a self-serving way. Areeda and Turner have characterized arguments of this genre as 'intrinsically speculative and indeterminate,' and have argued that '[n]o suitable administrative rules could be formulated to give them recognition.'[83] Although the argument may be valid in special circumstances,[84] these are surely the exception and not the rule.

Besides being speculative, the claim that technological progress will be promoted by protecting infant firms does not establish that welfare gains result. Do the discounted future period benefits more than offset the immediate losses that involuntary asset retirement by the dominant firm would entail? Where the prospects for future gains from innovation are small or problematic, a policy of forced retirement of product in support of infant firms seems dubious.

Another disability is the cost of enforcing the rule. If a requirement of involuntary asset retirement is to be the exception rather than the rule, those industries considered to be exceptions must be identified in advance or dominant firms will not know how to behave lawfully. Identification of these exceptions will be difficult even at a single point in time, much less over time. Although specific investigation of dominant firm industries in national markets would be possible because the number of such industries is relatively small, it would be impracticable to investigate and declare exceptions for the much larger number of local and regional geographic markets with dominant firms.

Finally, even if agreement could be reached in advance, a special predatory pricing rule for those industries declared to be exceptions is a questionable way of promoting greater pre-entry output or future technological progress. Alternative instruments for promoting competition and technological progress in these industries – including explicit subsidies, affirmative incentives for dominant firms to spin off technological ventures,[85] or, possibly, dissolution[86] – are apt to be as or more effective.

A policy of involuntary asset retirement under circumstances of the kind described in this section is a dubious undertaking. At the very least, those responsible for public policy formation in this area should (a) recognize the hazards of declaring exceptions and (b) give serious consideration to other public policy alternatives for promoting the intended benefits.

[83] Areeda and Turner, *supra* footnote 16, p. 897.
[84] Conceivably an underdeveloped country might decide to impose special restraints on established multinational firms if, by assisting indigenous firms, the skills needed to hasten development would be promoted. System gains would thus offset the local losses caused by an infant industry rule.
[85] Williamson, *supra* footnote 27, pp. 192–207.
[86] Ibid., pp. 223–6.

C. VOLUNTARY RETIREMENT OF PRODUCT

If regulation were costless, public policy would presumably require that the dominant firm sell its entire stock of product, Q. Any policy permitting the dominant firm to retire stock voluntarily runs the risk of causing welfare losses. Valuable assets with significant social value could be shelved or scrapped. But if regulatory solutions are disfavored, the possibility that the dominant firm will voluntarily retire product in the face of new entry must be entertained.[87]

A policy requiring a dominant firm to sell its entire stock in the face of entry will probably be a redundant constraint – although dominant firms confronted with such a requirement may produce less than they otherwise would in the pre-entry period. Voluntary asset retirement by a dominant firm faced with entry is an accommodating posture. Entrants may interpret asset retirement as an invitation to make further inroads, with the result that the dominant firm will have to retire even more product to prevent price deterioration. Where accommodation is anticipated to lead to substantial output increases by entrants, dominant firms may eschew a policy of voluntary asset retirement and instead sell Q at whatever price the market will bring.

IV. Predatory Pricing Among Established Rivals

There are three cases in which predatory pricing may be directed at established rivals. The first involves price cutting by established firms in a mature, but nevertheless loosely disciplined, oligopoly. The second involves price cutting by firms in an industry still in the early stages of development. The third case is the use of promotional prices by firms attempting to enter a new market. Each poses distinctive problems.

A. LOOSE OLIGOPOLY

The loose oligopoly condition can be further broken down into stable demand (or slow growth) and declining demand cases. In neither case do established firms have incentives to engage in the strategic prepositioning practised by dominant firms or collusive oligopolists anticipating entry. Hence the concern that predatory pricing rules will influence pre-entry

---

[87] This is especially likely to occur if the demand for the product in the range $Q + \Delta$ is inelastic. It is sometimes argued that monopolists will never set price in the range where demand is inelastic. This ignores the fact, however, that dominant firms sometimes price with an eye to entry. Also, even if pre-entry demand elasticity exceeds unity, post-entry demand elasticity (evaluated at $Q + \Delta$) may be below unity.

investment is irrelevant for loose oligopolies. Instead, cost-based rules are needed. The question then is what rule is appropriate for each condition.

Stable Demand

Any of a number of disturbances can upset pricing relationships among established oligopolists. For the most part, the ensuing price-cutting episodes do not occasion public policy concern. A predatory pricing issue arises only if price cutting persists and there is an indication that one or more firms is relying on a deep pocket in an effort to force the exit of some firms from the industry.

The appropriate test in such a situation is that prices should be remunerative. In the very short run this means that the price-cutting firm should never drop prices below average variable costs. An average variable cost test poses special hazards, however, if firms in the industry have different technologies. Firms that are more capital intensive will have lower average variable costs, *ceteris paribus*, since they have more fixed (nonvariable) capital costs. Since these firms may not be the most efficient firms in the industry, sustained low prices should be required to cover short-run average total costs. Where prices are maintained at low levels indefinitely, such prices should prospectively recover all costs in the long run.

Thus although a cost-based test is appropriate when there is sustained price cutting, neither short-run marginal cost nor its surrogate, average variable cost (which are the test criteria proposed by Areeda and Turner), is suggested. Rather, the relevant test is one of remunerative pricing. An average cost test both sorts out the efficiency of firms more accurately[88]

---

[88] Posner also makes this point, but not without considerable terminological confusion. Posner, *supra* footnote 3, p. 192. Thus he objects to the Areeda–Turner short-run marginal cost test because it purportedly: 'ignores the fact that short-run marginal cost is lower than long-run marginal cost . . . even when there is no excess capacity. In the short run, marginal cost does not include interest, rent, depreciation, and other overhead items, because they do not vary in the short run with the amount of output produced, but they are part of the long-run marginal cost of production, which is why a firm's short-run marginal cost is normally lower than its long-run marginal cost.' ibid., pp. 191–2.

This last reflects confusion between average total costs and average variable costs on the one hand and long-run marginal costs and short-run marginal costs on the other. Scherer, *Book Review*, *Yale Law Journal*, 86 (1977), pp. 974, 991 n. 90. Posner's statement would be correct if average variable cost is substituted for short-run marginal cost whenever it appears and average total cost replaces long-run marginal cost. The statement is technically incorrect, however, as it reads. The relevant distinction between short-run marginal costs and long-run marginal costs is *a temporal one*. In the short run plant scale is fixed. Producing successively more output from a fixed plant involves more intensive utilization of variable factors – multiple shifts may be introduced, scrappage rates may increase, scheduling problems and bottlenecks develop, etc. – with the result that the incremental cost of supplying the last unit easily becomes great and exceeds the cost of supplying this unit if plant scale were increased appropriately. Contrary to Posner, short-run marginal costs *exceed* long-run marginal costs at production levels that exceed design capacity. G. Stigler, *The Theory of Price*, 3rd edn (1966); pp. 156–8; New York: Macmillan; Viner, *supra* footnote 50.

and poses fewer problems of estimation by litigants. The efficiency advantage is that low-cost firms that are either labor intensive (and thus have high variable costs) or lack deep pockets will not be jeopardized by an average total cost pricing test. Only high-cost firms will be forced to exit. The cost estimation advantage is that all costs are taken into consideration. This scarcely assures a determinate result, but much of the accounting discretion allowed by a short-run marginal or average variable cost test is nevertheless reduced.

Declining Demand

The declining industry is a special case. Objectively viewed, some firms will have to exit. Efficiency is served if those with high out-of-pocket costs are forced to go early. Firms with specialized plant and high fixed costs, but low out-of-pocket costs, will remain. Society gains because the firms that are earliest to exit are those with the highest opportunity costs. An average variable cost test is thus appropriate.[89] It is noteworthy that the only case for which the Areeda and Turner tests and those proposed here agree is the very special case of a declining industry.

B. EARLY STAGE GROWTH INDUSTRIES

Perhaps the most difficult case to assess is the industry that is still in an early stage of development. Demand is growing rapidly, often accompanied by technological improvements of a significant kind. Firms that entered early and were profitable under excess demand conditions, but are unable to realize cost economies or maintain the progressive pace, may have to be 'shaken out'. This is a painful process and may occasion predatory pricing suits. The question is what criteria to apply.

The basic dilemma is that although firms with deep pockets may entertain dominant-firm aspirations and may attempt to accelerate the demise of small rivals by resorting to predatory pricing, there is a great risk that – since truth is especially difficult to ascertain in the early stages of growth – unmeritorious charges of predatory pricing will be brought by marginal firms. Lest the forces of economic natural selection be held in check by the application of rules designed to deal with more settled states of affairs, a double test is proposed. First, a remunerative pricing test should be applied to the would-be dominant firm. Since costs may fall rapidly in the early stages of an industry's growth, a price should be assumed to be nonremunerative only if it is below current costs as reduced

---

[89] This may be refined to require that price exceeds short-run marginal costs as well. But this is a technical refinement, the operational significance of which may be questioned.

to account for future unit cost reductions.[90] The second part of the test would require that the plaintiff demonstrate that it can attain cost levels competitive with the defendant firm's costs. A requirement of current cost equivalence between the would-be dominant firm and the plaintiff would be too severe, since nondominant firms may become effective competitors if given a reasonable chance. Firms experiencing substantially higher costs relative to other small rivals should be disqualified from bringing predatory pricing suits.[91]

C. PROMOTIONAL PRICING

Charges of predatory behavior are normally brought by entrants rather than established firms, but local firms with large market shares sometimes complain of predatory pricing when multimarket firms attempt to enter their territory. *Utah Pie Co.* v. *Continental Baking Co.*[92] is a conspicuous example. Promotional pricing thus raises the question: Should a new entrant be allowed to stage a promotional campaign that violates the cost-recovery test?[93]

Areeda and Turner characterize a promotional price as

---

[90] This is to allow for the possibility that costs may be falling rapidly as a result of (static) scale and (dynamic) learning-by-doing economies. If today's price does not cover yesterday's costs but exceeds tomorrow's, how is the price to be evaluated? Even a profit maximizing monopolist might set current price below current costs if future costs (and possibly future demand) are beneficially affected. Surely, however, a price is presumptively nonremunerative if it is below current costs as reduced by the discounted value of future unit cost reductions attributable to incremental current supply.

[91] A variant that may arise in demonstrating cost effectiveness concerns the case where the plaintiff procures an essential component from a vertically integrated rival. Achieving cost parity may then be complicated if either the internal transfer price and the market price of the component differ or if supply reliability differs between internal and external users. Inasmuch as the object is to sort on efficiency, both nonintegrated and integrated firms need by evaluated on comparable terms.

This assumes that the nonintegrated firm is prepared to make firm contracts with the integrated supplier. It is unrealistic to expect delivery in spot markets on terms that are equivalent (in price and regularity of delivery) to those that the integrated firm makes when product is transferred between internal divisions.

Furthermore, the integrated firm is not required to transfer products between divisions on market terms. To the extent that it does not and cost parity becomes an issue in litigation, an adjustment is plainly warranted for evaluative purposes.

[92] 386 US 685 (1967). For discussions, see Posner, *supra* footnote 3, p. 194; Areeda and Turner, *supra* footnote 3, pp. 726–7.

[93] Two caveats are warranted. First, the industry may experience an unanticipated fall in demand, in which case full-cost recovery may be temporarily infeasible. Second, the relevant costs for the entrant are those that will obtain after allowance has been made for unusual start-up expenses for administration, manufacturing, and distribution (though possibly not promotion).

a temporary, low price designed to induce patronage with the expectation that the customer will continue purchasing the product in the future at a higher [presumably cost-recovering] price. The promotional price may be below cost and is most easily illustrated by the seller who gives his product away without charge to some or all would-be customers.[94]

Such promotions may be the only effective way to overcome customer habit in industries where the product is differentiated by manufacturers. It is widely conceded that a promotional pricing exception may be warranted for products that are not, or are not perceived to be, homogeneous.[95]

Although a promotional pricing exception would relieve the entrant of the need to satisfy a remunerative pricing test from the very outset, such relief would be strictly temporary. The time limits on a promotional pricing effort would vary with the product and would require marketing expertise to establish. Only a few rough guidelines for a promotional pricing exception will be offered here. First, promotional prices to industrial users should rarely be necessary (a few 'demonstration' sales, perhaps, excepted). Appeal on the basis of the merits of the product should ordinarily be feasible from the outset. Second, promotional pricing for consumer durables is a doubtful undertaking, since repurchase will not occur for some time and imitation is apt to be a lagged and uncertain process. Consumer nondurables thus appear to be the area where promotional pricing is apt to be most attractive. The allowable length of a promotional pricing campaign for consumer nondurables should vary directly with the expected shelf life of the item. This may vary from a few weeks to, perhaps, a few months. But in no case should entrants expect to be able to effect massive market dislocations under the aegis of below-cost promotional pricing.[96] Only competition on the merits would warrant this; continued supply at a price below cost may be regarded as

[94] Areeda and Turner, *supra* footnote 3, p. 713.

[95] For a thoughtful discussion of promotional pricing and admissible dominant reactions thereto, see Areeda and Turner, *supra* footnote 3, pp. 713–16. Cooper also notes that below-cost pricing for promotional purposes warrants an exception. Cooper, *supra* footnote 3, p. 437.

It should also be recognized, however, that product differentiation complicates the problems of welfare evaluation enormously. Consumers may or may not benefit by the additional product variety that an entrant offers. The discussion of promotional pricing in the predatory pricing literature presumes that greater variety is beneficial. The presumption is followed here.

[96] As Commissioner Elman observed when the *Clorox* case was before the FTC, a dominant firm 'might tolerate the obtaining of a small foothold by a new entrant, but [it] can hardly [be expected to] sit by while a large share of the market is absorbed by the newcomer.' Procter & Gamble Co., 63 FTC 1534, 1552 (1963), 358 F.2d 74 (6th Cir. 1966), 386 US 568 (1967).

an indication of predatory intent on the part of the entrant and is presumptively unlawful.

V. Recent Cases and Commentary

Two types of predatory pricing have been distinguished in this chapter. One involves predatory pricing in relation to new entry. The basic model, set out in parts I and II, applies to products supplied continuously. This model was then extended in part III to consider generational equipment industries. The second type involves predatory pricing directed against established rivals. The loose oligopoly (in both steady-state and declining industries), growth industry, and promotional pricing conditions each warrant separate treatment within this category. These were examined in part IV. Three cases are examined here, illustrating four of these five conditions (omitting the growth industry situation).

A. RIVALRY AMONG ESTABLISHED FIRMS: LOOSE OLIGOPOLY

The recent case of *Hanson* v. *Shell Oil Co.*[97] was a challenge to predatory pricing in a loose oligopoly. Hanson argued that in 1961 Shell began a program to recover lost market shares in certain south-western states, where Shell's market share was about ten per cent,[98] by engaging in unlawful price competition.[99] The Ninth Circuit observed that 'Hanson presented no evidence which would suggest that the "specific intent" to monopolize existed.'[100] But the court took the argument further. Citing Areeda and Turner, the court held:

To demonstrate predation, Hanson had to show that the prices charged by Shell were such that Shell was foregoing present profits in order to create a market position in which it could charge enough to obtain supra-normal profits and recoup its present losses. This could be shown by evidence that Shell was selling its gasoline at below marginal cost or, because marginal cost is often impossible to ascertain, below average variable costs.[101]

The court further counseled that predatory pricing claims should not be upheld when they are used in a protectionist manner:

[97] 541 F.2d 1352 (9th Cir,. 1976).
[98] Ibid., p. 1360.
[99] Ibid., p. 1355.
[100] Ibid., p. 1358.
[101] Ibid. (footnote omitted).

The antitrust laws were not intended, and may not be used, to require businesses to price their products at unreasonably high prices (which penalize the consumer) so that less efficient competitors can stay in business. The Sherman Act is not a subsidy for inefficiency. Hanson's failure to show that Shell's prices were below its marginal or average variable cost was a failure as a matter of law to present a prima facie case under § 2.[102]

The possibility that the antitrust laws can be used in a protectionist way to discourage price rivalry was plainly recognized by the court and equally plainly rejected. Although the court's reliance on an average variable cost test was inappropriate considering the duration of the pricing conduct,[103] a cost-based test is necessary in a loose oligopoly to ascertain whether predation is present and, of equal importance, to prevent the predatory pricing law from being used as a shelter for inefficiency. In steady growth industries such as in *Hanson*, predatory pricing can be identified as sustained pricing below average total cost.

B. NEW ENTRY: STANDARDIZED PRODUCT AND PROMOTIONAL PRICING

Purex Corp. v. *Procter & Gamble Co.*[104] illustrates the issues that arise when new entry is attempted in a standardized product industry. The

---

[102] Ibid., pp. 1358–9 (footnote omitted).

[103] As pointed out above, an average variable cost test does not adequately sort out the relative efficiency of firms with differing intensities of fixed assets.

[104] 419 F. Supp. 931 (C.D. Cal. 1976). The district court's decision was part of a long litigation precipitated by Procter & Gamble's (P&G) acquisition in 1957 of the Clorox Chemical Company, makers of Clorox bleach. Ibid., p. 933. The Federal Trade Commission ruled that the acquisition acted 'to foreclose effective competition in the industry' and thus violated section 7 of the Clayton Act, 15 USC section 18 (1970), Procter & Gamble Co., 63 FIC 1465, 1569 (1963), 358 F.2d 74 (6th Cir. 1966), 386 US 568 (1967). The Commission ordered P&G to divest itself of Clorox within one year of the final order. Ibid., pp. 1585–7. The Sixth Circuit set aside the Commission's order, *Procter & Gamble* v. *FTC*, 358 F.2d 74 (6th Cir. 1966), 386 US 568 (1967), but the Supreme Court reinstated the decree. *FTC* v. *Procter & Gamble Co.*, 386 US 568 (1967). As a result, in 1969 Procter & Gamble was forced to divest itself of Clorox. 419 F. Supp. at 933.
Purex, Clorox's leading competitor in the bleach business, then brought a private treble damage suit under section 4 of the Clayton Act, 15 USC section 15 (1970) against P&G and P&G's wholly owned subsidiary, the Clorox Company, 419 F. Supp. at 933, Purex alleged that P&G and Clorox had violated not only section 7 of the Clayton Act (the issue previously determined by the Supreme Court), but also sections 1 and 2 of the Sherman Act, 15 USC, 1, 2 (Supp. V 1975). The district court held that the Supreme Court's adjudication of the section 7 violation only established that the effect of the P&G-Clorox merger '*may be* substantially to lessen competition, or to *tend* to create a monopoly. '419 F. Supp. at 933 [quoting Clayton Act section 7, 15 USC section 18 (1970)] (emphasis supplied by court). Since a plaintiff in a section 4 treble damage action must show that he *is* 'injured in his business . . . by reason of anything forbidden in the antitrust laws,' 15 USC section 15 (1970), the court held that Purex had to show actual injury in addition to violation of section 7, 419 F. Supp. at 934.

Purex complaint raised a number of issues, including an allegation that Procter & Gamble (P&G) – Clorox had unlawfully unencroached on Purex territories along the West Coast, but the 'conclusive' indication that Clorox engaged in predatory behavior involved its response to the Purex entry in Erie, Pennsylvania.[105] Inasmuch as Purex was a new entrant into this geographic market and the product in question was a consumer nondurable, Purex was presumably entitled to the temporary latitude afforded promotional pricing. And indeed Purex did use special promotions to launch its entry into this market. It was not alleged that these promotions were excessive;[106] the only litigated issue was whether the response by Clorox was unlawful.

Purex took several positions on the predatory pricing claim, one of which was that Clorox should not be permitted to charge a price or incur promotional expenses that yield a net loss.[107] The more basic question under the output restriction rule, however, is whether Clorox increased its sales in response to the Purex incursion. If Clorox had increased its sales of bleach above its accustomed volume, a presumption that this was a contingent response expressly designed to defeat entry would be warranted. Without such an increase, Clorox could be presumed instead to be conducting business at a steady level that would continue, entry or not.[108]

In addition to a remunerative pricing test, Purex also took the position that dominant firms (Clorox had a pre-entry market share in Erie in

---

Thus the court's opinion considered almost exclusively the issue whether the admitted section 7 violation, the P&G–Clorox merger, caused actual damage to Purex. P&G–Clorox's conduct in the Erie market, footnote 105 *infra*, only went to the issue whether Purex was damaged by actions Clorox could not have undertaken absent the merger. Ibid., pp. 941–2. The consideration of the alleged Sherman Act section 2, 15 USC, section 2 (Supp. V 1975), violation was relegated to two paragraphs at the end of the opinion. This does not affect the analysis in text since the court's discussion of the Erie incident, 419 F. Supp. at 940–2, addressed itself to P&G–Clorox's alleged 'anticompetitive predatory practice designed to prevent a new competitor from getting a foothold in the [Erie] market.' Ibid., p. 940.

[105] 419 F. Supp. at 940–2. Irwin Stelzer, an expert witness for Purex, testified on cross-examination as follows: 'I focused really on Erie ... [T]hat was considered the terrific example of what dominant firms shouldn't be allowed to do.' Trial Transcript at 2726-A.

[106] But the size of Purex's promotional expenditures was at issue in the case. Purex apparently spent over $3.00 per case of bleach sold on advertising and coupon discounts, while Clorox responded with expenditures and price reductions of about $.90 per case, 419 F. Supp. at 940. The court noted that it is an accepted principle in the business community 'that an established firm may use all fair means to protect its market, 'and found nothing reprehensible or anticompetitive in the Clorox response' because 'an unusually large attack may be expected to elicit a comparable response.' Ibid., p. 941. The court did not, however, address the lawfulness of the response in terms of either output or cost. Under the proposed criterion a $Q \leqslant Q$ test would have been appropriate.

[107] Plaintiff's Opening Brief, part II, pp. 183–5.

[108] Clorox prices during the introductory interval when the $Q \leqslant Q$ constraint is in effect should, of course, cover its average variable costs.

excess of 60 per cent) have an obligation to accommodate entry.[109] Since bleach does not lend itself to product innovations of a significant kind and Purex was a well-established producer of bleach in other geographic areas, no infant firm argument for the protection of Purex can reasonably be made. Rather, the argument reduces to a naked theory of umbrella pricing – in order to ensure the viability of a new entrant, the dominant firm is expected to maintain price. Since Purex was bringing additional (and substantially identical) product onto the market, P&G–Clorox would evidently be required to *reduce* output in an offsetting amount, in order to maintain price, under the theory of competition advocated by Purex. That the new entrant may be a high-cost supplier or that the dominant firm will hold excess capacity in these circumstances are evidently of no account. This approach is ill-advised. It makes the easy but egregious mistake of protecting competitors rather than competition.[110]

C. NEW ENTRY: GENERATIONAL EQUIPMENT

Telex Corp. v. *International Business Machines Corp*.[111] ilustrates the issues that arise when an entrant offers a product with a short life cycle by imitating the design of a device for which the dominant firm has discontinued production.[112] Again, although a number of conduct matters

[109] These views are set out in remarks made by Alfred R. Oxenfeldt, an expert witness for Purex. Trial Transcript at 2452–3. This testimony was summarized by the plaintiff's attorneys as holding that 'a newcomer must be given a chance to get established before the dominant firm responds.' Plantiff's Opening brief, part II, p. 183.

[110] Note that the output restriction rule is not an umbrella rule. It is sometimes mistakenly argued that the rule $Q \leqslant \mathbf{Q}$ is essentially equivalent to the rule $P \geqslant \mathbf{P}$, where the latter is plainly a price umbrella rule. This purportedly follows since price and quantity are inversely related through the demand function (as price increases, less of the product is demanded).

The error arises over a confusion between firm and market conditions. The output restriction rule applies to the dominant firm. But if the output of the dominant firm is unchanged ($Q = \mathbf{Q}$) and the entrant brings the quantity Δ onto the market, the dominant firm must reduce its output in response to entry if it is to hold its price unchanged. In a market for a homogeneous product, the post-entry output of the dominant firm will be $\mathbf{Q} - \Delta$ if the entrant supplies Δ and the $P = \mathbf{P}$ rule is in effect. Thus under the $P = \mathbf{P}$ rule the dominant firm makes a place for the entrant, while under the $Q \leqslant \mathbf{Q}$ rule the entrant must make a place for himself if the dominant firm refuses to be conciliatory.

[111] 367 F. Supp. 258 (N.D. Okla. 1973), 510 F.2d 894 (10th Cir. 1975).

[112] It is not entirely clear from a reading of Judge Christensen's opinion in *Telex* whether or not IBM's production of disk drives was fully completed when IBM cut its price. Also, the price cut was selective rather than general. IBM was experiencing increasing competition for its 2314 disk drive from plug compatible substitutes (including the Telex 5314 disk drive). Rather than cutting the price on all 2314s or allowing 2314s returned to IBM because of plug compatible competition to accumulate in storage, IBM decided to reconfigure the 2314, adding certain control functions, and market the resulting 2319A subsystem at a reduced price. A two-price system thus resulted: IBM maintained the price on those 2314 subsystems for which customers were willing to renew leases, while at the same time reducing the inroads made by plug compatible peripherals by marketing the 2319A at a lower price. *Telex Corp*. v. *International Business Machs. Corp*., 367 F. Supp. at 291–96.

were raised in the *Telex* case,[113] the basic issue was the existence of predatory pricing. Although it oversimplifies, I will take it as given that (a) IBM's production of the computer peripheral device in question was terminated before entry appeared[114] and (b) the device had negligible value in its best alternative (nonperipheral) use. The question facing the courts was what pricing latitude should IBM (and other dominant firms similarly situated) be permitted in the face of entry by firms like Telex.

The welfare analysis of part III discloses that, leaving aside infant firm issues, IBM should lease its entire stock of completed product (Q) at whatever price would clear the market. New entrants would invariably prefer that dominant firms be required to maintain their prices, because umbrella pricing facilitates easy entry. The misallocative effects of such pricing, however, argue against the adoption of an umbrella rule. Insisting that established firms must maintain their pre-entry prices until entrants are thought to be well established, despite the consequences of equipment retirement, comes perilously close to arguing that, whatever the efficiency consequences, more firms are always preferred to fewer in dominant firm industries.

Might an infant firm exception be warranted? Technological innovation is an important feature of the electronic data processing industry. Suppose, arguendo, that alternative antitrust instruments[115] are unavailable for promoting technological progress. Assume, moreover, that dominant firms receive adequate advance notification, and hence are aware of the bounds of lawful behavior. Three factors must be assessed to determine whether an exception is warranted. First, had Telex (or other peripheral manufacturers) made significant technological innovations? Second, are there

---

The assumption for the purposes of this analysis is that IBM had essentially completed production of the 2314 prior to the price reduction and that the cost of reconfiguring returned 2314s and adding control functions was a small fraction of the original manufacturing cost. Inasmuch as new plug compatible peripherals are designed to complement successive generations of computers, and given the assumptions stated above, the generational equipment model in part III would appear to be applicable. (If the facts should turn out to contradict the assumptions in significant degree, however, a further analysis of the economic implications beyond those set out here would be warranted.)

[113] The district court found IBM guilty of monopolization and attempting to monopolize in five specific respects:

1 The announcement and institution of the 2319A disc storage facility in September 1970.

2 The announcement of the 2319B disc storage facility in December 1970.

3 The announcement of the Fixed Term Plan long-term leasing program in May 1971.

4 The announcement and implementation of the Extended Term Plan, which was also a leasing plan, in March 1972.

5 IBM's pricing policies with regard to its memory products during 1970 and 1971.

Telex Corp. v. *International Business Machs. Corp.*, 510 F.2d 894, 900 (10th Cir. 1975), 367 F. Supp. 258 (N.D. Okla. 1973).

[114] Footnote 112 *supra*.

[115] p. 266 *supra*.

structural factors that incline such firms to be leaders or followers? And, third, if the answers to either of these questions disclose actual or potential leadership, would the gains from innovation be significant?

A complete answer to each of these questions is beyond the scope of this chapter, but a tentative evaluation is possible. The record in *Telex* indicates that Telex had mainly been a follower.[116] Also, there are structural reasons to believe that this may have been the 'natural' posture for peripheral manufacturers to adopt.[117] Even if an argument could be made that imitators have technological leadership potential, this does not establish that welfare gains will be realized by requiring dominant firms to maintain price when confronted with entry. Such an involuntary asset retirement policy yields net welfare gains only if the discounted future benefits of such a policy exceed the immediate welfare losses. The issues in *Telex* were never addressed in these terms.

VI. Rules of Law: Prior and Proposed

Areeda and Turner conclude their examination of the predatory pricing issue by proposing a series of rules, the most relevant of which are the following:

1. ....

    (b) A price at or above average cost should be deemed nonpredatory even though not profit maximizing in the short run.

    (c) A price at or above reasonably anticipated shortrun marginal and average variable costs should be deemed nonpredatory even though not loss-minimizing in the short run.

    ....

2. Recognizing that marginal cost data are typically unavailable, we conclude that:

    (a) A price at or above reasonably anticipated average variable cost should be conclusively presumed lawful.

---

[116] See the chronology of product introductions by IBM and Telex in *Telex Corp.* v. *International Business Machs. Corp.*, 367 F. Supp. 258, 271–72 (N.D. Okla. 1973), 510 F.2d 894 (10th Cir. 1975).

[117] The main frame manufacturers originate successive generations of new central processing units. Compatible peripherals are usually designed in the process. Leadership in peripheral design thus accrues naturally to firms responsible for state-of-the-art advances in central processing units. Furthermore, 'entry was initially easy for peripheral equipment manufacturers because they could choose to copy only proven successful products.' *Telex Corp.* v. *International Business Machs. Corp.*, 367 F. Supp. at 286. Considerably more detailed knowledge of the industry is needed, however, before these issues can be settled definitively.

(b) A price below reasonably anticipated average variable cost should be conclusively presumed unlawful.[118]

The Areeda–Turner rules do not distinguish predatory pricing in response to entry and predatory behavior among established firms. This distinction is basic; the rules of law proposed below expressly recognize it. The basic Areeda–Turner rules are formulated as marginal cost pricing tests, although Areeda and Turner concede that marginal cost is difficult to estimate and therefore offer average variable cost tests as an alternative. The rules proposed below eschew reliance on marginal costs.

A. ENTRY

The merits of the predatory pricing rules proposed below turn jointly on the efficiency arguments developed in earlier sections of this chapter and on the fairness attributes discussed in part VII, which follows. Some perspective on the rules may nevertheless be gained by a brief recapitulation of their properties:

1   the output restriction rule, even without an accompanying remunerative pricing test, represents a relatively severe restraint – certainly more severe than cost-based rules that permit dominant firms to offer contingent product in response to entry;
2   the remote possibility that the output restraint will not by itself preclude nonremunerative pricing in the immediate post-entry period can be forestalled by additionally stipulating that the dominant firm shall not price below its average variable costs;[119]
3   although the dominant firm is relieved of the output rstriction when the initial (18-month) restraint period has expired, it is simultaneously subjected to an average total cost remunerative pricing test, which assures that deep pocket considerations will not influence viability in the long run;
4   finally, promotional pricing exceptions aside, new entrants face two-

[118] Areeda and Turner, *supra* footnote 3, pp. 732–3.
[119] The argument that marginal cost should be the appropriate lower bound on prices is rejected for three reasons. First, the purported allocative efficiency benefits of marginal cost pricing are problematic in the short run. Second, even assuming that marginal cost could be estimated to the satisfaction of the litigants, involving the courts in a marginal cost pricing test implies using the antitrust laws to effect fine tuning. This is an undertaking of dubious merit. Footnote 16 *supra*. Third, the operationality of a marginal cost pricing test is seriously in question. Footnote 124 *supra*.

stage remunerative pricing tests identical to those set out in (2) and (3) above.[120]

Lawful Behavior

1.1 Short run: $Q \leqslant Q$

When dominant firms reduce their output or hold their (demand adjusted)[121] output unchanged in the face of new entry they shall be deemed to be behaving in a nonpredatory way provided that the resulting market price is not less than average variable cost.[122]

---

[120] As indicated, *supra*, entrants should not expect to effect massive market dislocations as part of a promotional entry effort. The special latitude afforded promotional pricing is merely intended to facilitate initial acceptance. Thereafter, a remunerative pricing test should apply.

It should be recognized that any entry effort – promotional or not – that combines a capital intensive technology (and hence low average variable costs) with deep pockets poses a potential difficulty. Conceivably, the entrant could offer product in the immediate post-entry period on terms that fully satisfy the remunerative pricing terms specified in rule 2.1,, while the dominant firms, with a less intensive technology, would be unable at the same price to recover its average variable costs. Lest the spirit of the remunerative pricing rules be abused (with counterproductive consequences), entrants attempting to exploit such average variable cost differences should be required to demonstrate that their cost advantages hold with respect to average total cost as well. If the latter test is failed, intermediate-term pricing at a level not less than that of the minimum average variable costs of the dominant firms could be stipulated. The viability of otherwise efficient dominant firms during the early post-entry period would not, therefore, be jeopardized.

The case can be made that new entrants should be granted a learning curve exception of the kind discussed in footnote 90 *supra*. The problem with this is that the necessary cost projections are difficult to make. Accordingly, there is a serious risk that new entrants (large or small) will abuse any such provision. I am inclined for this reason to restrict learning curve adjustment to early growth stage industries.

Although the issues addressed in this footnote are mainly of hypothetical (rather than operational) interest, it is noteworthy that the rules treat strategic behavior by dominant firms and entrants similarly; both are held to be objectionable. A restraint on admissible entry behavior is thus indicated where an entrant with a deep pocket and the requisite capital intensive technology attempts to subvert average variable cost pricing rules with a strategic purpose.

[121] See footnote 33 *supra* for a discussion of demand adjustment.

[122] A graphical display may be instructive. The short-run cost curves drawn below show the average total, average variable, and corresponding marginal costs of the dominant firm. The dominant firm is assumed initially to be producing at Q_o, and selling at a price P_o. When entry occurs, the dominant firm is permitted under the proposed rules to continue production at Q_o provided that the resulting market price exceeds P_v. If it does not, he must reduce output. If at Q_x the price still does not cover his costs, production will presumably be discontinued (since out-of-pocket costs exceed revenues). This last outcome is doubtful, however, since inability to cover minimum average variable costs implies either massive inefficiency on the part of the dominant firm or a strong likelihood that the new entrant is behaving in a predatory way (in which event the dominant firm is entitled to relief).

Note that whereas an average variable cost proviso is actually more permissive than a marginal cost pricing test (*AVC* is less than *SRMC* in the relevant region Q_x to Q_o), the output restrictions severely limit the range of action open to the dominant firm. Areeda and Turner's (surrogate) rules would allow the dominant firm to expand beyond Q_o provided that prices recovered variable costs. (fn. contin. overleaf)

1.2 *Long run*

Prices calculated to recover full costs over a sustained production interval, during which plant renewal and other expenses come due, will be deemed nonpredatory.[123]

The rationale for rule 1.2 is that output limits placed on the dominant firm in the short run are less easily justified, and more difficult to police, in the long run. When entrants have incurred the threshold costs of entry and have not been rendered nonviable by short-run strategic responses of dominant firms, they ought to be well positioned to participate in industry growth, achieve cost economies,

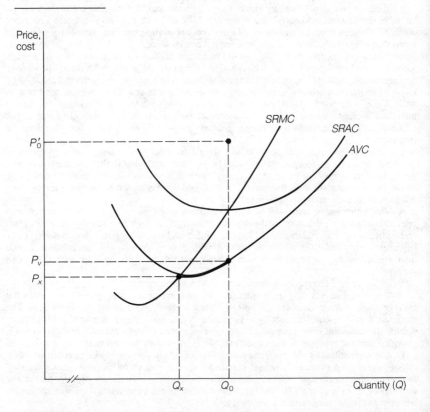

[123] The long-run rule applies to dominant firms and successful entrants alike. As discussed above, 12 to 18 months would appear to be a sufficient period for the output rule to govern.

and compete effectively. The restrictions on output expansion stipulated in rule 1.1 above are accordingly relaxed in the long run and are supplanted by an average total cost remunerative pricing rule.

Unlawful Behavior

2.1 Short run: $Q > Q$

Dominant firms that expand their (demand adjusted) output in the face of new entry will be deemed to be engaged in predatory behavior – even if the resulting market price exceeds the dominant firm's average variable cost.

2.2 Long run

Sustained production by dominant firms or successful entrants shall be deemed predatory if revenues are not fully cost recovering with respect to an appropriate assignment of all expenses incurred during the long-run interval.

Rule 1.1 is the basic rule. It does not disallow a conciliatory response, since accommodating output reductions are permitted. A conciliatory response is not mandated, however, except where the dominant firm is a high-cost supplier or the market-clearing price, were output to remain unchanged, would be less than the dominant firm's corresponding average variable costs. But the entering firm has no reason to anticipate that entry will be accommodated. To the contrary, the normal expectation is that such output as the entrant brings to the market will augment market supply in precisely that amount. Put differently, the dominant firm will not be expected to make a place for the new entrant by reducing its output in a partially or fully offsetting degree. The new entrant must thus be prepared to compete with the dominant firm at a common post-entry price below the prevailing pre-entry price. Rule 1.2 applies to the longer run and permits output expansion provided that the resulting prices fully recover cost.

Rule 2.1 is the counterpart of rule 1.1. Areeda and Turner would permit output expansion in the immediate post-entry interval if the resulting market price exceeds the dominant firm's marginal (or average variable) cost. Rule 2.1 prohibits output expansion. The welfare losses attributable to rules that permit contingent expansions of output are thereby avoided. (Dominant firms have an incentive to price higher and supply on inefficient terms in the pre-entry period if a positive output reaction is permitted. Aggregate post-entry product is also supplied at a higher cost under Areeda–Turner rules.)

The proposed rules are also superior in relative ease of enforcement. The Areeda–Turner rule, which permits output expansion, crucially relies on a price-to-cost test, which is exceedingly difficult to apply.[124] The proposed rule, by contrast, is much simpler: *Any (demand adjusted) output increase by the dominant firm is deemed predatory.* This is a much easier test statistic to develop.[125]

Rule 2.2 is concerned with behavior during the time period after the output restraint has expired. It makes allowance for the possibility that dominant firms (or successful entrants) with deep pockets will engage in long-term supply of a noncost recovering kind in the hope of eliminating rivals. Since supply can be sustained efficiently only if infrastructure-renewing costs are incurred (maintenance, replacement of plant and equipment, labor training costs, etc.), these costs should be taken into account in judging whether product is being supplied on economical terms. If these expenses are not being covered in the long run, a presumption of unlawfulness is warranted.

No special rule of law is needed to cover the generational equipment case discussed in part III. An entering firm should expect the dominant firm to sell its existing stock of equipment under the best terms it can secure. If demand is inelastic the dominant firm may well retire equipment when new supplies appear, thereby making a place for the entrant. There should be no presumption, however, that this will occur. To the contrary, the normal expectation is that the dominant firm's entire stock will be marketed, in which case the new product brought onto the market by an entrant will increase market supplies by precisely the amount of the entrant's output.

Although these rules cover dominant firm reactive behavior, an additional rule of law is required to cover the case where a firm (large or small) is attempting to enter a new market.

3 With the exception of promotional terms offered for a very short duration in conjunction with the sale of nondurable consumer goods, a new entrant should be expected to offer product on terms that are cost recovering.

Rule 3 allows the new entrant greater latitude by permitting very low

---

[124] Posner, *supra* footnote 3, pp. 190–1; Areeda and Turner, *supra* footnote 3, pp. 716–18, 733; Cooper, *supra* footnote 3, p. 438.

[125] The proposed short-run rule does include a variable cost proviso. A litigated case in which the dominant firm maintains or reduces output will thus require an examination of average variable costs. I would expect, however, that a major consequence of adopting the proposed rules would be a sharp drop in the number of litigated cases. Dominant firms will simply not respond aggressively to entry, and there is a presumption that nonresponse (holding output unchanged) is lawful. Except as market price falls drastically because of entry, the average variable cost floor is not apt to be breached (though this is more likely in highly labor-intensive industries). By contrast, dominant firms that increase output (as the Areeda–Turner rules permit) in a region of increasing marginal (and variable) cost are more apt to occasion litigation.

prices (even give-aways) for announcement purposes. The entrant can thus encourage customers to try the product on an experimental basis. This applies strictly to the short term. Part IV suggests some rough guidelines for assessing the allowable duration for a promotional campaign.

B. ESTABLISHED FIRMS[126]

Lawful Behavior

Occasional price wars of very limited duration do not pose predatory pricing threats to established oligopolists. Moreover, legal efforts to eliminate such behavior easily contribute to tighter oligopolistic pricing discipline. Accordingly, episodic price wars should be disregarded by the law. Attention should instead be focused exclusively on systematic pricing behavior among oligopolists.

1.1 *Intermediate run*
  (a) *Normal: $P \geqslant SRAC$*: Oligopolists charging prices that exceed short-run average costs shall be deemed to be behaving in a nonpredatory manner.
  (b) *Excess supply: $P \geqslant AVC$*: Oligopolists may reduce prices to average variable cost levels under conditions of chronic excess supply (such as develop in a declining industry).

  1.2 *Long run*
  Prices calculated to recover full costs over a sustained production interval during which plant renewal and related expenses are incurred will be deemed nonpredatory.[127]

Unlawful Behavior

Successive price wars, even though each is of very short duration, should be examined jointly rather than independently, in which case the intermediate-run test described below is relevant.

2.1 *Intermediate run*
  (a) *Normal: $P < SRAC$*: Sustained or frequently recurring pricing at less than short-run average costs will be deemed predatory.[128]

---

[126] The rules set out here apply to the case described as 'loose oligopoly'. Promotional pricing by new entrants, is covered by rule 3. The growth industry case poses special problems of its own. The pertinent considerations are set out above.

[127] Inasmuch as $SRAC$ is everywhere greater than or equal to $LRAC$, the long-run rule is redundant for the normal case. Lest the rules be misconstrued, however, the long run is included both here and in rule 2.2 for completeness.

[128] Where plants are operating beyond design capacities this is a more permissive test for predatory behavior than a short-run marginal cost test.

(b) *Excess supply*: $P < AVC$: Pricing at less than average variable costs will be deemed predatory, even under conditions of chronic excess supply.

2.2 *Long run*
Sustained pricing that is not prospectively cost recovering will be deemed predatory.

Since $SRMC > SRAC > AVC$ when plant is operated beyond the minimum cost point, for the normal case these rules are more permissive than the $SRMC$ rules of Areeda and Turner, but are more restrictive than their average variable cost surrogate. This points up a fact which, though apparent on reflection, warrants comment: AVC is often a poor surrogate for short-run marginal cost. Applying the AVC rule to the normal case allows much more output expansion than the $SRMC$ rule it is meant to approximate.[129] The proposed rules and the Areeda–Turner rules are identical only for the declining industry (excess supply) case.

VII. Fairness

The term predatory pricing reeks with implications of unfairness. Curiously, however, the fairness aspect of predatory pricing rules has received little attention in the recent literature. Partly this may be because fairness among oligopolists is difficult to characterize and the earlier literature complicated the task of characterization by failing to distinguish the new entry from the established rivalry cases. Partly it may be because fairness can be an obscure criterion.[130]

Deriving an 'optimal' predatory pricing rule based on notions of fairness poses formidable problems. A general criterion for assessing fairness is needed, but broad agreement on such a criterion is lacking. Although some might counsel that fairness be disregarded for this reason, a less ambitious option warrants consideration. Rather than derive the optimal rule, simply take the proposed rules as given and ask whether there are recognizable fairness differences between them. Comparative assessments

---

[129] As shown in the figure in footnote 122 *supra*, short-run marginal cost is equal to average variable cost at the output Q_x, but exceeds average variable costs at outputs greater than Q_x. This deviation, moreover, becomes progressively greater as output is expanded. Average variable cost thus becomes a progressively less satisfactory surrogate for marginal cost as output is increased above Q_o.

[130] As Professor Cooper notes, '[d]irect evidence of subjective motivations is always relevant in evaluating conduct, but inferences of motivation are ordinarily too dangerous to be accorded substantial weight.' He observes that the courts have repeatedly refused to expand reliance on intent beyond this limited role, 'instinctively recognizing that efforts to control the "fairness" of competition must encounter immense difficulties.' Cooper, *supra* footnote 3, p. 454.

of this kind are often feasible.[131] Since attitudes about fairness are apt to be stronger when relations between new entrants and dominant firms are involved and since the analysis has been primarily concerned with predatory pricing in the context of new entry, these remarks on fairness will be restricted to the new entry condition. It will be useful to consider the three broad classes of rules that apply in the new entry case: the protectionist rule ($P = \textbf{\textit{P}}$), the contingent supply rule ($P = MC$), and the business as usual rule ($Q = \textbf{\textit{Q}}$).

A. PROTECTIONIST RULE

The protectionist rule is that the dominant firm must take whatever actions are necessary to maintain market price when a new entrant appears. It involves a simple substitution of product supplied by the entrant for product previously supplied by the dominant firm. It violates a seemingly reasonable rule of industrial justice, namely, that entrants should expect to make their own way by offering incremental product in open markets.

B. CONTINGENT SUPPLY RULE

Of the possible bases for judging fairness, equality of opportunity is an appealing criterion. Posner's test for predatory pricing, excluding 'only a less efficient competitor,'[132] would appear to qualify under this standard. But this test misses the dynamics of the problem. Product that *could be supplied by an efficient dominant firm but is* offered only for purposes of defeating entry in markets where entry appears and deterring entry elsewhere is surely not equivalent to product supplied on a regular basis. To the contrary, contingent supply of a gaming variety – now it's there, now it isn't, depending on whether an entrant has appeared or perished – has the earmarks of a punitive purpose. Simple open market offers of incremental product by new entrants are not feasible when confronted by strategic behavior of this kind. It seems reasonable to regard such actions as pernicious and to declare them unfair and inadmissible.

---

[131] Note that the allocative efficiency advantage of the output restriction rule is a comparative one. Among the predatory pricing rules that have been proposed and are prospectively operational, it has the best properties. Some antitrust specialists will doubtlessly continue to favor 'comprehensive appraisals' of the kind described by Scherer, footnote 16 *supra*. The efficiency and fairness properties of such an approach are problematic and, I think, unascertainable.

[132] Posner, *supra* footnote 3, p. 193.

C. BUSINESS AS USUAL

The business as usual rule ($Q = \mathbf{Q}$) falls between the protectionist rule ($P = \mathbf{P}$, which implies $Q < \mathbf{Q}$) and the contingent supply rule ($P = MC$, which permits $Q > \mathbf{Q}$) in severity. Under this rule the dominant firm is advised that it can supply as much or as little as it wants, but that it should be prepared to supply on a regular basis. If, as seems reasonable, dominant firms have been supplying product under conditions in which production, distribution, and marketing are in balance, a continuation of the dominant firm's supply is surely inoffensive. Indeed, to expect someone to unbalance his operations (due to indivisibilities), lay off experienced workers, and hold capacity idle is tantamount to assigning a handicap to the established firm. Although horse races may benefit from efforts to equalize chances, the general presumption is that achievement should not be penalized. Efforts to cripple one firm to benefit another are widely believed to be unfair.

I conclude that fairness and efficiency both favor the $Q = \mathbf{Q}$ rule. Such harmony is perhaps not unusual; but neither is it always the case that what has the appearance of fairness and what contributes to efficiency warrant similar or identical behavior. It is nevertheless more satisfying when antitrust rules both yield consumer benefits (which is what efficiency is mainly about) and do not conflict with norms of industrial justice.[133]

VIII. Conclusion

Predatory pricing rules must distinguish between meritorius claims and claims that discourage legitimate rivalry.[134] Professors Areeda and Turner made a seminal contribution to the analysis of predatory pricing by establishing that systematic economic analysis can be applied to the thorny issues posed by predatory pricing. The straightforward application of 'settled' microeconomic propositions to public policy can sometimes be

---

[133] Restraints on promotional pricing also have a fairness rationale. Thus although new entrant status may properly entitle a firm to a brief promotional interval during which cost-recovering rules may be suspended, to ask for more is to rig the rules of the game in favor of those who have deep pockets. This is patently unfair (and also inefficient) and should be disallowed.

[134] Professor Scherer offers a similar summary of the objectives of predatory pricing law: '[t]he most workable competition in a [dominant firm industry] occurs when the dominant firm fears that it cannot deter entry from a high-price posture and is therefore led toward a continuing low-price, high-output strategy recognizing *inter alia* that no rules will force it to make room if entry does occur.' Scherer, 'Some last words on predatory pricing,' *Harvard Law Review*, 89 (1976) pp. 901, 902. But while it is relatively easy to reach agreement that these are the purposes to be served, designing a set of rules that are not defective in pre-entry or post-entry respects is quite another matter.

hazardous, however, Caution is warranted where the assumptions on which received doctrine is based are greatly at variance with the real world circumstances under examination.

The specific issue that arises here is whether the allocative efficiency benefits associated with continuous marginal cost pricing likewise apply when such pricing is of a temporary, strategic kind. I submit that marginal cost pricing loses its appeal when it is applied contingently as a strategic deterrent to entry. The predatory pricing problem needs to be formulated in strategic terms in order for the effects of alternative pricing rules to be accurately displayed. Such an analysis reveals that, when compared to the output rule proposed by this chapter, the Areeda–Turner marginal cost rules result in losses of social welfare in the periods before and after entry.

The output rule also has efficiency properties superior to other cost-based rules and to umbrella pricing. It is no more difficult to comprehend and is easier to apply than alternative cost-based rules. Rudimentary considerations of fairness also favor the output restriction rule over both cost-based and umbrella pricing rules. The output restriction rule provides a practicable way to sort out meritorious from protectionist claims of predatory behavior.

10

Pretrial Uses of Economists: On the Use of 'Incentive Logic' to Screen Predation

The use of economists to give expert testimony to inform the court and jury during antitrust trials is both widespread and controversial. One of the problems with such testimony is that it sometimes gets swept up with the adversarial quality of the courtroom.[1]

Although attorneys also use economists to assist them in evaluating pretrial issues, including the preparation of pretrial memoranda and motions, direct contact between economists and court at pretrial stages is rare. There is a growing opinion, however, that this is unfortunate and that the judicial process would benefit from earlier exposure to an assessment of the economic merits of a case. Several benefits can result.

Most important of these is that it forces the parties and the courts to focus on the economic issues early. Minor or mistaken issues can be filtered out and attention can thereafter be focused on major matters of real substance. An early separation of the wheat from the chaff reduces the likelihood of obscuration at trial stages, which saves time and avoids confusion. Occasionally, an examination of the economic merits may so dramatically clarify the issues that pretrial settlements that would not otherwise be reached can be agreed to. Asking economists to prepare pretrial memoranda on the merits has the advantage, moreover, of avoiding the adversarial dynamics of the courtroom. A more temperate and objective assessment should, as a consequence, thereby obtain.

I recently participated in a case in which the preparation of a pretrial memorandum on the economic merits appeared to contribute to a

© 1984 by Federal Legal Publications, Inc. Reproduced, with permission, from *The Antitrust Bulletin*, XXIX (1984), pp. 475–500, with amendments by the author
[1] The issues have reached even the popular press. See John A. Jenkins, 'Experts day in court,' *New York Times Magazine*, 11 Dec. 1983, pp. 98–106.

settlement. I shortly thereafter attended a conference on the Place of Economics in Legal Education,[2] in which the uses and misuses of expert economic witnesses – both in general and in relation to Judge Edward R. Becker's influential opinion in *Zenith Radio Corp.* v. *Matsushita Electrical Industrical Co.*[3] – were discussed. The possibility that greater pretrial uses of economists should be made, perhaps in conjunction with pretrial memoranda, was raised and elicited an interested response among conference participants.

The general arguments favoring such pretrial uses are those set out above. Here as elsewhere, however, it is often helpful to consider a specific example. The memorandum that I prepared and which was submitted to the court in the *Barry Wright* v. *ITT–Grinnell* litigation is therefore included in this chapter.[4] It is not offered as a model but as an illustration of how focusing attention on the economic merits of a case can sharpen perspectives.

The case in question alleges that ITT–Grinnell engaged in predatory behavior. Theories of predation have received a great deal of attention in law and economics journals in the past decade and numerous cases claiming predation have been brought before the courts. Although genuine predation involves complicated intertemporal behavior that can be difficult to assess, many cases are objectively lacking in merit. Specifically, many cases do not pass simple tests of 'incentive logic.' Forcing plaintiffs to confront these matters in pretrial stages, rather than rely on courtroom pyrotechnics and obfuscation, is arguably, if not plainly, in the interest of sound antitrust enforcement. This chapter has the purpose of stimulating commentary on the merits and limitations of using pretrial memoranda of the kind that follows. My sense is that the routine use of such memoranda would assist, perhaps greatly assist, the judicial process. But as with most reforms, skepticism is warranted. Potentially serious abuses and misuses of such memoranda, if they exist, should be exposed.

Normal business behavior involves rivalry and choices among alternative courses of action as events unfold and economic prospects become better defined. Winners and losers occur routinely as such rivalry proceeds and as firms and customers elect one course of action rather than another. Disappointments naturally occur as a consequence. Responses of four kinds can be distinguished.

---

[2] The conference was held in Denver, Colorado, 28–30 Oct. 1982, under the auspices of the Association of American Law Schools and the Emory University Law and Economics Center.

[3] 505 F. Supp. 1313 (E.D. Pa. 1980).

[4] Barry Wright originally sued both Pacific Scientific Corp. and ITT–Grinnell, accusing both of joint predation. Only ITT–Grinnell settled. Judge Walter Skinner subsequently decided the litigation in favor of the defendant. *Barry Wright Corp.* v. *Pacific Scientific Corp.*, 555 F. Supp. 1264 (D.C. Mass. 1983).

Some firms accept their disappointments with equanimity, as a manifestation of business risk. Others actively attempt to recoup market positions and profits by redoubling their efforts and/or shifting their market strategies. A third class files antitrust claims, with cause, that they have been the victims of predatory behavior. And a fourth class alleges that they have been victims of predation while in fact their disappointment is the consequence of normal rivalry.

Inasmuch as claims of predation are easy to bring and may involve complex factual matters that are subject to dispute, assessing such claims can sometimes be difficult. Fortunately, however, the merits of predatory pricing claims can be assessed in logical as well as factual respects. Those claims that rely on defective logic are naturally suspect. Such a plaintiff is arguably a sore loser and is asking the courts to award economic benefits that the competitive process, in sorting out winners and losers, has denied him. Public policy is properly concerned, however, not with the affairs of individual firms but with the process of competition.

The need for a complex factual inquiry is greatly relieved if this first-stage logic is not satisfied. Claims that satisfy the logic of predation, by contrast, are ones for which a follow-on assessment is needed. The second-stage question is whether the limits of acceptable rivalry were exceeded or not. This can also be assessed in two parts. First, can the events observed be explained without appeal to anticompetitive purpose or effect? The issue here is whether the events are the result of simple optimizing or if instead complex strategic purposes are being served. If this is uncertain or if it appears that strategic features could be significant, a detailed economic assessment of the relevant facts – which may entail an examination of prices, costs, output, and related economic features – is needed to evaluate the merits.

My discussion of *Barry Wright* v. *ITT–Grinnell* is in five parts. A brief chronology of the main events is described first. The logic of predation is examined next. Decision process aspects are then set out and evaluated. The economic data bearing on predation are then discussed. Some remarks on the operation of an enterprise system conclude the discussion.

1.   A Chronology and Related Factual Background[5]

1 ITT–Grinnell is the largest producer of pipe hanger systems for nuclear power plants in the United States. Shock arrestors or 'snubbers'

---

[5] The chronology and facts are consonant with those set out in Judge Walter Skinner's opinion in *Barry Wright Corp.* v. *Pacific Scientific Corp.*, 555 F. Supp. 1264 (D.C. Mass. 1983). The presentation has been slightly altered from that of the original memorandum to avoid reliance on confidential reports prepared by consultants to Barry Wright.

are critical components in these systems. Snubbers permit gradual movement of pipes in response to heat changes but resist rapid movement from earthquake or explosion.

2 Most snubbers in use through 1975 were hydraulic. ITT–Grinnell made its own.

3 Seal leakage and related maintenance problems developed in the hydraulic snubbers manufactured by another firm in 1974 and 1975. This was a serious concern, the downtime of nuclear facilities being very expensive.

4 Mechanical snubbers are functional substitutes for hydraulic snubbers and are not subject to seal leakage problems. They are subject, however, to mechanical failure to meet the dual requirements described above (item 1). Among US firms, International Nuclear Safeguards Corp. (INC) had introduced a mechanical snubber into commercial use in 1974. Pacific Scientific designed and produced a mechanical shock arrestor which used a novel and patented rotating inertial device by 1975. Pacific Scientific was successful, moreover, in persuading architects and engineers to specify mechanical snubbers to the exclusion of hydraulic snubbers in nuclear plant construction.

5 Pacific Scientific's share of the domestic pipe snubber market grew from 47 per cent in 1976 to 83, 84, and 94 per cent in the years 1977, 1978, and 1979, respectively.

6 ITT–Grinnell found itself dependent on Pacific Scientific for mechanical snubbers. Considering the hazards of sole-source supply and the fact that the margin realized by Grinnell on these mechanical snubbers was much less than it had enjoyed previously, ITT–Grinnell determined that it should find a second source. Its own efforts at developing a mechanical snubber being unsuccessful, it decided to support what appeared to be a promising effort by Barry Wright to develop a mechanical snubber.

7 Grinnell entered into the first of a two-phase contract with Barry in January 1976. The exploratory phase extended through August 1976. The second phase, which was agreed to in August 1976, provided that Barry develop a production capability by January 1977 for six sizes of snubbers. Grinnell would then be obliged to purchase its mechanical snubber requirements from Barry in a minimum amount of $9 million but not more than $15 million over the three-year period of 1977–1979. Upon delivery of $15 million of snubbers, Grinnell had the option to become

the owner of the Barry Wright snubber design, drawings, and assets at no additional charge.

8 Pacific Scientific offered to improve its discount to Grinnell in September 1976 if Grinnell would agree to place an order for $5.7 million in snubbers from Pacific in 1977. The initial agreement was cancelled, however, by the president of Grinnell. Pacific withdrew the discount upon reduction of the order to $1 million.

9 The Barry development experienced problems. Production of six sizes for January 1977 was not ready. Postponements were requested. Grinnell renewed discussions with Pacific and the discount terms were retrieved on $4.3 million of snubbers to be delivered in 1977, with options to purchase the same quantities at discount in 1978 and 1979. But a 100 per cent cancellation penalty was this time attached.

10 Contractual disputes between Barry and Grinnell followed. These were not successfully resolved. In two successive purchase orders in July 1977, Grinnell agreed to purchase its 1978 and 1979 mechanical snubbers from Pacific at the discount terms originally offered (as adjusted by a modest escalation factor).[6]

11 Barry Wright concluded that successful entry was precluded by these events and furthermore held that the behavior of Grinnell and Pacific was anticompetitive. It brought a lawsuit alleging both contractual and antitrust violations by ITT–Grinnell (and antitrust violations by Pacific). The main antitrust violations in which ITT–Grinnell was said to be implicated were: (a) the prices charged by Pacific and accepted by Grinnell were predatory; (b) the Pacific–Grinnell purchase orders were unlawful; and (c) Pacific agreed not to compete in the final market for snubbers with Grinnell. The thrust of these combined acts was that Barry Wright was unlawfully foreclosed from competing in the mechanical snubber market.

12 Here as elsewhere, qualified alternative sources of supply are preferred over a sole-source outcome. But while architecture-engineering firms, utilities, and hanger manufacturers would welcome and even assist a rival supplier, there are rational limits to what can be justified.

---

[6] Albeit gratuitous (and not included in the original memorandum), it did not seem to me feasible, based on the development experience, for Barry Wright to have a full line of snubbers ready before the end of 1979. Judge Skinner, upon hearing the testimony in *Barry Wright* v. *Pacific Scientific*, reached this conclusion.

II. The Logic of Predation

Predation is a very general term and the criterion by which predation is to be assessed is under dispute. It is widely believed for this reason that predation claims are difficult to evaluate. In fact, however, matters are not that bad. For one thing, there is broad agreement that predation efforts lack economic purpose unless specific structural preconditions can be shown to exist. For another, although the best criterion by which predation is to be judged is disputed, there is general agreement that fully remunerative sales, taking all relevant costs into account, are nonpredatory.

This second issue needs to be addressed, however, only if the structural preconditions are satisfied. If they are not, claims of predation can be regarded as presumptively protectionist: they represent an effort to have the courts award economic benefits that the plaintiff has been denied by legitimate competition in the marketplace. Since the hazard of misusing the courts for protectionist purposes is very real, the importance of performing a structural assessment is correspondingly great.

Structural issues of two kinds are germane to the assessment of predation. The first concerns the structure of the supply side of the industry; the second concerns the structure of demand. Since predation is rational only if the sacrifice of current profits can be recouped by increased future profits, the first question is whether the firm or firms against which the predation claims have been lodged occupy a sufficient market share and enjoy sufficient insularity to permit recoupment. Unless the firm or firms in question occupy a dominant market share and, upon the conclusion of a successful predation effort, do not risk the unwanted expansion of output by either fringe rivals or new entrants if prices are restored to earlier levels, attempted predation is without purpose.[7] High concentration coupled with high hurdles to entry thus describe the supply-side preconditions for a claim of predation to be taken seriously.[8]

The demand-side issue is whether customers are small or large in relation to the market. A common situation in which predation complaints

[7] This assumes that the relevant market for assessing predation is the market directly affected by the price reduction. The possible spread of direct effects to include indirect effects (e.g. to related lines of commerce) are thus ignored. This seems appropriate to the immediate case.

[8] This appears to be a consensus result. See chapter 9. Joskow and Klevorick (1979) p. 213; Ordover and Willig, 'An economic definition of predatory product innovation' (1981); F. Easterbrook, 'Predatory pricing and innovations; A comment,' in *Strategic Predation and Antitrust Analysis*, ed. S. Salop (1981), Washington, D.C.: Federal Trade Commission) J. Brodley and G. Hay, 'Predatory pricing: Economic theories and the evolution of legal standards,' *Cornell Law Review*, 66 (1981), p. 738.

arise is where customers are individually too small to influence the eventual competitive configuration of the market and collective action among them is difficult to orchestrate. Each customer in these circumstances behaves myopically, which is to say that at any given time each accepts the best sales terms that are currently offered without concern for the future. The dominant firm that slashes prices upon the appearance of an entrant may for this reason be able to prevent the entrant from making substantial inroads. Having successfully prevented new entry, the dominant firm then recoups its losses by increasing prices thereafter.

This myopic market-behavior logic breaks down, however, where customers are large in relation to the market. The basic proposition here has been succinctly put by Frank Easterbrook, as follows: 'No predatory strategy can work without the [unwitting] cooperation of consumers, who must desert the victim and buy from the predator even though that causes them to pay a monopoly price later on. If consumers are rational, they will not become instruments of their own harm. They will, instead, buoy up the intended victim with long term contracts.'[9]

Given the lawful limits on liquidated damages clauses,[10] large and perceptive customers will recognize that their interests and the profit calculus upon which the dominant firm relies – which entails sacrifice of immediate profits (low current prices) for future profit gains (high future prices) – are of opposite sign. Rather, therefore, than behave myopically, such customers will consciously support the attempted entry by a prospectively viable newcomer. One way of assisting the entrant would be to award it with long-term contracts. Another would be to assist its development efforts.

Obviously, however, the support given to entrants is both limited and conditional. Entry is not desired for its own sake but only as it offers the prospect of genuine relief. Fully effective entrants will be more highly valued than those that are marginal. And submarginal entry is not valued at all. To the extent that an entrant encounters development difficulties, experiences other cost disabilities, or will otherwise be unable to deliver product at good terms with assurance, customers will value his presence less. Accordingly, the amount and kind of support will vary with the circumstances.

Applying this two-part structural logic to the case at hand, we observe that Pacific enjoyed a large market share in 1977 but that this could hardly be regarded as secure. Only a few years earlier, INC had been the dominant firm. The possibility of new entry by domestic or foreign rivals was very real; and the possibility of being displaced by improved hydraulic

---

[9] Easterbrook, *supra* footnote 4.
[10] This caveat is elaborated in Williamson (1987), where I examine the Phillipe Ashion and Patrick Bolton (1987) model of the use of contract penalties to deter entry.

snubber designs was also a factor. Any effort by Pacific to borrow from the present in anticipation of future gains was therefore fraught with hazards. Instead, Pacific (and like-situated firms) was better advised to assess profitability effects in terms of immediate consequences.

This is reinforced by an examination of the demand side. Firms here – architecture-engineers, utilities, pipe hangers – were large and knowledgeable. Accordingly, they would value competition and, within reasonable limits, promote it. Indeed, this is precisely what ITT–Grinnell did. Not only did it actively support the Barry Wright development effort, but it consciously declined a 1977 purchase order with Pacific in favor of less attractive first-quarter terms. As the development and production realities of continuing with Barry Wright became more well defined, however, ITT–Grinnell reassessed the situation and, as described in section III below, made a determination to accept the Pacific offer. This was not a myopic decision whereby ITT–Grinnell unconsciously contributed to an adverse private and public policy result, but was a rational assessment of the merits.

The logic of predation thus sometimes relieves the need to become engrossed in a complex factual inquiry. At the very least, the Barry Wright complaint borders on protectionism. These concerns deepen when decision process aspects are introduced.

III. Decision Process Aspects

Suppose, arguendo, that the Barry Wright complaint was not defective in the above-described structural logic respects. Issues of two kinds then become germane. First, can the objectionable behavior be understood as the outcome of a simple economic decision process or does it appear to be the result of complex, strategic calculations where anticompetitive purposes and effects are responsible for the outcome? Second, what do the data disclose? The first of these is addressed here; the second is examined in section IV.

The decision process will be examined in two ways. First, the actual decision process will be scrutinized. Second, a related hypothetical will be examined: How would ITT–Grinnell have assessed the Pacific Scientific offer if it had continued its own mechanical snubber development program rather than supported Barry Wright's?

A. THE BARRY WRIGHT EXPERIENCE

The decision process of supporting Barry Wright can be examined in two stages. The first is the ITT–Grinnell assessment of its mechanical snubber alternatives in the fall of 1975. The alternatives that it identified were:

(a) continue its own snubber development; (b) copy the Pacific snubber; and (c) contract with Barry Wright to support its mechanical snubber. The first of these would entail a delay of two years. The second posed patent infringement hazards. The merits of the third turned on the prospects for early success and the terms of the contract. As of December 1975, the prospects appeared good, with production projected to begin late in 1976. And ITT–Grinnell margins of 40 per cent were contemplated.

That ITT–Grinnell decided to implement option 3 appears to be the result of a simple economic assessment of the merits. Put differently, there is no need to invoke strategic features – of a pre-emptive investment or punitive behavior kind – in order to understand this outcome. And Barry Wright was presumably benefited by this infusion of resources and expertise in relation to what it would have been without the ITT–Grinnell development agreement.

Bear in mind, however, that ITT–Grinnell was not interested in a second source of supply at any cost. Rather, what it sought from Barry Wright was price relief from Pacific and better security of supply. (To be sure, inventory accumulation is an alternative way to help safeguard supply. This, however, is a costly undertaking as compared with having access to a second parity source of supply.) Events did not go according to plan. As of mid-1977, ITT–Grinnell was essentially faced with four choices:

1   Commit 1978 and 1979 requirements to Pacific at discount prices.
2   Rely on Barry Wright to deliver 1978 and 1979 requirements, at the prices originally stipulated, and renegotiate the contract to appropriately reflect the delivery failures for 1977.
3   Commit 1978 to Pacific and await further developments before deciding on 1979.
4   Temporize, by deferring a final decision on Barry until, say, December 1977.

The consequences associated with these four alternatives are set out in table 10.1.

Option A offers the prospect of good prices through 1979 and negligible hazards of product failure,[11] delivery failure,[12] or contractual strain.[13] A drawback of this option is that Barry Wright may be a

---

[11] The Pacific snubber had a known performance record.
[12] Pacific used materials that were widely available and had a good record of labor relations with its nonunionized employees.
[13] The contract was relatively simple.

less viable or accessible second source of supply if this option is elected.[14]

Table 10.1 Economic assessment of options

Option	Prices			Hazards			Second-source ramifications
	1978	1979	1980 and beyond	Snubber failure	Delivery failure	Contractual strain	
A	good	good	uncertain	nil	nil	nil	worst
B	best	best	uncertain	serious	very serious	serious	best
C	good	uncertain	uncertain	some	some	serious	?
D	uncertain	uncertain	uncertain	?	serious	?	?

Option B offers the prospect of the best prices, assuming that Barry Wright is indeed able to produce the full set of mechanical snubbers that ITT–Grinnell will require in the quantities needed for both 1978 and 1979. Considering the delays already experienced and the fact that only three of the six snubber designs had passed the qualification tests, to say nothing of pilot production and acceptance testing, the possibility that delivery failures would occur was evidently very real. (If Barry Wright was unable to make the needed deliveries, ITT–Grinnell would have to return to Pacific. Spot-market purchases in smaller quantities typically command a price premium. Also, Pacific would not have the benefit of an assured order that would permit it to plan ahead and make the necessary investments to support larger production quantities. Actual prices would be higher on this account also.)

In addition, the Barry Wright snubber presumably carried with it a higher risk of failure after installation. (The INC experience is relevant here. More generally, the history of early installations of new designs – witness automobile recall experience – augurs for

[14] ITT–Grinnell's concern over second sources is somewhat mitigated, however, by three other factors: (a) ITT–Grinnell efforts to correct the defects in its hydraulic snubbers may be successful; (b) other domestic or foreign sources of supply of mechanical snubbers may become qualified; and (c) ITT–Grinnell might build up an inventory that would effectively extend its price and delivery protection beyond 1979.

caution.) Finally, the basic agreement would have to be agreeably realigned to reflect the 1977 delays. This poses the possibility of serious contractual strain. An unqualified decision by ITT–Grinnell to rely on Barry Wright for its 1978 and 1979 mechanical snubber needs has the best second-source features, however.

Option C assures good prices and poses few hazards through 1978, but matters are cloudy thereafter. Whether the viability of Barry Wright would be significantly improved by refusal of the 1979 discount offer by Pacific is unclear. Conceivably the prospect of securing ITT–Grinnell orders in 1979 would encourage Barry Wright to persevere through 1978. But the ITT–Grinnell/Barry Wright relation might have soured during this interval, as massive contract revisions would be required.[15]

Option D mainly postpones the agony of making a clear choice in the hope that matters would be greatly clarified six months later. The Pacific discounts, however, could be withdrawn, as Pacific would lack a firm basis upon which to plan its 1978 production, and ITT–Grinnell could experience 1978 delivery problems for that reason. Whether Barry Wright and Grinnell could iron out their contractual relation over this period is problematic. The case for temporizing is simply hard to make.

The upshot is that a simple economic assessment of the alternatives faced by ITT–Grinnell discloses that option A – namely, commit its 1978 and 1979 snubber orders to Pacific on discount terms that promise reasonable, albeit not exceptional, margins – has rather good properties. This is plainly not the option that ITT–Grinnell contemplated when the Barry Wright agreement was entered into early in 1976. But intervening events disclosed that the preferred scenario is unavailable and a realistic reassessment, in the light of intervening experience, is plainly needed. No devious, unlawful purposes have to be invoked in order to understand why ITT–Grinnell made the choice that it did. A simple profitability calculation suffices.

B. A HYPOTHETICAL

The decision process described above considers the rationality of the actual decisions reached by ITT–Grinnell. The one described here poses a hypothetical. Suppose that, rather than support the Barry Wright development, ITT–Grinnell had decided to complete its own snubber. Suppose further that its development experience was identical to that of Barry Wright. And suppose that ITT–Grinnell was presented in September

---

[15] Two sentences of text are here deleted to remove reliance on a confidential study of the plaintiff.

1976 and July 1977 with the identical discount offers from Pacific. How should ITT–Grinnell have responded to these?

Consider September 1976. The main difference here, probably, is that ITT–Grinnell would have issued a purchase order for its 1977 requirements in September 1976 rather than in January 1977. The reason for this is that the in-house development people could be expected to have been more candid in reporting on development difficulties and projecting manufacturing capabilities than were the ITT–Grinnell contacts at Barry Wright. This reflects a general difference in the completeness and candor of intrafirm as compared with interfirm communications.

Consider, therefore, the decisions to be made in mid–1977. These are essentially the four options set out in table 10.1, with the following differences: (a) ITT–Grinnell would be more apt to terminate its development effort if it chose option A, whereas there was some possibility that Barry Wright would continue under these circumstasnces; (b) the contractual strains referred to under options B and C would be mitigated if ITT–Grinnell were doing the development in-house; and (c) ITT–Grinnell would presumably make a careful assessment of the best alternative value of the investments that it had put in place in anticipation of its own mechanical snubber production.[16]

The first of these qualifications weakens the incentive to terminate the in-house development effort. That is, the possibility that Barry Wright would continue even without ITT–Grinnell business during 1978 and 1979 makes option A more attractive under the earlier assessment than under the hypothetical assessment. The second qualification operates in the opposite direction: since ITT–Grinnell would not experience in-house contractual strains if development were continued (say under option B), this favors in-house continuation. The third qualification is a wash if the Barry Wright assets are to be transferred to ITT–Grinnell at a price that reflects their best alternative value – which is presumably in the range of $65,000 (which is what ITT–Grinnell offered) and $1 million (which is what Barry Wright said it invested) – and if the legal and administrative costs of reaching a postcontractual settlement with Barry Wright are ignored (ignoring these favors option A under the in-house as compared with the Barry Wright alternative). The upshot is that none of these factors appears to be decisive and, such as they are, they are of offsetting sign.

Accordingly, the ITT–Grinnell decision, had it undertaken an in-house

---

[16] This ignores a fourth factor, which I will label 'bureaucratic inertia' for lack of a better term. In-house managers who have approved an internal development program may be defensive in reviewing the merits. Efforts to continue programs beyond reasonable limits may arise for this reason. This reflects a personal rather than a company rationality calculus, however, and hence will be ignored.

development effort with the identical development history of Barry Wright, would presumably be unchanged in July 1977 from what it was with Barry Wright. This confirms the lack of strategic features in the decision to terminate Barry Wright: ITT–Grinnell would have done to itself what it did to Barry, and it is elementary that firms do not inflict self-predation. (This last has special relevance to this case, since the assets, if the Barry Wright development had been successful, would have reverted to ITT–Grinnell upon delivery of $15 million in snubbers.)

IV. Assessing Predation

Suppose that the logic of predation issue is set aside. Suppose further that the examination of the decision process is disregarded. Attention is narrowly focused instead on the three events upon which predation is said to have been accomplished, to wit: (a) prices were set at predatory levels; (b) the purchase orders were of an unlawful kind and/or duration; and (c) Pacific induced ITT–Grinnell to accept a predatory outcome by (falsely) promising not to compete. Consider these seriatim.

A. PREDATORY PRICING

Other hanger companies, architecture-engineering firms, and utilities have not complained that the Pacific discounts to ITT–Grinnell were objectionable. The concern, if there is one, is entirely that expressed by Barry Wright.

Whether Pacific's prices were predatory can only be assessed in terms of a predatory pricing standard. Inasmuch as Barry Wright does not propose a standard, it is necessary to devise one. Since the appropriate standard for assessing predation is widely disputed and arguably varies with the circumstanes, several will be considered here.[17]

Among the possible criteria for evaluating prices are: (a) the established firm must maintain prices to facilitate new entry; (b) the established firm can reduce prices, but not below those of the entrant; (c) the established

---

[17] The criteria discussed in the text are all cost based. An alternative criterion is based on an examination of output. The question here is whether the dominant firm has increased output disproportionately upon the appearance of a new entrant. This is the so-called 'Williamson rule' (see Williamson, *supra* footnote 4; and Brodley and Hay, *supra* footnote 4). The application of the output criterion to snubbers is limited by three factors: (a) demand for snubbers is highly elastic; (b) demand projections in a new industry are difficult to make (among other things, unforeseen technological problems may arise – witness INC); and (c) it is usually inappropriate to assign dominant-firm status to a firm if its large market share has yet to appear or, after occurring, is of problematic significance. This last, of course, applies to the cost-based tests as well. It will be set aside for purposes of making the cost-based comparisons.

firm can reduce prices, but not below average total cost; and (d) the established firm can reduce prices, but not below marginal cost.

Although Barry Wright is not explicit, it appears to favor the first criterion. This is not, however, an acceptable standard. It is tantamount to umbrella pricing and is an invitation for inefficient firms to enter. The rigid price standard is patently protectionist and is generally recognized as such. To prohibit price cuts is to prevent a normal and indeed crucial benefit of competition from being realized. The fixed-price criterion stands antitrust economics on its head.

As discussed above, the Pacific prices were higher than the Barry Wright prices in all but a few cases.[18] Accordingly, the Pacific discounts pass this second test for predation – should it be thought that this is an appropriate standard (for which view, however, there is little support among students of the problem).

A comparison of Pacific's prices with its costs – either average total or marginal – requires that the relevant cost data be assembled. Assessing marginal costs is in any event difficult, and there is widespread dispute over whether this is an appropriate standard. Average-cost tests are easier to perform and many regard them as more defensible in 'normal' markets where demand is stable or growing. Assuming that accounting procedures are unobjectionable, the average-cost test will be satisfied if the product realizes a profit on the sales in question. (Judge Skinner concluded that 'Pacific made a substantial profit on the Grinnell sales.')[19]

This assessment of Pacific's prices confirms the logic of section II. Thus the logic of predation, given the structure of demand and supply in this industry, does not support selling below cost with the prospect of future recoupment. Neither does the evidence.

B. REQUIREMENTS CONTRACTS

Note that the contracts between Pacific and ITT–Grinnell to supply mechanical snubbers were not strictly requirements contracts. Instead, they were contracts for what ITT–Grinnell estimated to be its requirements. They did not preclude additional supply procurement from other sources. Note further that ITT–Grinnell proposed to Barry that it procure $3.6 million of its 1978 and 1979 snubbers from Barry. Inasmuch, moreover, as ITT–Grinnell attempted originally to secure all and subsequently attempted to purchase some of its mechanical snubbers from Barry Wright, the basis for the requirements complaint is not entirely clear. Be that as it may, it is nevertheless useful to address the question of whether a requirement contract can serve affirmative economic purposes.

[18] See footnote 9 *supra*.
[19] 555 F. Supp. at 1268, 1269.

The first economic purpose served by such contracts is that, as with all long-term contracts, it permits the parties to the contract to make more certain plans. The buyer has assured supply at a specified (or, if the contract includes escalator clauses, a formula) price. The buyer can often organize its economic activities more efficiently and effectively as a result. The seller is also assured of demand for its product and can plan its investment program accordingly. This is of special importance for investments that are highly specialized and hence cannot be used for alternative purposes without significant sacrifice of productive value.[20] Mechanical snubbers entailed nontrivial specialized investments in both physical and human assets. Pacific thus had a serious investment-planning interest in using contracts to better project its medium-term production requirements.

The second economic purpose served by requirements contracts is that they have attractive quantity flexibility features for the buyer while simultaneously protecting the seller against opportunistic exploitation. Quantity flexibility has advantages in a market where demand is variable and inventories are costly to hold. But sellers will be reluctant to grant quantity flexibiity without providing sales safeguards. Specifically, sellers will be concerned that buyers will exploit unrestricted quantity flexibility by buying from them when the contract price is low and buying from others should the contract price exceed the spot-market price (or other terms that become available). A requirements clause provides the seller with protection against such an outcome.

Whether a requirements contract serves anticompetitive purposes depends on the duration of the contract, the amount of commerce foreclosed, and the characteristics of the buyer. Contracts of long duration for a significant share of the market made with many small buyers arguably have stronger foreclosure properties. With respect to the Pacific contracts with ITT–Grinnell, note that the duration was for one and two years, which is not long in relation to the planning needs of the parties. The ITT–Grinnell business represented less than half of the domestic market. And whereas many small buyers might behave myopically and individually agree to separate requirements contracts that collectively effected a predatory outcome on rival suppliers, large and knowledgeable buyers would not.

The periods over which the contracts applied were thus at most of medium duration; more than half of the domestic market, to say nothing of foreign markets, remained open to competition. Moreover, the economic interests of other pipe hanger firms, architecture–engineering firms, and utilities in a second source of supply for mechanical snubbers

---

[20] The remainder of this paragraph has been revised to avoid reliance on confidential reports made by consultants to the plaintiff.

was arguably strong. A viable snubber supplier could thus sell to a substantial market that could be presumed to respond to new entry in an affirmative way. Claims of foreclosure do not withstand scrutiny.

C. COLLUSION

Barry Wright further contends that Pacific induced ITT–Grinnell to accept a predatory contract by falsely promising not to compete with ITT–Grinnell for final snubber sales. This claim can likewise be examined in terms of the logic as well as the data.

Logical tests of two kind apply. First, the issue of whether a substantial buyer would contribute to the predation of its market again arises. The same arguments advanced earlier apply here: self-inflicted predation is irrational.

Second, firms do not agree to participate in collusive arrangements against which unilateral cheating is easy. Put differently, unless it has access to effective countermeasurse, one-sided agreements not to compete that are both unlawful and can be violated with impunity are foolish – even to propose, much less to agree to.

The logic of the Barry Wright collusion claim is defective in both respects. Moreover, it is contradicted by the data: Pacific continued actively to sell snubbers directly to users and experienced considerable success. The upshot is that Barry Wright is joining an irrational-behavior claim (ITT–Grinnell did not perceive the consequences of self-inflicted predation) with Catch-22 reasoning (if direct sales by Pacific decrease, this is evidence of collusion; if instead they remain unchanged or increase, this is a result of cheating). Such an approach stands antitrust economics on its head.

V. Understanding Competition

Allegations of anticompetitive behavior are sometimes explained by a failure to understand the way in which an enterprise system functions. One of the key features of competition – of the normal, everyday, garden variety, procompetitive kind – is that it *generates both winners and losers.* Inasmuch as no one likes to lose, and since the lines between lawful and unlawful behavior are sometimes obscurely drawn, antitrust suits are often brought by those who come up short. Although sometimes these have merit, many do not. A series of factors is listed below that should help to underscore critical features of the competitive system and restore perspective on the antitrust claims of *Barry Wright* v. *ITT–Grinnell.* Some of these repeat points made in earlier sections.

A. FORTUITOUS EVENTS

Conditions of high profitability are not in themselves objectionable. For one thing, they signal opportunities. Additionally, they may reflect a valid patent or otherwise meritorious discovery. They are also sometimes explained by fortuitous events: being in the right place at the right time when a particular opportunity appeared. The 'unraveling' of hydraulic snubbers in the early 1970s was not expected but provided marvellous mousetrap opportunities. INC and then Pacific Scientific were the fortuitous beneficiaries. Such fortuitous outcomes ought not to be described as the result of deep planning (or comprehensive prepositioning) by one party and great ignorance by others. Rather, chance events are normal, albeit low-probability, outcomes in competitive systems and ought to be so regarded. A public policy problem is posed by these only if monopolistic consequences persist for very long periods of time thereafter and are unlikely to be upset by unassisted market forces. (Whether public policy should intrude in the long run is even widely disputed. But no one counsels for short-run intervention.)

B. EFFICIENT ADAPTATION

Firms commonly have targets, but they rarely have fixed targets – the achievement of which is essential, come what may. Instead, they select among options (sometimes keeping several open simultaneously) in terms of their assessment of the prospects associated with each; and they subsequently adapt as events unfold and as new information becomes available.

Adaptive, sequential decision making characterizes a well-working enterprise system. Confronted with unanticipated hydraulic snubber problems and a massive shift in favor of mechanical snubbers, ITT–Grinnell was faced with the temporary prospect of single-source supply. Rather than accept this passively, it explored ways of relieving this condition. Of those considered, the connection with Barry Wright evidently was the most promising.

That this development effort subsequently experienced serious difficulties does not imply that it should not have been attempted. Development work is commonly risky. (If it were not, it would be described as production.) The basic question is whether the undertaking represented informed risk bearing, and no one has suggested that it was lacking in merit when evaluated *ex ante*.

As slippage in the Barry Wright project developed and as contractual obligations expired, ITT–Grinnell naturally began to reconsider its options. Confronted with the *ex post* realities, it rationally decided to choose option A. Although this had adverse consequences for Barry Wright, it was scarcely a pernicious, anticompetitive result. Failure to adapt would suggest irrational commitment to a specific structural result rather than an economic assessment of the merits.

C. WINNERS AND LOSERS

But for the technical problems that Barry Wright experienced in bringing its development effort to timely completion and in producing high-quality snubbers in volume, Barry Wright would have been a big winner. But technical problems did occur, and the ITT–Grinnell business went elsewhere. Whether Barry Wright could thereafter have persevered successfully is outside the scope of these remarks. I merely observe that (a) Barry Wright's efforts are not necessarily discreditable because of adverse developments, (b) Barry Wright is not entitled to antitrust relief because the resulting structure of the industry is 'inferior' to what it would have been had the initial development effort succeeded, and (c) neither firms (suppliers; buyers) nor individuals (workers; others) in the private sector have an obligation to subsidize troubled firms (or troubled activities within firms) with which they deal, and use of public monies for such subsidies is rarely warranted.

To be sure, some firms ask for – and a few firms receive – public bailout assistance on the grounds that the public interest (national defense) would otherwise be jeopardized. And sometimes workers, other suppliers, or buyers will recognize that it is in their self-interest to accept inferior terms (a wage cut; a loan extension; an inferior product) because this preserves jobs or protects other specialized investments. But public policy, much less antitrust policy, does not hold that workers have an obligation to accept wage sacrifices, that banks have an obligation to extend loans on preferred terms to support projects that are objectively of high risk, or that customers have noncontractual obligations to continue procurement after production difficulties have set in. Rather, workers, suppliers, and customers are expected to consult their self-interest and decide accordingly. To hold otherwise is contrary to the basic principles upon which an enterprise system operates.

D. CONDITION OF ENTRY

Inasmuch as it commonly takes time to assemble the talent and resources needed to respond to market opportunities, entry into any given niche is often difficult in the short run. But it is inappropriate to describe entry as difficult quite generally if these short-run hurdles can be overcome at modest expense over a slightly longer planning horizon. More generally, the point is this: the condition of entry cannot be expressed in atemporal terms. Specifically, to characterize the condition of entry in terms of immediate hurdles will commonly exaggerate the difficulty of effecting entry over a longer and more relevant planning horizon.

E. UNWITTING PREDATION

It is a mistake to transfer predation reasoning that is appropriate to markets where customers are atomistic and unable to influence future supply conditions to markets where customers are large and knowledgeable and whose participation is essential to effect predation. Given that contrived contractual penalties are unlawful and unenforceable, large buyers cannot easily be induced to participate in predation schemes. Accordingly, allegations of predation under these conditions can be dismissed for failure to satisfy elementary tests of economic and competitive logic.

F. COMPETITORS VERSUS COMPETITION

The enterprise system plays hardball. Provided that the rules of the game are being observed, the experience of individual competitors is of no concern. Indeed, to intrude in the process by protecting individual competitors against hardball outcomes is contrary to competitive logic and prevents merit outcomes from being realized. Public policy analysts and the courts are properly concerned with social, not private, interests. The fate of individual competitors is relevant only as this relates to an assessment of whether the competitive process is operating in a meritorious way.

Batters like fat pitches, and competitors like fixed targets. But the rules of the game provide that fastballs, curves, and sliders are all OK. Adaptive rivalry is likewise to be expected and is a highly valued and essential feature of an enterprise system. Lawful rivalry always takes the form of offering more attractive terms (which commonly take the form of a price reduction). Only unlawful rivalry is objectionable. Spitballs are prohibited. So is predation.

Part IV
Commentary

History records that the economics of sound public policy are often sacrificed to political expediency. Antitrust is not exempt. I nevertheless believe that antitrust enforcement is *less* subject to politics than are many other regulatory activities. It has been gratifying to work on antitrust economics partly for this reason.

My reading of antitrust enforcement is that there have been massive changes during the past quarter of a century and that these have been informed by and even driven by contemporary economic analysis. The three essays in this section elaborate this opinion.

11
Comments on the Political Economy of Antitrust

I. Some Indications of Progress

Although there is an ebb and flow to antitrust, and recent changes may be reversed, it is my judgment that antitrust has made remarkable progress during the past decade – and I would say that a decade is about the appropriate interval at which to take such observations. Some of the areas in which progress has occurred include greater respect for economies in assessing social effects, better understanding of vertical integration and vertical restrictions, a deeper understanding of predatory pricing, greater skepticism with unadorned market share analysis, and a delimitation on entry barrier arguments.

A. TREATMENT OF ECONOMIES

The 1960s opened with the Federal Trade Commission taking the position that the 'necessary proof of violation of the statute consists of types of evidence showing that the acquiring firm possesses significant power in some markets *or* that its overall organization gives it a decisive advantage in efficiency over its smaller rivals.'[1] In other words, efficiency and the prospect of extending efficiency were regarded unfavorably by the FTC in assessing whether a merger should be permitted. This perverse use of efficiency reasoning has mainly disappeared since, but vigilance is warranted. The Justice Department made similar arguments in resisting the acquisition of the Mead Corporation by Occidental petroleum in 1978. The Government's lead attorney advised the court that the acquisition was objectionable because it would permit Mead to construct a large greenfield plant, which was the 'most efficient and cost effective'

Originally published in Tollison, *The Political Economy of Antitrust*, Lexington MA: D.C. Heath
[1] Foremost Dairies, Inc., 60 FTC 944, 1084 (1962), emphasis added.

investment, and that this would disadvantage Mead's rivals.[2]

I am prepared to believe, however, that this contorted view of antitrust economies is an aberration – a manifestation of 'creative lawyering' (see section on Market Share Analysis) – rather than a return to Foremost Dairy standards. For the most part, the past decade is one in which greater respect has been accorded to economies, both in the courts[3] and in the legislature.[4]

Parametric analysis of economies versus market-power effects has doubtlessly contributed to this result. Such analysis is useful in two respects. First, it shows the importance of being sensitive to economies if economic rather than emotive consequences are to be accorded serious weight. Secondly, and every bit as important, parametric analysis often permits difficult issues of quantitative net benefit assessment to be bypassed. Thus what difference does it make that demand elasticities are imperfectly known if, throughout the full range of relevant elasticities, the same net-benefit assessment obtains.

Put differently, thinking in net-benefit terms does not require that issues be addressed in fully quantitative terms. Conceptual benefits obtain by simply getting the issues straight, which would have avoided the mistakes made by the FTC in *Foremost Dairies* and by the Antitrust Division in resisting the Occidental–Mead takeover attempt. If trade-offs are involved, and if a net negative (or a net positive) assessment obtains over the relevant range of parameter values, a 'refined' net-benefit assessment is unnecessary. That the matter of economies as an antitrust defense does not elicit the same hostility now that it did in the 1960s is presumably because an appreciation for these conceptual gains, including the power of parametric analysis, is now more widespread.

B. VERTICAL MARKET RELATIONS

The antitrust atmosphere that prevailed in the area of vertical market restrictions in the 1960s was one of hostility. Donald Turner expressed it as follows, 'I approach territorial and customer restrictions not hospitably in the common law tradition, but inhospitably in the tradition of antitrust

---

[2] The phrase was employed by the Government's lead attorney, Barbara Reeves, in support of Count Four (Elimination of Actual and Potential Competition in Coated Free Sheet Paper), *US* v. *Occidental Petroleum Corporation* (Civil Action No. C-3-78-288).

[3] For a discussion, see O. E. Williamson, 'Economies as an antitrust defense revisited,' *University of Pennsylvania Law Review*, 125 (April 1977), pp. 728–9.

[4] Ibid., pp. 731–3. An economies defense was also incorporated in the recent no-fault monopoly proposal by the National Commission for the Review of Antitrust Laws and Procedures in its Report to the President and the Attorney General (Washington, DC, 1979), chapter 8.

law.'[5] Such reasoning was responsible for the mistaken arguments in *Schwinn*.[6]

In an unusual reversal of precedent, the Supreme Court has recently overruled *Schwinn* in the *GTE–Sylvania* case.[7] Among the reasons for this surely has been the growing awareness that 'nonstandard' modes of organization usually arise in response to economizing opportunities. Accordingly, except as rather special structural preconditions are satisfied, vertical restraints should not be regarded with animosity.

This position has taken a long time to be recognized. Among the contributing factors was the stream of criticism provided by the Chicago School (Director, Bork, Posner, and others, like Baxter) increasing appreciation for transaction-cost reasoning (Williamson, Phillips), and Turner's dramatic switch of position.[8] That reversals of bad precedent occur in the face of such criticism is surely a healthy indication of progress in antitrust.

C. PREDATORY PRICING

The leading predatory pricing case in the 1960s was *Utah Pie*.[9] Although the protectionist reasoning that the Court employed in this case has not been expressly reversed, the unsatisfactory quality of the opinion has been widely remarked[10] and considerable effort has been made to provide a more substantial economic basis for evaluating predatory pricing.

The standards that will eventually emerge are still unclear. As Paul Joskow has observed, the lower courts adopted the Areeda–Turner average-variable-cost rule for evaluating predatory pricing with undue haste:[11]

First, this rule has not been accorded generally favorable reviews by economists; the rave reviews come from the courts. It does not represent a triumph of economic efficiency over political considerations. Rather, I believe that this rule

---

[5] Turner expressed these views while he was Assistant Attorney General in charge of the Antitrust Division. The statement is attributed to him by Stanley Robinson, 1968 New York State Bar Association, *Antitrust Law Symposium*, p. 29.

[6] For a summary of the Government's main arguments in *Schwinn* and a critique thereof, see chapter 6.

[7] *Continental TV Inc.* v. *GTE Sylvania, Inc.*, 433 US 36 (1977).

[8] Turner participated in the Amicus brief with attorneys for the Motor Vehicle Manufacturers Association asking that the *Schwinn* decision be upset. Motion for Leave to File Brief and Brief for Motor Vehicles Manufacturers Association as Amicus Curiae, *Continental TV Inc.* v. *GTE Sylvania, Inc.*

[9] *Utah Pie Co.* v. *Continental Baking Co.* 386 US 685 (1967).

[10] See Bork (1978) New York: Basic Books, pp. 386–9. Also see Posner, *Antitrust Law*, pp. 193–4.

[11] Joskow (1980) Chicago: University of Chicago Press, p. 202.

has attracted so much judicial attention because it provides a way of disposing of cases that have arisen in an area where there are vague and conflicting rules proposed by political antitrusters, that often had to be applied to cases that seemed only to seek the preservation of particular competitors. I attribute the adoption of this particular rule to the desire of the judiciary to extract itself from the chaos of existing case law, not to their 'getting religion.' I attribute the elegant footnotes to their law clerks. I believe that we are seeing adopted what some of us view as an inappropriate rule from the perspective of economic efficiency because our friends the 'political antitrusters' were given too much rope. The courts were presented with vague notions about the value of small business, then were told that they shouldn't confuse individual competitors with competition, saw discussions of bigness *per se* confused with mergers of manufacturing of wooden spoons, heard the phrase competitive process a few times, and were left with nothing useful for coming to a decision. It was almost inevitable that a simple *per se* rule would be eagerly adopted, whether it evolved from appropriate considerations of economic efficiency or not. If average variable cost is a bad rule I suggest that we have it because of the void that was left in this area by the political antitrusters, not because of triumph of economic efficiency considerations in the interpretation of antitrust statutes.

To be sure, the courts were in a difficult bind. Faced with the need to decide cases, the courts could not wait until the Areeda–Turner rule had been tested by academic commentary. Fortunately, however, such commentary has been quick to appear.[12] Much of this has emphasized intertemporal efficiency. The likelihood that better tests for remunerative pricing will be adopted appears to be improving.[13]

D. MARKET SHARE ANALYSIS

When confronted with a difficult case that appears to be beyond the reach of the antitrust statutes, there is a strong temptation to resort to what John Shenefield has referred to as 'creative lawyering'[14] – which is a euphemism for bringing a contrived case. Such a temptation is especially great in the merger area, where the language of the statute is very broad.

[12] Among the relevant papers are F. M. Scherer, 'Predatory pricing and the Sherman Act: A comment,' *Harvard Law Review*, 89 (March 1976), pp. 869–90; chapter 9; Richard Schmalensee, 'On the use of economic models in antitrust,' *University of Pennsylvania Law Review*, 127 (April 1979), pp. 994–1050.

[13] Recent court decisions have been more cautious about accepting the Areeda–Turner test than were earlier ones. The Ninth Circuit opinion in *California Computer Products, Inc.* v. *International Business Machines Corp.* reflects this. Memorandum Opinion in *O. Hommel Co.* v. *Ferro Corp.* (Civil Action No. 76-1299) by the US District Judge William W. Know likewise expresses skepticism with the Areeda–Turner test.

[14] Hon. J. H. Shenefield, Testimony before the Subcommittee on Antitrust and Monopolies of the Committee on the Judiciary, United States Senate, 18 July 1978, p. 65.

If an adverse effect can be shown 'in any line of commerce, in any section of the country,' all that a creative lawyer needs to do is define his lines of commerce and geographic markets with sufficient imagination.

Knee-jerk reliance on market-share analysis, however, has also come under increasing criticism. Partly this is a reaction to the arbitrary standards of the 1960s and partly it reflects an appreciation that valued economizing purposes are frequently served by reconfiguring economic activity. The degree of disenchantment with a market-shares based approach to antitrust is illustrated by Richard Schmalensee's recent paper dealing with the *Rea-Lemon* case and Darius Gaskin's comments thereon.[15] The economizing purposes served by reconfiguring economic activity have already been remarked in connection with the discussion of vertical market relations. More generally, there is a growing awareness that transaction costs are central to an understanding of the organization of economic activity and that earlier antitrust traditions in which these considerations are ignored or suppressed miss much of what makes a high performance enterprise economy function.

E. BARRIERS TO ENTRY

Barriers to entry analysis as a guide to antitrust policy peaked in the 1960s. The term carries an anticompetitive connotation and the more militant members of the barriers to entry tradition plainly believed that any action that had the effect of impeding entry by new rivals or disadvantaging extant firms should be regarded as anticompetitive and should be proscribed. Mergers that yield efficiencies were among the objectionable practices. Advertising economies were held to be particularly offensive. This view was pressed by the Government and adopted by the Supreme Court in the 1967 decision regarding the illegality of Procter & Gamble's acquisition of Clorox.[16]

Confusion on this matter continues to this day. Thus Leonard Weiss, in contrasting Bain with Stigler on barriers to entry, insists that economies of scale be regarded as a barrier; 'To characterize such a situation as displaying "no barrier" is to give the term barrier to entry a meaning that is not very useful in evaluating market power.'[17] Why we should be preoccupied with market power to the exclusion of possible economies is not explained, but that is plainly the thrust of entry barrier analysis and its enthusiasts.

---

[15] Schmalensee, pp. 1004–16, and Gaskin, pp. 154–8, in *Antitrust Law and Economics*, ed. O. E. Williamson (1980).

[16] Bork (1978) New York: Basic Books, p. 310.

[17] L. W. Weiss, 'The structure–conduct–performance paradigm and antitrust,' *University of Pennsylvania Law Review*, 127 (April 1969), p. 121.

Fortunately, however, matters are changing. Bork, among others, has been instrumental in effecting the shift in emphasis, 'The question for antitrust is whether there exist artificial entry barriers. These must be barriers that are not forms of superior efficiency and which yet prevent the forces of the market ... from operating to erode market positions not based on efficiency.'[18] Thus merit outcomes, not structure *per se*, is what matters. The distinction between remediable and irremediable impediments to entry is important in this regard. Little useful public purpose is served, and a considerable risk of public-policy mischief results when conditions of an irremediable kind – that is, those for which no superior outcome can be realized – are brought under fire.

Remediable impediments, by contrast, are ones which, if removed, would lead to superior social outcomes judged in welfare (not market structure) terms. That this distinction is making headway is disclosed by the recent shift in position by Comanor and Wilson on advertising. Whereas previously they had emphasized the adverse-entry effects of advertising,[19] now they adopt a more symmetrical position and counsel that the effects of advertising should be evaluated in welfare rather than market structure terms, 'to the extent that consumer information is increased in the same process that monopoly power is attained, we may be unwilling to adopt specific policy measures directed against the latter for fear of adversely affecting the former.'[20] Furthermore, whereas previously the indictment against advertising tended to be quite broad, it is now recognized that the concerns are 'concentrated in a small number of industries' where advertising–sales ratios are unusually high.[21] Even here, a presumption of net negative consequences is unwarranted.

What this amounts to is that, here as elsewhere, trade-offs have to be recognized and that informed public policy will not mindlessly pursue 'desirable' market-structure outcomes at the expense of efficiency in its various forms. The view that economies must be recognized as a valid antitrust defense has thus gained ascendancy, despite great initial resistance and a few unreconstructed skeptics. This is a considerable shift from where antitrust enforcement stood in the 1960s. It is the principal basis for my claim that antitrust has witnessed great progress during the past decade.

[18] Bork (1978), p. 341.

[19] W. S. Comanor and T. A. Wilson, 'Advertising, market structure, and performance,' *Review of Economics and Statistics* (November 1967) pp. 423–40.

[20] W. S. Comanor and T. A. Wilson, 'Advertising and competition: A survey,' *Journal of Economic Literature*, 17 (June 1979), p. 472.

[21] Ibid., p. 470.

II. Concluding Remarks

My review of antitrust developments of the past decade is a relatively encouraging one. Affirmative regard for economies is now widespread and the importance of an economies defense is broadly recognized. This was not the case a decade ago. Vertical market restrictions and other unfamiliar business practices were regarded with suspicion during the 1960s. By contrast, the possibility that nonstandard practices are driven by transaction-cost economies is widely conceded today. Abuses of market-share analysis and barriers to entry arguments are much less common today. When abuses appear, moreover, they are quickly challenged. Thus whereas much antitrust argument was uninformed by rudimentary price theory and economizing notions in the 1960s, the role of microeconomics is securely established and the importance of economizing on transaction costs is widely recognized today.

The credit for this transformation is diverse. The Chicago School's tough-minded insistence that individual organization issues be viewed 'through the lens of price theory' is certainly a major contributing factor.[22] Advances in transaction cost reasoning and applications thereof to a variety of antitrust concerns have also been a factor.[23] The growing interest in industrial organization issues among the current generation of microtheorists has also contributed and, I conjecture, will play an even larger role as efforts are made to sort out what is at stake in the area of strategic behavior – that is, efforts by established firms to take up advance positions and/or respond contingently to rivalry in ways that discipline actual, and discourage potential, competition. Whether such behavior exists, what form it takes, how widespread each type is, and what antitrust ramifications attach thereto, are all open to dispute.

The reshaping of the structure–conduct–performance approach to make it more forward-looking and sensitive to trade-offs has also contributed to the progress.[24] And the increase in the size and quality of the economics staffs in the Antitrust Division and at the Federal Trade Commission have helped assure that bad economic argument gets recognized quickly and that more sophisticated analysis is brought to bear.

---

[22] For a development of this theme, see Posner, *Antitrust Law. Bork's recent book (The Antitrust Paradox)* is an important contribution to this tradition. The main limitation of the Chicago School has been its reluctance to make allowance for transaction costs, especially as this relates to strategic behavior. For a discussion, see my review of Bork's book in the Winter 1979 issue of the *University of Chicago Law Review*, 46 (1979), pp. 526–31.

[23] For a discussion, see chapter 5. Also see Williamson, *Antitrust Law and Economics*.

[24] See R. E. Caves and M. E. Porter, 'From entry barriers to mobility barriers,' *Quarterly Journal of Economics*, 91 (May 1977), pp. 241–62.

The notion that 'ideas, not vested interests' drive outcomes[25] is understandably attractive to academics. Plainly, however, there are public-policy arenas where this is mainly wishful thinking. In particular, realpolitik is apt to crowd ideas where the vested interests are easily organized and the individual stakes are large. Neither, but especially the former, is often the case with antitrust. Accordingly, ideas matter more for antitrust than for many other public-policy issues.

The upshot is that, although good analysis may not have won, it is surely winning. As recent and future refinements are tested and operationalized, I am confident that these will have a useful impact on antitrust as well. To be sure, there will be lags. And the hazards of creative lawyering will be with us always. Occasional setbacks notwithstanding, I do not expect the accomplishments of the past decade to be reversed. Vigilance is nevertheless warranted. Discovering and exposing efficiency consequences will remain among the leading tasks of antitrust scholars.

[25] J. M. Keynes, *The General Theory of Employment, Interest and Money* (1936) New York: Harcourt, Brace, p. 384.

12

Intellectual Foundations of Law and Economics: The Need for a Broader View

Edmund Kitch's interesting essay examining the intellectual foundations of law and economics opens and concludes on the same note: the merits of law and economics ought to be judged in relation to the competition. I agree with this and much of the intervening argument. But Kitch's characterization of law and economics can be disputed in both conceptual and factual respects. Since there is little to be gained by restatement of agreement, most of my remarks take the form of dissent.

With the exception of the introduction – which adds another datum, if one is needed, in support of George Stigler's observation that 'the lawyer views words ... as food for which the reader has an insatiable hunger'[1] – the essay is rather terse. Some of my differences with Kitch might have been avoided had he chosen to extend and qualify the argument. Other differences, however, are rather more basic. My comments are organized in three parts: areas of agreement, areas of contention, and a brief discussion of the research agenda.

I. Agreement

Although the merits of an intellectual tradition can be evaluated in a variety of ways, surely a comparative test is among the most important. Given the set of phenomena to be addressed, what does the competition have to offer? Although law and economics has its critics, a coherent alternative approach that fares well in the effort to explain and predict as wide a range of legal and economic phenomena has yet to emerge.

Reproduced with permission of copyright holder: © 1983 by the Association of American Law Schools, *Journal Legal Education*, 33 (1983), pp. 210–16.
[1] George J. Stigler, 'The law and economics of public policy: A plea to the scholars,' *Journal of Legal Studies*, 1 (1972), p. 1.

The critics of law and economics would be well advised to turn more of their attention to fashioning an alternative theory – which is not, however, to say that law and economies does not need or has not benefited from its critics.

Not only do Kitch and I agree on this point, but we also agree that the main basis for evaluating any 'market or regulatory arrangements' is in relation to 'other viable institutional alternatives.' This comparative institutional approach to the study of regulation was forcefully advanced by Ronald Coase in 1964:

Contemplation of an optimal system may suggest ways of improving the system. . . . But in general its influence has been pernicious. It has directed economists' attention away from the main question, which is how alternative arrangements will work in practice. . . . Until we realize that we are choosing between social arrangements which are more or less failures, we are not likely to make much headway.[2]

While it has taken some time for this viewpoint to gain ascendancy, it appears now to be widely accepted.

I also agree with Kitch that detailed knowledge is often important for understanding complex institutional phenomena. Both 'law reports and case records contain useful and carefully recorded information' that can be productively used for such a purpose. Tjalling Koopmans succinctly makes the point as follows: 'The task of linking concepts with observations demands a great deal of detailed knowledge of the realities of economic life.'[3] Some of these details are embedded in contracts, memoranda, correspondence, and the like that find their way into the record in law suits and investigations and can be more assiduously mined to good advantage.[4]

Kitch follows this point with the observation that legal history and comparative law should be developed more systematically. I concur and believe that the questions that Kitch poses at section I (10) should be central to the research agenda. I merely add that the study of business history is also useful grist for the law-and-economics mill. Work of the kind done by Alfred Chandler, Jr.[5] – which Robert Clark, I believe, would characterize as being of the 'middle range' (neither too sweeping nor too microanalytic[6] – is especially instructive.

[2] Ronald H. Coase, 'The regulated industries: Discussion,' *American Economic Review* 54 (1964), p. 195.

[3] Tjalling Koopmans, *Three Essays on the State of Economic Science (1957)*, New York, McGraw-Hill, p. 145.

[4] See Coase, *supra* footnote 2, pp. 195–6. Also see O. E. Williamson, 'Credible Commitments: Using Hostages to Support Exchange' (Unpublished manuscript, Oct. 1982).

[5] Alfred D. Chandler, Jr., *Strategy and Structure* (1966), New York, Doubleday; Alfred D. Chandler, Jr., *The Visible Hand* (1980), Cambridge, Mass.: Harvard University Press.

[6] Robert C. Clark, 'The interdisciplinary study of legal evolution,' *Yale Law Journal*, 90 (1981), p. 1265.

Finally, I agree with Kitch's remarks regarding the 'central unities of law' that a law-and-economics perspective helps to disclose and develop. This is surely an important intellectual contribution from which the study of the law can greatly benefit. The hazard is that economics will be interpreted too narrowly, in which unity may be realized at the expense of content.

II. Some Differences

My main concern with the way in which Kitch lays out the intellectual foundations of law and economics is that he imagines that economics speaks with one voice to the issues. The voice that he hears is that of his former colleagues at Chicago. I certainly agree that law and economics, individually and jointly, are greatly indebted to scholarship that has originated at Chicago – some of it in the face of massive dissent. (As Richard Posner put it, the law-and-economics program with which Aaron Director's name is associated was once regarded as 'little better than a lunatic fringe.'[7] But there are divisions even within Chicago, to say nothing of other differences outside of Chicago. Thus Posner acknowledges that there are differences between himself and John McGee on predatory pricing – where Posner is prepared to make allowance for strategic considerations which McGee neglects.[8] More important are the differences between George Stigler, who views industrial organization as applied price theory, and Ronald Coase, who insists that a 'direct approach' to the study of economic organization is needed in which transaction cost economizing is pre-eminently featured.[9]

Although an economizing orientation is maintained by both, the

[7] Richard A. Posner, 'The Chicago School of antitrust analysis,' *University of Pennsylvania Law Review, 127 (1979), p. 931.*

[8] Ibid.

[9] Ronald H. Coase, 'Industrial organization: A proposal for research,' *Policy Issues and Research Opportunities in Industrial Organizations,* ed. V. R. Fuchs (New York, National Bureau of Economic Research, 1972), pp. 59–73; Coase describes the direct approach to Industrial Organization as follows: 'This would concentrate on what activities firms undertake, and would endeavor to discover the characteristics of groupings of activities within firms. ... In addition to studying what happens within firms, studies should also be made of the contractual arrangements between firms (long-term contracts, leasing, licensing arrangements of various kinds including franchising, and so on), since market arrangements are the alternative to organization within the firm. The study of mergers should be extended so that it becomes an integral part of the main subject' (p. 73).

This is a very different research agenda than the applied price theory approach to industrial organization – which emphasized the study of 'pricing and output policies of firms, especially in oligopolistic industries' (ibid., p. 62). What I have referred to elsewhere as transaction cost economics (see the references in footnote 20 *infra*) has been implementing the research agenda described by Coase during the last decade.

differences between the applied price-theory approach and the comparative institutional assessment of transaction costs are profound. Inexplicably, these differences are ignored by Posner in his recent survey of antitrust economics at Chicago.[10] Even more surprising, these issues never surface in the recently edited transcript 'The Fire of Truth: A Remembrance of Law and Economics at Chicago, 1932–1970.'[11]

As between these two approaches, the direct approach is both less well developed and, for many law-and-economics purposes, more promising. Further, it is noteworthy that these two approaches scarcely exhaust the possibilities. Several other economic approaches to the study of industrial organization and related law-and-economics issues warrant remark. These include recent efforts to tighten up the concept of 'barriers to entry' that was central to the Harvard tradition in this field;[12] the study of economics as a process, which is associated with Austrian and evolutionary approaches to economic institutions,[13] the uses of agency theory[14] and information economics[15] to study economic organizations; neoclassical efficiency assessments of legal rules,[16] and eclectic blends of economics with feasibility analysis to inform such complex issues as predatory pricing.[17]

---

[10] Posner, *supra* footnote 7.

[11] Edmund W. Kitch, ed., 'Transcript of a discussion held March 21–23, 1981.' Los Angeles, California,' *Journal of Law and Economics* 26 April 1983; pp. 163–233.

[12] See Richard E. Caves and Michael E. Porter, 'From entry barriers to mobility barriers: Conjectural decisions and contrived deterrence to new competition, *Quarterly Journal of Economics*, 91 (1977), p. 201; A. Michael Spence.. 'Entry, capacity, investment, and oligopolistic pricing,' *Bell Journal of Economics*, 81 (1977), p. 534. Avinash K. Dixit, 'A model of duopoly suggesting a theory of entry barriers,' *Bell Journal of Economics*, 10 (1979), p. 20 and B. Curtis Eaton and Richard G. Lipsey. 'Exit barrier are entry barriers: The durability of capital as a barrier to entry,' *Bell Journal of Economics*, 11 (1980) p. 721; O. E. Williamson, 'Antitrust enforcement: Where it has been, Where it is going,' *Industrial Organization, Antitrust, and Public Policy*, ed. J. V. Craven (1982), Boston, Kluwer-Nyhott.

[13] Israel M. Kirzner, *Competition and Entrepreneurship* (1973) University of Chicago Press, Chicago); Richard R. Nelson and Sidney G. Winter, *An Evolutionary Theory of Economic Change* (1982) Cambridge, Mass.: Harvard University Press.

[14] Michael C. Jensen and William H. Meckling, 'Theory of the firm: Managerial behavior, agency costs, and ownership structure,' *Journal of Fin. Econ.*, 3 (1977), p. 305; Stephen A. Ross, 'The determination of financial structure: The incentive signaling approach,' *Bell Journal of Economics*, 8 (1977), p. 23.

[15] Michael Rothschild and Joseph E. Stiglitz, 'Equilibrium in competitive insurance markets,' Quarterly Journal of Economics, 80 (1976), p. 629. Sanford J. Grossman and Oliver D. Hart, 'Corporate financial structure and managerial incentives,' ed. J. J. McCall, *The Economics of Information* (1982), University of Chicago Press, Chicago;; p. 107–40.

[16] Peter A. Diamond and Eric Maskin, 'An equilibrium analysis of search and breach of contract.' *Bell Journal of Economics*, 10 (1979), p. 282. Steven Shavell, 'Damage measures for breach of contract,' *Bell Journal of Economics*, 11 (1980), p. 446.

[17] Joskow and Klevorick (1979, p. 213). Steven C. Salop, ed., *Strategy, Predation, and Antitrust Analysis* (1981), Federal Trade Commission, Bureau of Economics, Washington, DC.

The upshot is that law and economics speaks with many voices. Often this is because different approaches are better suited to different problems. Sometimes, however, different economic approaches speak to identical issues differently.[18] Such differences should be acknowledged rather than ignored or papered over. One has no hint of either variety in the relevant approaches of conflict among them from the Kitch paper.

Turning now from this general objection, consider the following particulars:

1 Kitch contends that 'marginal rather than gross or average effects are the important effects' and that 'past costs are sunk costs and have no bearing on decisions in the present.' Both statements need to be qualified. Thus, Coase's famous essay on social cost discloses the need to examine both marginal and total effects, with special emphasis on the latter.[19] And recent scholarship has emphasized that fixed costs are not necessarily sunk: the critical question is whether the assets in question can be effectively redeployed in alternative uses or by alternative users.[20] Where durable assets can be redeployed, the alternative value to which they can be put is properly considered in deciding on whether to continue or terminate an existing business.

2 Kitch argues that parties who are already engaged in an exchange relation can frustrate the purposes of a new law because, 'since they have already incurred the costs of bargaining, the marginal cost of adding a new topic – the new law – to their agenda is low, and it is plausible to expect complex multiparty arrangements to offset its effects.' There is much to be said for the view that it is necessary to go beyond immediate effects to consider eventual effects. A partial equilibrium versus a general

---

[18] See the exchange between Richard R. Nelson and Richard A. Posner in 'Symposium on antitrust law and economics,' *University of Pennsylvania Law Review*, 127 (1979).

[19] Ronald H. Coase, 'The problem of social cost,' *Journal of Law and Economics*, 3 (1960), p. 1. Also see Rosalind A. Seneca, 'Inherent advantage, costs, and resource allocation in the transportation industry, *American Economic Review*, 63 (1973) p. 945. The general point is this: when choices are being made between discrete alternatives, which is commonly the case when alternative institutions are under review, both marginal and total conditions need to be checked. See Williamson, Credible Commitments, *supra* footnote 4.

[20] See chapter 2; O. E. Williamson, *Markets and Hierarchies: Analysis and Antitrust Implications: A Study in the Economics of Internal Organization* (1975), Free Press, New York; O. E. Williamson, 'Transaction cost economics: The governance of contractual relations,' *Journal of Law and Economics*, 22 (1979), p. 231. Benjamin Klein, Robert A. Crawford and Armen A. Alchian.' Vertical integration, appropriate rents, and the competitive contracting process.' *Journal of Law and Economics*, 21 (1978), p. 297. Lester G. Telser, 'A theory of self-enforcing agreements,' *Journal of Business*, 53 (1981), p. 27. Benjamin Klein and Keith B. Leffler, 'The role of market forces in assuring contractual performance,' *Journal of Political Economy*, 89 (1981), p. 615. Curtis Eaton and Richard G. Lipsey, 'Capital commitment, and entry equilibrium,' *Bell Journal of Economy*, 12 (1981), p. 593.

equilibrium approach to the study of the corporation income tax is an example. But sometimes immediate effects are really very important (parties can be expropriated in the short run). And changes in the law can shift bargaining strength even for parties that are engaged in continuing exchange (witness the Wagner Act). Thus although it is useful to recognize that parties have an interest in restoring efficient trading (e.g., merging so as to evade taxes on the transfer of intermediate product), this is not always feasible or may be costly to effectuate. The fact that setup costs have already been incurred does not imply that subsequent negotiations will go smoothly.

3 Kitch contends that 'markets have strong efficiency properties.' I do not know what to make of such a statement taken by itself. rather, Kitch should heed his own advice. Here as elsewhere, a comparative institutional standard should be maintained. Such an orientation discloses that markets have good efficiency properties when used as the governance structure for organizing some transactions, that hierarchical or administrative modes have good efficiency properties for other types of transactions, and that mixed modes (franchising, nonstandard contracting) have good efficiency properties for still others. Furthermore, and of special importance to the study of economic organization, headway has been made – and prospectively will continue to be made – in matching up governance structures with transactions in a discriminating (mainly transaction cost economizing) way.[21]

4 Kitch makes repeated reference to self-interest seeking as an important behavioral assumption in the economic analysis of complex phenomena. This is correct. But different types of self-interest seeking need to be distinguished. And self-interest-seeking arguments can be and sometimes are used to excess.

As I understand him, the type of self-interest seeking to which Kitch refers is mainly of a simple or up-front kind. This is what Peter Diamond had in mind when he observed that standard 'economic models ... [treat] individuals as playing a game with fixed rules which they obey. They do not buy more than they know they can pay for, they do not embezzle funds, they do not rob banks.'[22] Such self-interest seeking needs to be distinguished from opportunism, which is a more subtle form of behavior that involves self-interest seeking with guile. Failure to make allowance for self-interest seeking of this deeper kind has been rseponsible for misconceptions of some economic phenomena – of which the purported

---

[21] See the references in footnote 18 *supra*.

[22] Peter A. Diamond, 'Political and economic evaluation of social effects and externalities: Comment,' ed. Michael D. Intrilligator, *Frontiers of Quantitative Eonomics* (1971), North-Holland Publishing Company, Amsterdam; pp. 30–2.

efficacy of franchise bidding for natural monopolies is one illustration.[23]

5 Related to this last is Kitch's claim that 'rather elementary price theory' has been used to document 'a stunning series of failures in the structure of economic regulation. ... These demonstrations focused on agencies that restricted entry (airlines, trucks, communications common carriers), restricted pricing freedom (railroad, utility regulation, Robinson-Patman Act), or prevented the creation of private property rights (broadcast regulation).'

I agree that elementary price theory has been used for these purposes and has been instrumental in reshaping views on the needs and purposes of regulation. Specifically, the literature to which Kitch has reference has helped to demonstrate that regulation has commonly served special interests (often those of the regulated firms) rather than the public at large. This is an important achievement. But I would add the following qualifications:

(a) The characteristics of the assets are critical in evaluating the efficacy of deregulation. Trucks and airplanes are usefully distinguished from local electricity, gas, and water distribution in this connection. Although durable investments in all of these industries may be great, trucks and airplanes are mobile and most are general purpose. The investment in local distribution of utility services, by contrast, is sunk (highly specific). Transition problems aside, truck and airline deregulation is relatively easy to effectuate. Local distribution, by contrast, is much more problematic.

(b) The definition of property rights can be difficult. The private sector unsuccessfully wrestled with the creation of private property rights in broadcasting for 30 years before federal regulation was introduced.[24] To be sure, a well-working market in electromagnetic spectrum might have evolved if given 30 additional years. The particular way in which regulation was introduced and implemented might have been improved upon. And current reforms may be warranted. But rather elementary

---

[23] See O. E. Williamson, 'Franchise bidding for natural monopolies – in general and with respect to CATV,' *Bell Journal of Economics*, 7 (1976), p. 73, for a discussion of the misconceptions associated with the purported efficacy of franchise bidding to supplant regulation in circumstances where assets are highly specific. Paul L. Joskow and Richard Schmalensee's recent study, *Deregulation of Electric Power: A Framework of Analysis* (Energy Laboratory, MIT, Sept. 1982), examines the efficacy of franchise bidding in the electric power industry and concludes that the enthusiasts of deregulation have not done their comparative institutional homework. Upon examining the characteristics of the assets and the uncertainties to which electric power is subject, they conclude that market contracting will be beset with a host of problems.

[24] Ronald H. Coase sets out the history of this private effort to deal with electromagnetic spectrum in his article 'Federation communication commission,' *Journal of Law and Economics*, 2 (1959), p. 1.

price theory is not, by itself, up to doing the job. It is misleading to pretend otherwise.

III. The Research Agenda

I contend that the study of law and economics will benefit from adopting a broader conception of the issues that reliance on rudimentary price theory can support. This is in the spirit of Karl Llewellyn's views, expressed 50 years ago, that the study of contract would benefit from shifting the focus from a preoccupation with technical rules (marginal analysis) to an examination of institutions of contract and of the purposes to be served (the study of governance).[25] It is also consonant with Ronald Coase's prescription that industrial organization rely less on applied price theory, which in his judgment operates at too high a level of aggregation to deal with the interesting problems of economic organization in a useful way, and adopt a direct approach to the problem instead.[26] It is furthermore consonant with some of the more probing studies of law, economics, and organization with which Guido Calabresi has been concerned.[27]

Although the comparative institutional approach to the study of alternative modes of organization to which I refer relies heavily on efficiency analysis – with special attention to transaction-cost features – other social values are permitted (in some cases encouraged) to intrude.[28] Such an intellectual undertaking involves more than law and economics. An adequate understanding of many of the issues can be realized only by adopting a law-economics-and-organizations perspective, making allowance for what Frank Knight has felicitously referred to as 'human nature as we know it.'[29] It further involves examining economic and social organization at a sufficiently microanalytic level that details of the 'middle range' are permitted to matter.[30] Albeit useful for many purposes, the elementary price theory to which Kitch refers is simply inadequate for many others. The promise of a law-economics-and-organizations perspective – to which legal scholars have many advantges in relation to

[25] Karl N. Llewellyn, 'What price contact? – Essay in perspective, *Yale Law Journal*, 40 (1931), p. 704.
[26] Coase, *supra* footnote 9.
[27] Guido Calabresi and Philip Bobbitt, *Tragic Choices* (1978), W.W. Norton, New York. Guido Calabresi and A. Douglas Melamed,' Property rules, liability rules, and inalienability: One view of the cathedral.' *Harvard Law Review*, 85 (1972), p. 1089.
[28] Ibid.
[29] Frank H. Knight, *Risk, Uncertainty and Profit* (1965), Harper & Row, New York.
[30] Clark, *supra* footnote 6.

their economist counterparts[31] – needs to be and, I am confident, will be developed.

---

[31] Roger Cramton quotes Kingman Brewster to the effect that lawyers 'focus on the fact that public officials and tribunals are going to be fallible at best and incompetent or abusive at worst' ('The effectiveness of economic regulation: A legal view,' *American Economic Review*, 54 (1964), pp. 182, 185. Ronald Coase remarks that this is perhaps 'too jaundiced a view of human nature ... a welcome corrective to what is assumed in much economic discussion' (Coase, 'The regulated industries,' *supra* footnote 2, p. 196). I have discussed the issues by contrasting simple self-interest seeking of the type referred to by Diamond (see text accompanying footnote 22 *supra*) with a condition of opportunism, which involves self-interest seeking with guile and is responsible for many of the complex governance structures in modern economics. See Williamson, *Markets and Hierarchies*, *supra* footnote 20, pp. 26–37.

13

Antitrust Enforcement: Where it has Been; Where it is Going

Antitrust, which once enjoyed widespread support, has come under withering attack from a variety of quarters recently. Many of the critics regard antitrust as an anachronism, and openly counsel that it be abolished. But some hold the opposite view. They urge that antitrust enforcement be strengthened, and recall the Warren Court years with nostalgia.

Critics of the first kind appear to be dismayed over the difficulties experienced by US auto, steel, and other industries as compared with the robust successes of the Japanese. A reshaping of the relations among firms and between business and government along the lines of the Japanese model is widely held to be attractive. The details of the Japanese model remain somewhat obscure, however, and its transferability to the US scene is problematic. Until the model is more fully worked out, its net benefits assessed, and its transferability demonstrated, it would appear to be judicious to regard reforms along these lines as speculative. For the purposes of this chapter therefore, my examination of antitrust will remain within the framework of US experience.

A decade is a useful interval over which to observe and report on antitrust developments. The 1960s, 1970s, and 1980s can each, I think, be usefully characterized as an antitrust era. Specifically, concentration and entry barrier analysis flourished in the 1960s. Efficiency analysis gained ascendancy in the 1970s, and I expect the 1980s to be the period when the analysis of strategic behavior comes of age. Arguments that antitrust should be abolished would be easier to understand had there been no substantial progress during the 1970s or if the problems of the 1980s were inconsequential. Inasmuch, however, as antitrust made remarkable progress during the 1970s and since difficult problems of

Research on this chapter was facilitated by a grant from the National Science Foundation. Reprinted from *Industrial Organization, Antitrust and Public Policy*. ed. John Craven, Klurver–Nihjoff Publishing, Boston (1983), pp. 41–68, with permission.

strategic behavior remain unresolved, calls for the abolition of antitrust are premature if not uninformed.

Antitrust enforcement in the 1960s is briefly examined in the first section of this chapter. The reforms of the 1970s are reviewed next. Some of the concerns and recent developments relating to strategic behavior are then treated and unresolved enforcement dilemmas for the 1980s are addressed. Concluding remarks follow. I argue that, whereas reliance on entry barrier arguments was excessive in the 1960s, much of this was redressed by a shift of attention to efficiency, in all of its forms, in the 1970s. Difficult strategic behavior issues have, nevertheless, surfaced and this area is presently in great flux.[1] Considerable research resources have recently been directed at these issues – as a result of which there is a prospect for better resolution in the latter part of this decade.

I. The 1960s

The 1960s was the era when market-power analysis flourished. This was partly due to earlier theoretical, empirical, and policy studies in which entry barriers were prominent, but it was also because antitrust economics was sorely lacking in two other respects. First, there was a general undervaluation of the social benefits of efficiency. Second, there was a widespread tendency to regard efficiency very narrowly – mainly in technological terms. An awareness of transactions costs, much less a sensitivity to the importance of economizing thereon, had scarcely surfaced. Instead, the firm was held to be a production function to which a profit maximization objective had been assigned. Subject to rudimentary economy-of-scale considerations, the efficient boundaries of firms were taken as given. Accordingly, efforts to reconfigure firm and market structures that went beyond these natural boundaries were assessed almost exclusively in market-power terms.

The intellectual basis for market-power analysis was provided by Joe Bain in the 1950s, especially in his book *Barriers to New Competition* (1956). Many of the antitrust ramifications of this approach to industrial organization were set out by Carl Kaysen and Donald Turner very shortly thereafter in their book *Antitrust Policy: An Economic and Legal Analysis* (1959). The decade of the 1960s witnessed further applications of this line of reasoning and widespread adoption of entry barrier arguments by the courts.

Illustrations of the success of entry barrier reasoning are the *Procter & Gamble* and *Schwinn* cases, both of which were decided by the Supreme

---

[1] A shift of the traditional entry barrier approach in the direction of strategic behavior was signaled by the influential paper of Richard Caves and Michael Porter (1977).

Court in 1967.[2] The first of these cases was anticipated by the Federal Trade Commission's opinion in *Foremost Dairies*, where the Commission ventured the view that the necessary proof of violation of section 7 'consists of types of evidence showing that the acquiring firm possesses significant power in some markets *or* that its overall organization gives it a decisive advantage in efficiency over its small rivals.'[3] Although Donald Turner, among others, was quick to label this as bad law and bad economics (1975, p. 1324) in that it protects competitors rather than promotes the welfare benefits of competition, the Commission carried this reasoning forward in *Procter & Gamble* and linked it with barriers to entry in the following way:[4]

In stressing as we have the importance of advantages of scale as a factor heightening the barriers to new entry into the liquid bleach industry, we reject, as specious in law and unfounded in fact, the argument that the Commission ought not, for the sake of protecting the 'inefficient' small firms in the industry, proscribe a merger so productive of 'efficiencies.' The short answer to this argument is that, in a proceeding under section 7, economic efficiency or any other social benefit resulting from a merger is pertinent only insofar as it may tend to promote or retard the vigor of competition.

This emphasis on entry barriers and the low regard accorded to economies also appears in the Supreme Court's opinion. Thus the Court observed that Procter's acquisition of Clorox may[5]

... have the tendency of raising the barriers to new entry. The major competitive weapon in the successful marketing of bleach is advertising. Clorox was limited in this area by its relatively small budget and its inability to obtain substantial discounts. By contrasts, Procter's budget was much larger; and, although it would not devote its entire budget to advertising Clorox, it could divert a large portion to meet the short-term threat of a new entrant. Procter would be able to use its volume discounts to advantage in advertising Clorox. Thus, a new entrant would be much more reluctant to face the giant Procter than it would have been to face the smaller Clorox.
Possible economies cannot be used as a defense to illegality.[6]

The aforementioned insensitivity to transaction cost economizing was

---

[2] *Federal Trade Commission* v. *Procter & Gamble Co.*, 386 US 568 (1967); *United States* v. *Arnold Schwinn & Co.* 388 US 365 (1967).

[3] Foremost Dairies, Inc., 60 FTC 944, 1084 (1962), emphasis added.

[4] Quoted from Bork (1978, p. 254).

[5] *Federal Trade Commission* v. *Procter & Gamble Co.*, 386 US 568, 574 (1967).

[6] Although perverse applications of economies reasoning are much less common today, occasional aberrations nevertheless appear. See footnote 28, for an example.

coupled with a preoccupation with entry barriers in reaching the *Schwinn* decision. Donald Turner, who was then the head of the Antitrust Division, succinctly expressed the prevailing attitude toward nonstandard or unfamiliar business practices as follows: 'I approach territorial and customer restrictions not hospitably in the common law tradition, but inhospitably in the tradition of antitrust law.'[7] This view, which I shall refer to as the inhospitality tradition, was widely held among antitrust specialists during the 1960s. Rather than presume – or at least investigate the possibility – that vertical restrictions served affirmative economic purposes, it was assumed instead that they were designed to enhance market power. Specifically, the Government argued that 'Schwinn's strenuous efforts to exclude unauthorized retailers from selling its bicycles suggest that, absent these restraints, there would be a broader retail distribution of these goods with the resulting public benefits (including lower price) of retail competition.'[8] Since the Government believed that it was 'unnecessary to create quality images' because products that are objectively superior would be self-evident, and since product differentiation can adversely affect the condition of entry, Schwinn's efforts to effect differentiation were held by the Government to be contrary to the public interest.

Accordingly, antitrust enforcement in the 1960s can be described as a period during which market-power concerns were virtually determinative. The benefits of economies were wilfully disregarded, and the evidence of economies was narrowly restricted to those with technological origins. A series of reactions, many of which were needed correctives, was set in motion by the excesses to which this type of reasoning was given.

II. The 1970s

The reconceptualizing of antitrust issues that occurred during the late 1960s and early 1970s is sketched below. This mainly entailed a shift away from entry barriers to address economic organization from the standpoint of what economic purposes are being served. Two of the cases that were decided during the 1970s in which this shift is reflected will be briefly described.

A. EFFICIENCY ANALYSIS

The reforms of antitrust enforcement in the 1970s had their origins in critiques of the 1960s. These include (a) the insistence of the Chicago

---

[7] The quotation is attributed to Turner by Stanley Robinson 1968 NY State Bar Association, Antitrust Symposium, p. 29.

[8] Jurisdictional Statement for the United States at 14, *United States* v. *Arnold Schwinn & Co.* 388 US 365 (1967). For a discussion, see Williamson (1979a, pp. 980–5).

School that antitrust issues be studied through the lens of price theory;
(b) related critiques of the entry barrier approach; (c) application of the
partial-equilibrium welfare-economics model to an assessment of the trade-
offs between market power and efficiency; and (d) a reformulation of the
theory of the modern corporation whereby transaction-cost-economizing
considerations were brought to the fore. An additional contributing factor
was the reorganization of the economics staff of the Antitrust Division.
Whereas previously the staff economists were used almost exclusively to
support the legal staff in the preparation and litigation of cases, they were
now asked to assess the economic merits of cases before filing.

The Chicago School approach has been set out by Richard Posner
(1979) elsewhere. Although it is possible to quibble with Posner's rendition
of Harvard versus Chicago (as these were viewed in the 1960s), it is
nevertheless clear that the efficiency orientation favored by Aaron Director
(and his students and colleagues) has stood the test of time rather well.
Thus whereas Director's views on tie-ins, resale-price maintenance, and
the like were widely regarded as suspect – 'In some quarters the Chicago
School was regarded as little better than a lunatic fringe' (Posner, 1979,
p. 931) – this approach enjoys wider respect today.[9] But Chicago, or at
least the diehard branch, has, in the process of applying price theory to
antitrust, insisted on an uncommonly narrow formulation. (Specifically,
as discussed below, the diehard-Chicago approach to the study of strategic
behavior is myopic and simplistic. This has a bearing, however, more on
the enforcement issues of the 1980s than to those of the 1970s.)

Given Chicago's price theory orientation, many of the criticisms of the
entry barrier approach understandably originated there as well. Objections
of two kinds were registered. The first of these held that the basic entry
barrier model, as set out by Bain (1956) and elaborated by Franco
Modigliani (1958), purported to be but did not qualify as an oligopoly
model. As George Stigler put it, the entry barrier model solved the
oligopoly problem by murder: 'The ability of the oligopolists to agree
upon and police the limit price is apparently independent of the sizes and
numbers of oligopolists' (1968, p. 21). Put differently, the model did not
address itself to the mechanics by which collective action was realized.
Instead, it simply assumed that the requisite coordination to effect a limit-
price result would appear. As discussed below, recent models in the entry
barrier traditon have avoided this problem by explicitly casting the analysis
in a sitting monopolist–duopoly framework. Addressing the issues of entry
in this more limited context has analytical advantages, but applications
outside of the dominant-firm context are appropriate only upon a showing

[9] The recent Areeda and Turner antitrust treatise is an example. See Posner (1979, pp.
933–8) for a discussion of the earlier Kaysen and Turner book as compared with the Areeda
and Turner treatise.

that the necessary preconditions to effect oligopolistic coordination are satisfied.

The other objection to entry barrier analysis relates to public policy misuses of entry barrier reasoning. That the condition of entry is impeded is neither here nor there if no superior structural configuration – expressed in welfare terms – can be described. However obvious this may be on reflection, this was not always the case. Rather, there was a widespread tendency to regard barriers of all kinds as contrary to the social interest. But as Robert Bork has put it, 'The question for antitrust is whether there exist artificial entry barriers. These must be barriers that are not forms of superior efficiency and which yet prevent the forces of the market ... from operating to erode market positions not based on efficiency' (1978, p. 311, emphasis added).

The distinction between remediable and irremediable entry impediments thus becomes the focus of attention. Little useful public policy purpose is served, and considerable risk of public policy mischief results, when conditions of an irremediable kind are brought under fire. Mistaken treatment of economies of scale illustrates what is at stake. Thus, suppose that economies of scale exist and that the market is of sufficient size to support the larger of two technologies. Since superior outcomes will be attributable to the less efficient technology only under very unusual conditions, net social benefits ought presumably to be attributed to these scale-economy conditions. To describe such economies as barriers to entry, however, does not invite this conclusion; to the contrary, mistaken welfare judgments are encouraged. Many of the enthusiasts of entry barrier analysis have been reluctant to concede such hazards.

That efficiency benefits were held in such low regard in the 1960s is partly explained by the widespread opinion that, as between two structural alternatives – one of which simultaneously presents greater market power and greater efficiency than the other – the more competitive structure is invariably to be preferred. This view was supported by the implicit assumption that even small anticompetitive effects would surely swamp efficiency benefits in arriving at a net valuation. The FTC opinion that 'economic efficiency or any other social benefit ... [is] pertinent only insofar as it may tend to promote or retard the vigor of competition'[10] – where competition is defined in structural terms – is a clear indication of such thinking.

Application of the basic partial-equilibrium welfare-economics model to an assessment of market power versus economies trade-offs disclosed that to sacrifice economies for reduced market power came at a high cost (Williamson, 1968). Although the merits of this framework remain open to dispute (Posner, 1975, p. 821), the general approach, if not the

[10] See footnote 4 *supra*.

framework itself, has since been employed by others. Bain was among the first to acknowledge the merits of an economies defense in assessing mergers (1968, p. 658). Wesley Liebeler (1978), Robert Bork (1978), and Timothy Muris (1979) have all made extensive use of the partial-equilibrium trade-off model in their insistence that antitrust enforcement that proceeds heedless of trade-offs is uninformed and contrary to the social interest.

A common argument against trade-off analysis is that the courts are poorly suited to assess economic evidence and arguments of this kind (Bok, 1960). In fact, a simple sensitivity to the merits of economies is sufficient to avoid the inverted reasoning of *Foremost Dairies*; and although errors of the *Schwinn* kind are avoided only upon recognizing that economies can take transaction cost as well as technological forms, the mistakes of the inhospitality tradition also become less likely once this step has been taken.

Whereas technological innovations were easily accommodated within a production function framework (and economists have devoted considerable attention to these matters) organizational innovation is alien to this framework (and, as of the early 1960s, had been generally neglected). The publication of Alfred Chandler's book *Strategy and Structure* (1962) represented the opening wedge in an effort to develop a deeper understanding of the importance of organizational innovation and its relation to the study of the modern corporation. Chandler focused on the shift from the traditional hierarchical structure (or unitary form) to the multidivisional (or M-form) structure. This innovation first appeared in the 1920s and was imitated and widely adopted thereafter. Chandler argued that the new structure had deep rationality properties that permitted the firm to realize superior results in both strategic and operating respects. It was uninformed and untenable to argue that internal organization was a matter of indifference after the appearance of Chandler's book.

Independently, Armen Alchian (1969) and Richard Heflebower (1960) also recognized that organization form had an important bearing on economic performance. They advanced the proposition that corporations were discharging functions ordinarily associated with the capital market. The internal-resource allocation, incentive, and control attributes of the modern corporation were subsequently discussed and developed by others (Williamson, 1970, 1975). This in turn led to a more general study of firm and market structures whereby the issue of mediating transactions was addressed not as a datum but as an economizing issue. Although this insight owes its origins to Ronald Coase's classic 1937 paper, it was not until the 1970s that the issues were operationalized.

Whereas both the production function approach and inhospitality tradition regarded markets as the natural, hence efficient, way by which to mediate transactions between technologically separable entities, this presumption was unacceptable once firms were described not as production functions but as governance structures. Whether transactions should be mediated by markets, hierarchies, or mixed modes was thus an issue to be investigated by assessing the transaction-cost ramifications of each. Such a comparative institutional undertaking involved (a) dimensionalizing transactions, (b) describing alternative governance structures, and (c) recognizing that transaction costs would be economized by matching governance structure with transactions in a discriminating way (Williamson, 1971, 1975, 1979b).

This approach to the study of economic organization disclosed that many nonstandard or unfamiliar business practices that were, at best, puzzling, when assessed in technological terms, were in fact the outcome of rational transaction-cost-economizing efforts. Vertical integration, vertical market restrictions, and aspects of conglomerate and multinational organization were all re-examined to advantage. Organizational innovations that had hitherto been regarded as presumptively unlawful, under the inhospitality tradition, were thus accorded greater sympathy. Indeed, subject to the condition that certain structural thresholds (mainly high concentration coupled with barriers to entry) are not exceeded, a presumption that organizational innovations have the purpose and effect of economizing on transaction costs is warranted.[11] This is a rather drastic departure from the mistaken views of the 1960s.

B. TWO CASES

It is a credit to the growing sophistication of antitrust that the 1970s witnessed a shift away from asserted, but often only imagined, entry barrier effects to consider the affirmative purposes served by new business configurations. This occurred both with respect to mergers-for-economies as well as vertical market restrictions (and other nonstandard business practices). The 1975 decision of the Federal Trade Commission to vacate the administrative law judge's order and dismiss the complaint in the *Budd Company* case illustrates the shift in mergers-for-economies

---

[11] Developing this takes us beyond the scope of the current chapter, but it has been addressed elsewhere (Williamson, 1981). Among the leading organizational innovations during the past 150 years that have important transaction cost economizing attributes are (a) the appearance of managerial hierarchies in the railroads in the 1860s; (b) selective forward integration out of manufacturing into distribution that occurred at the end of the nineteenth century; (c) the invention of the multidivisional structure in the 1920s and its subsequent diffusion following the Second World War; (d) the extension of multidivisionalization to manage diversified lines of commerce (the conglomerate); and (e) the further application of this to promote technology transfer in the multinational enterprise.

thinking.[12] The complaint had stressed Budd's importance as a potential entrant into narrowly defined lines of commerce and held that the benefits conferred by Budd on the acquired firm (Gindy) disadvantaged small rivals. The Commission rejected the complaint counsel's narrow definition of the market and regarded the acquisition as procompetitive – in that the acquisition relieved Gindy of financial and other handicaps that it had experienced previously. The upside-down valuation of economies in *Foremost Dairies* and *Procter* was thus recognized as a perversion of sound antitrust economics.

The Supreme Court's decision in 1977 in the *GTE–Sylvania* case also corrected mistaken reasoning of the 1960s, specifically that of *Schwinn*. Contrary to *Schwinn*, the Court held that[13]

[vertical] restrictions, in varying forms, are widely used in our free market economy. As indicated above, there is substantial scholarly opinion and judicial authority supporting their economic utility. There is relatively little authority to the contrary. Certainly there has been no showing in this case, either generally or with respect to Sylvania's agreement, that vertical restrictions have or are likely to have a 'pernicious effect on competition' or that they 'lack ... any redeeming virtue'. ... Accordingly, we conclude that the per se rule in *Schwinn* must be overruled.

The 1960s preoccupation with competition, often amounting to no more than a concern over competitors coupled with a naive view of the modern corporation, was thus substantially redressed.

III. Strategic Behavior: A Progress Report

The main issue on the research agenda for industrial organization during the next decade is the study of strategic behavior – by which I mean efforts by established firms to take up advance positions or respond contingently to rivalry in ways that discipline actual and discourage potential competition. Whether such behavior exists, what forms it takes, how widespread each type is, and what antitrust ramifications attach thereto, are all open to dispute.

Although a great deal of research talent has been directed to these issues in the past few years and real progress has been made, we still have a long way to go before the main issues can be thought to be settled. Unlike efficiency analysis, where industrial organization could draw upon

---

[12] Budd Co. [1973–1976 Transfer Binder] Trade Regulation Reporter CCTT, para. 20, 998 (FTC No. 8848 18 Sept. 1975).
[13] *Continental TV Inc. et al.* v. *GTE–Sylvania Inc.* 433 US 36, 45 (1977).

applied welfare economics for assistance, the study of strategic behavior poses puzzles that are quite novel. The need for new theory has not gone unnoticed and a number of applied theorists have been developing new models designed to answer these requirements.

Although this work is progressing rapidly, it is still in early stages of development. As matters stand presently, established firms have considerable latitude in responding defensively to new rivalry. Unlike the entry barrier era of the 1960s, where courts were quick to find anticompetitive purpose lurking behind innocent and efficient practices, the courts in the 1970s have been very cautious in evaluating claims of predation and strategic abuse by dominant firms.[14] This is partly because agreement is lacking on criteria for discerning admissible from excessive competitive replies to new rivalry. Additionally, there are problems in translating proposed criteria to operational measures that the courts can apply with confidence. Related to both of these is the hazard, to which the courts have been alert, that firms that complain they are subject to predatory pricing (and other unlawful practices) may, in fact, be seeking protectionist relief from legitimate, albeit complex, rivalrous behavior. Also, the enforcement ramifications of some of the new models have yet to be worked out.

A. DIEHARD CHICAGO

The distinguishing characteristic of what Posner has referred to as 'diehard Chicagoans' (1979, p. 932) is a reluctance to confront strategic behavior in any but a very narrow context. The favored approach, as illustrated most recently by the commentary of John McGee (1980), has been to insist upon studying strategic behavior issues in myopic terms.[15]

Predatory Pricing

McGee's survey of the recent predatory pricing literature is mainly negative with one conspicuous exception. McGee advises readers that 'Robert Bork's formulation of the problem commands attention' (1980, p. 293) and concludes that, 'In his masterful analysis of the US antitrust laws, Robert H. Bork shows why predatory price cutting would be rare or nonexistent even if there were no legal rules against it' (1980, pp. 316–17). Although I agree that Bork has made important contributions to the study of antitrust,[16] McGee and I differ on our assessment of

---

[14] For references to the relevant cases, see Ordover and Willig (1981, p. 70, n. 2).

[15] Although McGee was not among those identified by Posner as being a member of the diehard school, McGee has since volunteered that he qualifies for membership (1980, p. 292, n. 15).

[16] See my review of Bork's book in Williamson (1970a).

Bork's treatment of strategic behavior in general and predatory pricing in particular.

Thus Bork poses the problem of predatory pricing by considering a firm with an 80 per cent market share that 'wishes to kill a rival with 20 per cent in order to achieve the comforts and prerogatives of monopoly status' (1978, p. 149). He concludes, upon examining the rationality of such an undertaking, that predatory pricing of this kind is 'most unlikely to exist' (1978, p. 155). But the case that Bork considers is a very special and relatively uninteresting kind. As discussed below, the full ramifications of predatory pricing are not disclosed by focusing on a dominant firm's efforts to destroy a rival that has already committed itself by investing in specialized human and physical capital (and hence needs only to recover its variable costs to remain viable during the predatory siege).

McGee is nevertheless attracted to this formulation and therefore regards predatory pricing as insignificant. Indeed, his preferred legal rule on predatory pricing is to ignore it altogether (McGee, 1980, p. 317). Upon recognition, however, that some rule must be adopted, McGee understandably endorses the most permissive predatory pricing rule that has yet to be proposed: the Areeda–Turner marginal-cost-pricing rule.[17] In fact, this rule has found favor in many courts. But as Paul Joskow has explained, this has occurred because of a pressing need to fill a void and 'not because of the triumph of economic efficiency considerations in the interpretation of antitrust statutes' (1980, p. 202).

Voids can be filled, of course, in many ways. One of the reasons the courts were attracted to a marginal-cost-pricing rule, I conjecture, is that they perceived the dangers that more stringent rules would encourage protectionist abuses and accordingly favored a very permissive standard. In the process, however, of reducing the risk of what Joskow and Alvin Klevorick (1979, p. 223) refer to as 'false-positive' error – that is, incorrectly declaring something predatory that in fact is efficient – the courts have accepted a huge risk of 'false-negative' error – that is, allowing behavior that is, in fact, predatory to continue.

Although a consensus on this issue has not yet developed, there is widespread concern that a marginal-cost-pricing standard is defective.[18] A basic problem with this criterion is that it appeals to static-welfare-economics arguments for support while predatory pricing is unavoidably

[17] This rule is mainly associated with the 1975 paper of Phillip Areeda and Donald Turner. McGee, however, observes that he originated the rule ten years earlier (McGee, 1980, p. 290).

[18] Janusz Ordover and Robert Willig, in a recent paper, develop cost-based criteria that they contend are in the spirit of Areeda and Turner (Ordover and Willig, 1981, pp. 9, 16). In fact, however, their double test – the price exceeds both average and marginal cost – is much more stringent, and they nowhere propose average variable cost as a suitable surrogate, the operational result at which Areeda and Turner arrive.

an intertemporal issue. As William Baumol succinctly puts it, static analysis of the kind in which Areeda and Turner rely is 'inadequate ... because it draws our attention from the most pressing issues that are involved' (1979, p. 2). The 'nub of the problem ... [is] the intertemporal aspect of the situation' (1979, p. 3).

The Condition of Entry

As a result of persistent criticism, much of it originating with Chicago, it is now widely recognized that the entry barrier arguments of the 1960s were much too sweeping. But such a demonstration does not establish that this entire tradition should be rejected. The possibilities that remediable impediments to entry might arise, and that such circumstances are identifiable, ought to be considered. Consistent with his neglect of strategic factors, Bork seems unwilling to entertain such possibilities. This unwillingness is due chiefly to his implicit assumption that labor and capital markets operate frictionlessly, so that every market outcome is presumptively a merit outcome and further discussion is pointless. Once transaction costs are admitted, however, the assumption of frictionlessness no longer applies, the possibility of introducing strategic impediments to entry arises, and the main argument needs to be qualified. To be sure, the exceptions may not be numerous and the difficulties of informed or efficacious intervention may be great. Such defects might better be tolerated, therefore, rather than made subject to public policy review and attempted rectification. But this is a separate argument. Neither Bork nor others of the antientry barrier belief have addressed the entry barrier issues on these grounds. Since the frictionlessness assumptions on which Bork implicitly relies are unacceptable to many students of antitrust, continuing dispute over the nature and importance of entry barriers is to be expected.

Recent Headway

Objections that have been or could be leveled at early entry barrier models and related applications to predatory pricing include: (a) the structural preconditions are not carefully stated; (b) whether it is more attractive to bar rather than accept entry is assumed but not demonstrated; (c) attention is focused on total costs, but the composition of costs and the characteristics of assets matter crucially and have been neglected; (d) the incentives to engage in predation are weak; and (e) cost asymmetries between established firms and potential entrants are asserted but rarely addressed. Recent work has made headway with each of these issues.

Structural Preconditions. As discussed above, the early entry barrier models purported to be oligopoly models. But the question of how oligopolists managed to achieve effective concurrence of market action –

with respect to price, output, investment, and so forth – was not addressed. The relevance of those models outside of the dominant firm context was thus questionable.

Recent models in the entry barrier tradition have essentially abandoned the oligopoly claim. The issues are posed instead in a duopoly context between a sitting monopolist and a potential entrant. Those who would apply these models to oligopoly presumably have the heavy burden of demonstrating their applicability.

Similar care has been taken in assessing claims of predation. The hazard here is that the legal process will be misused to discourage legitimate rivalry. There is growing agreement that the structural preconditions that must be satisfied before claims of predation are seriously entertained are very high concentration coupled with barriers to entry (Williamson, 1977, pp. 292–3). Joskow and Klevorick (1979, pp. 225–31) and Ordover and Willig (1981) concur and propose a two-tier test for predatory pricing. The subset of industries for which strategic behavior warrants public policy scrutiny would thus appear to be the following: (a) the sitting monopolist–duopolist situation; (b) regulated monopolies; (c) dominant-firm industries; and (d) what William Fellner has referred to as 'Case 3 oligopoly' (1949, pp. 47–9) – which is an industry where an outside agency (for instance, a union) enforces collective action.[19]

Rationality of Pre-entry Deterrence. In principle, entry can be deterred in any of three ways: (a) by expanding output and investment in the pre-entry period, thereby discouraging the incentive to enter; (b) by threatening aggressive post-entry responses; and (c) by imposing cost disadvantages on rivals. The second of these is addressed below. The first is in the spirit of Bain and Modigliani and has been dealt with more recently by Avinash Dixit, who models the entry problem in a duopoly context (1979, 1980). This permits him simultaneously to display and assess the profitability and feasibility of having the sitting monopolist adopt any of three postures: (a) behave in an unconstrained-monopoly fashion; (b) expand output and investment so as to deter entry; and (c) accept entry by taking up a Stackelburg-leadership position in relation to the entrant. Dixit demonstrates that entry deterrence is optimal when fixed costs are of intermediate degree; the complaint that entry deterrence is an imposed, rather than derived, result can be dismissed if the requisite conditions are satisfied.

Costs, Assets, and Credibility. The standard entry barrier model assumes that potential entrants have access to the same long-run average total cost curve as do estabished firms. But the composition of costs between fixed

---

[19] It has been argued that the United Mine Workers performed this function in the bituminous coal industry (Williamson, 1968).

and variable is ignored. This poses the following anomaly: extant firms and potential entrants are indistinguishable if all costs are variable. The only effective entry-deterring policy in circumstances where all costs are variable is setting price equal to total cost, which is to say that entry deterrence is without purpose. The crucial role of fixed costs in early deterrence is evident from an examination of Dixit's (1979) formulation of the entry problem.

Even granting that entry deterrence sometimes is optimal, another question arises as to how large a monopoly distortion can develop by reason of temporal asymmetry (the sitting monopolist has assets in place at the outset) and fixed-cost conditions. Schmalensee has recently addressed this issue and shows that the pre-entry present value of excess profits that can be realized by established firms 'cannot exceed the capital (start-up) cost of a firm of minimum efficient scale,' and that scale economies are therefore of little quantitative importance from a welfare standpoint (1980, pp. 3, 8). This result is questionable, however, because it ignores the reputation-effect incentives discussed below.

A related issue that has come under scrutiny is the matter of credible threats. This goes to the issue of what post-entry behavior is appropriately imputed to the sitting monopolist. As Curtis Eaton and Richard Lipsey observe (1980, p. 721), both credible and posturing threats take the same form – 'If you take action X, I shall take action Y, which will make you regret X.' But credible and noncredible threats are distinguishable in that the party issuing the threat will rationally take action Y only if credibility conditions are satisfied. If the Nash response to X is indeed to take action Y, the threat is credible. But if, despite the threat, X occurs and the net benefits accruing to the party issuing the threat are greater if he accommodates (by taking action Z rather than Y), then the threat will be perceived as posturing rather than credible. Since such threats will be empty, Eaton and Lipsey have urged that analysis of strategic behavior focus entirely on threats for which credibility is satisfied. The translation of this argument into investment terms discloses that the sitting monopolist must invest in durable, *transaction-specific assets* if he is to successfully pre-empt a market and deter entry.[20]

Reputation Effects. Bork's original assessment of the benefits of predation, McGee's commentary thereon, the Areeda–Turner criterion for assessing predation, Schmalensee's measures of welfare distortion, and the Eaton and Lipsey treatment of credible threats all address the issue of entry and predation in a very narrow context. A large, established firm is confronted

---

[20] Asset specificity can take three forms: site specificity, physical asset specificity, and human asset specificity. For a discussion of these issues in transaction cost terms and an assessment of their organizational ramifications, see Williamson (1979b).

with a clearly defined threat of entry and its response is assessed entirely in that bilateral context. The rationality of killing a rival (Bork, 1978) or of deterring an equally efficient firm (which has not yet made irreversible commitments) becomes the focus of attention (Eaton and Lipsey, 1980, 1981). If, however, punitive behavior carries signals to this and other firms – in future periods, in other geographic areas, and, possibly, in other lines of commerce – such analyses may understate the full set of effects on which the would-be predator relies in his decision to discipline a rival. Assessing this requires that the issue of predation be addressed in a teaching and learning context – which, since teaching and learning models are not well developed, is not easy, and is somewhat speculative.

Recognition that reputation effects can be important has nevertheless been growing and there has been some headway in dealing with the issues. The general point has been made by Christian von Weizsacker in the context of what he refers to as the extrapolation principle (1981, pp. 72–3):

One of the most effective mechanisms available to society for the reduction of information production cost is the principle of extrapolation. By this I mean the phenomenon that people extrapolate the behavior of others from past observations and that this extrapolation is self-stabilizing, because it provides an incentive for others to live up to these expectations. ... By observing others' behavior in the past, one can fairly confidently predict their behavior in the future without incurring further costs ...

[This] extrapolation principle is deeply rooted in the structure of human behavior. Indeed it is also available in animal societies. ... The fight between two chickens does not only produce information about the relative strengths in the present, but also about relative strength in the future.

Whereas Eaton and Lipsey and others have emphasized that only credible threats will effectively deter rivals and that credibility is realized by making pre-emptive investments, reference to reputation opens up the possibility that behavior matters. If, however, all of the objective factors pertinent to rivalry are fully disclosed, what is it that a firm can credibly do to alter preceptions?

The answer to this puzzle, as to many others in economics, is that the fiction of complete knowledge facilitates analysis, but sometimes obscures the core issues. Obscuration is a special hazard where competition of a small-numbers kind with repeat play is involved.

David Kreps and Robert Wilson have addressed the issues by observing that the general problem with so-called noncredible threats is that 'the competitor realizes that if faced with a *fait accompli* of entry, the monopolist will find it optimal to accept this entry. Thus the believability of the threat is tenuous; perhaps the competitors will simply call the monopolist's bluff and enter' (Kreps and Wilson, 1980, p. 2). But while others terminate the analysis here, Kreps and Wilson go on to pose the following dilemma: 'if the monopolist carries out the [noncredible] threat, then he will become known for being tough, and this will deter subsequent challenges and therefore be to his long-run advantage. Today's entrant, realizing that the monopolist will meet today's challenge in order to deter challenges in the future, believes that the threat is credible and thus does not enter' (1980, p. 2).

Kreps and Wilson evaluate the behavioral aspects of credibility by considering a series of examples of noncooperative games. The two crucial features are (a) there must be uncertainty regarding the sitting monopolist's payoffs, and (b) the game involves repeated play. While the specific source of uncertainty is not important, they nevertheless offer several possibilities: 'There may be uncertainty concerning the monopolist's production function. The monopolist may derive nonpecuniary benefits from fighting, or he may gain pecuniary benefits indirectly in another of his activities. He may simply be irrational ... [or there may be] uncertainty about the monopolist's discount rate' (p. 24).

With respect to repeated play, they observe that 'the play of early rounds may be overwhelmingly influenced not by immediate payoffs but by considerations of what information is being transmitted' (p. 58). This incentive to develop a reputation for toughness is especially great where the sitting monopolist 'plays against a sequence of different opponents, none of whom [has] the ability to foster a reputation' (p. 58). Accordingly, whereas credible-threat conditions must be fully satisfied in a full-information game, quasi-credibility may do if there is payoff uncertainty and repeat play.[21]

Applications pose the question of whether the circumstances where reputation-effect incentives are strong can be recognized. An important consideration is whether local entry is being attempted into a small sector of the total market in which the established firm enjoys dominance. Exploratory entry into a local geographic market, or into one or a few products in a much broader line of related products, would presumably enhance the appeal of a teaching response. The likelihood that the observed behavior is strategic is increased in the degree to which (a) the response is intensively focused on the local disturbance (is carefully crafted to apply only to the market where entry is attempted) and (b) goes beyond

---

[21] Assessing investment behavior is made more complex as a consequence. Thus even if a firm is 'unable to use excess capacity or a highly developed sales network profitably ... *if* its opponents think that the firm might be able to use that capacity/sales network to engage in profitable predation, then the firm may wish to develop that capacity/sales network' so as to confirm the fear (Kreps and Wilson, 1980, p. 61).

a simple defensive response (for example, holding output unchanged in the face of entry) to include a punitive aspect (for example, increasing output as the reply to entry).

Cost Asymmetries. Areeda and Turner (1975) and, more recently, Ordover and Willig (1981, pp. 13–14) take the position that the predatory impact of a price reduction by a dominant firm can be judged by whether such a reduction will exclude an equally efficient rival. As I have argued elsewhere, this is a peculiar criterion for assessing the welfare benefits of contingent increases in output– 'now it's here, now it isn't, depending on whether an entrant has appeared or perished' (Williamson, 1977, p. 339). I did not, however, comment on the costs incurred by the entrant except in passing (1977, pp. 296, 303–4). This is a regrettable oversight, since Ordover and Willig, like Areeda and Turner before them, argue that whenever an incumbent's costs are lower than the entrant's, 'a price just below the rival's cost does earn the incumbent some profit ... and therefore induces exit without violation of our standard of predation' (1980, p. 14). Inasmuch as they make no reference to the contrary, Ordover and Willig appear to have reference to the full pecuniary costs experienced by the rival. In consideration of the series of strategic-cost disadvantages that an entrant experiences or may be made to bear in relation to an established firm, this is surely a dubious criterion.

There are two points here, the first of which is that history matters in assessing costs. Temporal cost differences can arise in operating cost, cost of capital, and learning-curve respects. The second point is that the established firm may, by its own actions, be responsible for cost differences of the first two kinds and may contribute to the third.

Operating-cost Asymmetries. The possibility that a potential entrant experiences cost disadvantages by reason of strategic forward integration into distribution has been addressed by Bork (1978, pp. 156–8). Thus suppose that the dominant firm experiences identical costs whether its product is distributed by integrated or independent dealers. Forward integration may nevertheless be attractive because this has the effect of raising the costs to potential rivals. If potential entrants that would otherwise enjoy cost parity (say in terms of manufacturing costs) must, because of foreclosure, simultaneously create a distribution capability to effect entry, and if *additional* costs are incurred in creating a side-by-side distribution network that would be avoided by utilizing (or expanding) existing, but nonintegrated, distribution capacity, forward integration may be presumed to have been undertaken for the purpose of creating strategic operating-cost asymmetries.

Capital Cost Differentials. Assume, for the purposes of the argument here, that the potential entrant would experience identical distribution costs to those of the established firm if it were to enter both manufacturing and distribution stages rather than manufacturing alone. Suppose also, however, that the would-be entrant has demonstrated competence only at the manufacturing stage. Two-stage entry thus requires it to raise funds for an unfamiliar second stage to which the capital market can be expected to attach a risk premium (Williamson, 1975, pp. 110–12; 1979b, pp. 962–4). Accordingly, cost parity between established firm and potential rival can be upset by capital cost differentials.

The capital costs of would-be entrants can further be increased if established firms can quasi-credibly threaten to engage in post-entry predation. If the 'suppliers of capital to [potential] entrants perceive that the risks in the particular markets are greater than they had previously thought them to be, the cost of capital to new entrants will rise' (Joskow and Klevorick, 1979, p. 231).

Learning Effects. The proposition that costs are a function not merely of the scale and scope of a firm's activity but also of the cumulative output was set out by Armen Alchian in 1959. Only recently, however, have the strategic ramifications been addressed. One of the complications that is introduced by learning effects is that the test of remunerative pricing by dominant firms in early-stage growth industries is much more difficult (Williamson, 1977, p. 323). Current costs need to be reduced by the discounted effect on future costs in making the assessment. As Michael Spence puts it, 'When there is a learning curve, the short-run output decision is a type of investment decision. It affects the accumulated output, a stock, and through it, future costs and market position' (1981, p. 1).

But there is more to it. First and foremost, the established firm, which enjoys the benefits of lower costs by reason of accumulated output, will never be confronted with an equally efficient rival if costs comparisons are made in the immediate post-entry period and learning curves are important. Second, out of recognition of the intertemporal cost effects, the established firm may have an incentive to engage in aggressive pricing designed to 'reduce the return to competitors investing in expanded market shares' (Spence, 1981, p. 41). Additionally, the established firm may upset efforts to achieve cost parity by threatening (perhaps with good cause) to bring law suits should the entrant attempt to shorten the learning period by hiring away key employees.

The upshot is that the *equally efficient rival criterion is primarily suited to static circumstances where historical differences and contrived cost asymmetries may be presumed to be absent*. This scenario is evidently favored by those who take a narrow view of predation and advocate a marginal cost pricing standard. To the extent, however, that actual circumstances are not accurately described in this way, allowance for cost differences may be necessary if an informed assessment of predation is to be realized.[22]

IV. Unresolved Dilemmas

The study of strategic behavior has made remarkable progress since the late 1970s. A number of troublesome problems nevertheless remain. These include: (a) whether efforts to curb predation should focus primarily on price and output, or if other aspects of rivalry should be included; (b) inasmuch as rules governing predation set up incentives for established firms to preposition, should allowance be made for prepositioning in assessing the merits of alternative rules; and (c) whether victims of mistaken predation should be accorded protection.

A. DIMENSIONS

Although they are not independent, the study of strategic behavior is usefully split into *ex ante* and *ex post* parts. *Ex ante* behavior takes the form of pre-entry investment (in capacity, research and development, promotion, the offer of multiple brands, and so on) while *ex post* behavior involves specific adaptations by dominant firms contingent upon entry. As between the two, aggressive strategic behavior in *ex post* respects is widely believed to be the more reprehensible, but there are complicating factors here as well.

Christian von Weizsacker's work on innovation is instructive in this regard. He distinguishes between progressive and mature industries and observes that the positive externalities of innovation are especially strong in a progressive industry due to the 'possibility of generating the next innovation' (1981, p. 150). A welfare assessment of the intertemporal incentives to engage in innovation in a progressive industry leads von Weizsacker to conclude that 'a pricing action by an incumbent, which by reasonable standards is not considered a predatory action in a nonprogressive industry, [*a fortiori*] cannot be called a predatory action in a progressive industry' (1981, p. 210).

A somewhat different aspect is emphasized by Ordover and Willig, who, in an important paper, contend that *ex post* 'manipulation of the

---

[22] F. M. Scherer observers that 'Entry at or near the minimum optimal scale into significant oligopolistic markets is [rare] ... Indeed, it is sufficiently rare that it usually receives considerable attention in the relevant trade press' (1980, p. 248). Many models of predatory pricing ignore this and argue that only output that is produced by an equally efficient rival is socially valued.

product set can frequently be more effective than price cutting as an anticompetitive tactic' (1981, p. 18). Two types of tactics are examined. The first entails 'the introduction of a new product that is a substitute for the products of the rival firm and that endangers its viability by diverting its sales. The second tactic is employed in the context of systems rivalry. It consists of the constriction in the supply of components that are vital to consumers' use of the rival's product, coupled with the introduction of systems components that enable consumers to bypass their use of the rival's products' (p. 19). Although both their criterion for assessing predation as well as the practicability of implementing their rules for assessing strategic R&D and the upward repricing or withdrawal of pre-existing components complementary to a rival may be disputed, the issues have nevertheless been structured in a useful way. Follow-on studies will surely make use of this framework.

But what should be done in the meantime when the law is confronted with problems that run well ahead of the theory? SCM Corporation asked for compulsory licensing relief in its complaint that Xerox had excluded SCM from the plain-copier market,[23] and Berkey Photo argued that unannounced product innovations by Kodak placed it at an unfair disadvantage.[24] The FTC has also brought some rather ambitious strategic behavior suits. A collusive strategy of brand proliferation formed the basis of its complaint against the principal producers of ready-to-eat cereals (Kellogg, General Mills, General Foods, and Quaker Oats),[25] and the FTC subsequently charged duPont with making pre-emptive investments in the titanium-dioxide market.[26]

Except for cases that are patently protectionist (and some of these have a protectionist flavor), there are no happy choices. Put differently, trade-offs proliferate and our capacity to evaluate them is very primitive. Thus, although some reject these suits with the observation that 'Plaintiffs arguments in the high-technology cases of the 1970s rests implicitly on an atomistic theory of competition which posits an organized economy with no changes in technology, no shifts in consumer tastes, no change in population – and no future that is essentially different from the past' (Conference Board, 1980, p. 18), this is really a red herring. Strategic behavior is an interesting economic issue *only* in an intertemporal context where uncertainty is featured. The high-technology cases are plainly of this kind, and arguably involve strategic calculations in which private and

---

[23] *SCM Corp.* v. *Xerox Corp.* (DC Conn 1978) 1978–2 Trade Cases, Para. 62, 392.
[24] *Berkey Photo, Inc.* v. *Eastman Kodak Co.* (DC NY 1978) 1978–1 Trade Cases, par. 62, 392.
[25] *FTC* v. *Kellogg et al.*, Docket No. 8883.
[26] *FTC* v. *E. I. du Pont de Nemours & Co.*, Complaint, Docket No. 9108, 5 Aprill 1978 CCH Trade Regulation Reporter, transfer binder, Federal Trade Commission Complaints and Orders, 1976–1979, Par. 21, 407.

social valuations differ. The courts have understandably been cautious in moving ahead in this area. Assuming that these are matters that can be re-examined as a deeper understanding of the issues and a capacity to make informed trade-offs develops, this would appear to be the responsible result.

B. PREPOSITIONING

A primary focus on *ex post* price and output behavior does not, however, mean that *ex ante* investments should be ignored entirely. Indeed, if comprehensive comparisons of the welfare ramifications of alternative predatory pricing rules are to be attempted, differential *ex ante* consequences, if they exist, should presumably be included.

The ways by which firms will preposition in relation to different rules have been addressed by Spence (1977), Salop (1979), Dixit (1979, 1980), and Eaton and Lipsey (1980, 1981) in relation to entry deterrence in general and by Williamson (1977) as entry deterrence applies to predation. The general argument here is that an 'established firm can alter the *outcome* to its advantage by changing the initial conditions. In particular, an irrevocable choice of investment allows it to alter its post-entry marginal cost curve, and thereby the post-entry equilibrium' (Dixit, 1980, p.96). This line of reasoning has been applied to the study of predation with the following result: each predatory pricing rule predictably gives rise to 'pre-entry price, output, and investment adjustments on the part of dominant firms whose markets are subject to encroachment. To neglect the incentives of rules whereby dominant firms made *pre-entry adaptive responses of a strategic kind* necessarily misses an important part of the problem' (Williamson, 1977, p. 293).

There is less than unanimity, however, over whether these prepositioning effects should be taken into account. Recent supporters of the marginal cost/equally efficient rival pricing rule (McGee, 1980; Ordover and Willig, 1981) ignore the prepositioning ramifications of alternative rules. Whether this is because they believe them to be unimportant or beyond the purview of responsible analysis is unclear. For the moment, the matter of prepositioning incentives and their relevance for rule assessment is under dispute.

C. MISTAKEN PREDATION

A troublesome question arises where predatory pricing is attempted in circumstances where the structural preconditions described previously are not satisfied. I will refer to this class of events as 'mistaken predation,' in that even if the predator is successful in driving a rival from the market it will fail to realize anything but very transient market power benefits.

A significant excess of price over cost cannot be supported for any but a short period of time where rivals are many and entry is easy. Where this obtains, an attempt at predation is mistaken because a correct assessment of the net benefits will disclose that they are negative.

The fact that attempted predation is mistaken does not, however, guarantee that it will never occur. Where it does, should the victims be entitled to relief by bringing suit and recovering damages? The application of the type of reasoning employed by Joskow and Klevorick would suggest a negative answer. The hazard is that many of the suits brought by firms in competitive industries would have the purpose of relieving these firms from legitimate rivalry rather than attempted predation. Since mistaken predation will presumably be rare or, at least, not repeated, the 'false positive errors – that is ... errors that involve labeling truly competitive price cuts as predatory' (Joskow and Klevorick, 1979, p. 223) would appear to be high and augur against allowing suits of this kind. Some firms would be victimized as a result, however, and other students of predation may assess the hazards differently.

V. Conclusion

The 1960s was a decade when antitrust was preoccupied with measures of concentration and entry barriers. Such a narrow formulation facilitated easy enforcement – to the extent that Justice Stewart was moved to observe that 'the sole consistency that I can find under section 7 is that the government always wins'[27] – but sometimes at the expense of an informed welfare assessment of the issues. Three factors contributed to this condition. First, it was widely believed that oligopolistic collusion was easy to effectuate. Second, wherever entry barriers were discovered they were held to be anticompetitive and antisocial, there being a great reluctance to acknowledge trade-offs. And third, the business firm was thought to be adequately described as a production function to which a profit maximization objective had been assigned.

These views had two unfortunate consequences. For one thing, anything that contributed to market power – offsetting benefits notwithstanding – was held to be unlawful. Second, nonstandard or unfamiliar business practices that departed from autonomous market contracting were also held to be presumptively unlawful. If the natural way by which to mediate transactions between technologically separable entities is through markets, surely any effort by the firm to extend control beyond its natural (technological) boundaries must be motivated by strategic purpose.

Matters changed in the 1970s, as a greater appreciation for efficiency

[27] Dissenting opinion in US v. Von's Grocery Inc. 384 US 270 (1966).

benefits developed, and as the conception of the firm as a governance structure took hold. The perverse hostility with which efficiency differentials were once regarded gave way to an affirmative valuation of efficiency benefits,[28] and business practices that were previously suspect, because they did not fit comfortably with the view of the firm as a production function, were reinterpreted in a larger context in which – implicitly, if not explicitly – transaction cost economizing was introduced. As a consequence, antitrust errors and enforcement excesses of the 1960s were removed or reversed in the 1970s.

Despite progress with these matters, antitrust cannot settle back to a quiet life. Other difficult antitrust issues relating to strategic behavior have recently surfaced, and existing criteria for assessing the lawfulness of strategic practices are actively under dispute. Significant headway with a number of strategic behavior issues has nevertheless been made and more is in prospect. The study of strategic behavior has been clarified in the following significant respects: (a) severe structural preconditions in both concentration and entry barrier respects need to be satisfied before an incentive to behave strategically can be claimed to exist; (b) attention to investment and asset characteristics is needed in assessing the condition of entry – specifically, nontrivial irreversible investments, of a transaction-specific kind have especially strong deterrent effects; (c) history matters in assessing rivalry – both with respect to the leadership advantage enjoyed by a sitting monopolist as well as in the incidence and evaluation of comparative costs; and (d) reputation effects are important in assessng the rationality of predatory behavior.

This last has a bearing on two crucial aspects of the strategic behavior issue. For one thing, those who argue that strategic behavior can be disregarded unless credible threat conditions are fulfilled have overstated the case. This is not to suggest that the study of credible threats cannot usefully inform the analysis of strategic behavior. But if knowledge is imperfect then dominant firms can alter expectations by posturing (as well as by objectively fulfilling credibility conditions), in which event precommitments need not be as extensive as the credible threat literature would indicate. Second, myopic assessments of strategic behavior understate the incentives to engage in predation. Those who focus on the incentive to kill a specific rival are ignoring what may often be the stronger incentive – that is, to develop a reputation that will subsequently help to deter this and other firms in later periods, in other geographic markets,

---

[28] Vigilance is, nevertheless, necessary lest retrogression occur. Thus the Government's lead attorney advised the court in *US* v. *Occidental Petroleum* (Civil Action No. C-3-78-288) that the acquisition of Mead by Occidental was objectionable because it would permit Mead to construct a large 'Greenfield plant, which was the most efficient and cost-effective treatment,' and that this would disadvantage Mead's rivals.

and in other lines of commerce.

Among the issues actively under dispute in the study of strategic behavior are the following: (a) whether the equally efficient rival criterion is a useful one;[29] (b) whether the assessment of predatory pricing rules should make allowance for prepositioning incentives;[30] (c) whether strategic behavior should focus primarily on *ex post* contingent responses or can also be responsibly extended to include *ex ante* investments;[31] and (d) what remedies should be sought.[32] Clarification on these as well as sharpening of the issues enumerated in the preceding paragraph can be expected as the 1980s progress. I expect that antitrust enforcement regarding strategic behavior will be in much better shape at the end of the decade as a result of intervening scholarship. I furthermore anticipate that the continued need for antitrust will be demonstrated – and, alarmist cries for the abolition of antitrust will be discredited – in the process.

---

[29] Lest there by any doubt, I regard this as a seriously flawed criterion.

[30] I believe that they should, though this complicates the analysis.

[31] My own view is that antitrust is best advised to focus – at least for the present – on *ex post* contingent behavior. Behavior that goes beyond being merely defensive to include a punitive aspect is especially reprehensible and, arguably, is also the easiest to assess. Accordingly, contingent behavior that is directed not merely at the immediate rival but has a teaching-and-learning aspect is properly made the principal focus of antitrust enforcement against predation – at least until the state of the art for modeling and assessing strategic behavior is significantly advanced from where it stands presently.

[32] Not only are welfare assessments of *ex ante* entry-deterring behavior very subtle (von Weizsacker, 1980, 1981), but meaningful relief for *ex ante* investments may be difficult to fashion. Unless, therefore, a clear showing of welfare losses is made and efficacious relief can be devised, caution would appear to be warranted before pressing antitrust to hold that *ex ante* investments are unlawful.

Bibliography

Adelman, M. A. 1961 The Antimerger Act, 1950–60, *American Economic Review, Papers and Proceedings*, LI, 236–44.

Aghion, P. and Bolton, P. 1987 Contracts as a barrier to entry. *American Economic Review*, 77, forthcoming.

Alchian, A. A. 1959 Costs and Outputs. In *The Allocation of Economic Resources: Essays in Honor of Bernard Francis Haley* eds M. Abramovitz et al., Stanford, California: Stanford University Press, 23–40.

—— 1961 *Some Economics of Property*. Santa Monica, RAND Corporation.

—— 1965 The basis of some recent advances in the theory of management of the firm. *Journal of Industrial Economics*, 14, 30–41.

—— 1969 Corporate management and property rights. In *Economic Policy and Regulation of Corporate Securities*, ed. H. G. Manne. Washington, DC: American Enterprise Institute for Public Policy Research, 337–360.

—— and Demsetz, Harold 1972 Production, information costs, and economic organization. *American Economic Review*, 62, 777–95.

Arreda, P. and Turner, D. F. 1975 Predatory pricing and related practices under Section 2 of the Sherman Act. *Harvard Law Review*, 88, 697–733.

Arrow, Kenneth J. 1965 *Aspects of the Theory of risk-bearing*. Helsinki: Yrjo Jahnssonin Saatio.

—— 1969 The organization of economic activity. In *The Analysis and Evaluation of Public Expenditure: The PBB System*. Joint Economic Committee, 91st Congress, 1st Session. Washington, DC: US Government Printing Office.

Baiman, Stanley 1982 Agency research in managerial accounting: A survey. *Journal of Accounting Literature*, 1, 154–213.

Bain, Joe 1956 *Barriers to New Competition*. Cambridge: Harvard University Press.

—— 1958 *Industrial Organization*. New York: John Wiley and Sons.

Barzel, Yoram 1982 Measurement costs and the organization of markets. *Journal of Law and Economics*, 25, 27–48.

Baumol, W.J. 1965 *The Stock Market and Economic Efficiency*, New York: Fordham University Press.

—— 1979 Quasi-permanence of price reductions: A policy for prevention of predatory pricing. *Yale Law Journal*, 89 1–26.

——, Panzer, John, and Willig, Robert 1982 *Contestable Markets*. New York: Harcourt, Brace, Jovanovich.

——, Heim, Peggy, Malkiel, B. G., and Quandt, R. E. 1970 Earnings retention, new capital, and the growth of the firm. *Review of Economics and Statistics*, November, 345–55.

Becker, G. S. 1965 A theory of the allocation of time. *Economic Journal*, September, 493–517.

Ben-Porath, Yoram 1980 The F-connection: Families, friends, and firms and the organization of exchange. *Population and Development Review*, 6, 1–30.

Blake, H. M. and Jones, W. K. 1965a In defense of antitrust, *Columbia Law Review*, LXV, 377–400.

—— and —— 1965b Toward a three-dimensional antitrust policy, *Columbia Law Review*, LXV, 422–66.

Bok, D. 1960 *Section 7 of the Clayton Act and the merging of law and economics. Harvard Law Review*, 74, 226–355.

Bork, R. H. 1965 Contrasts in antitrust theory: I. *Columbia Law Review*, LXV, 401–16.

—— 1966. The rule of reason and the per se concept: Price fixing and market division, II. *Yale Law Journal*, 375–475.

—— 1969 Vertical integration and competitive processes, in *Public Policy Toward Mergers*, eds J. Fred Weston and Sam Peltzman. Pacific Palisades, California: Goodyear Publishing Company, 139–49.

—— 1978 *The Antitrust Paradox*. New York: Basic Books.

—— and Bowman, W. S. 1965 The crisis in antitrust. *Columbia Law Review*, LXV 363–76.

Bridgeman, Percy 1955 *Reflections of a Physicist*. New York: Philiosophical Library.

Brown Shoe v. *United States*, 370 US 294 (1962).

Brozen, Yale 1970 The antitrust task force deconcentration recommendation. *Journal of Law and Economics*, October, 279–92.

Buchanan, James 1975 A contractarian paradigm for applying economic theory. *American Economic Review*, 65, 225–30.

Caves, R. E. and Porter, M. E. 1977 From entry barriers to mobility barriers. *Quarterly Journal of Economics*, 91 241–62.

Chandler, A.D., Jr. 1962 *Strategy and Structure*, Cambridge, Mass.: MIT Press.

—— 1966 *Strategy and Structure*. New York: Doubleday and Co. Inc., Anchor Books Edition.

Clarkson, Kenneth W., Miller, Roger, and Muris, Timothy 1978 Liquidated damages vs. penalties. *Wisconsin Law Review*, 351–90.

Coase, Ronald H. 1937 The nature of the firm. *Economica*, November. Reprinted in *Readings in Price Theory*, eds G. J. Stigler and K. E. Boulding. Homewood, Ill., Richard D. Irwin, 331–51.

—— 1960 The problem of social cost. *Journal of Law and Economics*, 3, 1–44.

—— 1972 Industrial organization: A proposal for research. In *Policy Issues and Research Opportunities in Industrial Organization*, ed. V. R. Fuchs. New York: National Bureau of Economic Research.

—— 1984 The new institutional economics. *Journal of Institutional and Theoretical Economics*, 140, 229–31.

Comanor, W. S. 1965 Research and technical change in the pharmaceutical industry. *Review of Economics and Statistics*, XLVII, 182–90.

Commons, John R. 1934 *Institutional Economics*. Madison: University of Wisconsin Press.

DeAlessi, Louis 1983 Property rights, transaction costs, and X-efficiency. *American Economic Review*, 73, 64–81.

Demsetz, Harold 1966 Some aspects of property rights. *Journal of Law and Economics*, 9, 66–83.

—— 1968 Why regulate utilities? *Journal of Law and Economics*, 11, 55–66.

—— 1969 Information and efficiency: Another viewpoint. *Journal of Law and Economics*, 12, 1–22.

Dewey, D. 1961 Mergers and cartels: Some reservations about policy. *American Economic Review, Papers and Proceedings*, LI, 255–62.

Director, Aaron and Levi, Edward 1956 Law and the future: Trade regulation. *Northwestern Law Review*, 51, 281–317.

Dixit, A. 1979 A model of duopoly suggesting a theory of entry barriers, *Bell Journal of Economics*, 10, 20–32.

—— 1980 The role of investment in entry deterrence. *Economic Journal*, 90, 95–106.

Eaton, B. C. and Lipsey, R. G. 1980 Exit barriers are entry barriers: The durability of capital. *Bell Journal of Economics*, 11, 721–9.

—— and —— 1981 Capital, commitment, and entry equilibrium. *Bell Journal of Economics*, 12.

Edwards, C. D. 1955 Conglomerate bigness as a source of power. *Business Concentration and Price Policy*. Princeton: Princeton University Press.

Fama, Eugene and Jensen, Michael 1983 Agency problems and residual claims. *Journal of Law and Economics*, 26, 327–50.

Federal Trade Commission Staff Study 1969 *Economic Report on Corporate Mergers*, Washington, DC: Federal Trade Commission.

Fellner, William 1947 Prices and wages under bilateral oligopoly, *Quarterly Journal of Economics*, 503–32.

—— 1949 *Competition Among the Few*. New York: Alfred A. Knopf, Inc.

Ferguson, C. E. 1964 *A Macroeconomic Theory of Workable Competition*. Durham, NC: Duke University Press.

Fitzroy, Felix and Mueller, Dennis 1985 Cooperation and conflict in contractual organizations. *Quarterly Review of Economics*, forthcoming.

Friedman, Milton 1953 *Essays in Positive Economics*. Chicago: University of Chicago Press.

Fuchs, Victor 1972 *Policy Issues and Research Opportunities in Industrial Organization*. New York: National Bureau of Economic Research.

Fuller, L. 1963 Collective bargaining and the arbitrator. *Wisconsin Law Review*, 3–46.

Furubotn, Eirik and Pejovich, Svetozar (eds) 1974 *The Economics of Property Rights*. Cambridge: Balinger.

Georgescu-Roegen, Nicholas 1971 *The Entropy Law and Economic Process*. Cambridge, Mass.: Harvard University Press.

Goldberg, Victor 1976 Regulation and administered contracts. *Bell Journal of Economics*, 7, 426–48.

—— 1980 Rational exchange: Economics and complex contracts. *American Behavioral Scientist*, 23, 337–52.

Grossman, Sanford and Hart, Oliver 1986 The costs and benefits of ownership: A theory of vertical integration. *Journal of Political Economy*, 94, 691–719.

Hadley, A. T. 1897 The good and evil of industrial combination, *Atlantic Monthly*, LXXIX, 377–85.

Hamburg, D. 1966 *R & D: Essays on the Economics of Research and Development*. New York: Random House.

Harris, Milton and Townsend, Robert 1981 Resource allocation under asymmetrical information. *Econometrica*, 49, 33–64.

Hayek, Friedrich 1967 *Studies in Philosophy, Politics, and Economics*. London: Routledge and Kegan Paul.

Heflebower, R. B. 1960 Observations on decentralization in large enterprises. *Journal of Industrial Economics*, 9, 7–22.

Hirshleifer, J. 1970 *Investment, Interest and Capital*, Englewood Cliffs, New Jersey: Prentice Hall.

Holmstrom, Bengt 1983 Differential information, the market and incentive compatibility. Unpublished manuscript.

Horowitz, I. 1962 Firm size and research activity. *Southern Economic Journal*, XXVIII, 298–301.

Hurwicz, Leonid 1972 On informationally decentralized systems. In *Decision and Organization*, eds C. B. McGuire and R. Radner. Amsterdam: North Holland Publishing Co.

—— 1973 The design of mechanisms for resource allocation. *American Economic Review*, 63, 1–30.

Jensen, Michael 1983 Organization theory and methodology. *Accounting Review*, 50, 319–39.

—— and Meckling, William 1976 Theory of the firm: Managerial behavior, agency costs and ownership structure. *Journal of Financial Economics*, 3, 305–60.

Johnson, R. E. 1966 Technical progress and innovation. *Oxford Economic Papers*, XVIII, 158–76.

Joskow, Paul 1977 Commercial impossibility, the uranium market and the Westinghouse case. *Journal of Legal Studies*, 6, 119–76.

Joskow, P. L. 1980 The political content of antitrust: Comment. In *Antitrust Law and Economics*, ed. O. E. Williamson. Houston, Tex.: Dame Publishers, 196–204.

—— 1985 Vertical integration and long-term contracts: The case of coal burning electric generating plants. *Journal of Law, Economics, and Organization*, 1, 33–79.

—— and Klevorick, A. K. 1979 A framework for analyzing predatory pricing policy. *Yale Law Journal*, 89, 213–70.

—— and Schmalensee, Richard 1983 *Markets for Power*. Cambridge, Mass.: MIT Press.

Kaplow, Louis 1985 Extension of monopoly power through leverage. Program in Law and Economics, discussion paper no. 4. Harvard Law School, Cambridge, Massachusetts.

Kaysen, C. 1965 The present war on bigness: I. *The Impact of Antitrust on Economic Growth*, Fourth National Industrial Conference Board Conference on Antitrust in an Expanding Economy, New York, 31–8.

—— 1968 Models and decision-makers: Economists and the policy process, *Public Interest*, 80–95.

—— and Turner, D. F. 1959 *Antitrust Policy: An Economic and Legal Analysis*, Cambridge, Mass.: Harvard University Press.

Kendrick, J. W. 1961 *Productivity Trends in the United States*. Princeton: Princeton University Press.

Kenney, Roy and Klein, Benjamin 1983 The economics of block booking. *Journal of Law and Economics*, 26, 497–540.

King, Mervyn 1977 *Public Policy and the Corporation*. London: Chapman and Hall.

Klein, Benjamin, Crawford, Robert, and Alchian, Armen 1978 Vertical integration, appropriable rents, and the competitive contracting process. *Journal of Law and Economics*, 21, 297–326.

—— and Leffler, Keith B. 1981 The role of market forces in assuring contractual performance. *Journal of Political Economy*, 89, 615–41.

Knight, Frank H. 1965 *Risk, Uncertainty and Profit*. New York: Harper and Row.

Kreps, D. M. and Wilson, R. 1980 On the chain-store paradox and predation: Reputation for toughness. GSB Research Paper No. 551, Stanford, California.

Kronman, Anthony 1985 Contract law and the state of nature. *Journal of Law, Economics, and Organization*, 1, 5–32.

—— and Posner, Richard 1979 *The Economics of Contract Law*. Boston: Little, Brown and Co.

Leibenstein, H. 1966 Allocative efficiency versus 'X-efficiency'. *American Economic Review*, LVI, 392–415.

Liebeler, W. C. 1978 Market power and competitive superiority in concentrated industries, *UCLA Law Review*, 25, 231–1300.

Llewellyn, Karl 1931 What price contract? – An essay in perspective. *Yale Law Journal*, 40, 704–51.

Macaulay, Stewart 1963 Non-contractual relations in business. *American Sociological Review*, 28, 55–70.

McGee, J. S. 1980 Predatory pricing revisited. *Journal of Law and Economics*. 23, 289–330.

McKenzie, Lionel 1951 Ideal output and the interdependence of firms. *Economic Journal*, 785–803.

Macneil, Ian 1974 The many futures of contract. *University of Southern California Law Review*, 47, 691–816.

Malmgren, H. B. 1961 Information, expectations and the theory of the firm, *Quarterly Journal of Economics*, 399–421.

Manne, Henry G. 1955 Mergers and the market for corporate control. *Journal of Political Economy*, April, 110–20.

Mansfield, E. 1963 Size of firms, market structure, and innovation. *Journal of Political Economy*, LXXI, 556–76.

—— 1964 Industrial research and development expenditures: Determinants, prospects, and relation to size of firm and inventive output. *Journal of Political Economy*, LXXII, 319–40.

March, J. G. and Simon, H. A. 1958 *Organizations*. New York: John Wiley.

Markham, J. W. 1955 Survey of the evidence and findings on mergers. *Business Concentration and Price Policy*. Princeton: Harvard Graduate School of Business, 141–82.

Marschak, Jacob 1968 Economics of inquiring, communicating, deciding. *American Economic Review*, May, 1–18.

Masten, Scott 1984 The organization of production: Evidence from the aerospace industry. *Journal of Law and Economics*, 27, 403–18.

Meade, James E. 1952 External economies and diseconomies in a competitive situation. *Economic Journal*, 54–67.

Mirrlees, James 1976 The optimal structure of incentives and authority within an organization. *Bell Journal of Economics*, 7, 105–31.

Modigliani, F. 1958 New developments on the oligopoly front. *Journal of Political Economy*, 66, 215–32.

Monteverde, Kirk and Teece, David 1982 Supplier switching costs and vertical integration in the automobile industry. *Bell Journal of Economics*, 13, 206–13.

Muris, T. J. 1979 The efficiency defense under Section 7 of the Clayton Act. *Case Western Reserve Law Review*. 30, 381–432.

Muris, Timothy 1981 Opportunistic behavior and the law of contracts. *Minnesota Law Review*, 65, 521–90.

Myerson, Roger 1979 Incentive compatibility and the bargaining problem. *Econometrica*, 47, 61–73.

Nelson, Richard and Winter, Sidney 1982 *An Evolutionary Theory of Economic Change*. Cambridge, Belknap Press.

——, Peck, M. J. and Kalachek, E. D. 1967 *Technology, Economic Growth, and Public Policy*. Washington, DC: Brookings Institute.

Nozick, Robert 1980 *Anarchy, State, and Utopia*. Cambridge, Mass.: Harvard University Press.

Ordover, J. A. and Willig, R. D. 1981 An economic definition of predatory product innovation. In *Strategic Views of Predation*, ed. S. Salop. Washington, DC: Federal Trade Commission.

Ouchi, William 1980 Markets, bureaucracies, and clans. *Administrative Science Quarterly*, 25, 129–41.

Palay, Thomas 1985 Avoiding regulatory constraints: Contracting safeguards and the role of informal agreements. *Journal of Law, Economics, and Organization*, 1, 155–75.

Pollak, Robert 1983 A transaction cost approach to families and households. Unpublished manuscript.

Posner, R. A. 1969 Oligopoly and the antitrust laws: A suggested approach. *Stanford Law Review*, Jun, 1562–606.

—— 1970 A statistical study of antitrust enforcement. *Journal of Law and Economics*, October, 365–420.

—— 1975 The social costs of monopoly and regulation. *Journal of Political Economy*, 83, 807–25.

—— 1979 The Chicago School of antitrust analysis. *University of Pennsylvania Law Review*, 127, 925–48.

—— and Rosenfield, Andrew 1977 Impossibility and related doctrines in law: An economic analysis. *Journal of Legal Studies*, 6, 83–117.

Radner, Roy 1970 Problems in the theory of markets under uncertainty. *American Economic Review*, 454–60.

Richardson, G. B. 1960 *Information and Investment*. Oxford: Oxford University Press.

Ross, Stephen 1973 The economic theory of agency: The principal's problem. *American Economic Review*, 63, 134–9.

Salop, S. 1979 Strategic entry deterrence. *American Economic Review*, 335–8.
Salop, Steven and Scheffman, David 1983 Raising rival's costs. *American Economic Review*, 73, 267–71.
Scherer, F. M. 1965 Firm size, market structure, opportunity, and the output of patented inventions. *American Economic Review*, LV, 1097–125.
—— 1970 *Industrial Market Structure and Economic Performance*. Chicago: Rand McNally.
Schmalensee,, R. 1978 Entry deterrence in the ready-to-eat breakfast cereal industry. *Bell Journal of Economics*, 9, 305–27.
—— 1980 Economies of scale and barriers to entry. Sloan Working Paper No. 1130–80, Cambridge, Mass.
Shepherd, W. G. 1984 Contestability vs. competition. *American Economic Review*, 74, 572–87.
Simon, Herbert A. 1957 *Models of Man*. New York: John Wiley and Sons.
—— 1957 *Administrative Behavior*. 2nd edn. New York: Macmillan.
—— 1978 Rationality as process and as product of thought. *American Economic Review*, 68, 1–16.
Smith, Vernon 1974 Economic theory and its discontents. *American Economic Review*, 64, 320–2.
Speidel, Richard E. 1981 Court-imposed price adjustments under long-term supply contracts. *Northwestern University Law Review*, 76, 369–422.
Spence, A. M. 1977 Entry, investment and oligopolistic pricing. *Bell Journal of Economics*, 8, 534–44.
—— 1981 The learning curve and competition, *Bell Journal of Economics*. 12.
—— 1983 Reviewing contestable markets and the theory of industry structure. *Journal of Economic Literature*, 21, 981–90.
—— and Zeckhauser, Richard 1971 Insurance, information, and individual action. *American Economic Review*, 61, 380–7.
Stigler, G. J. 1951 The divison of labor is limited by the extent of the market. *Journal of Political Economy*, June, 185–93.
—— 1956 Industrial organization and economic progress. In *The State of the Social Sciences*, ed. L. D. White, Chicago: University of Chicago Press, 269–82.
—— 1958 Monopoly and oligopoly by merger, *American Economic Review, Papers and Proceedings*, XL, 23–4, reprinted in *Readings in Industrial Organization*, eds R. E. Heflebower and G. W. Stocking. Homewood, Ill.: Richard D. Irwin, 69–80.
—— 1963 United States v. Loew's Inc.: A note on block booking. *Supreme Court Review*, 152–63.
—— 1968 *The Organization of Industry*. Homewood, Illinois: Richard D. Irwin.
Stocking, G. W. 1955 Conglomerate bigness: Comment. *Business Concentration and Price Policy*. Princeton: Princeton University Press.
Stuckey, John 1983 *Vertical Integration and Joint Ventures in the Aluminum Industry*. Cambridge, Mass.: Harvard University Press.
Turner, D. F. 1965 Conglomerate mergers and section 7 of the Clayton Act, *Harvard Law Review*, 78, 1313–95.
—— 1969 The scope of antitrust and other economic regulatory policies. *Harvard Law Review*, April, 1207–44.
—— and Williamson, O. E. 1971 Market structure in relation to technical and

organizational innovation. In *Proceedings of the International Conference on Monopolies, Mergers and Restrictive Practices*, ed. J. Heath. London: HMSO.

United States v. *Philadelphia National Bank*, 374 US 312 (1963).

von Weizsacker, C. C. 1980 A welfare analysis of barriers to entry, *Bell Journal of Economics*, 11, 399–421.

—— 1981 *Barriers to Entry*, New York: Springer-Verlag.

Wachter, Michael and Williamson, Oliver 1978 Obligational markets and the mechanics of inflation. *Bell Journal of Economics*, 9, 549–71.

Whinston, Andrew 1964 Price guides in decentralized organizations. In *New Perspectives in Organization Research*, eds W. W. Cooper, H. J. Leavitt, and M. W. Shelly. New York: John Wiley, 405–48.

Williamson, O. E. 1964 *The Economics of Discretionary Behavior: Managerial Objectives in a Theory of the Firm*. Englewood Cliffs, N.J.: Prentice Hall.

—— 1965 Innovation and market structure. *Journal of Political Economy*, LXXIII, 67–73.

—— 1967 Hierarchical control and optimum firm size. *Journal of Political Economy*, LXXV, 123–38.

—— 1967 A dynamic stochastic theory of managerial behavior. In *Prices: Issues in Theory, Practice and Public Policy*, eds A. Phillips and O. E. Williamson. Philadelphia: University of Pennsylvania Press, 11–31.

—— 1970 *Corporate Control and Business Behavior*. Englewood Cliffs, NJ: Prentice Hall.

—— 1975 *Markets and Hierarchies: Analysis and Antitrust Implications*. New York: Free Press.

—— 1976 Franchise bidding for natural monopoly – in general and in relation to CATV. *Bell Journal of Economics*, 7, 73–104.

—— 1979a Bork, The antitrust paradox: A policy at war with itself. *University of Chicago Law Review*, 46, 526–31.

—— 1979b Transaction–cost economics: The governance of contractual relations. *Journal of Law and Economics*, 22, 233–61.

—— 1979c Williamson on predatory pricing II. *Yale Law Journal*, 88, 1183–200.

—— 1981 Cost escalation and contracting. Center for the Study of Organizational Innovation, University of Pennsylvania, discussion paper no. 95.

—— 1981 The modern corporation: Origins, evolution, attributes. *Journal of Economic Literature*, 19, 1537–68.

—— 1983 Credible commitments: Using hostages to support exchange. *American Economic Review*, 73, 519–40.

—— 1984a The economics of governance: Framework and implications. *Journal of Institutional and Theoretical Economics*, 140, 196–223.

—— 1984b Corporate governance. *Yale Law Journal*, 93, 1197–230.

—— 1985 *The Economic Institution of Capitalism: Firms, Markets, Relational Contracting*. New York, Free Press.

—— 1987 Delimiting Antitrust. Unpublished manuscript.

—— Wachter, Michael, and Harris, Jeffrey 1975 Understanding the employment relation. *Bell Journal of Economics*, 6, 250–78.

Wright, J. C. G. 1969 Products and welfare. *Australian Economic Papers*, Dec.

Index

Index compiled by J. Balinski